A STATE BUILT ON SAND

DAVID MANSFIELD

A State Built on Sand

How Opium Undermined Afghanistan

HURST & COMPANY, LONDON

First published in the United Kingdom in 2016 by
C. Hurst & Co. (Publishers) Ltd.,
41 Great Russell Street, London, WC1B 3PL
© David Mansfield, 2016
All rights reserved.
Printed in India

The right of David Mansfield to be identified as the author of
this publication is asserted by him in accordance with the
Copyright, Designs and Patents Act, 1988.

A Cataloguing-in-Publication data record for this book is
available from the British Library.

978-1-84904-568-1 *paperback*

www.hurstpublishers.com

This project is funded by
the European Union

To
Joanne, Ben and Nathan

CONTENTS

CONTENTS

CONTENTS

ACKNOWLEDGEMENTS

This book would not have been possible without the support of a lot of different people. Most notable is the European Commission and their generous support to the Afghan Research and Evaluation Unit (AREU). Giacomo Miserocchi at the European Commission (EC) stands out in particular as someone who fundamentally believed that documenting almost two decades of fieldwork in Afghanistan and experience in the drugs policy world was a useful exercise that needed support. AREU and its staff have helped in the completion of this task and provided long-term support to my fieldwork in rural Afghanistan.

There are others who have supported my research over an extended number of years: individuals in a range of institutions who stand out for their commitment to developing a more detailed understanding of how policies and programmes were working on the ground in Afghanistan. Many did this despite knowing that senior managers or other agencies were not always keen to know or be presented with evidence of impact. These individuals shall remain anonymous here but I am forever thankful for the funding they have provided and the support they gave to simply documenting the lives and livelihoods of rural Afghans without any desire to influence the findings of the research.

In terms of the substantive part of the work in Afghanistan, particular thanks go to my colleagues and now close friends at the Organisation for Sustainable Development and Research (OSDR) who have spent a considerable amount of time with me in rural Afghanistan, enduring my predilection for asking far too many questions. The support given by Hajji Sultan Mohammed Ahmady, Ghulam Rasool, Hajji Hasti Gul and Azizullah for well over a decade is immeasurable. They have been patient throughout and have kept me out of trouble on many occasions. I am truly thankful for their commitment and friendship over such an extended period of time. There are a number of other colleagues at OSDR, individuals who live and work in some of the most insecure parts of the country and who have shown such generosity in sharing their time and knowledge. None of this work would have been possible without them.

There are also Richard Brittan and the team at Alcis Ltd, particularly Matt Angell, Dilip Wagh and Tim Buckley. The work they do with geospatial imagery and analysis is truly pioneering, and when combined with well focused fieldwork and a detailed understanding of the ground, it can provide an unrivalled understanding of the nature of change in the lives and livelihoods of the population in some of the most conflict-affected parts of Afghanistan.

There is a group of colleagues who have offered considerable advice and input on the numerous papers that I have written over the past eighteen consecutive growing seasons. Special thanks go to Michael Alexander, Rory Brown, William Byrd, Pierre Arnaud Chouvy, Matt Dupee, Pierre Fallavier, Paul Fishstein, Anthony Fitzherbert, Tom Franey, Arunn Jegan, David Macdonald, Dipali Mukhopadhyay, Ronald Neumann, Ian Patterson, Ghulam Rasool and Richard Will. These individuals have put a considerable amount of time into providing comments, and their insights are much appreciated. The work is so much better for their contributions.

My good friend and academic supervisor Jonathan Goodhand also merits particular thanks with regard to the substantive part of my work and its evolution over the last decade. Jonathan has always been patient and supportive, as well as tolerant of my failure to meet deadlines. He has constantly pressed me to look beyond the findings of my last piece of fieldwork and pointed me in the direction of wider literature and ideas that have proved to be invaluable for developing a better understanding of the complex reasons why opium bans endure in one area and collapse in others. I have learned a lot from our work together.

Of course there are also the countless farmers and rural communities that have welcomed me and my colleagues over the last eighteen years of fieldwork. They have shared their time, their experiences and the details of their lives and livelihoods, and have shown incredible hospitality despite many having so little to spare. Some have warned us of security problems, even imminent dangers, and for that I will be eternally grateful.

There are others who have been instrumental to the body of work that makes up this book, providing support at critical junctures: Michael Alexander, David Macdonald and Richard Will, 'partners in crime' during those formative years at the United Nations Office on Drugs and Crime, UNODC; Michael Ryder, Peter Holland, Guy Warrington, Andy Smith, Dave Belgrove, Ian Patterson, Robert Magowan and Tom Franey for their unwavering commitment to doing the best job possible; I learned a lot from them during my time at the UK Foreign and Commonwealth Office, and they made the experience so much more pleasant than it could have been and it subsequently became; Christoph Berg at GTZ, a person who was ahead of his time and willing to press for a different approach to rural development in drug crop-producing and abandon the concept of alternative development despite the fact that to do so would not serve his interests; Paul Fishstein and Andrew Wilder for establishing the foundations for the empirical work at the Afghan Research and Evaluation Unit (AREU), and along with Nigel Pont their support while in Boston; Robert Vierkant and Said Maqsoudi of the US Department of Defence for much needed support in writing up work on the Taliban ban and some of my old field notes; Jean Luc Lemahieu at UNODC for the dinners and all the entertaining and informative debates we have had on the drugs issue in Afghanistan over the course of many years; finally, Rory Stewart and the Kennedy School for their invitation to undertake a fellowship at Harvard, which led to new opportunities in Boston for me and my family, for which we will always be thankful.

There is a further group of professionals who have made life so much easier and richer for their inputs: John Gallini and the late, great Mark Fischer for their invaluable legal advice; Ken Freshman and Deborah Schultz who made the numbers add up; Ann Buxbaum for her expert editorial support with this book, as well as previous papers; and finally Michael Dwyer and the team at Hurst who were so instrumental in turning my manuscript into a meaningful book. All of these professionals have been a pleasure to work with.

Last but far from least, I wish to thank my family. They have not only endured the stress of my frequent visits to Afghanistan, particularly as the security situation deteriorated, but perhaps even worse have had the experience of living with me while I tried to make sense of my work and write this book. My wife Joanne has been a source of strength, unequivocal support, ideas and inspiration throughout, including during my work in Afghanistan; this book would certainly not have happened without her. More importantly, she and our two boys, Ben and Nathan, bring a joy and meaning to my life that is immeasurable. To my mother, Maureen Mansfield, for her enduring and unconditional love and support; and to my late father, John Neville Mansfield, to whom I can only apologise for not finishing this work sooner so that you could have seen it. You continue to be an inspiration to me and I miss you very much.

PREFACE

I have spent over 23 years working on illicit drug crop cultivation. This has not been an easy line of work; it has not been structured by a career path, an academic theory or a literature that could have helped guide my way. Instead it has been a journey shaped by a collection of disparate opportunities that have arisen over more than two decades, which I have used, with dogged persistence, to develop a deeper understanding of the rural communities that cultivate drug crops and how they respond to efforts to prevent them from growing opium poppy.

The work I have done over this period of time has been shaped by my observations and the results of empirical work in rural areas rather than by ideology, preconceived policy positions or the constructs of the programmes and projects that fall under the current banner of drug control interventions. I have in particular avoided the cut and thrust of what has often appeared to be a rather polemic debate on international drugs policy and practice, where all too often the detail of the complex life stories of those living in some of the most challenging circumstances possible—where communities are exposed to an array of physical, economic and ecological risks in some of the most remote parts of the world—are largely ignored by academics and policy-makers who have never met those involved in drug crop cultivation and the families they support.

I have also steered clear of those who have sought to use Afghanistan as a Trojan horse to establish precedents in drugs policy that range from licit cultivation to the introduction of aerial spraying to the establishment of some kind of hemispheric balance with the eradication effort in Colombia. I have on many occasions found myself and my work shunned by both those in favour of reform and those pressing for a more aggressive eradication effort in Afghanistan. It often seems that neither of these factions finds empirical work that charts the complex and diverse responses to current drug control interventions of particular value in their efforts to press forward with a predetermined policy position.

Personally, I am of the opinion that a conversation that gives primacy to legal frameworks (regulations either to allow opium poppy or to destroy it because it is prohibited under Afghan and international law) is somewhat ahead of itself. The idea that the Afghan state might have the coercive power to tax and control licit opium poppy cultivation in the areas where it is grown—many of which have little to no history of paying tax or being subjugated by the state—seems misplaced. Similarly, the belief that an Afghan state that does not enforce a ban across its territory somehow lacks 'political commitment' or 'will' is one that ignores hundreds of years of Afghan history, as well as the history of state formation in many parts of the world (Thoumi, 2003: 76). The suggestion that the Afghan state can assert its authority over its territorial boundaries through a campaign of aerial spraying seems even more disconnected from the realities of state–societal relations in Afghan history, the increasingly precarious bargains that underpin the current Afghan government, and the lessons learned from more contemporary efforts to ban opium production in the country.

In particular, I hope that this exposition of almost two decades of work with rural communities in Afghanistan illustrates the empirical, methodological and theoretical progressions that I have made as I have tried to make sense of the world that those cultivating opium poppy inhabit.

Too often I have engaged with a drugs literature that has been rather preoccupied by a policy debate that often appears ethnocentric and that gives little voice to those who are actually engaged in drug crop cultivation in some of the more marginal and conflict-ridden parts of the world. Treated as the passive recipients of economic and political signals—instructed to take up or abandon opium by either the market or armed actors—the farmers and rural communities that produce opium and coca are depicted as lacking agency and unable to influence the world in which they live. This is not a portrayal that I recognise.

Contrary to claims by some in the media and many academic accounts, I have found that it has not been 'traders', 'warlords' or even 'the Taliban' who have been the catalyst in the diffusion of opium poppy across Afghanistan, with assertions that these parties have provided seed, fertiliser and training. Instead, it has more often than not been farmers who have brought opium poppy cultivation into areas of Afghanistan where opium has not been produced before, driven by population pressures in their home villages, patterns of reciprocal labour arrangements or migratory movements, and the availability of land to sharecrop or rent at reasonable prices in areas where opium has not previously been grown in abundance.

It has also been farmers who have agitated against the rural elite when their leadership has continued to play a role in supporting state authorities in banning opium production. Resistance is not a uniform response, but it is particularly common in those areas where non-hierarchical social structures prevail and where the impact of a ban has led to a large proportion of the population experiencing significant losses in welfare. These are often very public transcripts, in which community members remind the rural elite that they are only 'first amongst equals', and that others—often a cousin and long-term rival—might do a better job representing the community's interests to the state.

Protests by farmers have also taken the form of collective resistance, sometimes violence, against those armed actors who look to impose a ban on opium production.

In sum, far from being passive and without agency, farmers can be an important constituency within the complex and ever-shifting mosaic of bargains that represents political order in rural Afghanistan. History shows us that those with coercive power can impose their will on the rural population, but they often need to tread carefully if they are to sustain their reign. I would argue that the imposition of taxes, conscription and opium bans has been possible in those areas with an agricultural surplus, hierarchical social structures and a history of state encapsulation. However, a ban on opium in areas where it inflicts, to quote Scott (1976: 196), 'patterns of collective insecurity that affect substantial numbers of peasants' on a population with 'strong communal traditions', and a history of challenging the hegemony of the state, is likely to lead to protest, violence and ultimately rural rebellion. Containing this rebellion can be a challenge once those with coercive power are seen to be politically and militarily vulnerable, and it may only be a short time before this unrest spills over, challenging the hegemony of the state in the lower valleys.

All of these factors point to a far messier process of policy-making than many would like. It does not offer broad-brush policy options, or simple and pithy narratives easily digested by senior policy-makers and academics who often continue to see efforts to curtail drug crop cultivation as a series of boundaried interventions that can neatly fit under the mandate of specialised counternarcotics institutions with clear mandates and corresponding budgets. Instead, it requires contextualising drug crop cultivation within the particular histories, livelihood portfolios and political configuration of specific localities.

It demands recognising that efforts to reduce drug crop cultivation should not be at the forefront of a state's efforts to engage with rural communities on their peripheries but that it should be recognised as an outcome of a wider process of state formation and rural development.

1

ESTABLISHING THE CONTEXT

Introduction

This research examines the complex socio-economic and political processes behind bans on illicit drug crop cultivation in conflict-affected states, the differentiated impacts of these bans on livelihoods and political (dis)order, and the wider implications for international policies aimed at counternarcotics and statebuilding. The research is motivated by a desire to improve our understanding of the risks that banning drug crop cultivation might incur in creating a political equivalent to the 'butterfly effect' in source countries, where small variations in the political fabric at the periphery gather enough pace to send reverberations and destabilise the sub-national, national and regional political order.

The predominant discourse on drug crop cultivation and efforts to control it, is rarely grounded in the day-to-day realities of those who farm opium poppy or coca and experience the effects of prohibition. Instead, the focus is directed largely to fluctuations in cultivation, measured through aggregated statistics. The physical destruction of the crop is often placed at the forefront of efforts to control supply; the aim of these efforts is to reduce the total amount of opium or coca available for processing and, by raising the risks of cultivation, to deter farmers from growing drug crops in subsequent growing seasons.

Some of the academic literature on illicit drugs, though critical of mainstream policy, is similarly ungrounded in its analysis. The efficacy of investing in either repression or rural development programmes to deter drug crop

1

production is challenged, with reference to the 'balloon effect': the temporal or spatial displacement of supply. This critique argues that efforts to reduce drug crop cultivation are at best a futile exercise, and at worst, as stated by Kleiman (cited in World Bank, 2011: 224), exacerbate security and governance problems by raising prices and 'conferring competitive advantage on traffickers with the most guns and the most influence'.

Both these 'master narratives' overly simplify the complex and dynamic processes of change that occur when a ban on drug crop cultivation is imposed. Questions of politics and power are commonly reduced to a simplistic binary division between two opposing sides—the state and insurgents—in which there is a battle for control over territory, and over the rural population engaged in the cultivation and trade of drug crops. These narratives lack a fine-grained appreciation of the varying household and community responses to drug bans. Similarly, there is a need for a more sustained and sophisticated analysis of the process of transition that some farmers experience, graduating out of drug crop cultivation and diversifying both crops and income, often in the absence of any direct counternarcotics interventions.

The positions of both the mainstream drug control community and those critical of supply-side measures are built on the economic principles of global supply and demand, and a model of farmer decision-making driven by the desire to maximise income on the one hand and, on the other, by the coercive acts of the state and other armed actors. Primary data is largely limited to global and national estimates of production and to quantitative data of often unreliable provenance, given the insecure terrain in which drug crops are grown and the sensitive subject matter being examined. Questionable aggregate statistics have limited validity in explaining the varied livelihood trajectories of those directly involved in drug crop cultivation, or the reasons why some households and communities transition out of drug crop cultivation while others often violently resist counternarcotics efforts.

A further weakness in the analysis of supply-side efforts in source countries lies in a failure to understand the diverse political and economic geography of the areas in which drug crops are grown, and the impact of different state–societal relations, social structures and resource endowments on both how bans are imposed and communities' responses to the bans. These differences are especially clear in areas of what Risse et al. (2011: 245) refer to as consolidated statehood, where there is a long history of state encapsulation and more favourable economic conditions, and areas of limited statehood where domestic sovereignty is constrained and access by state institutions is negotiated.

There is also a propensity for the literature to neglect the profoundly political process involved in imposing a ban; to ignore the array of informal and formal institutions involved and to disregard the different reasons why these institutions are engaged in efforts to ban opium poppy; and why some of them withdraw their support for a ban over time. There is a tendency to assume either passivity on the part of power-holders in source countries—the narrative of the 'innocent bystander' coerced by US hegemony to pursue a policy of prohibition—or to argue that collusion, corruption and engagement in the drugs trade compels state and non-state actors to engage in counternarcotics efforts. All too often these narratives assume that the motivations of actors and institutions in source countries are shaped solely by competition over control of rents generated by the drugs trade (Snyder, 2006).

Effective bans are assumed to be the result of overwhelming coercive power, combined with shifts in economic incentives. However, this assumption misses the complex political processes that underpin the imposition of a ban in source countries. It fails to recognise the elite bargains that are constantly being reshaped by external interventions (or anticipated interventions); by the interests of sub-national, national and even international actors; by exogenous events; and, in some locations, by the actions of rural constituents who may be positioned to depose their leadership and fracture political coalitions. This failure to acknowledge the wider political and economic environment also reflects the teleological orientation and 'drugs fetishism' contained within much of the literature, where the world is seen largely through the prism of drug production and drug control measures, and little consideration is given to the wider context.

This research attempts to address these deficiencies by drawing upon and combining political economy and livelihoods perspectives, allied with sustained, longitudinal empirical research. The research examines the complex and dynamic political processes involved in prohibiting cultivation in a single source country: Afghanistan. A case study approach is adopted in order to analyse four different bans on opium production: the Taliban prohibition of 2000/1: the two bans imposed in Nangarhar province in eastern Afghanistan in 2004/5 and 2007/8, following the collapse of the Taliban regime; and the effort to reduce cultivation in the 'Helmand Food Zone' between 2008 and 2011.

Detailed analysis of these bans reveals the complex reasons for their imposition at particular moments in time; how institutions with different interests, mandates and constituents aligned behind efforts to enforce a ban; and the role that prohibition itself played in reshaping the economic and political terrain, leading to different political settlements and differing outcomes on the ground.

The research places opium bans within the broader socio-economic and political context in which they occur. This means analysing both the domestic (national, provincial, sub-national and local levels) and international settings which have shaped the characteristics, dynamics and outcomes of opium bans. It also provides a granular analysis of the impact of these bans on a diverse rural population, exploring how farmers in different socio-economic groups and locations have responded to efforts to prohibit opium poppy over time; their sources of income and social protection; changes in patterns of food consumption, healthcare and assets; and their collective response to the state's efforts to control drugs.

Rationale

This research positions efforts to prohibit drug crop cultivation at the centre of a complex and multi-level interaction among three factors: external interventions, domestic political economy and local livelihoods. The research draws upon three bodies of literature: (i) illicit drugs and counternarcotics; (ii) political economy and statebuilding; and (iii) rural livelihoods.

Illicit drugs and counternarcotics

There is a disparate body of work on drug crop production and supply-side efforts. A significant part of this literature uncritically reflects and reinforces the international conventions calling for nation states to commit human and financial resources to curb the production, trafficking and use of illicit drugs, and is produced by drug-control organisations, such as the United Nations Office on Drugs and Crime (UNODC), as well as various parts of the United States Government (USG). The academic literature on drug production is more discordant and is based on a wide range of disciplines, in particular economics, politics, history, geography and criminology.[1] Much of it is critical of the prevailing drug control regime, questioning the efficacy and ethics of current supply-side efforts in drug-producing countries.

Both kinds of literature have significant gaps when it comes to analysing efforts to ban opium and coca. The first and most obvious gap is the paucity of primary data on the lives and livelihoods of those cultivating illicit drug crops. There is a tendency to focus on changes in aggregate level statistics, comparing national and regional data, which ultimately tells us little about how reductions in cultivation have taken place; the factors that led farmers to reduce or abandon illicit drug crop production; the likelihood that these factors will persist over time; and ultimately whether reductions in levels of cultivation will be sustained, or whether production will simply return in subsequent years. Limited empirical data at the household and community levels and an over-reliance on aggregate data from institutions involved in drug control have arguably led to problems of bias (Gootenburg, 2005: 121) and 'policy-based evidence' (Cramer and Goodhand, 2011).

The second gap is the absence of robust political economy analysis that deals explicitly with power relations and politics in drug-producing areas.[2] Where politics is taken into account, it tends to be treated as an externality that gets in the way of the effective implementation of counternarcotics policies. Analysis focuses on questions to do with 'state failure' and the contest between states and insurgent groups for control of drug-producing areas (Staniland, 2012: 243). Non-state politico-military groups are often portrayed as one-dimensional and monolithic—the FARC in Colombia, the Wa in Burma, the Taliban in Afghanistan. Their coercive power and ability to impose their will on their ranks and on the rural population within their territory are often taken at face value. The depiction of both the state and insurgents as institutions with cohesive structures and hierarchies is inadequate. It stands in stark contrast to the hybrid, or 'twilight' institutions (Lund, 2006) found in areas of limited statehood, where power is diffuse rather than concentrated, and where the lines between state and non-state, as well as between private and public entities, are blurred. A sharp distinction between state and insurgents is rarely seen in practice, when the same individual can simultaneously be a government official, a private actor and an insurgent supporter, and where social affinities and patronage networks pervade both state and insurgent groups.

The third gap is a product of the teleological orientation of much of the drugs literature and its tendency to focus on the efficacy of specific counternarcotics interventions and institutions. The work of economists such as Reuter (2010), Caulkins (2010) and Mejia (2010) features heavily here. Much of the critique of supply-side efforts focuses on the monetary value of very specific measures included in the current lexicon of counternarcotics, such as eradication and alternative development (Felbab Brown, 2010; Inkster and Comolli, 2012). Such a bounded and evaluative approach tends to overlook the 'on-the-ground dynamics' and 'local messiness' in drug crop-producing areas (Kalyvas, 2006). There is a need to move beyond a reductionist position on the kinds of measures that may or may not contribute to households transitioning out of drug crop cultivation, and to broaden the analytical lens to include the wider socio-economic, political and environmental processes that are at work in areas of production, including external interventions that may have no counternarcotics objectives, but have profound effects on the dynamics of drug cultivation and bans.

In considering how bans are imposed and why they may unravel, there is a need to improve our understanding of the many formal and informal institutions that support prohibition in drug-producing areas. The language of 'the war on drugs' implies a more concerted, coherent and coordinated effort than is often seen in practice and conceals the muddled and competitive policy processes characteristic of government bureaucracies in conflict-affected states. It is also important to develop a more intimate knowledge of the diverse rural households and communities that are involved in drug crop cultivation and the broad range of institutions that shape decision-making at the household level.

Political economy and statebuilding

Research on the political economy of conflict and statebuilding provides a useful analytical lens for positioning opium bans in relation to processes of statebuilding and state contestation (Goodhand and Mansfield, 2010; Heyman and Smart, 1999; Meehan, 2011; Lund, 2006). It is important to differentiate between statebuilding and state formation. Statebuilding is understood here as a conscious, planned and often externally supported attempt to build an apparatus of control. In the post-Cold War period there have been a growing number of experiments in exogenous statebuilding, including Kosovo, East Timor, Iraq and Afghanistan. Statebuilding has become a point of convergence for a range of actors and policy arenas, including peacebuilders, development donors, counternarcotics agencies and counterinsurgency experts. In spite of their different objectives, there are commonalities between the technical interventions designed to 'fix' failed states (Ghani and Lockhart, 2008) and the measures that fall under the lexicon of counternarcotics interventions. Both sets of interventions are intended to strengthen state institutions so that they can gain greater control over their territory and eliminate a wide range of social ills, including drug crop production, organised crime, terrorism and insurgency.

State formation, on the other hand, is an historical or immanent process, the largely unconscious outcome of conflicts, negotiations, compromises and trade-offs between competing politico-military elites and socio-economic groups (Goodhand, 2012: 333). Processes of state formation, banditry, warlordism and illegal practices have frequently been close companions (Gallant, 1999). This perspective takes us away from the idealised notion of the Weberian state with the ability to impose its will, tax its population and deliver services within its administrative boundaries. Rather than being autonomous entities that float above society, states are seen to consist of 'a multiplicity of actors, interests and institutions in constant conversation with the heterogeneous elements that form society as we know it' (Migdal, 1994: 9). This depiction of the state as a constellation of different and competing elements, with shifting centres of power, provides a more convincing framework for examining how prohibition policies become salient for a variety of institutions and actors competing for power, resources and legitimacy.

This analysis is further bolstered by the literature on political settlements and political geography, which offers an explanation of the uneven nature of state power and why some areas—what Risse et al. (2011) refer to as 'limited statehood'—maintain a greater level of autonomy from state institutions than others. This work explores the arrangements that are established between state institutions at the centre and non-state actors at the periphery. It examines local histories, political structures, elite composition, the distribution of rents and the resource endowments that communities have at their disposal, as a way of improving our understanding of state–societal relations (Boone, 2003; Barkey, 1994). When combined with the work of scholars such as Scott (1976, 1990, 2009) and Wolf (1966) on peasant resistance and rebellion, this body of literature offers important points of reference for any enquiry into state efforts to ban drug crop production, and community responses, across what is typically a widely divergent geographic and political terrain.

Political economy analysis also highlights the role that international organisations play, often inadvertently, in shaping the central state's relationship with the institutions and populations within its borders. Risse et al. (2011) and de Waal (2009), for example, challenge the notion of the international community as neutral arbiters and mediators in conflict-affected states, and instead explore how international military and civilian engagement can distort and destabilise the fragile coalitions that tie together local elites and those at the political centre. This work may help illuminate the underlying power dynamics which explain how bans are imposed in areas of limited statehood, and how they may unravel as the political and economic equilibrium shifts.

Rural Livelihoods

This work builds upon a strong body of empirical research in rural communities which challenges some of the economically reductionist arguments used to explain drug crop cultivation. As both a conceptual and methodological framework, the livelihoods model provides a rounded and holistic approach to understanding the complex role of drug crops in providing access to a wide range of assets for those involved in their cultivation. The livelihoods perspective draws on concepts such as coping, adaptation, diversification and, in particular, resilience. Rather than offering a definitive, mono-causal explanation of the causes of cultivation, it aims to unpack the complex factors behind dependency on drug crop cultivation and how these factors influence the prospects for enduring reductions in cultivation in a complex socio-economic, political and ecological terrain.

Hypothesis and Questions

This research aims to compare and study four different drug bans implemented over a thirteen-year period. It is hypothesised that one of the keys to understanding how and why these bans were implemented is the nature of political settlements at the international, national and local levels, the history and perceived legitimacy of the state presence in the area concerned and the significance of rents generated by the opium economy relative to other sources of economic activity. Furthermore it is hypothesised that the dynamics and sustainability of opium bans will be fundamentally different in areas of consolidated statehood, compared to areas of limited statehood.

This research addresses three central questions, discussed in detail in Chapter 4:

1. What are the local, regional, national and international processes that contribute to the imposition of a ban on opium poppy cultivation at a particular moment in time?
2. How do different households and communities respond to efforts to ban opium production in Afghanistan, and in particular what are the conditions that lead to violent unrest by rural communities?
3. What are the wider implications of the research findings for counternarcotics interventions and statebuilding more broadly?

In the effort to answer these questions, this research is designed to achieve four objectives. First, it aims to plug an empirical gap by providing a longitudinal study of households and communities engaged in opium poppy cultivation, and by documenting efforts to curb production within the diverse and dynamic political, economic, societal and ecological terrain in which the crop is grown. In doing so it aims to capture the aspirations, values and experiences of those who cultivate illicit drug crops—whose first-hand experience illustrates the effects of prohibition and the varied responses it elicits.

Second, the research aims to contribute to a growing understanding of rural livelihoods and demonstrates how a livelihoods perspective can provide a nuanced analysis of drug cultivation and drug bans. It provides a rare longitudinal analysis of a highly complex and dynamic political terrain where the population is exposed to conflict, engaged in what is considered an illegal activity, and in some cases actively involved in direct political action, including acts of violence against the state and international military and civilian forces.

Third, the research aims to enhance the political economy literature pertaining to conflict and statebuilding, by documenting the multiple and fluid centres of political power involved in imposing bans in a source country like Afghanistan. It maps how the different priorities of these centres of power have coincided and, in some cases, then ruptured; it offers a better understanding of how bans on drug crops are imposed in practice and why the coalitions that support prohibition might subsequently collapse. In doing so, it adds to the literature on political settlements and brokerage in areas of limited statehood. It examines how international interventions and obligations have inflated the price of loyalty in areas where the state often has few stable partners, systematically undermining efforts at state formation. It will also contribute to the debate on how best to integrate politics and power into the livelihoods approach in conflict-prone environments, providing new theoretical and methodological perspectives.

Finally, this research aims to generate methodological insights into the challenges of conducting research in conflict-affected areas. It draws together a number of methodological tools and merges in-depth qualitative fieldwork with high-resolution remote sensing imagery. It is unique in offering insights into the ways that synergies can be developed between quite different data-collection techniques.

Methodology

Chapter 4 details the research focus and design; the varied methods of collecting data; and the methodological and ethical considerations imposed by a changing security environment. It suffices here to recognise that the research has been undertaken over an extended period and draws on a variety of methods. It has been shaped by the challenges of exploring what is an illegal activity in insecure and contested spaces and has been informed by an existing body of empirical work from which conceptual, methodological, ethical and practical lessons have been drawn (Goodhand, 2000; Zaitch, 2001; Siegel, 2008). It has been an inductive and iterative process shaped by observations and the results of empirical work.

All researchers have their own sets of biases. However, my consistent exposure to and deep contact with farmers and farming communities in Afghanistan, as well as experience with the policy community, has helped me to maintain a critical distance from the drugs fetishism found in mainstream narratives and much of the drugs literature.

In particular, my immersion in the drug policy community and the wider statebuilding effort in Afghanistan has also supported an examination of the 'theatre of drugs policy'. I have borne witness to the ways in which different institutions and actors can, at times, subsume the counternarcotics agenda to pursue competing goals, and how counternarcotics organisations can co-opt the narrative and agendas of counterinsurgency, statebuilding, development and other issues to help justify their own policies and programmes. This experience has made me aware of the danger of bias in the often polarised debates on drugs and drug control; a bias that I have counteracted through regular fieldwork and engagement with the ground realities in rural Afghanistan.

Structure

This book is divided into eleven chapters. Chapters 2 and 3 map out the theoretical framework for the research. Chapter 2 reflects on the wider literature on statebuilding and political power to analyse opium bans not simply as a function of coercion but as the product of complex and varied socio-economic and political processes. Chapter 3 shows how the rural livelihoods perspective can illuminate the complex role of drug crops and their prohibition in different socio-economic, political and ecological terrains.

The methodology for the research is described in detail in Chapter 4. This chapter documents the challenges associated with collecting primary data in rural Afghanistan, and how a lack of basic demographic data and the diversity in local circumstances have shaped the way that fieldwork has been conducted.

Chapter 5 offers a brief history of the Afghan state, drug crop production and efforts to control it. It highlights the diverse patterns of production and the different approaches to drug control that have been pursued over time and by different donors in different regions.

Chapter 6 begins the empirical work. It documents the complete cessation of opium production imposed by the Taliban in the 2000/1 growing season, through a process of negotiation, coercion and the promise of development assistance. Chapter 7 offers a detailed account of two efforts to ban opium production in Nangarhar in 2004/5 and 2007/8, following the fall of the Taliban: it focuses on the role of international, national, sub-national and local elites in encouraging and facilitating the prohibition of opium poppy. Chapter 8 documents the unravelling of the second ban on opium production in Nangarhar between 2010 and 2013. This chapter explains how the ban collapsed in areas of limited statehood and remained intact in areas where there was a strong state presence and where the local elite's interests were heavily tied to the success of the state.

Chapter 9 examines the many disparate institutions that were behind the effort to ban opium production in the 'Helmand Food Zone' between 2008 and 2013. It examines how drug control became such a pressing priority for so many institutions and how reductions in cultivation became intimately tied to the wider statebuilding effort and individual performances of international and national actors. Chapter 10 charts the livelihood trajectories of different population groups—particularly the land-poor—in central Helmand in response to the state's efforts to eliminate both opium production and the concurrent counterinsurgency effort.

And finally, Chapter 11 brings together the different strands of enquiry into a comparison of these four bans and highlights the broader implications of the research. It shows how coalitions of international, national, sub-national and local institutions with different interests and mandates establish the conditions under which a ban can be imposed and sustained in areas of consolidated statehood, but how in areas of limited statehood the very act of prohibition distorts the political marketplace and undermines efforts at state formation.

2

POWER, CORRUPTION
AND DRUG CROP CULTIVATION

Introduction

This chapter goes beyond traditional analyses to place opium bans within socio-economic and political processes that vary by both terrain and state–societal relations, and that involve many actors with competing interests. It draws upon the wider political economy literature to offer an explanation for the diffuse dynamics behind drug control efforts and their varied impacts on the ground. It does so by initially examining the literature on statebuilding, and the narrative of 'weak' and 'fragile' states that has been used to justify international interventions in Kosovo, the former Yugoslavia and east Timor, as well as to provide a rationale for counternarcotics efforts in the drug crop-growing areas of Colombia and Afghanistan. The challenge to 'mainstream state talk' (Boege et al., 2008: 4), instead of starting from an idealised notion of the Weberian state, engages with the empirical reality of the state in countries like Afghanistan, where domestic sovereignty is contested and the state is one of several actors, compelled to engage in intense bargaining processes with many competitors in order to maintain some semblance of political order across its territory.

The literature on political geography shows that statebuilding processes have been extremely uneven, particularly in borderlands, and highlights the different kinds of political configurations that have evolved in areas where social and political structures have limited the state's capacity for direct rule. The literature also highlights the role of international actors in shaping and distorting political coalitions that are formed to impose a ban on opium poppy; it shows how prone to rupture these coalitions are in rural areas where economic and political power is diffuse and contested. The chapter recognises that rural households and communities are not simply 'objects of history' (Moore, 1966: 453) but active participants in local and sub-national politics. It ends with a short review of the literature on rural protest and what it has to say about the structural conditions that provoke violent protest and agrarian insurgency.

Explanatory accounts of drug crop cultivation often focus on its relationship to the coercive power of state or non-state actors. For instance, in Afghanistan, in the early 1990s local politico-military actors such as Nasim Akhundzada in Helmand, and Hajji Qadir in Nangarhar are credited with preventing cultivation as much as encouraging it (McCoy, 1980: 458). Similarly, the Taliban is widely credited with increasing levels of cultivation in the south in 1995, through the concentration of the means of violence in the areas under its control; later reductions in levels of cultivation are attributed to its successful imposition of a complete ban on production in 2001 (Felbab Brown, 2010).

Comparable explanations for fluctuations in cultivation in other source countries can be found in the official literature of drug control institutions and in more scholarly work. In Colombia, rising production has over the years been attributed to the Medellin and Cali cartels, the Colombian Revolutionary Armed Forces (FARC), and the paramilitaries (Kirk, 2004: 100; Tullis, 1995: 69). In Peru in the 1990s, *Sendero Luminoso*—the Shining Path—reportedly established quotas on cultivation and acted as an intermediary with Colombian cartels, engaging in a form of collective bargaining to force up market prices (Streatfeild, 2001; 392; Strong, 1992). In Burma, changing levels of cultivation have been attributed to the armed factions of Lo Hsing Han, Khun Sa and subsequently the Wa (McCoy, 1972; Buxton, 2006: 970). It is not uncommon to see references to these actors providing agricultural inputs, such as seed, fertiliser and credit, as well as using coercion and intimidation to co-opt rural communities into drug crop cultivation (Tullis, 1996; Felbab Brown, 2010).

Underpinning these explanations for drug production is the narrative of the weak or failed state, where armed actors have de facto sovereignty and have succeeded in gaining some degree of market control over the drugs trade. Indeed, according to McCoy (1980: 480):

> In the actual drug production zones of the Andes, Afghanistan or Burma, determining control over the drugs trade is a relatively easy matter. By simply hiking

through the Afghan-Pakistan borderlands, for example, a New York Times reporter or a DEA [Drug Enforcement Administration]agent can quickly learn that Mullah Nasim (Akhundzada) *rules* the poppy fields of the upper Helmand valley or that Hekmatyar *owns* the half dozen heroin refineries at Kohisultan. The fact of *territorial control* makes involvement in drug dealing too obvious to conceal in these opium highlands. (Emphasis added.)

This depiction of territorial control over drug production by individual warlords and armed actors has led national governments and multilateral institutions to negotiate bans on cultivation. Examples include the attempt by Congressmen Lester Wolff and Joseph Nellis to negotiate with Khun Sa in 1977; earlier efforts to deal with Lo Hsing Han (Lintner, 1999: 313–15; Renard, 1996: 61); discussions between the US Ambassador to Pakistan and Nasim Akhundzada in 1989 (McCoy, 1980: 458; Peters, 2009b: 55–6); and the numerous meetings between the former Executive Director of UNODC, Pino Arlacchi, and representatives of the Taliban regime in the mid to late 1990s. In all these instances, policy-makers have viewed power as being concentrated in the hands of non-state actors in rural areas, leading them to believe that comprehensive eradication will bankrupt insurgent groups (Schweich, 2008; Smith, 2013: 207).

However, such explanations often ascribe more coercive power to armed actors than they actually possess. As Catherine Brown notes (1999: 251):

the exotic image of the 'Golden Triangle' with its 'drug barons' commanding powerful drug funded armies, particularly the portrayal of Khun Sa as the 'drug kingpin' of the region, trivialises and obscures the political and economic complexities of the situation.

It is my hypothesis that political power in areas of drug crop cultivation is often more negotiated and decentred than is frequently appreciated and that efforts to negotiate or enforce bans may not have the intended effect of establishing control over state peripheries or eliminating cultivation. Rather, negotiating and imposing these bans may create the political equivalent of the 'butterfly effect', establishing small variations in political settlements at the periphery that gather enough pace to destabilise the sub-national political coalition that supported a ban on production.

Behaving Like a State: Drug Control and Statebuilding

Historically statebuilding has been a violent and contested process that has entailed centralising the means of coercion and capital within a given territory (Goodhand, 2009). As Tilly (1985: 175) notes:

...the builders of national power all played a mixed strategy: eliminating, subjugating, dividing, conquering, cajoling, buying as the occasions presented themselves. The buying manifested in exemptions from taxation, creation of honorific offices, the establishment of claims on the national treasury, and a variant of other devices that made magnate's welfare dependent on the maintenance of the existing power structure. In the long run it all came down to massive pacification and the monopolisation of the means of coercion.

In contrast, contemporary statebuilding is frequently seen as a technocratic and exogenous process. Initially launched as 'peacebuilding' under UN Secretary General Boutros Boutros Ghali in 1992, it consisted of a series of interventions with the goal of 'rebuilding the institutions and infrastructure of nations torn by civil war and strife'. The agenda was broadened in 2000 with the Report of the Panel on United Nations Peace Operations (the Brahimi report) and the call for more proactive engagement in what were considered 'weak' and 'failing' states (Suhrke, 2011: 6–8; Paris and Sisk, 2007: 2). In 2001 the doctrine of 'responsibility to protect' was defined. This argued that sovereignty was a responsibility rather than a right; it suggested that foreign intervention was not only legitimate but was a necessity in states where the population 'is suffering serious harm as a result of internal war, insurgency, repression or state failure' (International Commission on Intervention and State Sovereignty, 2001; Mukhopadhyay, 2014). It is precisely this call for a proactive engagement in failed and failing states, with an ever widening agenda of activities and objectives aimed at building societies organised by democratic values and free market economics—frequently referred to as 'the liberal peace'—that has been at the forefront of efforts in Afghanistan since 11 September 2001.

Overseas drug control has a much longer history than the statebuilding efforts seen since the 1990s. The desire to limit the cultivation, trade and use of illicit drugs dates back to the International Opium Convention signed in The Hague in 1912.[1] Controlling illicit drug crop cultivation has been a central part of the architecture of this and subsequent international conventions on illicit drugs. For example, the 1961 Single Convention on Narcotics Drugs, as amended in 1972, called on all states to 'prohibit the cultivation of opium poppy, the coca bush and cannabis' and to 'seize any plants illicitly cultivated and destroy them, except for small quantities required...for scientific or research purposes' (UN, 1961: 12). These demands were reiterated in the 1988 Convention Against Illicit Traffic and Narcotics Drugs and Psychotropic Substances which called on states to 'take appropriate measures to prevent illicit cultivation of and to eradicate plants containing narcotic or psychotropic substances, such as opium poppy, coca bush and cannabis plants culti-vated illicitly in its territory' (UN, 1988: 14). In 1998 the 'Special Session of the General Assembly Devoted to Countering the World Drug Problem Together' reaffirmed the need for states to 'implement and enforce' Article 14 of the 1988 Convention and 'take appropriate measures to prevent the illicit cultivation of plants containing narcotic and psychotropic substances and to cooperate to improve the effectiveness of eradication efforts *inter alia*, giving support to alternative development' (UN, 1998: 33).[2]

Aside from these international obligations to which most drug crop-pro-ducing nations are signatories, separate bilateral arrangements with Western governments—most notably the USG—also outline the measures that major drug-producing or transit nations need to comply with (US Department of State, 2013: 2–3). These commitments ensure that a country's performance against drug control objectives are codified in law[3] and are subject to an annual review in which each country is assessed and reported on. Failure to comply can bring a number of sanctions imposed by the US Congress that may include the suspension of aid, the imposition of stricter trade controls, and an obligation by US missions at International Financial Institutions (IFIs), such as the World Bank and International Monetary Fund, to vote against the provision of loans, grants or financial support.

The policy narrative on illicit drug production is underpinned by an ideal-ised notion of the nation state, similar to that which has informed peacebuild-ing efforts since the early 1990s (Suhrke, 2011: 7). Within this framework, 'weak', 'fragile' or 'failed' states are those where the state does not have the necessary legitimacy and capacity to centralise the means of coercion, secure its borders or protect its population.

These states are seen to be producers of 'public bads' including terrorism, protracted violence and human rights abuses, as well as illicit drug produc-tion,[4] and the remedy for weak or fragile states is to be found in the 'state-building' efforts of modern diplomacy, military interventions, as well as the technical and financial assistance of Western bilateral development pro-grammes and the work of international institutions such as the United Nations. In theory, these interventions are aimed at strengthening state insti-tutions so that a state can gain control of its territory, increase its revenue through taxation, and deliver the public goods and services that it is assumed will help gain legitimacy with the population. As such, the state is seen as the guarantor of order (Hopkins, 2008: 175).

Within this idealised concept, illicit drug crop cultivation is seen to thrive in territories where state power is contested by armed non-state actors, or where state actors are seen either to lack the necessary political commitment or to have been so corrupted that they do not enforce the legal norms established by the international drug control conventions. Both counternarcotics and statebuilding interventions aim ostensibly to build the capacity of state institutions to gain greater control over their territories. Through the process of state territorialisation the threats to global insecurity, often found on the margins of the nation state, can be eliminated. One of the justifications for eliminating drug production is to bankrupt insurgent movements and enable state institutions to (re)gain control over their unruly peripheries.

Often the remedies outlined for those countries producing drug crops are indistinguishable from those advocated by Western donors and international agencies in pursuit of statebuilding objectives. For example, strengthening police and military forces, support for the judiciary, and the delivery of public goods and services in the form of rural development—what Giustozzi (2011: 5) has referred to as 'virtuous state building'—are bound up with notions of good governance and are at the forefront of counternarcotics efforts. Further similarities between the counternarcotics and statebuilding agendas include the belief that, with the right kind of technical support, equipment and funding, the causes of state 'fragility', like the drivers of drug production, can be resolved. In this environment, greater investment and personnel are always justified, and the scope and depth of the mission is likely to expand when interventions do not achieve their stated goals—what Suhrke (2011) has characterised as a 'critical mass doctrine'.

Increasingly linked to the wider statebuilding effort, there is a recognised set of counternarcotics interventions that include interdiction, eradication, alternative development and demand reduction. These are often seen as bounded interventions that fall under the mandate of the drug control community in the form of UNODC and such bilateral institutions as the International Narcotics and Legal Affairs Section (INL) of the USG. Under the auspices of such institutions, specific counternarcotics programmes are developed and budgeted, with performance measures linked to different activities. Implementation is often undertaken by a variety of institutions including private civilian and military contractors, in partnership with the governments of the source countries.

In a country that is a major supplier of drug crops, a successful counternarcotics programme will bring about a reduction in levels of cultivation by encouraging farmers to abandon cultivation, and/or will achieve high levels of eradication. In this context, rural development interventions offer incentives to farmers to transition from drug crops to legal crops. Some alternative development projects in Pakistan and Thailand go further, facilitating transition to non-farm income.

While seen by many as simply rural development programmes targeted at those who produce opium and coca, alternative development initiatives can be qualitatively different, primarily because of the imperative to reduce levels of cultivation within the life of the programme. In some cases, donors attach conditionality to the receipt of development assistance, requiring rural communities and even individual households to commit to reductions in cultivation in order to receive assistance at all, or even to abandon production before development inputs are provided.

The mechanistic agreements and short-term development assistance on offer have led to a growing recognition that this kind of development often becomes a vehicle for strengthening the patrimonial system in source countries. These kinds of alternative development programmes are often supported by efforts to reinforce the coercive capacity of the state. They may include dissemination counternarcotics messages as well as technical assistance and equipment to support crop destruction. These interventions, based upon an imperative to deliver quick and dramatic reductions in drug crop cultivation, are in tension with the proclaimed values and goals of liberal peacebuilders, including democracy, human rights, security, good governance and a market-based economy.

Counternarcotics programmes therefore run in parallel with a range of other forms of interventions, including rural development programmes designed and implemented by development organisations. These programmes may have quite different objectives, including counterinsurgency (COIN), but, like many conventional development programmes, they may give little consideration to their effects on the causes of drug crop cultivation. COIN operations may offer support for armed groups that extract rent from the drugs trade but are willing to conduct combat operations against insurgent groups. And rural development programmes may undermine efforts to reduce drug crop cultivation in the short term by, for example, providing access to improved irrigation or road networks that increase yields and facilitate trade.

Shaped by the same structures and processes that demand value for money against specific goals and performance measures, institutions that fund and implement these interventions typically resist efforts to curtail their investments if cultivation increases, arguing that this is not within their institutional mandate. Experience shows that most institutions implementing these programmes will be particularly unhappy to have their operational space undermined by active efforts to destroy the standing crop (Brailsford, 1989a; Mansfield, 2002a).

In this complex and crowded institutional environment, adaptive behaviour can be seen not only among farmers as they respond to a variety of interventions and exogenous and idiosyncratic shocks, but also among the varied institutions and actors at local, sub-national, national and international levels that have different and competing interests. Policy areas such as counternarcotics, counterinsurgency, food security and economic growth may not be mutually reinforcing despite the optimistic assumptions of liberal peacebuilders. There are contradictions and trade-offs between objectives, time frames, sequencing and priorities; competition over finite funds; and frequently tensions between personalities. Understanding this institutional environment and the factors that shape the policy process is critical to developing a clearer picture of how bans are imposed and why they may subsequently collapse.

Fulfilling International Drug Control Obligations in Countries with Limited or Contested Domestic Sovereignty

In spite of these tensions, there has been a growing convergence between statebuilding and counternarcotics policy when it comes to implementation on the ground. Even the destruction of the standing crop and the imposition of bans on drug crop cultivation are justified as interventions that will strengthen the legitimacy of the state by enforcing legal norms across national territory and weakening criminal and/or insurgent groups that threaten the state's monopoly over violence (Schweich, 2008; UNODC/MCN, 2007). An effective ban on drug crop production is therefore viewed as an important symbolic act—a telling visual display of the state's capacity to impose its policies within its territorial boundaries.

As such, the absence of illicit cultivation is interpreted not only as an indicator of successful drug-control efforts but also as a proxy measure of state strength and legitimacy. In this sense, sovereignty and recognition are bound up with the ability to provide security and prevent the export of 'public bads' like terrorism and drugs. Thus, performance that meets counternarcotics objectives conveys to an international audience that the state can perform its core functions. As Migdal (1994: 9) notes:

> Examples abound of 'hybrid' polities whose rulers went out of their way to present the appearance of a Weberian state to the international system, while representing something quite different to their domestic constituents.

In Afghanistan, this conjoining of reductions in cultivation with references to 'strong' and 'committed' governors (UNODC/MCN, 2008) has received plaudits from the central government in Kabul and Western donor nations. This theme is mirrored in the 2011 World Development Report (2011: 36–367), where emphasis is placed on domestic political leadership in combatting crime, corruption and developmental crises.

Conversely, increasing levels of drug cultivation are taken to signify declining state power and a growth in the strength of non-state actors involved with the drug economy. Continued or resurgent cultivation becomes a powerful shorthand for state failure, particularly in the case of opium poppy. This is why images of national or international security forces, or of physical infrastructures like arterial roads or government building, surrounded by the crop in full flower, are a common feature of media articles, as well as the covers of books on illicit drugs and the failure of drug control efforts.

Given the way that persistent drug crop cultivation is framed within the debate on weak and fragile states, it is worth examining the academic literature on statebuilding for a more complete analysis of the uneven and diffuse nature of state and non-state power in a source country like Afghanistan. This work shows how states without a monopoly over the means of violence try to maintain political order in a frequently volatile 'political market place' (de Waal, 2009).

This literature leads us down a different analytical track in seeking to explain why opium bans are implemented and may subsequently collapse; it takes us away from normative language and references related to farmgate prices, aberrant behaviour, corruption and a lack of political commitment of those in positions of state power. Instead, it locates efforts to ban opium and their subsequent return to cultivation within the context of a wider and dynamic process of political bargains and brokerage involving multiple centres of power. It also offers some explanation as to why the political coalition in support of a ban on opium remains more stable in some areas of a province than in others; an explanation that is subsequently examined in the empirical chapters of this research.

The Diffuse and Uneven Nature of State Power

A central theme in the language and conceptual framework of international drug control treaties and obligations, as well as in the official narratives and literature on drugs, is the notion of a Weberian state, viewed as a single actor with a legitimate monopoly over the means of violence within its territorial boundaries. As such, the state has what Krasner (1999: 4) refers to as 'domestic sovereignty'—'the formal organization of political authority within the state and the ability of the public authorities to exercise effective control within the borders of their own polity'.

However, in many parts of the world, the nation state has *de jure* sovereignty but has not achieved full territorial control of areas within its own borders where *de facto* sovereignty may lie with others (Jackson, 1990). In some marginal, remote areas, the state has limited presence, perhaps due to low population densities and/or the lack of potential for rent extraction (Scott, 2009). In other areas, particularly border regions, territorial control may be disputed by neighbouring states or by armed groups within the country. Transnational networks and organisations may also constrain the state's monopoly over coercion and taxation. These may include the commercial interests of the extractive industries, the smuggling of licit and illicit commodities by cross-border criminal organisations, and the presence of international peace-keeping forces and/or private security companies, all of which may challenge 'Westphalian sovereignty' (Krasner, 1999).

Risse (2011: 4) contends that, while most developing states have achieved full territorial control, or 'consolidated statehood', there remain areas 'of limited statehood': territorial, sectoral, social and temporal space in which 'the central authorities lack the ability to implement and enforce rules and decisions or in which the legitimate monopoly over the means of violence is lacking'. Many drug crop-producing nations thus have 'international sovereignty'— where territorial boundaries are recognised and they are accountable for what happens within their borders but lack the coercive force and administrative capacity to implement the international treaties and bilateral commitments to which they are signatories.

The empirical elements of this research show a tension between, on the one hand, the need for the Afghan state to project the appearance of state power and 'behave like a state' by banning opium poppy, and, on the other hand, its weak domestic sovereignty, which is particularly fractured and contested in borderland regions where drug crop cultivation is concentrated. This tension helps explain why prohibition can prove so short-lived in many parts of Afghanistan, and why prohibition undermines state formation in some of the more peripheral and most contested parts of the country.

Central to my analysis is an understanding of the nature of the state and how order is established and maintained in areas where the means of violence have not been concentrated. North et al. (2009) suggest that developing societies deal with the 'violence problem' by absorbing the key wielders of violence into an effective political coalition which manipulates the economic system in order to produce rents for a few privileged insiders—what North et al. refer to as 'limited access orders'. Under this arrangement, 'the dominant coalition within a political settlement creates opportunities and order by limiting the access to valuable resources (land, labour, and capital) or access and control of valuable activities (such as contract enforcement, property rights enforcement, trade, worship and education) to elite groups' (Di John and Putzel, 2009: 14).

Viewing the state as a constellation of competing elements with shifting centres of power provides a more accurate starting point for examining prohibition policies. Given their international responsibilities and the repercussions of failing to comply with bilateral and multilateral drug control requirements (Snyder, 2006: 951–2), major drug-producing countries like Afghanistan are obliged to find ways to engage with areas of limited statehood that exist within their territorial boundaries. Expanding and consolidating territorial control into these areas would require a degree of coercive power that the state cannot bring to bear; or, if it were to try to do so, that would impose a financial and military burden that could threaten the government's capacity to administer, coerce and tax in its own economic and political heartlands. In this context, the central government may need to make alternative arrangements and reach accommodations with local elites, agreeing to greater autonomy—a process that Scott refers to as 'indirect rule'—in order to ensure a degree of acquiescence and compliance with the state's primary interests, in particular the protection of its borders against military incursions, but also on occasion a ban on drug crop production.

The critical question is: How does the state engage with the different rural realities that exist within its own territory, particularly those areas where state power is contested and where there is a history of violent resistance to efforts by the central government to impose its writ? In his work on Somalia, Menkhaus (2007: 78) refers to 'the mediated state' in which the government relies on partnerships (or at least coexistence) with diverse local intermediaries and rival sources of authority to provide core functions of public security, justice and conflict management in much of the country. However, without sufficient coercive and financial power on the part of the state, it remains unclear what form these partnerships will take, how durable they will be, and how the state can gain traction with the rural elite and its constituency in its demands for action against drug crop cultivation—a policy that inevitably has economic effects on the rural population.

23

The spatial distribution of power in source countries like Afghanistan is vividly captured in Scott's (2009) analysis of 'state' and 'non-state space'. He describes how pre-existing power structures, the dispersion of the population and a lack of an economic surplus can undermine the state's efforts to encapsulate parts of its own territory. Some scholars (Hammond, 2011; Lieberman, 2010) challenge Scott's explanation of why populations migrated to the highlands of Southeast Asia, and his attribution of migration to these 'shatter zones' as a rejection of the policies and practices of the state. In response, Scott points to the potential for violent resistance to state interference in these areas; a claim that clearly has historical relevance in parts of rural Afghanistan (cf. Barfield, 2010).

Scott (2009) argues that, in contrast to the 'state-governed peoples' of the valley societies, physical terrain, combined with an isolated tribal and more egalitarian social structure, has thwarted the formation of a dominant elite with which the state can engage and establish a more permanent physical presence in highland communities. These are what Scott terms 'the self-governing peoples' where the state has had to find ways to manage dissent rather than attempt to impose the policies of the central government. As Staniland (2012: 256) notes, 'Population security and statebuilding sound good in the metropole but often look very different at the periphery; seemingly technocratic policies like governance and service provision are in fact short-hand for state coercion, homogenisation, surveillance and extraction'.

Scholars such as Karen Barkey (1994), Catherine Boone (2003) and Paul Nugent (2002) also document the variable nature of state power and show how state strategies of engagement are shaped by the terrain, borders, leadership, social structures and resource endowments of different areas within the national territory. They do not, however, offer as polarised an image of state–societal relations as Scott; rather, they use historical data to provide an insight into the blurred boundaries between state and non-state/anti-state actors and into the different arrangements the central state has made with those in positions of power in the regions.

Barkey(1994), for example, reflects upon the temporal nature of societal resistance to state intrusion in her study of the Ottoman Empire in the seventeenth and eighteenth centuries. In her historical analysis she documents how bandits, once a source of unrest and a threat to social order, were subsequently co-opted by offers of rewards and position. She highlights the state's potential to expand its domestic sovereignty over time through a constant process of coalition-building and deal-making. This process was aided by the motivations of bandit groups themselves who, Barkey argues, were not interested in directly challenging state rule and collaborating with other societal groups whose interests were compromised by the state, but instead looked to improve their own bargaining position and gain concessions and privileges from the state (Barkey, 1994: 20–21).

Focusing on the political topography in post-colonial Africa, Boone (2003) argues that state penetration into rural areas is facilitated by the concentration of people and resources. She notes: '...in a hierarchical peasant society, rural leaders are political actors whom the centre must engage either as allies or as rivals'. She contends that differences in economic opportunities, class and communal structure, and the economic autonomy of a rural elite, will produce different 'patterns of political battling and bargaining between regimes and rural elites' (Boone, 2003: 9).

Boone contends that in areas of economic surplus where there are hierarchical rural societies, the state will look to share power with a rural elite that is economically dependent on the state, but will usurp an elite that has economic autonomy and is therefore in a position to challenge the authority of the state. In areas where rural society is not hierarchical but where commercial agricultural production occurs, the state will not look to establish a physical presence but will govern from the centre through what Boone refers to as 'administrative occupation' (2004: 36–7). Finally Boone's schema (2003: 33) anticipates a scenario in some rural areas where localities are left to their own devices; where the centre does not seek to 'engage or impose' but 'abdicates authority'—what she refers to as a strategy of 'non-incorporation'.

As we shall see in subsequent chapters, this description of areas of non-incorporation, which Scott (2010) also terms 'non-state space', seems particularly relevant to the more remote and marginal areas of Afghanistan where poor soils and limited landholdings have militated against agricultural surpluses and state encapsulation. Boone, however, does not anticipate a strategy of non-incorporation in 'a zone of commercial agriculture, especially in an area of export crop production'; she assumes that 'the state will have an interest in taxing producers and in monitoring the accumulation of wealth in private hands' (Boone, 2003: 33). She is writing about licit crop production; in the case of illegal drug crops, state actors are forced to pursue strategies of both accommodation and sanction, and as Snyder (2006: 950) argues, public extraction (or a state monopoly) is not an option where a high-value resource is deemed illegal by international law.

What is perhaps not adequately conveyed in Boone's typology is the potential for the institutional arrangements between state and local elites to alter over time. Political geography constantly evolves, and in a post-conflict setting, the state may be forced to renegotiate the rules of the game with new rural elites that emerged during the years of conflict and have greater economic, political and military autonomy. Therefore, where a new class of 'violence entrepreneurs' (Giustozzi, 2005: 10) have emerged and alternative forms of authority, economic activity and regulation have been established, the dual legitimacy problem faced by state elites is likely to be most intense. Although the state is bound by international obligations and demands to curb illicit drug production and local forms of authority, political order and domestic legitimacy may depend upon stable and interdependent relationships with peripheral elites.

To develop a better understanding of why bans on drug crops can be imposed and sustained in some areas and not in others, it is necessary to capture the fluid and dynamic nature of the interactions between the central state and local actors occupying different kinds of geographic space. In contemporary Afghanistan, multiple international actors operate according to different agendas, including counterinsurgency, counter-terror, the war on drugs, and statebuilding. It is also important to understand how the competition among these international institutions impacts on domestic sovereignty and the state's interactions with sub-national and local elites.

The Complex and Distorted Political Marketplace

The literature on political settlements and coalition-building offers an essential contribution to any analysis of efforts to curb cultivation in a source country like Afghanistan, where a variety of centres of political power are involved in implementation, and where deal-making and bargaining are an integral part of any effort by the state to gain the appearance of territorial control and elicit the acquiescence of many actors.

Therefore, governance networks are extremely dynamic and multi-levelled and to an extent everyone is 'partially-sighted', with no one having complete control over the process. Resources such as drugs which flow through these networks have unpredictable and contingent effects. As North et al. (2009) note, in basic limited-access orders, elites are constantly oscillating into and out of the dominant political coalition. Few of these actors, particularly those at the local and sub-national levels, are prepared to fully commit to any single policy, let alone efforts to ban opium; they often prefer to maintain a strategic distance from direct decision-making. This preference for what Suhrke (2006) refers to as 'spot contracts' is not only to protect the political capital of elites should the other actors in this fragile coalition fail to live up to their commitments, but also to maintain a degree of independence that allows them to retain their value as brokers and mediators between their current state patrons and the rural constituencies from which they draw their legitimacy.

North et al. (2009) usefully highlight the importance of a dominant coalition that establishes political order by concentrating the means of violence and limiting access to rents. Their analysis does not, however, sufficiently disaggregate the different centres of political power within this coalition—how they compete and interact among themselves, how they engage with the wider world in which they operate, and how interactions alter over time and space. Moreover, drug crops present a particularly challenging commodity on which to establish a stable political coalition. As a 'diffuse resource' (Auty, 2001) spread over a wide geographic area, easily extractable and with a high value, it is difficult for any group to monopolise. As Le Billon (2001: 571) notes, 'This [geographic] fragmentation has an important impact on armed conflict economies based on resources as leaders may face difficulties in keeping their allies and controlling their subordinates'.

De Waal's (2009 and 2010) model of the 'political marketplace' provides another useful lens for viewing the spatial and temporal dimensions of governance networks. The idea of the political marketplace is based upon a model of patrimonial governance, where allegiances are traded between provincial elites and the metropolitan centre. It is a marketplace based on the currency of loyalty which can be bought and sold in exchanges between centre and the periphery. In parallel with the work of Parks and Cole (2010: 18) on 'secondary political settlements', de Waal's model explores how provincial elites might use votes in an election, the revenue from economic activity, or even violence to extract the highest price they can from the metropolitan elite, while at the same time the metropolitan elite looks at ways to minimise the amount they will pay, using many of the same tools against the provincial elite. Recognising the temporary nature of any bargains made in the absence of an 'inclusive buy-in of all elites by the best resourced actor in the market place', de Waal (2009: 102–4) talks of the need for renegotiation when 'market conditions shift'.

In the context of what are often locally implemented efforts to ban opium production, de Waal's (2009: 103) analysis also reflects on the 'marketplace of loyalties that operates at sub-national and local levels, where provincial elites secure the support, including votes and guns, of their constituents in return for jobs, and licenses to trade or pillage'. He reflects on the potential for 'multiple rival power centres' within each metropolitan elite, although he does not further develop these aspects of his model.

The model explicitly recognises the role that international actors play in 'distorting the political marketplace' by acting as 'players, not referees', particularly where the international intervention is of a size that it ends up competing with the metropolitan elite, inflating the price of loyalty and rendering agreements unstable. Given the role that international actors have played in the imposition of opium bans and their presence in many rural areas in the form of both civilian and military agencies in post-2001 Afghanistan, the inclusion of this international dimension is critical to an understanding of the full range of parties in the political coalitions that lie behind prohibition and what effect these have on the resilience of the bans and the coalitions that underpin them.

The model can be further extended. First, in addition to bargaining between centre and periphery, the marketplace involves complex interactions between and within local elites, involving the making and remaking of 'tertiary political settlements'. Second, these settlements have a transnational dimension involving linkages upwards to international actors and across the border to state and non-state actors in neighbouring countries. While Barnett and Zurcher's (2008) 'peacebuilder's contract' goes some way to modelling the bargaining relationships between international actors, national elites and peripheral elites, it is helpful to return to Risse et al. and the concept of limited and consolidated statehood. Like de Waal, Risse (2011: 3) recognises the multiplicity of state, non-state and international actors engaged in areas of limited statehood; where sovereignty is shared and where governance 'links the local with national, regional and global levels' in what is termed 'multilevel governance'. Of particular value is the level of disaggregation and dynamism offered within the architecture of multilevel governance.

Risse (2011: 245) identifies four levels in multilevel governance, where 'actual or suspected policy decisions and actions at one level shape the expectations, the behaviour and actions of actors at other levels'. The first level is the interaction between different local actors; the second is the interaction between local and international actors; the third is the interaction between the different international actors operating at the local level; the fourth consists of the different international organisations and representatives of donor governments working with national ministries at the centre.

Conceptually Risse's approach helps move us beyond the kind of dichotomous model presented by Snyder (2006), where state and private actors compete or collaborate over the extraction of rents from 'lootable' commodities such as illicit drugs. Snyder points out the importance of those in state power being seen to comply with the demands of the international drug-control regime, while perhaps benefitting from payments for protection from private actors and receiving bilateral assistance for their counternarcotics efforts at the same time. However, further disaggregation is required to chart the far more complex institutional environment in which drug crop cultivation and drug control efforts take place in a country like Afghanistan, where multiple actors—including foreign governments and multilateral organisations—engage directly with local communities and rural elites, as well as with a variety of central and sub-national state actors.

As such, multilevel governance is a necessary adjunct for understanding the complex and fluid bargains that occur across different spatial and political space within countries like Afghanistan. This allows for agency and contingency, in which different actors often misread the policy decisions and actions of others, and where international actors are always constrained by their lack of intimate knowledge of local conditions and circumstances (Risse et al., 2011: 253). It also offers a model where the political marketplace is fluid and dynamic; where there are multiple and competing interests at work and, in the context of this research, where the effort to curb drug crop cultivation is one of many objectives around which different political actors might coalesce.

Risse's model is not a rigidly hierarchical one as local, national and international levels all interact and only international organisations are perceived to have the 'freedom to roam' between the different actors and levels. In the context of Afghanistan, it is clear that there are further interactions to consider in which international organisations and actors are not involved. These interactions may differ according to the political geography of the area. In areas of consolidated statehood, local elites are likely to operate through the state apparatus in which, in line with Boone's arguments, they have typically been absorbed and which they have come to represent. However, in areas of limited statehood, local actors may have gained direct access to a variety of institutions with political power at the national and even international level and can bypass those that occupy positions at the sub-national level.

In Afghanistan, this privileged access is often due to the strategic location of some areas of limited statehood. For example, much of the country's border, aside from the formal border crossings, consists of areas where both national and international actors are particularly active, attempting to secure the allegiances of those who reside there by providing weapons and largesse, in order to prevent the infiltration of armed actors from neighbouring countries (most notably

Pakistan). It could be argued that locations that cultivate drug crops are likely to be areas of limited statehood with privileged access to national and international actors, enabling their rural representatives to avoid a hierarchy of sub-national elites and institutions. These are areas where the state does not have direct territorial control but where it does have strategic interests in complying with its international obligations. They may even be areas where international actors are directly engaged in the delivery of development assistance, or in diplomatic initiatives aimed at moral suasion to prevent drug crop cultivation.

While the position of the rural elite in these areas is often contested locally and leaders may even change over time due to family rivalries and disputes, party affiliation and camaraderie (*andiwal*) during the war against the Soviets have provided these rural notables with direct links to those in the provincial administration and in Kabul. In this sense, the local elite should be understood as individual members of families of distinction within the village and the tribe or sub-tribe, who are seen as able to represent the village's interest in part by drawing on patronage and favour from those elites with power at the provincial and national levels.

The result is that some local actors may have considerably more influence than either Risse or de Waal projects. Taking advantage of their capacity to engage directly with a wide spectrum of institutions and the intense competition for their loyalty, they may form or—for the sake of negotiations—appear to form coalitions with different international, national, and cross-border actors as a way of gaining greater leverage. Local actors in these areas are likely to be involved with many different negotiations with a number of different parties, looking to extract as much rent as they can while, at the same time, better positioning themselves with other parties, so as to find the political space in which they might renege on any past deals that are incurring a financial or political cost, and make new deals that offer greater returns.

The 'shifting market conditions' that de Waal refers to are both exogenous and endogenous, a consequence of just how complex and dynamic the political marketplace can be in a terrain like that of Afghanistan, where multiple international actors are operating with diverse and competing interests, and all looking to persuade local elites to co-opt the rural population into doing their bidding. I would further argue that, when combined with drug crop cultivation within a border area, the price of loyalty may be hyper-inflated, and any political bargains made with local actors in these areas are likely to be extremely fragile. This is due both to the different interests of the national and international actors and to the kinds of societal structures that are often found in this kind of terrain, where, in the words of Barrington Moore (1966: 453), the rural population 'is not simply an object of history' but is an active participant, particularly where private and collective interests are threatened, as explored in the next section.

Political economy models and frameworks like the limited access order and political marketplace tend to reduce politics to the interplay of material resources and access to the means of coercion. In so doing, they downplay the importance of ideas, beliefs and norms which are often held collectively and may trump individual material interests. These models also assume that actors in the marketplace act rationally and have access to complete information. Yet in situations of multilevel governance, players in the market are partially sighted and are constantly double-guessing or misperceiving the policy decisions and actions of others; these misperceptions can shape their own expectations and behaviour (Risse et al., 2011: 245). Therefore, to understand the political marketplace in countries like Afghanistan, one must first appreciate the discursive and the symbolic and recognise how legitimacy is constructed by drawing upon culturally embedded discourses and repertoires of action. David Mosse (2004), writing about development projects, has argued that the perceived success or failure of projects may have more to do with crises of representation and the inability to mobilise sufficient support for and belief in the legitimacy of such projects, rather than with more prosaic and seemingly central concerns about whether or not they deliver tangible benefits.

It is also critical to keep in mind that efforts to ban drug crops are intimately tied to perceptions of state success and of the performance of individual leaders within the domestic and international arenas. Drug control can serve as a means by which elites can present themselves as credible interlocutors and behave in a 'state-like' way to gain patronage and support, almost regardless of what their past or current misdemeanours might have been. To the outside world a ban is a visual expression of power, control and territorialisation. The interactions that domestic political leaders have with the international community and the public support they receive for their efforts to ban drug crops can reinforce the image of leadership to both external and internal audiences. Locally farmers in areas of limited statehood may have a quite different understanding of state power, shaped by history and current experiences, but they may adjust these in the face of an international intervention and its support for prohibition. Understanding these different perceptions, and how and why they change over time and location, is critical to understanding how prohibition is imposed even in some of the most contested areas, and why it may subsequently collapse, in some cases quite dramatically.

The Rural Population: Active Participants in the Political Marketplace

Despite the critical role that history, resources and societal structures play in shaping the interactions between the state and local centres of power, particularly in the areas of limited statehood, there are only a few isolated accounts of the role that local elites play in imposing bans on drug crop cultivation, of the coalitions between sub-national and local elites in support of prohibition and of the durability of the political (dis)agreements that underpin these coalitions.[5] Even less attention is given to local political settlements and how the distribution of economic and political power at the village level can either buttress or undermine efforts to impose a ban in a given area. Rural households and communities are largely absent from the analysis of the deeply political processes involved in imposing a ban on opium poppy cultivation across a wide geographic area in which state power is typically contested.

As noted earlier, much of the drugs literature presents an overly simplified account of rural communities as political actors, focusing largely on farmers' reactions to crop destruction. For example, in Afghanistan, UNODC claims that it is largely government coercion that compels farmers to desist from opium poppy cultivation, which implies that the state is successfully concentrating the means of violence and is able to impose its will on a rural population (UNODC/MCN, 2011: 61). In contrast, critics of drug control efforts, particularly eradication, claim that the destruction of the opium crop has prompted farmers to reject the state and join the insurgency (Holbrooke, 2008; Bergen, 2011: 192). The Taliban in particular is said to have gained support by offering protection to rural communities at risk of losing their crop, and by counteracting government corruption associated with the eradication effort. As such, the rural population is depicted as subject to the coercive powers of either the state or of insurgent groups.

One problem with these accounts is that they depict both the state and insurgents as institutions with cohesive structures and hierarchies, when these institutions are hybridised and the lines between state and non-state, as well as private and public, are blurred. Social affinities and patronage networks pervade both state and insurgent groups, and the same individual can simultaneously be a government official, a private actor and, for example, a Taliban supporter. As de Waal (2009: 101) notes, this makes for much more amorphous institutions and structures than are usually portrayed:

> The distinction between institutional and patrimonial governance is as true for
> insurgents as for governments and is as valid in wartime as during peace.... In coun-

tries with institutionalised governance, any rebel forces that survive to challenge a government will themselves be disciplined, hierarchical, capable of coordinating political and military strategy, and be able to call a halt to violence when they choose to do so. In countries with patrimonial governance, both government and rebels are likely to operate in the same way: using kinship and patronage, and licensing proxies. Once begun, these ill-governed wars are remarkably difficult to stop.

Further, superimposed on the image of the state and insurgents as monolithic is the sense that both are exogenous entities, offering their assistance to a rural population that has a choice between two sides in a conflict. The insurgents are presented as offering the capacity for violence to repel the state's eradication efforts. In exchange, the rural population is expected to provide the insurgents with financial and political support allowing it to increase its territorial control.

The rural population is portrayed as distinct and separate from both state and insurgents. This depiction ignores how bonds of kinship, patronage and collective action, including acts of violence, often shape the policies and practice of the different centres of power—some affiliated with the state, some with the insurgency, many striving to maintain independence—that coexist in a given locality. Finally there is the predisposition that the drug-related literature shows towards drugs fetishism and teleology, placing far too much emphasis on drug crop cultivation and drug control efforts—particularly crop destruction—in shaping the political terrain.

In many drug crop-producing countries, including Afghanistan, the threat of crop destruction has played its part in alienating the rural population (Farrell and Giustozzi, 2013: 852). However, whether this has automatically prompted farmers to join insurgents is less clear. The empirical evidence points to different responses to efforts to destroy drug crops in different areas within a country and over different time periods. For example, in some areas of Afghanistan efforts to ban opium poppy were largely accepted; there was little resistance either to the state's and local elites' efforts to coerce the local populations not to plant opium poppy, or to subsequent efforts to destroy the opium crop that was successfully planted. In contrast, in other parts of the very same province and in subsequent years, these same interventions prompted violent reactions that led to armed rebellion in areas that had previously responded to efforts to ban opium with only minor acts of defiance. In this context, it is important to distinguish between acts of resistance to government efforts to ban drug crop cultivation and actual rebellion against the state, and thereby to recognise the role that the rural population plays in the political marketplace, attempting to shape political settlements at the local and sub-national levels.

It is possible to see evidence of 'acts of everyday resistance' (Scott, 1990) in response to efforts to ban opium poppy and coca in a number of drug crop-producing nations. For example, in Afghanistan, households and communities may engage in attempts to deter eradication by irrigating their fields, thereby preventing the tractors from destroying the crop. In Colombia, farmers coppice their crops after spraying, or are said to cover them in molasses in an attempt to limit the damage caused (cited in Keefer et al., 2010: 282). In Thailand, it is reported that a favourite practice has been to plant opium within the boundaries of another village so as to divert blame should the plants be discovered (Gillogly, personal communication, 1996). Farmers may offer bribes or provide protracted shows of hospitality as a way of delaying or deterring an eradication force.

In some areas collective responses to eradication may take the form of compensating farmers whose land is adjacent to the road or district centre for the loss of their crop. Along what might be conceived as a continuum of repertoires of peasant resistance to eradication, actions may vary from stone throwing or the burning of tyres or vehicles, to placing mines in fields.

These acts of violent and non-violent resistance are not necessarily revolutionary; they are frequently about defending the status quo rather than overturning it. They typically aim to tilt the balance in favour of rural communities in their negotiations with the authorities, possibly pressing for greater development assistance (and thereby further penetration by the state). They are, of course, intended to limit the state's efforts to destroy the crop, but on occasion they are also acts of resistance encouraged by the political elites and designed for public humiliation and eventually dismissal of opponents in the local authorities. Far from being acts of rebellion, they could in fact be seen as an attempt to change the market conditions and renegotiate terms between rural communities, local elites, and sub-national and national authorities in the political marketplace.

These acts of resistance, supported by much of the literature on agrarian change, show that rural households and communities are not passive, simply responding to the whims of local and sub-national politico-military elites(Scott, 2003: 44; Keefer et al., 2010: 16). They are, in fact, actors in their own right in the political marketplace, engaged in activities designed to acquire political and economic advantage over fellow villagers and neighbouring communities, and to influence the actions and decisions of local and sub-national elites with regard to the state's efforts to ban drug crop cultivation.

What provokes the rural population to shift from the 'everyday politics' of resisting the imposition of a ban on drug crops, to engaging in armed opposition to the state? What impels them either to take up arms themselves or invite organised armed opposition into the area not simply in order to establish better terms in their exchange with the authorities, but to expel state institutions from the area altogether? What are the underlying structural conditions and circumstances that make some areas or socio-economic groups more likely to rebel than others? And why do some communities take up arms immediately, while others only look to repel the state after a number of years of prohibition? Are there other more important processes at work than the imposition of an opium ban itself?

The political economy literature highlights the importance of disaggregating the political landscape and examining the nature of the political bargains that have been reached between national, sub-national, local and international actors. This disaggregation calls for a more granular understanding of the composition and structure of rural communities in order to improve understanding of the different socio-economic, political and ecological processes that might lead to rural rebellion.

Class-based explanations of rural rebellion advanced by the likes of Stinchcombe (1961) and Paige (1975) may provide only a partial explanation in contexts like contemporary rural Afghanistan where, on the surface, violent rebellion in response to opium bans and any subsequent uptick in the insurgency appear to be more closely linked to a specific (but growing) geographic territory than to any particular socio-economic group. Moreover, in the case of Afghanistan, it is hard to disagree with Wolf (1969: 290) in his rejection of Stinchcombe's and Paige's assertion that the protagonists of rural rebellion are to be found in an alienated class of agricultural wage labourers, including sharecroppers and tenant farmers, on the basis that 'a rebellion cannot start from a situation of complete impotence'. Wolf (1969) like Scott (1976) and Skocpol (1982: 354) celebrates the material and organisational advantages of the 'middle peasant', arguing that these small landowners have the 'tactical leverage' on which rural rebellions are built.

However, the coincidence of particular patterns of land ownership and violent resistance to efforts at prohibition does not explain why the rural population in some geographic areas might shift from broadly accepting the state's efforts to impose an opium ban, with only minor resistance, to staging violent uprisings against the state in subsequent seasons. It is argued here that this shift from resistance to revolt is likely a consequence of the societal structures that prevail within rural communities in areas of limited statehood, as well as of the impact that a ban on opium has on the welfare of the population when taken in tandem with the other shocks to which the population is often subjected.

Central to this argument is the work of James C. Scott and his depiction of societal structures in non-state spaces, or areas of limited statehood where the absence of an agricultural surplus and difficult physical terrain have deterred the state from direct rule. Scott (2009) suggests that it is an error simply to subsume the political and economic interests of the rural population under those of the rural elite in this kind of terrain. In these more remote areas, rural elites act more as brokers than as patrons. They draw on the bonds of kinship and affinity with their fellow villagers. They have not benefited from formal positions within the administration and accumulated land. Socio-economic differentiation exists within these communities but shows none of the extremes that can be found in the low-lying areas where the penetration of markets, the state and colonial powers have supported the establishment of a landed elite and a corresponding class of agricultural wage labourers and tenant farmers who owe fealty to their landed patrons.

Of particular significance is the fact that the population in non-state space belongs to acephalous tribal communities where, in the context of Afghanistan, elites are considered 'first among equals' rather than what Mamdani refers to in his critique of British indirect rule in colonial Africa as 'personal despots'.[6] While these local elites have constituents, they also have competitors and adversaries who are adept at capitalising on their opponent's failure to deliver to the population. In these areas, as in others, the rural population is looking to its local leadership to access economic resources from outside the area, or at least to establish the secure conditions under which they can manage their lives and livelihoods (Scott, 1972b: 105).

There is a broad consensus between Scott (1976) and many other scholars of agrarian change (e.g. Jenkins, 1982: 487) that the foundations for peasant rebellion can be found in the economic insecurity of the rural population. Scott (1976: 7–11) claims that where subsistence livelihood is not secured, the loss of legitimacy for the local elite 'is often swift and complete'. Therefore in areas of limited statehood, local elites are not only confronted with a more tenuous hold on political power, but with a rural population that operates close to subsistence level. As Scott (1972a: 35) notes:

> When the peasants' welfare has not declined, when social links, say to politicians and bureaucrats, offer alternative mechanisms of security, when urbanization and industrialisation provide real opportunities for those who can no longer be accom-

modated within the village, agrarian elites may lose legitimacy more or less peacefully. A buoyant economy, rural development programs and electoral party patronage thus represent for the peasant opportunities and services which make the worsening terms of trade with agrarian elites less painful. If on the other hand, the peasant's welfare is declining, if his subsistence is threatened and if few alternatives are open, the process may be vastly more explosive.

Following these arguments, it might be expected that attempts to compel farmers to desist from cultivating opium in areas of limited statehood, where there may be no viable alternatives, will impose significant costs on the rural population, thereby diminishing the political capital of local elites that are seen to have supported prohibition. In this kind of economic and political terrain, local elites may have to consider the livelihood trajectories of the most influential segments of the rural population and assess how interventions will impact on the current political order, before continuing to support efforts to ban opium production. In fact, it is my argument that, in the absence of the coercive power to enforce a ban on opium, local elites have had to be far more responsive to the economic interests of the rural population than many have assumed.

Such is its vulnerability that the local elite's political survival may require it to withdraw from the coalition that has supported a ban on cultivation if it does not wish to be rejected, and then replaced, by adversaries within the community. Of course, the local elite may also have its own reasons for withdrawing from the coalition that has supported the ban. These reasons may include the breakdown in relationships with the centre or the provincial administration over the share of rents or the distribution of patronage to political opponents, or simply a need for the local elite to maintain a separation from the state and ensure that their loyalty is not taken for granted and is suitably rewarded. When confronted with what is often only a temporary concentration of coercive power, and the demand that they support national or global actors in their desire to eliminate opium poppy, local elites may attempt to limit their involvement and, if an opium ban is maintained, shift their alliances to those local and regional actors that emerge in opposition to the prohibition of opium production, so as to be seen to be supporting the interests of their rural constituents.

These factors point to an extremely dynamic and interactive political terrain at the local level. Rural households and communities are not necessarily subjects of the local elite but can be active participants in the political process. The literature on agrarian change and rural rebellion indicates that farmers in areas of limited statehood are not only capable of challenging the local elite but will engage in individual acts of resistance as well as collective action that can shape political settlements between local, sub-national and even national elites. The literature suggests that where their subsistence is threatened, farmers may take up arms or draw on the support of insurgent organisations that will allow them to accrue direct material benefits, which may mean a return to opium poppy cultivation.

In sum, the complex interrelationship between the economic welfare of the rural population, the political order and peasant resistance and rebellion—as well as how this varies over time, space and socio-economic conditions—dictates that any empirical enquiry into efforts to ban drug crop cultivation has to be firmly embedded in an analysis of the impact of prohibition on the lives and livelihoods of the different rural communities directly involved. This area of study will be the subject of the next two chapters.

Conclusion

Explanations for changing levels of drug cultivation in Afghanistan and elsewhere are all too often simplistic and uninformed. Inhibited by a failure to examine and critique the methodological limits of the data on opium production from official organisations like the United Nations, as well as by ignorance of the economic and agricultural realities of the opium poppy crop, master narratives tend to ascribe too much power to the actions of national and sub-national political actors. The enforcement of an effective ban is perceived as the result of the concentration of the means of violence in the hands of state actors or 'violence entrepreneurs'. The subsequent collapse of a ban and the resurgence of cultivation are interpreted as a loss of political will, a lack of commitment or a function of corruption. This chapter has shown that such an account has severe limitations.

The literature on statebuilding and political settlements highlights the need to focus on the spatial dynamics of power in drug-producing areas: the political coalitions that underpin the state and the complex bargaining processes mediated by brokers who link the centre to the periphery and the national to the local. This chapter has shown how unstable this order may be, particularly in areas where the physical terrain, combined with tribal isolation and a more egalitarian social structure, has thwarted the formation of a dominant elite with which the state can engage and establish a more permanent physical presence.

In the context of liberal peacebuilding and statebuilding efforts in Afghanistan, stability in areas of limited statehood can be further undermined by a crowded and competitive institutional environment where international agencies, both civilian and military, are neither neutral nor well informed about local specificities. Both de Waal's (2009) model of the political market-place and Risse et al.'s (2011) framework of multilevel governance provide analytical lenses through which to examine the many institutions that compete for influence in these areas—areas that have gained increased significance given their location at the interstices of nation states where transnational crime, terrorism and drug crop cultivation can coexist. There is a need to improve our understanding of the messiness in the local political bargains that underpin efforts to impose a ban on drug crop cultivation: to disassemble the political marketplace into its constituent parts; examine the often competing interests of the relevant local, sub-national, national and international institutions; and to explore the interactions between these institutions, charting how and why their priorities and their capacity to establish political order change over time.

This chapter has challenged the tendency to portray those who cultivate drug crops as passive, subject to the violent actions of either state actors or insurgent groups. It has summarised the rich body of scholarly work on peasant resistance and rebellion that belies the notion of rural households and communities as separate from the political and military actors engaged in a conflict. It has explored the acts of 'everyday politics' that farmers engage in and argued that even violent resistance to eradication should not necessarily be seen as rebellion against the state. Instead, it has shown that violence can be an act of negotiation by rural communities looking to strengthen their position in their dialogue with both local elites and the authorities, on occasion hoping to protect their crops but also pressing for greater development assistance and therefore further penetration by the state. The chapter has also examined the structural factors that make some rural populations more susceptible to peasant rebellion than others; it has described how a combination of local political structures, resource endowments and exposure to co-variant shock can lead to violent revolt, insurgency and attempts to topple those in state power.

The chapter has provided a map of the complex and dynamic political terrain within which bans on drug crop cultivation are imposed. As subsequent chapters will show, establishing a political coalition under which a ban can be enforced is a significant challenge. Maintaining that coalition over time and across a wide geographic space that has distinct political histories, social structures and resource endowments, as well as quite different exposures to shocks and crisis, can be all but impossible.

It is my contention that the political bargains which underpin the banning of opium are inherently precarious and ultimately destabilising when they are imposed in areas that meet three criteria: (i) where market conditions are constantly in flux, in large part due to the impact an opium ban can play in creating what Scott (1976: 205) refers to as 'patterns of collective insecurity'; (ii) where 'multiple rival power centres exist', not only within the metropolitan elite but also amongst rural leaders'; and (iii) where the coercive power and patronage of international actors have been instrumental in shaping the behaviour of sub-national and rural elites, as well as of the rural population itself. Understanding the kind of terrain where these conditions are most likely to coalesce and the point at which they begin to align is critical to the hypothesis of this research and to answering the three research questions that underpin it.

3

RURAL LIVELIHOODS PERSPECTIVES
ON DRUG CROP PRODUCTION

Introduction

This chapter draws on literature on rural livelihoods and agrarian economics. It offers an alternative way of examining and understanding drug crop cultivation and shows how the rural livelihoods framework can transcend the more limited focus on the economic primacy of drug crop cultivation, illuminating the complex role that opium poppy plays in providing access to a range of assets for those involved in its cultivation. The chapter shows the utility of a livelihoods perspective for capturing this multifunctional role in different socio-economic, political and ecological terrains and for observing how communities respond to efforts to ban drug crops.

This chapter examines how the literature on rural livelihoods can provide a more complete understanding of divergent patterns of cultivation found in drug crop-producing countries, and a framework for interpreting different household and community responses to prohibition efforts. Like the previous chapter, it offers those policy-makers and scholars who are less familiar with the realities of rural life in conflict-affected areas of the developing world some benchmarks by which to judge the statistics and narratives that have become such a mainstay of the debate on opium production in Afghanistan, and that have shaped the range of counternarcotics, counterinsurgency and statebuilding policies.

The chapter is divided into three sections. The first section describes how drug crop cultivation and farmers of opium poppy and coca are discussed in much of the literature and identifies the limits of this literature. The second section explores how the sustainable livelihoods perspective moves us away from definitive, mono-causal explanations toward those that examine in detail individual and collective household responses to a ban. The third section looks at how the livelihoods perspective can be refined to include the wider political and security dimensions of the lives of the rural population in drug crop-producing countries, as well as the factors that inform their involvement in opium poppy and coca cultivation.

Terms such as 'poor', 'marginalised' and 'vulnerable' are labels that are often used to describe farmers of opium poppy or coca by development practitioners and policy advocates (GTZ, 2003; Transnational Institute, 2005). On the other hand, descriptors such as 'rich', 'profitability', 'high price' are contained in many of the statements of policy-makers within the drug control community (UNODC/MCN, 2007).

Academics may succumb to the lure of these simplified portrayals of farmers of drug crops. For example, Brass (2008: 189), who cites gross earnings of US$12,600 per hectare of coca, writes about 'rich peasants' who 'benefit substantially from the coca crop'. Other scholars refer to the 'poverty' of those cultivating illicit drug crops but do not specify the severity, duration and dimensions of deprivation experienced by the population (Steinberg, 2004). Nor is there any explanation of how poverty manifests itself in the different terrains in which drug crops are grown within a single source country, or how the level of poverty and its distribution among the population in a given area might impact on drug control efforts compared to another location where the population has a different socio-economic profile.

These narratives fail to capture the diversity of drug cultivating contexts and the varied patterns of opium poppy and coca cultivation within a single source country. They also simplistically portray those who cultivate drug crops as primarily economic actors driven by the desire to maximise income (UNODC/MCN, 2012: 54; Caulkins et al., 2010: 23; Naim, 2005: 69), either for the purpose of conspicuous consumption—'the greedy',[1] or as a means of escaping poverty—'the needy'.

Risk is largely considered in the context of the state acting to destroy the crop (Thoumi, 2003; Mejia, 2010). How different households and communities living under different circumstances and political orders experience and manage the risk of the imposition of a ban or crop destruction is largely neglected, as are the diverse risks and opportunities that households and communities associate with engaging in activities related to 'the legal economy'.

The data produced by UNODC tends to reinforce the portrayal of 'the farmer' as a rational economic actor. In Afghanistan, a variety of metrics help build an image of opium farmers as income maximisers, in accordance with neoclassical economic theories of the firm. These metrics include a summary of the responses farmers offer when asked directly why they cultivate opium poppy (UNODC/MCN, 2011: 60–62)—most notably high price; comparisons of the gross returns on wheat and opium poppy; and estimates of the annual gross income of those who cultivate opium poppy and those who do not (Buxton, 2006: 103; UNODC/MCN, 2013).

The labelling of the population of a drug producing country as either 'opium poppy farmers' or 'non-opium poppy farmers' by UNODC (UNODC/MCN, 2010: 68–71) reinforces this simplistic portrayal of farmers' livelihoods, implying that those who grow opium poppy are landed and producing nothing else, while those who do not grow opium poppy on their own land are not working on the opium crop of others (McCoy in Steinberg et al., 2004: 66).[2] Not only are both inferences untrue, but there is much in the current portrayal of drug crop-producing households that, to quote Durrenberger (1980: 134) in his discussion of Chayanov's seminal work on the peasant economy, 'do not match the realities observed'.

Assessing Changes in Patterns of Drug Crop Cultivation from Afar: The Limits of the Current Literature

There is a disparate body of work on drug crop production. The focus of this literature is threefold: (i) the production of illicit drug crops, such as coca and opium; (ii) the international regime established to control these drugs; and (iii) the impact that drug production and the drug control regime have had on wider socio-economic and political processes. Drug control organisations such as UNODC, as well as various parts of the US government (most notably the I.N.L. Section of the US Department of State), are a significant part of this drugs literature. They represent the voice of the international conventions, calling for nation states to commit human and financial resources to curb the production, trafficking and use of illicit drugs.

The academic literature on drug production is more discordant. It is based on a wide range of disciplines: economics, politics, history and geography. Some of the more detailed studies of the production and trade in drugs offer rich political histories that are country-specific, such as Westermeyer (1983) and Painter (1994), while others present comparative work covering a number of countries in a region, including McCoy's classic study of the politics of heroin in South East Asia (1980), and Clawson and Lee's (1996) review of the cocaine industry in South America.

More generic work examines production at a global level and reviews the effectiveness of different efforts to reduce the harms of drug crop production, as well as efforts to curb it (Felbab Brown, 2010; Buxton, 2006). The academic literature on drugs also includes a strong body of scholarly work from the discipline of economics, including Reuter (2010), Caulkins et al. (2010) and Mejia and Posada (2010). Much of this work evaluates and criticises the current prohibition regime. A number of these studies, such as Paoli et al. (2009), Keefer and Loayza (2010) and Babor et al. (2010), are ambitious evaluations, examining the efficacy of a wide range of interventions that fall under the current label of drug control across a number of different source countries.

In recent years the literature on drug crop production has been expanded by a growing body of journalistic and autobiographical reports, primarily concerning Afghanistan. Some of these reports focus on drug crop production and are produced by those who have been directly involved in drug-control efforts, such as Hafvenstein's (2010) description of his work in Helmand province between 2004 and 2005, and Peters (2009a, 2009b) account of the relationship between the Taliban and opium production in the southern provinces of Afghanistan. Other reports are more general but include detail on the challenges that senior Western officials, both military and civilian, faced in their efforts to understand and respond to the phenomena of drug production in a source country like Afghanistan (Neumann, 2009; Cowper-Coles, 2011: 80–87; Eide, 2012: 117–19; McChrystal, 2013: 319–41).

At the heart of the drugs literature lie the reports and estimates of UNODC, and to a lesser extent the figures produced by the US government. Most policy-makers, academics and the media draw upon UNODC when writing about drug crop production, citing a variety of quantitative statistics, including estimates of the hectarage of coca and opium poppy grown, price data and yields. In addition to reliance on the official data, and the explanations of cultivation offered by drug control bodies such as UNODC, there is also a heavy reliance on journalists for information on the lives of those farmers who grow drug crops. In fact, much of the academic work on drug production is based on these two sources of secondary data and is written by scholars who have conducted limited primary research in the rural areas where drug crops are grown. In the case of Afghanistan, almost all the literature discussing drug crop production is based on data from these and other secondary sources, or has been compiled by authors who have conducted short visits to Kabul or a mission to one or two provincial capitals (Inkster and Comolli, 2012; Mercille, 2012; McCoy, 2003; Caulkins et al., 2010; Felbab Brown, 2010; Paoli et al., 2010).

There is, however, a further body of literature that is of particular relevance here. This is not an exhaustive literature—it is limited to a small number of detailed studies. Nor does this literature focus specifically on illicit drug crops; rather its interests lie with the study of anthropology and rural development in drug crop-producing areas. These are empirical studies that offer rich detail on the lives and livelihoods of those who grow drug crops but contextualise production within the wider socio-economic, political, cultural and ecological terrain in which opium poppy and coca are grown. Walker's (1992) edited volume on the highlands of Thailand, along with the works of Geddes (1970), Dessaint (1975, 1976) and Jones (19901a,1991b), stand out as excellent examples of the kind of scholarly work that has been conducted with households and communities engaged in drug crop cultivation. Further academic work has examined the political economy of drug production and efforts to control it in source countries, without a focus on rural communities. The work of Pain (2004, 2006a, 2006b, 2007a), Goodhand (2000, 2005, 2009), Kramer (2012) and Chouvy (2011) stands out; all of them have spent considerable time conducting primary research in drug-producing areas.

There is also an important but limited 'grey literature' that delves into the day-to-day realities and challenges faced by individuals and communities in drug crop-producing areas. This work can be found in the project documentation of multilateral, bilateral and non-governmental development organisations, including their appraisals and monitoring and evaluation reports. It has been produced by development practitioners who have typically worked for organisations in areas where opium poppy and coca have been grown, such as the northern highlands of Thailand, the tribal administered areas of Pakistan, the Yungas and Chapare in Bolivia, or Afghanistan. In these reports, individuals such as Fitzherbert and Phillips (UNDCP, 1995c) have provided important insights into the lives and livelihoods of those who grow illicit drug crops, albeit over limited time frames.

Some of my own research in Afghanistan, originally for the UN International Drug Control Programme (UNDCP) and subsequently for a wide range of other organisations, is located within this subset of the drugs literature. While authors such as McCoy (2003; 2004: 71) would consider my initial research principally about drug crop production, I would not categorise it as such.

Instead, I would argue that my work ensues from the more holistic approach found in the rural development and anthropological literature. This work can be distinguished from the mainstream drugs literature by its emphasis on primary research in drug-cultivating areas, as well as its focus on the wider processes of change and transformation of rural households and communities.

A major shortcoming of the literature on drug crop production has been its failure to engage directly with the rural communities that inhabit drug crop-growing areas and to document the changes in drug crop cultivation and the complex processes that lie behind these changes. In fact, the dearth of fine-grained analysis of the households and communities engaged in illicit crop production leads to a disconnect between the varied aspirations, values and experiences of the households and communities that cultivate illicit drug crops and the narratives usually found in the drugs literature.

Much of this literature is guilty of drugs fetishism—viewing the world solely through the prism of drug production and drug control measures. Little or no consideration is given to the wider socio-economic, political and environmental context inhabited by those individuals and communities that cultivate opium poppy and coca. Indicative of this fetishism is the reductionism with which the communities that cultivate drug crops are described. In the case of Afghanistan, drug control agencies such as UNODC depict rural households in binary terms, as either 'poppy farmers' or 'non poppy farmers'. Their livelihood activities are circumscribed by a comparison of the gross returns on opium and wheat (UNODC/MCN, 2013: 63–4) and by statistics which assert that it is simply 'high price' that motivates farmers to cultivate opium poppy: a caricature that is frequently perpetuated in the media and in some of the scholarly literature (Caulkins et al., 2010; Keefer and Loayza, 2010: 95–134).

In part, this drugs fetishism is a function of the evaluative nature of much of the drugs literature, too often shaped by the opposing parties in the ongoing debate on the effectiveness of the international drugs control regime. In this discourse, supply reduction efforts are viewed from a teleological perspective, where measures such as eradication and alternative development are assessed against the role they may or may not play in influencing levels of drug crop cultivation. Much of this evaluative work is conducted at an aggregate level, drawing on UNODC's estimates of levels of cultivation and production. The drug control community defends its position as one of containment, claiming that without eradication and alternative development, drug crop cultivation would be much higher (UNODC/MCN, 2008: 3). On the other hand, scholars such as Reuter (2010) and Barbor et al. (2010) tend to dismiss any reductions in drug crop cultivation as localised and a function of wider economic processes, such as the rapid economic growth in Thailand during the 1990s, or political events in other source countries creating the conditions for cultivation to shift. As Reuter (2010: 114) notes from a UNODC evaluation in 2005:

> There is little empirical evidence that the rural development components of Alternative Developments on their own reduce the amount of drug crops cultivated. Agriculture, economic and social interventions are not seen to overcome the incentive pressure exerted by the market conditions of the illicit drugs trade. Where reduction in drug cropping occurs it seems other factors, including general economic growth, policing etc., can be identified as contributors to the change that takes place.

This is a world where drug control interventions are seen as discrete and bounded; alternative development is viewed as a set of interventions located in a specific geographic space with a clear budget, time frame and a primary objective of reducing drug crop cultivation. It is not recognised as a means of state territorialisation and market penetration that exposes often remote and marginalised rural communities to the wider socio-economic and political processes that contribute to changing patterns of drug crop cultivation. It is this same drugs fetishism that interprets the behaviour of farmers growing illicit drug crops and sees the intercropping of opium, coca or cannabis with other crops as a method of preventing detection by satellites and deterring eradication (Mejia and Posada, 2010: 7), rather than as a strategy for the better management of land, labour and even pests (Mansfield, 2009b).

There is also a tendency in the drugs literature, particularly in the work of economists such as Reuter (2010) and Caulkins et al. (2010), to ignore changes in cultivation that occur at the local or even sub-national level, or to dismiss them as a largely irrelevant 'balloon effect'—actions that will be compensated for by increases in cultivation elsewhere. Windle and Farrell (2012: 868–74) point to the problems of simply dismissing local reductions and assuming that there is no net benefit from a relocation of cultivation from one area to another. They conclude that such an assessment is 'formulated on a rather shallow understanding of the dynamic nature and dimensions of displacement and diffusion effects' and go on to argue that 'in some cases it has led to an extreme-case-pessimist characterisation of law enforcement as being entirely ineffective, and it is possible that an uncritical use of the term may have gained credence among parties that have a preference and an interest to perceive drug law enforcement efforts as failing'. From a purely drug control perspective, they point to the challenges associated with relocating cultivation to other areas and the potential that the scale of reductions in one area may not be offset by increases in another—a situation that can be seen in different parts of Afghanistan (Windle and Farrell, 2012: 872).

Located firmly in the milieu of the debate on the international drug policy regime and the analysis of international and national estimates of production, it is apparent that neither the drug policy community nor the academic literature invests sufficient effort in examining changing patterns of cultivation within a country or even in exploring the methodological limits of the estimates of drug production provided by an official body like UNODC (Thoumi, 2005). The result is a tendency to analyse drug trends in different national and regional contexts, to infer causal relationships between reductions in one area or country and rises in another, and to ignore the possibilities that fluctuations in supply may be more a function of methodological changes or poor-quality data rather than an intended or unintended consequence of drug control efforts per se.

It is striking that, amidst this preoccupation with estimates of aggregate levels of cultivation and broad explanations for shifting patterns of production, little to no consideration is given to the complex processes by which farmers actually transition out of opium poppy and coca cultivation; what effect the movement out of drug crops has had on the wellbeing of different social and economic strata within rural communities; how this transition impacts on state–societal relations; and why many farmers do not return to drug crop cultivation despite the higher profit margins that might be available after a rise in farmgate prices.

These questions have been of keen interest to me for both practical and intellectual reasons. During almost two decades of fieldwork, I have become familiar with many households and communities in different parts of rural Afghanistan who have 'graduated out' of drug crop cultivation, while at the same time, according to their own estimates, experiencing an improvement in their quality of life. Apart from complaints about day-to-day corruption, concerns over the likely trajectory of security following the withdrawal of NATO in 2014 and the rising cost of living, these farmers do not wish for the collapse of the Afghan government and are not involved in violent protest against it. However, I am also familiar with many farmers who have not successfully made this transition; they have experienced significant losses in welfare and have engaged in 'everyday acts of resistance' (Scott, 1990) in response to efforts to ban opium poppy and what they see as state intrusion. Their concerns have ultimately culminated in violent resistance against the government of Afghanistan, including offering support to the insurgency, and even joining it.

Therefore, the vast majority of the drugs literature ignores the divergent trajectories that can be found amongst different households and communities in drug-producing areas. Much of the data cited is national and adopts an historical perspective to explain patterns of production, in some cases offering a comparison between different source countries. A few sub-national studies exist, such as Dion and Russler's (2011) assessment of cultivation in Colombia, but even these draw on secondary data from the UN and other bodies. Household or village-level data on the role of opium in rural livelihoods is rare and limited to UNODC household surveys. To date there are no longitudinal studies that examine the livelihood trajectories of communities engaged in drug crop cultivation and how these communities respond to both efforts to curb cultivation imposed by the state and the wider socioeconomic, political and ecological events to which they are exposed.

As with the literature on conflict-affected states, much of the existing drugs literature does not hear the voices of those who are directly engaged in drug crop cultivation or are the primary targets of drug control efforts in source countries. This literature tends to favour the 'state-centric views' of drug control institutions and to reproduce the narratives of the powerful (Luckham and Kirk, 2013: 341, 346). In these explanations much is lost, including the previously described myriad of local political bargains and agreements required to impose a ban across a wide and diverse geographic and political terrain. It is my contention that in parallel to Kalyvas's (2006) work on civil war and the importance he gives to examining the micro-dynamics of violence and conflict, there is a need to engage with the 'on-the-ground dynamics' and 'local messiness' in drug crop-producing areas in order to avoid being seduced by 'master narratives' and 'the simplified macro-historical accounts' that dominate explanations of patterns of drug crop production and assessments of efforts to curb it.

It should be recognised that, as explored further in the next chapter, there are significant challenges to conducting primary research in drug-producing areas. Insecurity, state action against cultivation, and remote and inhospitable terrain all militate against in-depth research with drug crop-producing communities. What is less clear is why the drugs literature does not do more to challenge the secondary sources that are cited: the views of government officials who only leave their compound when accompanied by armed protection;

the narratives of local armed actors (and their adversaries); and, in particular, the statistics and explanations of drug control institutions such as UNODC. The methodological limitations of research conducted by UNODC (itself shaped by drugs fetishism), in which farmers are asked direct and closed questions about drug crop cultivation, are ignored by scholars with little experience of conducting primary research in drug crop-producing areas.

Reliant on secondary data of variable quality, these scholars tend to treat growers as being without agency, responding to price signals and/or the political actions of state and non-state actors operating in their area. Even where household decisions are discussed, the individual households responsible for cultivating opium poppy or coca are viewed in the context of neoclassical economic theories of the firm, assuming the single goal of profit maximisation (UNODC/MCN, 2007; Caulkins et al., 2010; Keefer et al., 2010). Little consideration is given to the diversity that exists within and between rural communities; to the differences in economic returns on drug crop cultivation, depending on the factors of production and patronage networks a household can draw upon; or to the ways in which the role of opium in accessing land, labour and credit impacts on cropping decisions over an extended period.

The result is a literature that continues to focus on the primacy of economic interests. Statements about the insurmountable profit to be earned from plant-based drug crops still prevail, despite evidence to the contrary—even in the literature that claims to be informed by a political economy perspective (Buxton, 2006: 102; McCoy, 2003). Analysis of those who cultivate illicit drug crops and causal explanations for changes in cultivation are further weakened by simplistic crop-by-crop comparisons (Renard, 2001), by ignorance of the methodological limitations of much of the data on drug production, and by a failure to draw on the wider literature on the complex and diverse nature of rural livelihoods, including how households manage risk in areas of chronic insecurity (Wood, 2003).

Reshaping our Understanding of Drug Crop Cultivation and Those Who Cultivate Drug Crops

There is a rich body of literature in agrarian studies and rural livelihoods that adopts a holistic approach to the study of farmer behaviour, embedding it within the deep cultural, historical, political, social and ecological terrain of the rural population. Much of this work documents how formal income maximisation theories fail to explain the behaviour of farmers (Chayanaov, 1966;

Scott, 1976; Wolf, 1966, 1969; Bartlett, 1980: 547). Based on empirical work, it highlights the risk-averse nature of farmers and their preference for subsistence security over high income—what Scott (1976) has referred to as 'safety first' (Scott, 1976; Popkin, 1979; Chayanov, 1966; Ellis, 2000; Wood, 2003, 2007). Fafchamps (1992: 90) argues that 'because staples constitute a large share of total consumption and have low income elasticity, farmers are adamant about protecting themselves against food price risk. In most cases this is optimally achieved by emphasising food self-sufficiency.' These findings are supported by primary research in a range of geographical settings, including India, Mexico, Vietnam, Russia and the Andes (Binswanger, 1978; Moscardi and de Janvry, 1977; Scott, 1976; Bebbington, 1999: 2039).

In fact, far from complying with the neoclassical theory of the firm and seeking to maximise economic returns, Chayanov (1966) argues that farmers rejected a marginal gain in labour income when family demands had already been met and further increases in the labour expended would lead to an unacceptable level of drudgery (Durrenberger, 1980: 137). He pointed to the priority that farmers gave to a stable subsistence over that of a higher risk/ higher return strategy. He reflected on the way that farmers combined crops and cropping seasons so that labour demands were commensurate with the labour inputs available within the household at the precise time that they were required, rather than pursue a strategy of hiring labour during peak periods in an attempt to increase their income (Chayanov, 1966: 149).

Wolf (1966) also challenges the relevance of neoclassical economic theory to agrarian communities, asserting that 'peasants run a household, not a firm' (Wolf, 1966: 102). He argues that farmers divide their wealth among three investments: a replacement fund for biological survival; a ceremonial fund to shore up village-level solidarity; and a final fund from which rent could be paid to landlords, money lenders and the state. The ceremonial fund—which Scott (1976) later called the 'moral economy' and which subsequently became known as social capital—serves to build reciprocity within the village and to support farmers in better managing risk. It entails investing in a wide network of social relationships in order to obtain favours, reciprocity and patronage that can be drawn upon when required.

These alternative explanations of farmer behaviour, running contrary to the neoclassical theory of the firm, have subsequently been developed and further refined through primary research and conceptual work in areas as diverse as village studies, farming systems research, agro-ecosystem analysis, rapid and participatory rural appraisals, political ecology and many others. In the 1990s, this wide and disparate body of work was brought together under what Scoones (2009: 172) has referred to as the boundary term of 'livelihoods'. It has been instrumental in developing a better understanding of how rural communities actually live, and it is my contention that the livelihoods framework is particularly valuable for examining the causes of drug crop cultivation and the effect of efforts to ban it.

Using the Sustainable Livelihoods Approach to Improve Understanding of Drug Crop Cultivation and Efforts to Ban It

The sustainable livelihoods approach evolved out of a growing body of theoretical and applied research in developing countries. It became embedded in the debate on poverty alleviation among academics and development practitioners during the 1990s, rejecting the notion of poverty simply as a function of low levels of income or consumption and viewing it as multidimensional. This definition of poverty incorporated notions of rights; raised questions as to how people access their basic needs for health, education, clean water and physical security; and conceptualised poverty as an inability of people to realise their potential as human beings (Ellis, 2000: 77).

This more contextual understanding of the lives of the poor drew heavily on Amartya Sen's (1981) work on capabilities, entitlements and assets in his study of famine, as well as Robert Chambers' work on vulnerability and risk in the 1980s and 1990s. The concept of vulnerability—defined as 'exposure to the risk of becoming poor'—captured the dynamic forces influencing livelihood security and the experiences of the poor (Kantor and Pain, 2011: 5).

This perspective on poverty, and particularly the work of Sen and Chambers, inspired a body of research into the ways in which people in developing countries secure their livelihoods. This research has typically adopted an analytical structure for considering the different assets that people might draw upon; the numerous activities that they engage in; the multiple locations they operate from; the range of outcomes (not just income) that they pursue; and how these are all shaped by the wider macro-environment that they inhabit but over which they have little control.

Through more longitudinal work, the livelihoods approach has provided the basis for an assessment of the types of activities that households undertake and whether these activities deliver outcomes that allow assets to be accumulated or indicate increasing vulnerability and the potential for assets to be lost or stripped.

Various frameworks have been developed for livelihoods analysis, but they all have a number of common features. The approach developed for, and subsequently adopted by the Department for International Development (DFID) is perhaps the best known (Carney, 1998). At the core of the framework (see Figure 1) are the different assets that a social unit—usually the household—draws upon to pursue a variety of livelihood strategies. The framework identifies five types of capital assets: human, natural, financial, physical and social. To quote Ellis (2000: 8):

> In brief, natural capital refers to the natural resource base (land, water, trees) that yields products utilised by human populations for their own survival. Physical capital refers to assets brought into existence by economic production processes, for example, tools, machines, and land improvements like terraces or irrigation canals. Human capital refers to the education level and health status of individuals and populations. Financial capital refers to stocks of cash that can be accessed in order to purchase either production or consumption goods, and access to credit that might be included in this category. Social capital refers to the social networks and associations in which people participate, and from which they can derive support that contributes to their livelihoods.

The DFID framework presents these assets in the form of a pentagon that schematically shows the relationships among these capital assets and the variation in people's access to them. These assets are then used in various strategies in order to pursue a range of livelihood outcomes, such as more income, increased well-being, reduced vulnerability, improved food security, etc.

Acknowledging the multiple livelihood strategies that people adopt, the framework allows for a number of different activities to be undertaken in parallel and different outcomes to be pursued at the same time. At the level of the household, where there are multiple family members, livelihood strategies can be particularly complex. Household members may produce crops and raise livestock on their own land, and consume and sell these products. They may also work on the land of others as part of a reciprocal arrangement or in return for wages. They might collect firewood from common land during periods of agricultural underemployment. The household might also own assets such as a car, tractor or oxen that they lease out to others in return for rent. There could be family members working in urban areas, some of them residing there temporarily or permanently, others involved in buying and selling livestock, owning a shop, or engaged in cross-border trade.

While the activities that are adopted are informed by people's preferences and their portfolio of assets, they are also influenced by the 'vulnerability context' and by what DFID refers to as 'transforming structures and processes'.

Figure 1: Sustainable rural livelihood: Framework

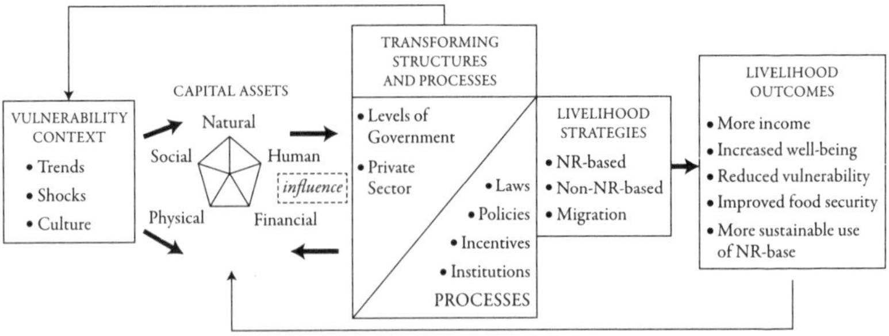

The vulnerability consists of the 'external environment in which people exist': the shocks, seasonality and trends that lie beyond their control. The transforming structures and processes are the 'institutions, organisations, policies and legislation that shape livelihoods', which, like the vulnerability context, are seen to be beyond the control of affected households and communities (Carney, 1998).

The framework's inclusion of the vulnerability context and transforming structures and processes recognises the need to examine the macro-environment in which household decisions are made, as well as to understand how this macro-environment shapes livelihood outcomes both in the immediate term and following later iterations. The inclusion of feedback loops where livelihood outcomes are subsequently translated into assets, and where transforming structures and processes shape the vulnerability context, further reflects the dynamism in the model and the importance of longitudinal analysis rather than static 'snapshots' of the lives and livelihoods of the population under study.

A Livelihoods Perspective on Drug Crop Cultivation

There are a number of significant advantages in using the livelihoods approach to improve understanding of the causes of drug crop cultivation and the effect of efforts to ban it. Primarily, as both a conceptual and methodological tool, the livelihoods approach focuses on examining and understanding the experience of households and communities at the local level. It does not make broad assumptions about why households and communities make certain choices, but examines household decision-making *in situ*. It does this within the context of the different types of capital and activities that households can draw upon, given their personal circumstances, but also within the wider socio-economic, political and ecological context that has an impact on the livelihood opportunities of different groups within a community. This people-centred focus is critical for developing a better understanding of the different livelihood outcomes that farmers pursue and how these are shaped not just by aspirations, but also by policies, processes and institutions.

This is particularly important in Afghanistan, where access to assets and markets is shaped by informal institutions, as well as by conflict and violence, rather than by price alone (Wood, 2005). Land, for example, cannot simply be purchased on an open market in response to the potential for increased profits, following a rise in the price of an agricultural commodity such as opium. Those who own land are reluctant to sell it because it is not simply an agricultural input; it embodies deep historical, cultural and political significance. As in many rural communities, the sale of land is typically seen as a desperate measure which symbolises a break in lineage and represents a loss of face within the community. In rural Afghanistan, land ownership is closely entwined with representation in local traditional decision-making bodies. Nor is it possible simply to sell land on an open market. Local traditions govern who can use and purchase land. A farmer compelled to sell his land should offer his family members and neighbours first refusal before offering the land to others. Tradition, as well as the capacity for violence, has shaped the spate of land grabs in the former desert lands of Afghanistan, including in the provinces of Farah, Kandahar, Nimroz, Helmand and Nangarhar. This former desert land, which has increasingly been seized, commoditised and sold, is not available to all. While it is still formally recognised as belonging to the government, access is determined not by an individual's capacity to pay for the land, but by the available personal, tribal and political networks.

In the context of drug crop cultivation, these local perspectives have been missing. Analysis of how households and communities respond to changes in drugs policy, such as the imposition of a ban, has been based on assumptions and not studied *in situ*. For example, Windle and Farrell (2012: 868) argue that there is a tendency to use the term 'balloon effect' dismissively, rather than as a concept properly informed by theory and evidence.

This brings us to a second advantage of the livelihoods approach: that it offers a holistic framework from which to avoid drugs fetishism and examine the totality of the lives and livelihoods of those living in drug crop-producing areas. This is helpful on two counts. First, it recognises that those households cultivating drug crops should not simply be defined by that fact—that they may well be engaged in a wide range of other activities, some of which may not be agrarian. This leads to an acknowledgement that there is more to rural livelihoods than crop production and that 'alternative crops' and 'crop substitution'—labels that persist in much of the drugs literature—fail to reflect the current reality in many source countries.

A more holistic framework also compels us to look at the wider policies, institutions and processes that influence drug crop cultivation, and not simply at those that fall under the current banner of drug control. For instance, there may well be wider economic processes at work that influence levels of drug crop cultivation. These might include increasing wage labour opportunities in distant urban areas which increase the outflow of family labour from a drug-producing area; environmental shocks, such as drought, which limit the amount of irrigated land available; a rise in food prices that prompts a move away from cash crop production towards staples; or a local political bargain between the central state and local powerbrokers that, although not primarily aimed at drug control, favours the imposition of a ban on drug crop cultivation at that time.

All of these processes may well be concurrent and run in tandem with other factors, each of which will have a different effect on the livelihood opportunities of a divergent rural population. The livelihoods approach helps to understand the impact of these factors on both livelihood strategies, including drug crop cultivation, and livelihood outcomes, and to observe how this varies across different terrain and population groups. It ensures a better understanding of causality, particularly when assessing drug control efforts.

In the study of drug crop cultivation in Afghanistan, a third benefit to using the livelihoods approach is its emphasis on assets 'not simply as resources that people use to build livelihoods; [but how] they give them the power to be and act' (Bebbington, 1999). For example, my own use of the livelihoods framework (UNDCP, 1998a, 1998b; Mansfield, 2002a) established an understanding of the multifunctional role of opium poppy in rural livelihoods that mirrored the broader debates on the complex and holistic nature of rural livelihoods. This work revealed that opium production is not simply a source of income but the means by which the poor, through sharecropping arrangements, can gain access to land which can be used for food production and consumption, as well as for the cultivation of cash crops, like opium, for sale. It highlighted the role of the by-products of opium—the straw and seed—in the household economy. It also showed that we need to look beyond the income earned by individuals and households from directly producing opium on their own farms, and examine the wage labour earning opportunities created by opium production during the weeding and harvest seasons, which often employed farmers from areas where opium poppy was not cultivated at all (UNDCP, 1998b, 1999b; Mansfield, 2002a, 2008b).

Further aspects of my work revealed that those cultivating opium poppy were given preferential access to credit in the form of advance payments on their future crop. The livelihoods approach also highlighted the role that opium has played in increasing socio-economic differentiation—enabling the land-wealthy to accumulate assets by drawing on the significant financial advantages of employing farmers to sharecrop opium on their land; by providing advance payments on the crop; and by selling their surplus opium long after the opium harvest, when prices have risen. These fortunate landowners have, in turn, reinvested their earnings in the purchase of other assets, such as vehicles and tractors, shops and trade, providing further income and adding to their financial capital. The income from opium poppy has offered some the means to provide loans to family members, neighbours and others; it has funded trips to Mecca for Hajj, thereby strengthening patronage networks and building the social capital of the household (Mansfield, 2002a; UNODC, 2004).

The livelihoods approach and its focus on local perspectives offers a fourth advantage, in that it allows us to examine the diversity that exists among the rural population—in particular, those growing opium poppy—and to explore how 'different people in different places live' (Scoones, 2009: 172). Here again we can move away from the model of the 'average farmer' and assumptions about the values and aspirations that govern his behaviour. Instead we can examine decision-making within the different rural realities that exist in drug-producing areas. This is particularly important in rural Afghanistan where socio-economic, political and environmental conditions can vary across relatively short distances, particularly in provinces where there are highly variable patterns of violence due to the ongoing conflict.

For example, some areas in a province may have a reliable source of irrigation year round, fertile land, and easy access to urban centres, with the agricultural and labour markets that this entails. These areas may be relatively secure and their populations are likely to be recipients of a range of government services. Other areas nearby may be subject to an ongoing presence of armed anti-government groups, have poor soil and unreliable (and costly) irrigation, and little public- or private-sector investment. The tribal make-up of an area may also vary. One community may consist largely of tribes with a long history in the province, with access to patronage systems within government and insurgent groups. A neighbouring village, however, may comprise several tribal groups from across the country and find itself marginalised by state and anti-state actors alike.

Within each of these communities there will be households whose particular resource endowments allow them to manage and recover from the different shocks that are a regular feature of life in rural Afghanistan. They will have access to the political and economic capital that renders them less vulnerable to intimidation by insurgent groups and less likely to be the targets of state law enforcement efforts or attempts at predation. They will also be better placed to take advantage of any public- and private-sector investments made in their area. But in these same communities there will also be households that are disadvantaged because they are landless, do not have access to local patronage systems, have high dependency ratios, and/or have been resettled from areas outside the province. These households are potentially more vulnerable to shocks and in response are more likely to adopt coping strategies that undermine their future earning capacity.

Opium poppy cultivation currently persists across these different areas and socio-economic groups, but it may not be as embedded in some livelihood strategies as it is in others. Examining opium poppy cultivation across the different terrains in which it is grown, mapping the way in which bans are imposed and understanding how different households and communities respond to these bans helps us understand why we see such divergent responses to prohibition and how local socio-economic, political and ecological conditions shape these responses.

Finally, the livelihoods approach places considerable emphasis on livelihood outcomes and longitudinal analysis. Questions of how livelihoods change over time are critical. Researchers want to know which populations have livelihoods that are resilient to environmental shocks, changes in government policy or the onset of war, and to be able to identify those groups that are not only more likely to experience these events but will also pursue activities that denote increasing vulnerability and stress. In the context of drug crop cultivation, this understanding of how different households and communities respond to efforts to reduce cultivation is critical for those within the drug control community, as well as for development practitioners and those interested in conflict and stability in conflict-prone areas.

In rural Afghanistan, all households are exposed to risk—the possibility that adverse effects will occur as a result of natural events or human activities

(Holzmann et al., 2003: 6). Stress and shock represent the materialisation of risk, but along different timescales. Stress is ongoing and represents a continuous or slowly increasing pressure that is generally within a 'normal' range of variability, while shock is intense and sudden. Risks can be natural or the result of human activity; they can affect individuals (idiosyncratic) or particular groups (co-variate), or they can affect most or all of the population (macro). Risks can reoccur over time (repeated) or occur concurrently with other risks (bunched). They can also materialise infrequently but have a dramatic effect on welfare (catastrophic) or occur frequently but have limited impact (non-catastrophic). A household's capacity to manage risk is dependent on its assets and capacities and the nature of the risk or risks to which it is exposed.

In parts of rural Afghanistan, government efforts to implement a ban on opium production represent a shock to the rural population. It can have consequences for both those cultivating the crop on their own land and for a range of other socio-economic groups within and outside the area in which the ban is imposed. Given the range of other shocks and stresses that a household, community or area may be exposed to—including drought, conflict and, in recent years, a dramatic rise in the price of wheat—it is not possible to analyse in isolation the causes of reductions in opium poppy cultivation or the sustainability of those reductions. It is necessary to understand the range of stresses and shocks to which households and communities are exposed and to identify how these affect livelihood strategies and levels of opium poppy production.

Livelihood concepts such as adaptation, resilience and coping strategies are particularly useful for examining the qualitative changes that households experience in response to shocks. A resilient livelihood has the flexibility to adapt and recover from exposure to shock. A livelihood that is not resilient results in households pursuing coping or survival strategies that undermine future earning capacity by depleting productive assets and leaving the household more vulnerable than before. Coping strategies may force people to make decisions favouring security and shorter-term gains that limit their future options, including building alliances with local elites and non-state actors in what Wood (Gough and McGregor, 2007: 113) has referred to as 'dependent security'.

These concepts help shift the line of academic inquiry away from one that attempts to offer a definitive explanation of the causes of cultivation, which, as we have seen, are often couched in neoclassical theories of the firm and the income-maximising peasant farmer, to one that examines the relationship between household responses to a ban and dependencies on drug crop cultivation as a means of earning a living. This kind of inquiry might, in turn, tell us about the prospects for enduring reductions in cultivation across the different socio-economic, political, and ecological terrains in which these crops are grown, as well as provide a prognosis of the types of individual and collective actions we may see in response to efforts at prohibition and how these actions might differ over space and time.

Criticism of the Livelihoods Approach: The Need to Bring Politics to the Forefront

The livelihoods approach is not without its critics, including some of those who have been its strongest advocates and have considerable experience using the framework in the field. On the surface, it also appears that the approach is no longer the centre of influence that it once was within bilateral development organisations like DFID (Solesbury, 2003).

Scoones (2009: 181) points to the fact that livelihoods approaches have often been 'dismissed as too complex', 'too local' and not 'appropriate to the new aid modalities of direct budget support and the Paris agenda'. One challenge for livelihoods research has been that of scaling up, moving beyond an analysis of micro-level decision-making—the capital, activities and strategies of individual households—and generating findings that are relevant to the development of national or sub-national policies (Kanji et al., 2005: 8; Baumann, 2000: 32). Much of the research has focused on specific areas or groups, and, according to Scoones, attempts to link the micro with the macro have been 'more of an ambition than a reality' (2009: 187).

The focus on the household has also resulted in a tendency to overstate individual agency and not recognise the structural parameters within which household decisions are made (Gough et al., 2006: 23). According to Schmink (1984), the use of language such as 'livelihood strategies' has reinforced the idea that decisions are deliberate or conscious when they may in fact be reactions to shocks or simply shaped by 'habitus'—defined by de Haan and Zoomers (2005: 41) as a system of 'acquired dispositions, primarily defined by social class and acquired through socialisation'.

In order to understand the role of social class, gender, caste or identification with other groups in informing household decisions, as well as to overcome the problems of scaling up, scholars like de Haan and Zoomers (2005) propose adopting the concept of 'livelihood pathways' to denote that patterns of livelihood activities arise from both a conscious and a subconscious process of coordination among particular social groups, and to describe 'livelihood trajectories' for the life paths of individual actors. To improve understanding of these processes, they argue for the need for more comparative research:

> In current research, livelihoods are usually analysed in relation to a single location, seeking to understand the geographical, socio-economic and cultural micro-situation. More emphasis should be placed on comparative research, or, a systematic comparison of livelihood decisions in different geographical, socio-economic, cultural or temporal contexts, so that patterns can be recognised as pathways, which go beyond the specific case. (de Haan and Zoomers, 2005: 44).

Distinguishing between the livelihoods of different social groups and their particular histories also begins to overcome a further criticism of livelihoods analysis: its failure to integrate politics and power adequately and directly into the livelihoods framework. Both practitioners and scholars recognise that the livelihood approach offers an entry point for the study of how politics and power shape livelihood opportunities and outcomes, through an analysis of 'transforming structures and processes'. However, there is a broad consensus that it is inadequate simply to view politics as a background or context and that there has been a general reluctance to 'take the next step from institutions to power' (de Haan and Zoomers, 2005).

Baumann (2000: 5) has argued that the livelihoods framework 'is incomplete without an analysis of politics and power relations' and, along with Collinson (2003) and Moser (2006: 23), they have attempted to make the study of politics more explicit by including political capital as an asset within the livelihoods framework, along with natural, social, physical, financial and capital assets, thereby transforming DFID's asset pentagon to a hexagon. These writers link political capital closely with rights. They argue that people's access to assets depends on their political capital, which is not fixed over time, population, or location, and which therefore needs to be closely tied to the household and the other assets in their portfolio. There are also people and groups that resist change to policies, institutions and processes; consequently there is a need to understand how those who believe they will be either 'winners' or 'losers' might react in response to a policy change, and how this reaction might be manifested. This all points to a concerted effort to integrate questions of political economy into the livelihoods framework (Collinson, 2003).

The need to integrate politics and power into livelihoods analysis more effectively is all the more pronounced when working in areas of chronic conflict, such as drug producing areas. Lautze and Raven-Roberts (2006) and Young (2009) have reconceptualised vulnerability as endogenous to livelihood systems, and argue that 'assets may become life- and livelihood-threatening liabilities in times of conflict' (Young et al., 2009: 21). They cite numerous examples derived from empirical work where assets have been stripped and lives lost due to criminal or political interests, but also, as in the case of Darfur in Sudan, as part of the tactics of war. In their exploratory research, Young et al. (2009: 71) refer to activities such as predatory raids or other violent acts as 'livelihood maladaptations' that fuel tensions and drive further conflict. They argue that 'livelihoods and conflicts are inextricably linked' in complex emergencies and that one cannot be understood without understanding the other.

Building on the limited coverage of livelihoods research, Maxwell and Vaitla (2012) point to the absence of longitudinal research in 'risk-prone' areas or in situations of 'actual humanitarian emergencies'. They note the reliance on one-off localised assessments or large surveys which have proved to be inadequate to understanding the dynamics of livelihood change in these settings. They refer to the need to move away from what is often seen as a linear model of livelihoods and adopt 'a livelihoods cycle' which they argue will better capture the 'direct feedback between consumption, investment and savings decisions and assets' (2012: 3); they also propose to locate the vulnerability context and the transforming structures and processes (referred to as 'policies, institutions, and processes') more centrally within the livelihoods analysis. This is another attempt to compel livelihoods researchers to look more closely at the impact of politics and power on livelihoods outcomes and vice versa.

As we have seen in the previous chapter, in the context of this research, politics and power are critical to understanding such varied responses to efforts to ban drug crop cultivation, particularly in areas of limited statehood. The diverse political geography of Afghanistan, the multiplicity of formal and informal institutions at the local level and the complex political process all underpin efforts to ban drug crop cultivation and shape household and community responses to prohibition. These factors dictate that an understanding of politics and power has to be at the centre of the analysis.

Beyond an understanding of how political power is distributed and articulated across the diverse political terrain in Afghanistan, there is a need to explain how and why the different centres of power shift over time, how these shifts relate to changes in the lives and livelihoods of the rural population and what effect these have on efforts to ban opium production. For example, what prompts the breakdown in an alliance between the international, national, sub-national and local elites which facilitated the imposition of an opium ban in the first place? How do local livelihood outcomes support these alliances, or, in some cases, fracture the political settlements that underpinned prohibition at the local level and, subsequently, over a larger geographic area? What role do other economic and environmental shocks, as well as local conflict over resources, play in undermining the local economy and political order that supported the imposition of an opium ban?

It is an ambitious task to undertake this kind of holistic analysis with its many moving parts in such insecure terrain, and to ensure that its findings have a resonance beyond an individual community or district. The analysis is a composite of multiple pieces of research in rural Afghanistan conducted over many years. It has required an intimacy with the policy environment in both Afghanistan and in Western capitals over an extended period, as well as an iterative, cautious and patient approach to engaging in the local messiness of the politics of rural Afghanistan. The next chapter describes the methodological approach that has been pursued to this end.

Conclusion

Attempts to correlate broad socio-economic and political data with opium production have typically failed to explain the many complex factors that influence levels of cultivation and how these vary over time, space and socio-economic group. Cropping decisions are far more complex than the current data on gross returns on opium and coca portray. Rural households are involved in a range of activities, many of which produce either goods to be consumed or a direct income stream, and some of which are aimed at building and strengthening social networks that can be drawn upon later. In Afghanistan, many farmers do not see their choice as binary—opting for either the higher returns from opium or the lower returns from wheat.

The absence of a more detailed account of the lives and livelihoods of those who cultivate plant-based drugs renders explanations for changes in the levels of opium and coca production problematic. It remains unclear why some households within a given area persist with opium poppy and coca cultivation while others do not, or why levels of cultivation in one district fall in a given year while production increases in the neighbouring district. As a result, shifts in cultivation are too often attributed to price fluctuations and/or political actions at regional and district levels, when the causes may actually involve a complex interplay among socio-economic, cultural, environmental and political factors. There is a need to move beyond the current impasse and develop a more informed understanding not only of the diverse circumstances and motives that influence drug crop cultivation, but also of the different pathways that households follow when they transition out of opium and coca production.

This chapter has outlined the need for a conceptual and methodological framework that grounds an analysis of drug crop cultivation and efforts at prohibition in the experiences of those farmers and communities directly involved. It has touched on the rich history of scholarly work on agrarian change that challenges the reductionist economic assumptions that currently dominate the portrayal of decision-making in rural households. It has outlined a contemporary body of empirical work and an analytical framework that proposes a people-centred and holistic approach to the examination of the lives and livelihoods of rural populations in developing countries.

This chapter has argued that the livelihoods approach offers distinct advantages for examining both drug crop cultivation and efforts to ban it in the complex and dynamic socio-economic, political and ecological terrain of a country like Afghanistan: a focus on the assets, values and aspirations of the local population; a holistic view of the interface between the macro-environment and micro-decision-making; a capacity to explore, document and value the diversity within and between rural communities; and an emphasis on longitudinal research and the study of livelihood outcomes. These advantages combine to make the livelihoods approach an appropriate method and theoretical model for understanding the causes of drug crop cultivation and the impact of efforts to ban it.

Reflecting on the previous chapter's discussion of the literature on political geography, peasant resistance and rebellion, as well as the work on political settlements, this chapter has also shown the need to develop the livelihoods approach so as to make politics and power central to the analysis of drug crop cultivation. It has also begun to highlight some of the methodological challenges of studying a highly complex and dynamic political terrain where the population is exposed to conflict, engaged in what is considered an illegal activity, and in some cases is ready to engage in direct political action themselves, including acts of violence. These are challenges that will be explored in detail in the following chapter.

4

RESEARCH METHODOLOGY

Introduction

This chapter documents the challenges associated with collecting primary data in rural Afghanistan. A solid methodological approach must adapt to the changing political and security situation in different parts of the country; the constant process of identifying and refining knowledge gaps; the development and use of new and affordable technologies; and the shifting positions of the multiple institutions involved in drug control policy and operations. The methodology for this research has taken these factors into account; it also reflects my own cumulative experience over seventeen years of on-the-ground research.

Since 1997, I have had access to both the rural communities that cultivate opium poppy in Afghanistan and the policy-making community, both in Afghanistan and in Western capitals. This experience has provided a unique insight into both the policy process and the impact of efforts to ban opium production on rural households and communities. Exposure to both policy-makers and those cultivating opium poppy led me to look beyond the academic literature on drug control, which tends to evaluate interventions aimed at reducing illicit drug crop cultivation strictly in terms of their efficacy as instruments of drug control. I have positioned my empirical work within the wider economic, political and institutional environment in which efforts to prohibit opium are implemented (Thoumi, 2002: 163).

This chapter is by its very nature somewhat retrospective. It documents the evolution of the research process as it has been adapted to the changing security situation in rural Afghanistan and the growing challenges associated with investigating an activity that has become increasingly subject to punitive action by the Afghan state and its sponsors. It provides a detailed account of the challenges of conducting research in such an environment, the limitations of the data and how data collection has had to adjust to the changing circumstances in Afghanistan. It is a chapter that is of value to both those who are looking to engage in empirical inquiry in conflict-affected areas where drug crops are grown, but also to policy-makers and scholars who with regard to Afghanistan have tended to cite and use research findings without due consideration of the methodological limitations of the work.

The chapter is divided into four sections and a conclusion: (i) the development of the research focus and hypothesis; (ii) the research design, with a discussion of the research challenges in rural Afghanistan and how these have been overcome; (iii) data collection in practice, including the different sources of primary data and the measures taken to manage bias during its collection; (iv) the effect of the changing security environment on data collection and measures taken to ensure a coherent ethical position.

Focusing the Research

The Exploratory Phase

The exploratory phase of this research lasted for seven years. It encompassed fieldwork in rural Afghanistan between 1997 and 2001, as well as a number of consultancies for the Foreign and Commonwealth Office (FCO) from 2001 to 2004. This phase led to the main body of research between 2004 and 2013, as detailed in the empirical chapters, 6–10.

The first element of the exploratory phase consisted of a number of thematic studies that I produced for what was then UNDCP. These 'Strategic Studies' involved fieldwork across different parts of Afghanistan in my capacity as project manager for the Afghan Opium Poppy Survey.[1] Given the pioneering nature of this work and the challenges of working in Afghanistan at the time, the studies were iterative and flexible in substance and methodology. Using a case study approach, fieldwork was conducted at multiple research sites, and respondents with different asset portfolios were interviewed. This approach was used to overcome the absence of even the most basic population and demographic data in rural Afghanistan and to allow what Yin (1994: 31) refers to as 'analytical generalisation'.

Over the course of the project, the list of policy-relevant research questions expanded as each study produced new data and different lines of inquiry. During this period I established the relationships with both colleagues and communities in Afghanistan needed to conduct research on such sensitive issues as the role of women in opium production and the structure of the farmgate trade in opium in the provinces of Helmand, Kandahar and Nangarhar. Each study built on the findings of prior studies and sought to cross-verify the findings in different locations and with different groups of respondents. For example, the Strategic Study on credit (#3) addressed the different financial mechanisms available to those borrowing, while part of the subsequent study on the farmgate trade examined those who provided the loans.

The second component of the exploratory phase involved a number of consultancies for the FCO, including my participation in a multi-donor mission to look at the impact and sustainability of the Taliban prohibition during the 2000/1 growing season (Donor Mission, 2001). The review of the Taliban prohibition included interviews with some of the main protagonists involved in the opium ban, within both the Taliban and the international community, as well as primary data collection with farmers and communities in Nangarhar, Kandahar and Helmand provinces.

Further consultancies with the FCO involved extensive reviews of the 'grey literature' on opium production in Afghanistan and other source countries, and a review of licit cultivation in India and Turkey. This latter work included primary data collection with those cultivating opium poppy legally in India and Turkey, as well as with the agriculturalists providing technical support to farmers to help them improve yields. All of this paved the way for the main body of research beginning in 2004, providing valuable data with which to verify research findings in rural Afghanistan.

The Research Hypothesis

The main body of research compares and studies four drug bans implemented over fourteen years in three provinces of Afghanistan. It is hypothesised that three factors are key to understanding how and why these bans were implemented: the nature of political settlements at the international, national and local levels; the history and perceived legitimacy of the state presence in the area concerned; and the significance of rents generated by the opium economy relative to other sources of economic activity. A further hypothesis is that the dynamics and sustainability of opium bans will be fundamentally different in areas of consolidated statehood, compared to areas of limited statehood.

This research seeks to address three questions:

1. **What are the local, regional, national and international processes that contribute to the imposition of a ban on opium poppy cultivation at a particular moment in time?** This question aims to develop a deeper understanding of how coercion, persuasion and reward are used in brokering bans on drug crop cultivation across the diverse socio-economic, political and ecological terrains of rural Afghanistan, and how these tools are used to build support for the enforcement of a ban across a coalition of local, subnational, national and international actors. It also examines the role of international institutions in mobilising the demand that a ban be imposed, and explores how different international and domestic organisations and agencies—often with quite different mandates—coalesce around calls for lower levels of drug crop cultivation, typically on a temporary basis.

2. **How do different households and communities respond to efforts to ban opium production in Afghanistan, and in particular what are the conditions that lead to violent unrest by rural communities?** This question examines why some households and communities are more resilient to a ban on opium production than others, and under what circumstances a ban on opium poppy cultivation can be sustained without significant losses in welfare and increasing levels of violence. It aims to document the livelihood portfolios of the different socio-economic groups and communities engaged in opium poppy cultivation and how these impact on both the coping strategies adopted in response to a ban and the degree of rural resistance that manifests within local communities.

3. **What are the wider implications of the research findings for counter-narcotics interventions and statebuilding more broadly?** This final question explores the policy implications of the research and what the efforts to ban opium poppy cultivation tell us about the diffuse nature of political power in rural Afghanistan. It asks what the current efforts to reduce drug crop cultivation can realistically hope to achieve, and over what time frame, given the wider socio-economic and political processes of transformation and change that either support communities in their graduation out of drug crop cultivation or drive a resurgence of opium production.

The Research Design

Researching Illegal Activities

There is a growing body of literature pertaining to conducting research with those directly involved in illegal activities (Zaitch, 2001; Von Lampe, 2008;

Rawlinson, 2008; Siegel, 2008; Chin, 2007; Rodgers, 2001; Jacobsen and Landau, 2003). Much of this literature highlights the formidable challenges of gaining access to those engaged in what the state has deemed an illegal enterprise, as well as the questionable reliability of the data that this research produces. However, many of those who have conducted primary research on illegal activities stress the limitations of relying on the data of law enforcement institutions and highlight the need to develop first-hand accounts of those directly participating in criminal activities (Siegel, 2008: 23, 26; Rawlinson, 2008: 13; Von Lampe, 2008: 3; Zaitch, 2001: 13).

In terms of access, the illegality of opium production has been less of a constraint on research than many academics and policy-makers might appreciate, and certainly much less of a challenge than the deteriorating security situation in rural Afghanistan. In part, it has been possible to maintain access to opium poppy-growing areas and those cultivating the crop due to the fact that over the last two decades there have been periods when opium poppy cultivation was tolerated by the state, if not widely accepted. During these periods, farmers have not been subject to punitive action or risked their crop being destroyed.

Afghan farmers themselves also see opium poppy cultivation and the concept of legality quite differently from the official position of the Afghan government and that of officials from Western nations. While in discussions most farmers recognise that opium production is *haram* (forbidden) under Islam, or even illegal according to Afghan law, they will question the legitimacy of enforcing a ban on cultivation given their economic situation and some of the more egregious activities of which government officials are accused.

This does not mean that the legal status of opium production was not an issue during the course of my research. For example, efforts to ban opium poppy in Nangarhar under Governor Hajji Din Muhammad in the 2004/5 growing season, and his successor, Gul Aga Shirzai, in 2007/8, did lead to greater unease among farmers. The fact that interviewers asked about changes that respondents had experienced in their lives ensured that the discussions focused on issues that were of greatest concern to them, dispelled any criticism that the research was opium-led, and dissipated the threat of violence (Edwards, 2010: 9).

Avoiding 'Drugs Fetishism'

Although opium poppy cultivation is typically seen by respondents in Afghanistan, as well as on occasion by those in state institutions, as more acceptable than other types of illegal activities, the research design avoided direct questions on opium production.

The decision to pursue a more indirect line of inquiry with regard to opium was in part to avoid what Goodhand (2000: 15) has referred to—in research on war zones—as the danger of 'conflict fetishism', where there is an 'automatic assumption [by researchers] that violence is the problem and the only lens through which to look at people's lives'. He points out that 'those affected by conflict frequently remind researchers and aid workers that there are other aspects to their lives—that war is not the only point of reference' (ibid.). Similarly, those who cultivate opium poppy cannot simply be defined as 'opium farmers', particularly given the wide range of other activities that they pursue as part of their overall livelihood and the tendency for farmers to move in and out of opium poppy cultivation when the situation allows or requires it.

The consequences of drugs fetishism can be seen in much of the research conducted by counternarcotics agencies in Afghanistan, as well as by researchers in other countries (Chin, 2007: 97). UNODC in particular asks respondents direct drug-related questions. For example, it enquires why a particular farmer does or does not cultivate opium poppy (UNODC, 2012/MCN: 57–8) and asks village headmen to quantify the number of farmers who cultivate opium and to estimate the amount of opium held as inventory in a given village (UNODC/MCN, 2012). This kind of direct line of inquiry is clearly subject to social desirability bias; it also presents challenges with regard to data that is sensitive and rarely shared, and is by its very nature unseen (such as the amounts of opium stored), even by other members of the same community.

Experience has shown that when the interview concentrates on opium production and farmers are asked direct opium-related questions—particularly income-related ones—there is a tendency to exaggerate the economic advantages of the crop, both as a way of negotiating future development assistance and out of self-aggrandisement. Jacobsen and Landau (2003: 9) along with other researchers warn that this kind of reactivity—'where the active presence of the researcher potentially influences the behaviour and responses of informants'—needs to be managed if the results of research are not to be compromised (Barakat et al., 2002: 994).

Instead, Barakat et al. (2002) and other researchers, including Goodhand (2002) and Wood (2006), advocate a more indirect and flexible approach to research in areas affected by conflict, particularly when pursuing sensitive lines of inquiry:

> Where there are strong reservations or mistrust over certain topics, direct questions are not put. Instead the interviewer prompts spontaneous discussion by the use of

'cue questions', such as remarks or indirect enquiries, that allow respondents to broach the subject in their own way if they choose. No preconceived questions, specific order or schedule is imposed upon the respondents. Rather they are encouraged to relate their opinions in a way that draws on their own experiences. (Barakat et al., 2002: 999).

Adopting a Livelihoods Approach

In Vlassenroot's work on war and social research, he describes the livelihoods approach as one that:

> ... looks at where people are, what they have, what their needs and interests are, and it evaluates the strategies they use within the broader political and economic framework to achieve their desired outcomes. The analysis of these livelihoods thus requires a differentiated and multilevel research that examines the changes in socio-economic interaction patterns over time; it is based on empirical investigations into the evolution of households and community strategies, in which the micro-level findings (the livelihood) are mirrored against the macro context (the political economy) to explain the social, economic and political factors relating to poverty and vulnerability. (Vlassenroot, 2006: 196)

While some of the conceptual advantages of the livelihoods approach have been outlined in the previous chapter, it is also worth highlighting four methodological benefits. First, my own experience in Afghanistan and other illicit drug crop-producing countries, as well as the work of others (Goodhand, 2000: 13), confirms the importance of avoiding a direct line of questioning around opium and coca production. The livelihoods approach avoids the biases associated with drugs fetishism and the kind of direct line of questioning pursued by UNODC. My research experience in Afghanistan has shown that where opium is produced, respondents will typically include it when recounting the different crops that they grow and sell. By conducting interviews in the field during the planting and harvest season for the winter crops, including opium poppy, it is also possible to verify, and where necessary challenge, the veracity of a respondent's answers.

Second, the rural household remains the most accessible unit of analysis when looking at the opium economy in Afghanistan. The livelihoods approach focuses on the wider experiences of rural respondents, and so has been critical in establishing rapport and building trust between the 'researcher' and the 'researched'. When invited to discuss changes in their lives and livelihoods over the preceding twelve months, respondents rarely decline. Many, particularly the resource-poor, welcome the chance to be heard. They complain that much of the dialogue between NGOs, government officials, internationals and their own community is dominated by the rural elite. The fact that interviews are conducted in the field with respondents as they work, and not in group settings where the village elders often dominate, reinforces the message that the research is aimed at 'generating data which gave authentic insights into people's experiences' (Jacquemin, 1999: 304).

Third, the livelihoods approach allows the research to document household capabilities and assets, the different shocks that households and communities are exposed to, and their responses. A critical part of this work has been to document the different coping strategies that households adopt in response to what can, in some circumstances, be concurrent and repeated shocks. This approach has revealed how resilient different livelihoods are to shocks, how a ban on opium production affects household and community welfare, and ultimately the likely sustainability of low levels of opium production in a given area over time. It provides information on the wide variety of interventions that are implemented in areas where drug crop cultivation is concentrated in Afghanistan. It also allows an examination of the multiple and often competing programmes that farmers and communities are subject to—not just those aimed at drug control—and analyses the different responses. This is a significant advance on much of the evaluative work on supply-side interventions in the counternarcotics literature, which typically neglects these wider programmes and shocks and assesses changes in cultivation only against a specific counternarcotics intervention—a product of 'drugs fetishism'.

Finally, the livelihoods approach allows primary data collected through household interviews to be cross-verified and strengthened, using remote sensing data and other primary research in rural areas in Afghanistan. For example, remote sensing data on cropping patterns in central Helmand were complemented by more granular field data on specific crops and crop budgets. A rapid feedback loop between the initial results of the fieldwork in rural areas and the remote sensing data from either satellite imagery or helicopter overflights has allowed the data collection by both methods to be further refined.

Making Politics More Central

As detailed in Chapter 3, the livelihoods approach has been criticised for not making politics and power more central to its analysis (Scoones, 2009; Baumann, 2005; Lautze and Raven-Roberts, 2006). Those examining drug crop cultivation in rural Afghanistan have to wrestle with the challenges of scaling up from questions of micro-level decision-making to those relevant to the macro-policy environment. They also have to deal with the practical problems of studying a highly complex and dynamic political terrain that may involve conflict, purportedly illegal activity, and direct political action, including acts of violence. For these reasons, this is a population that is neglected in the literature on rural livelihoods; as yet there is no primary research on those cultivating illicit drug crops over an extended period of time.

Like the work of many livelihood researchers at the time, my initial research during the Taliban regime in the 1990s concentrated on the capital, activities and livelihood strategies of households, as I examined the role that opium poppy played within household livelihood strategies and how these varied by socio-economic group.[2]

However, with the imposition of the Taliban ban on opium in the 2000/1 growing season my perspective changed. During the Taliban ban, as well as while researching subsequent efforts to ban opium after the Taliban's collapse, conversations with farmers revealed the details of the political brokerage that was taking place both within rural areas and between those areas and subnational, national and international actors.

These conversations revealed the complex bargaining at different levels of governance that establish the basis for these bans, the different—and often temporary—coalitions that underpin them, and the multiple and competing interests of those involved. I came to the realisation that while there was still a pressing need to map the livelihood strategies of households in different areas in order to understand livelihood outcomes in response to a ban, this work was not sufficient to understand the complex and profoundly political process which shapes the imposition of a ban on opium and how households and communities respond to it. During these discussions it became apparent that 'power was everywhere' (Scoones, 2009: 180) and that an examination of how an opium ban is imposed, and why it may subsequently collapse in some places and not in others, would require an analysis of politics at several different levels.

The first element of political analysis was the diverse political geography within Afghanistan, given the significant differences between state–societal relations in some more remote parts of the country and those in the more accessible communities in the main river valleys. To understand why this might be, it was necessary to develop a more informed view of the history of these different areas through both the literature and my fieldwork within rural communities, as well as with researchers and key informants working in the relevant areas. It was essential to choose research sites that reflected the different political terrains in a province and to select respondents from a cross-section of the community, including local elites and more marginal groups. This diversity would provide broader insights into how the state and its efforts to ban opium were seen and how community members reacted to the local elite where the leadership continued to play a role in supporting the ban on opium production.

The second analytical element was institutional politics and the proactive role that different Afghan actors were playing in imposing bans. Represented by some as the passive victims of US hegemony, and demonised by others for corruption, it was clear that the government of Afghanistan had many moving parts, each with different motivations for imposing a ban and different roles in its implementation. My exposure to the policy community and to rural elites and communities in Afghanistan suggested that the picture was more complex than that of the Afghan state simply mimicking the demands of bilateral donors to reduce opium poppy cultivation. Drugs were part of the 'political marketplace', in which allegiance to those calling for prohibition, and subsequent compliance with an opium ban, were in part traded for political patronage and increased development assistance. It was a highly competitive environment where short-term deals were being brokered by those with formal and informal power across the different layers of society, from the village to the presidential palace, in an attempt to change the international narrative on Afghan drug production and to gain what they believed would be preferential access to economic and political power. Developing a closer understanding of the different actors involved in the imposition of a ban drew on my role as a participant in the policy discussions within the international community and between various donors and the Afghan government, as well as on my insights from fieldwork with rural communities and their own view of the formal and informal institutions involved in the imposition of the ban.

The third element of political analysis was the wider political environment in which prohibition was being imposed. After all, bans are not imposed in a vacuum, and at the same time as prohibition was being implemented, other events were unfolding across the different geographical spaces and political constituencies in which these deals were being struck. All of these events had the potential to reshape and possibly fracture the alliances on which an opium ban is built. This realisation led to a closer look at the complex interactions among political forces in Kabul, Jalalabad and amongst the Nangarhari rural elite; the role played by those imposing (or suspending) the enforcement of the ban in a given area; and how the exchanges between these political forces were affected by a range of other factors. These factors included elections and the patronage they offered, (dis)agreements over rent extraction and, of course, the welfare of rural constituencies due to the effects of the opium ban and other exogenous and idiosyncratic shocks that communities might be subject to. On top of these factors were overlaid the multiple and often competing interventions of civilian and military international actors.

Therefore, I did not start my research with the same theoretical framework and clear understanding as I ended it. The political terrain changed dramatically over the course of my work, and my accumulated knowledge of this terrain was acquired over years, not months. Moreover, it was not easy to research these overtly political processes within a frame of reference that goes beyond bans on opium to include conflicts such as land disputes, civilian casualties, incursions by insurgents and reactions to local and sub-national elites. I had to be responsive to the challenges of examining sensitive political issues with rural households and communities, local elites and national and international policy-makers. I needed regular triangulations of my research findings with a small number of well-informed Afghan and international researchers to check the veracity of the work.

This experience highlights that, while there are calls to make politics more explicit within the livelihoods approach, it is far from easy to do in practice. Gaining access has become more difficult over time. At the local and sub-national levels there is both the challenge of insecure space and that of moving beyond the narratives of the powerful who tend to be located in the provincial centres and national capitals. There are problems in cross-verifying the data and information from fieldwork in rural areas, which may amount to gossip, rumour and conspiracy theories. And finally, there is need for caution, in avoiding direct questions about sensitive subjects; and for patience, in saving some queries and questions until 'next time', when greater confidence and trust have been built. At the national and international levels, there has always been a need to review secondary data and to subject the narratives of policy-makers to the same critical eye required for reviewing the results of fieldwork. Cross-verification of data has required a continued engagement with both policy-makers and rural communities over a protracted period of time and over different geographic terrains (de Haan and Zoomers, 2005: 44).

Embedded Case Studies

As cited in Chapter 3, a further criticism of the livelihoods approach has been the tendency to focus on single population groups, failing to produce results that have resonance with a policy community more concerned with the macro-environment (Scoones, 2009). I have sought to overcome this criticism through comparative research of livelihood decisions and outcomes in different geographic, socio-economic and political contexts over an extended period of time.

Data collection in rural areas was designed to be explanatory and inductive. The exploratory research phase showed the extreme diversity in socio-economic, political and environmental conditions within any given province in Afghanistan. Insecurity and the continuing absence of the most basic demographic data also ruled out conducting large-scale surveys using probability sampling techniques (Berg, 2007: 42: Barakat et al., 2002: 993). Edwards points to just how unreliable and potentially misleading any attempt at random sampling in Afghanistan would be:

> In the realms of 'social sciences', survey research tries to approximate [data that conveys a degree of certainty], but particularly in places like Afghanistan, such research—especially when couched in the statistical language of percentages and coefficients—conveys a spurious sort of precision that is likely to mislead those who take it seriously. (Edwards, 2010: 12)

My own experience and the work of others also advised against more quantitative surveys and data-collection methods when investigating an issue like opium poppy cultivation in the increasingly insecure terrain of rural Afghanistan (Goodhand, 2000: 13; Barakat et al., 2002). To overcome these challenges, the research adopted a multiple case study approach that was shaped by maximum variation sampling. The individual case studies, the embedded units within them and the individual households selected for interviews were based on maximum variation sampling so that 'any common patterns that emerge from great variation are of particular interest and value in capturing the core experiences and central shared aspects' (Patton, 1990: 172).

The provinces of Nangarhar in the Eastern Region and Helmand in southern Afghanistan were selected due to my experience in these two provinces as significant opium producers during the 1990s. Nangarhar was of particular interest as an area where opium poppy cultivation was 'entrenched' but where, following concerted efforts by the provincial authorities in the 2004/5 growing season, there was a significant downturn in the level of cultivation followed by a rebound in 2007. This cycle was repeated with negligible levels of cultivation in 2008 and 2009 and with limited resurgence of cultivation in 2010.

In contrast, the population in Helmand had experienced much higher levels of eradication but did not see a fall in the levels of cultivation until the 2008/9 growing season, when the substantial shift in the terms of trade between opium and wheat led to a dramatic reduction in the amount of opium produced (Mansfield et al., 2011). Between 2009 and 2011, further significant reductions in opium poppy cultivation were associated with the counternarcotics efforts of Governor Gulab Mangal and the increased presence of international and national security forces. My ongoing work for the FCO and the Afghan AREU supported fieldwork in the provinces each year during both the planting and harvest seasons.

Within Nangarhar, embedded sub-units were selected, consisting of research sites in five districts chosen for maximum variation, juxtaposing locations where the population had different assets, exposure to stresses and risks, and different experiences of interventions, including counternarcotics efforts. The selection of research sites required a thorough knowledge of the area derived from exploratory research and using remote sensing data. The relatively permissive security situation at the beginning of the research period made it possible to obtain varied research sites, ranging from the more remote and mountainous parts of districts such as Khogiani and Achin—where state presence is minimal and where landholdings are particularly small—to areas such as upper Kama and lower Surkhrud which represent well-irrigated areas located close to Jalalabad city. In each district, research sites were selected that were both upstream and downstream of the irrigation source, so as to provide a better picture of how populations with different resources and economic opportunities responded to a ban on opium production.

In Helmand, geo-spatial data was used to select a total of 28 research sites that had quite different experiences of both development and counternarcotics efforts, and where the population had contrasting resource endowments. However, in Helmand the research design was limited to the more secure districts of Lashkar Gah, Nad e Ali, Nawa Barakzai, Nahre Seraj and Marjeh. These were the areas where counternarcotics efforts have been focused in what has become known as the Food Zone Programme. In 2010, seven research sites north of the Boghra Canal were included. These were areas where the land had previously been desert, was irrigated by tube wells, where development assistance was not provided and where anti-government elements (AGE) dominated. The research sites in this area, as well as those unaffected by eradication and the provision of agricultural inputs, acted as a control group by which to judge the counternarcotics efforts in the Food Zone.

In each embedded unit, households were selected by maximum variation sampling, with an emphasis on obtaining a cross-section of different socio-economic groups within each research site. This made it possible to explore which groups were more resilient to the imposition of a ban; to determine which were more likely to benefit from assistance or be more vulnerable to interventions such as crop eradication; and to improve understanding of their involvement and reactions to any collective decision-making and responses to the state's efforts to curb opium poppy cultivation (Barakat et al., 2002: 995).

In total fifteen farmers were interviewed in each district of Nangarhar during each round of fieldwork, conducted every six months between the 2004/5 and 2012/13 growing seasons. Further interviews were also conducted with shopkeepers and labourers in the bazaars of Markoh, Kahi and Jalalabad to aid understanding of the impact of a ban on the wider economy. In Helmand, fifteen farmers were interviewed in each research site every six months from May 2008 until the end of the 2012/13 growing season.

Working with Local Researchers

Fieldwork in Nangarhar was conducted with the same four local researchers from 2004 to 2009. After April 2009, my mobility in Nangarhar was largely confined to the districts adjacent to the provincial centre of Jalalabad, with some limited travel to the district of Shinwar. My long-term contacts in the more distant areas were hesitant to have me visit, concerned that I would be subject to attack but also that criminal or anti-government elements would hear of my visit and threaten them. Consequently, the bulk of the primary research in the field since then has been conducted by a small team of Afghan researchers with whom I worked for over a decade. The core group of researchers have worked with each other for almost 25 years, are from rural areas in eastern Afghanistan, and are all trained agriculturalists who retain farming land in their own villages.

The security situation in Helmand was such that, since fieldwork began in 2008, it has always been undertaken by a group of six researchers. Four of them are farmers from central Helmand and have been able to travel freely across the province, including in the area north of the Boghra Canal. Two others are from Kandahar but have family and extensive contacts in the canal command area. All have in-depth knowledge of the areas in which they are working and familiarity with the farming systems in place.

With the fieldwork increasingly facilitated by Afghan researchers, my relationship with them became critical. The duration of my work in Afghanistan, the sense of my commitment to the country, the longevity of our working relationship, and my time in remote rural areas with key members of the team were important for building trust with this group and served as a basis for cross-verification of data. The preparation and debriefings between myself and local colleagues strengthened our working relationship and were a critical element in the research process. Preparation entailed a continuing dialogue with local researchers about the scope and nature of the research before the development of an interview guide, its translation into Pashto, and training in its use. The team were also told before each round of work that if the security situation was not permissive in any of the research sites, they were not to visit.

During the post-fieldwork debriefings, the data from each interview was translated and written up verbatim before being reviewed. This provided an opportunity to compare the data from different research sites and socio-economic groups with the researchers. Debriefings were conducted on site after each day of fieldwork, allowing us to adjust the research to that day's findings if necessary. With the deterioration in the security situation, I also conducted interviews in Jalalabad with farmers from the research sites in order to cross-verify and build on the results of the fieldwork of local researchers.

Debriefings for the Helmand fieldwork were conducted in Kabul. The FCO's duty of care required me to reside at the Provincial Reconstruction Team (PRT); as Afghan colleagues were unable to visit each day, fearful of being seen by anti-government elements, we decided to relocate the debriefings. My own experience of conducting research in the province during the 1990s and continued engagement in fieldwork in other provinces provided a useful check on research findings. Most importantly, with Alcis Ltd's integration of high-resolution geo-spatial imagery and analysis onto a single system, known as GeoExplorer, it was possible to review research findings from specific locations with local researchers. This offered further opportunities to verify data and examine issues of specific interest.

Collecting Primary Data

Drawing on Experience among the Policy Community

Some of the most challenging aspects of this research relate to negotiating access to the officials and policy-makers who shape drugs policy in Afghanistan. Official narratives typically present policy outcomes and do not document the complex processes that shape the final policy decision. The many—often competing—actors and organisations involved, the multiple levels at which policy is negotiated, and the disconnect between what is presented on paper and what is subsequently implemented are often lost in official policy statements and the narratives of public officials. The high turnover of staff in Afghanistan makes it particularly difficult to chart the policy process retrospectively and the reasons why certain decisions were made at specific points in time. Moreover, the important role that individual agency plays in the policy-making process is typically not documented in the memoirs and personal accounts that have been a growing part of the literature on the international intervention in Afghanistan since 2001 (Cowper-Coles, 2010; Schweich, 2008; Collins, 2015).

The prohibition of opium cannot be assessed simply by its impact on drug control outcomes in the short term, or even its effect on those who cultivate it. The literature has been particularly weak in documenting the wider political and institutional context in which the prohibition of opium has taken place in illicit drug crop-producing countries such as Afghanistan (Thoumi, 2002: 162). For example, the evaluation of the Taliban prohibition by Farrell and Thorne (2002) drew criticism for the authors' failure to address the unintended consequences of the dramatic reduction in opium production, the wider context in which the ban was enforced, and how this ultimately impacted on its sustainability (Jelsma, 2005; Thoumi, 2005). In general, the literature has failed to consider or document the multiplicity of international, national, regional and local institutions involved, many of which have no direct mandate for drug control; it has instead simply attributed the drive to ban opium to the hegemony of the USG and the international drug control regime (McCoy, 1991; Buxton, 2010).

Contrary to the literature's depiction of prohibition as the product of a coherent and authoritative international drug control regime, it has been a fragile coalition of institutions, with quite different motivations, that have pressed for dramatic reductions in opium production in Afghanistan over the last decade. To understand the impact of the policy process on the imposition and sustainability of prohibition in a given area, it is necessary to identify the different institutions involved; the reasons for their engagement in drug control efforts, no matter how indirect; and the ways in which a ban might serve their wider mandates and interests.

Neumann (2010) offers invaluable insights into the policy-making process in Afghanistan during the period in which he was US Ambassador in Kabul. He highlights the competitive and iterative nature of the policy process; the multiple and often competing actors involved in both Kabul and Western capitals; the embedded policy positions that can develop; the pressure to act, and act quickly, against unfavourable metrics; and the inevitable impact of the election cycle of Western nations on policy decisions. Those working in Afghanistan recognise the factors described and might further emphasise the high turnover of international staff, the restrictions on travel within the country, and the consequences of these factors for making informed policy judgements (Suhrke, 2011).

Those working specifically on the issue of drug production and trade in Afghanistan might further add the inevitable limitations of developing evidence-based policy when dealing with an underground economy in which there is always incomplete information; working with statistics—particularly national ones—that are at best 'guesstimates' but are so frequently cited as evidence of policy 'success' or 'failure'; and the challenges of engaging in a policy dialogue with people who have such deep-rooted views on the subject despite having rarely, if at all, spent time in rural Afghanistan.

To develop a chronology of the policy process and the institutions involved in the implementation of the bans on opium in Afghanistan, I drew on my direct experience working for a range of organisations, including UNODC, FCO, AREU, DFID, the Canadian International Development Agency (CIDA), the Dutch Foreign Ministry, the Aga Khan Development Network (AKDN), the World Bank, the Asian Development Bank and the European Commission.

This work involved engaging with officials and senior policy-makers involved in drug control in Afghanistan for more than a decade, including two former Executive Directors of UNODC. Furthermore, as a UNODC employee of the Afghanistan programme during the 1990s, and later a member of the donor's mission investigating the Taliban ban in the 2000/1 growing season, I met with some of the senior leadership in the Taliban regime, and with district governors and tribal elders who were involved in the implementation of the ban.

After December 2001, I also provided technical support to the UK government—formerly the 'lead' and then the 'partner' nation on counternarcotics in Afghanistan. This role gave me access to senior policy-makers and officials, particularly between 2001 and 2008. Since 2005, I undertook consultancies for several bilateral, multilateral and non-government organisations that were directly involved in the drugs issue or that implemented rural development programmes in opium poppy-growing areas. Throughout this time I again had direct access to a range of Afghan officials, as well as a variety of policy-makers involved in counternarcotics and development efforts for bilateral and multilateral institutions.

This experience, by its nature, is partial. It is shaped by the individuals and the institutions that I had contact with, as well as by the correspondence and documentation to which I gained access. It does, however, provide a unique insight into the policy environment and the wide range of actors that shape drugs policy in Afghanistan. The length of my exposure to this constantly changing policy community also provided an opportunity to compare the different opium bans implemented in Afghanistan, as well as the different institutions and political processes involved in their implementation. My direct involvement with data collection in provinces, including Nangarhar, during the implementation of these bans also allowed each ban to be reviewed from the perspective of the different primary stakeholders in the rural areas (some of which may not have been affected by the ban at all), and from the standpoint of the secondary stakeholders in institutions in Kabul and Western capitals.

In charting the institutional context that shaped drugs policy in Afghanistan, and the implementation of a variety of opium bans over the last seventeen years, I did not formally interview the main protagonists. Instead, I drew on my experience with these individuals and the policy process and the documentation at my disposal. As such, my engagement has been shaped by what Burawoy (1998: 5), in his description of the extended case method, refers to as 'the real events, struggles and dramas that took place over space and time'. I have made use of the growing body of secondary data from researchers, practitioners and policy-makers who have been actively engaged in Afghanistan over an extended period of time (Neumann, 2009; Leslie and Johnson, 2002; Cowper-Coles, 2010; Fitzherbert, 2004; Mukhopadhyay, 2014). I have also had drafts of my research reviewed by a number of individuals who were more intimately involved in policy decisions.

Structuring and Funding Data Collection in Rural Afghanistan

Conducting research on opium poppy cultivation in rural Afghanistan has never been an easy task. As with any 'illegal' or 'underground' activity, data collection is vulnerable to the biases of both those involved in drug production and the organisations responsible for its control. Matters are made all the more difficult in Afghanistan by the absence of robust data on the most basic variables, including population size and composition, making sampling problematic (Kandiyoti, 1999). Since 2001, the growing pressure to act against opium cultivation and its trade has increased the already heightened sensitivities associated with enquiring about any behaviour that might result in punitive action by the government or international community. And the deteriorating security situation in much of rural Afghanistan since 2008 has made empirical work with those cultivating opium poppy particularly challenging.

Household data was collected through the interlinked research consultancies that I designed and that were funded by a number of donors, as detailed in earlier sections of this chapter. At the core of this integrated research strategy was the empirical work conducted each planting season since 2002 and funded by the FCO, as well as work during the harvest season funded by Gesellschaft für Technische Zusammenarbeit (GTZ), AREU, and Development Alternatives Incorporated (DAI).

It is important to note that none of the funding organisations sought to influence the methodology or outcomes of the research. I had complete autonomy regarding research design and approach. As one official phrased his enquiry, 'I am not interested in good news or bad news, I just want the news.'[3] The research has been viewed as evaluative in nature, and has helped shape donors' understanding of what has and has not worked. The results of the research typically remained part of the 'grey literature' and were not published by its funder as part of any effort to present a narrative on the efficacy of a particular policy (Thoumi, 2002: 162).

A core principle that I adhered to throughout this research was the pursuit of objectivity and the importance of managing bias, while at the same time recognising, as Thoumi (2002: 163) reminds us:

> It may be argued that it is virtually impossible to eliminate all biases from illicit drug research, however, any social scientist in contrast to a social activist, has two responsibilities: to distance him or herself from the politics involved and to spell out his own biases and prejudices, that is, the implicit assumptions in his or her approach at the issue to be researched. Only this way the limitations of the study and the meaning are clear.

This research is an attempt to simply present the evidence; any bias that it contains is methodological and not ideological.

Collecting and Cross-verifying Household Data

Interviews with rural households have primarily focused on the portfolio of livelihood activities and the different shocks that households may have experienced. In opium-producing areas, respondents will typically acknowledge that they cultivate opium poppy when discussing the crops that they grow and will offer information on the process and impact of a ban on opium production when discussing the shocks to which they have been exposed.

Although respondents were candid in their discussions on opium production, the research adopted a number of strategies to improve the collection of data and its reliability, particularly given the challenges of the ongoing conflict. First, individual interviews concentrated on the direct experience of the respondent and his household rather than on a wider geographic area; this practice reflected the experiences of organisations like the Swedish Committee, whose extensive research in the late 1980s and early 1990s showed that answers become increasingly more speculative as the geographic area broadens (Swedish Committee for Afghanistan, 1992: 1).

Second, interviews with farming households were undertaken in the field while farmers tended their crops. This had several advantages. It helped manage security risks, as researchers were less conspicuous in the fields than in the residence or village centre. It also helped to minimise the repeated interruptions and potential bias prevalent in interviews conducted in the household compound. Group discussions with farmers were avoided, as they tended to be dominated by community elites, were found to be inappropriate for discussing sensitive issues and increasingly represented a security threat (Goodhand, 2000: 13; Shairzai et al., 1975: 13; Stevens and Tarzi, 1965: 1).

Third, as the security environment deteriorated and the local authorities took more punitive action against those cultivating opium poppy, it became necessary for contact with respondents to become more discreet. Interviews were conducted without a formal survey and were conversational in style, and while similar information was sought from each respondent, the order differed based on the particular circumstances of the person being interviewed. This less formal style of interview reduced the potential for social-desirability bias that has been shown to impact the results of more quantitative research techniques, such as polling in chronically insecure provinces (Pinney, 2010).

Fourth, interviews were not written up on site but after the researcher and respondent had parted company. This was not intended to be secretive or clandestine; rather, it acknowledged that what Kovats Bernat (2002: 210, 215) refers to as 'low-profile data collection' puts respondents at ease. In this instance, it reduced the security risks to researchers, including myself (Bourgois, 1990: 52; Zaitch, 2001: 13; Siegel, 2007: 25). Although delayed write-ups can present some challenges with regard to recall or memory bias, such issues were diminished by the experience of the fieldworkers.

Fifth, data collection was conducted over a number of consecutive years at the same time each year, coinciding with both the planting season for opium poppy in November/December and the opium harvest in April/May. These two distinct periods in the agricultural calendar were found to be advantageous for data collection as farmers were familiar with the performance of the previous season's crops and were already considering what would be cultivated during the next growing cycle. Collecting data over consecutive seasons also helped develop a longer-term perspective on the impact of the prohibition on opium, including a greater understanding of the socio-economic and political processes which have supported some farmers' transition out of opium production and led to the deprivation of others.

Finally, other sources of data were drawn upon to cross-verify and refine the data. For example, to cross-check the information on crops sales and how agricultural markets function, wholesale and retail traders were interviewed in the main bazaars in each district covered by the fieldwork, as well as in the cities of Jalalabad, Lashkar Gah, Gereshk and Kabul. Agricultural labourers, including those harvesting the opium crop, were also interviewed in a number of locations in both Helmand and Nangarhar, to give a better explanation of the impact of efforts to ban opium and the availability of off-farm and non-farm income opportunities over time. Photography also provided time series data of particular fields or valleys.

Remote sensing data was also used to cross-verify household data and ascertain the degree of crop diversification that followed the enforcement of an opium ban in specific research sites. Helicopter reconnaissance over Nangarhar and Helmand by Alcis Ltd was particularly helpful in providing data on cropping patterns in key valleys and research sites. Other remote sensing data were used for further investigations of qualitative findings, including infrastructural developments, the implementation of development assistance, the incidence of crop failure and drought, land seizures, eradication and the growth in land under agricultural production. This body of data has proved to be invaluable, particularly as the security situation deteriorated and made some locations inaccessible to the researcher.

Collecting Data on the Political Economy

Acquiring data on the political economy began with rural respondents themselves. Framing data collection around the changes in lives and livelihoods that households had experienced over the preceding agricultural season and the causes of these changes prompted a variety of responses, many of which related to interactions and disputes between individuals, villages, and local, subnational and even national elites.

These initial responses were often found to focus on particular experiences or events that were of significance to the individual, such as eradication (or perhaps the lack of it), conflict over land, acts of predation, violence or—latterly—insurgency. These responses proved helpful in identifying and ranking issues that respondents viewed as important to their overall wellbeing. They also served as an entry point for discussing local configurations of power, the complex and changing relationships between groups and individuals within the local area, and the connections with formal and informal institutions in the province and in Kabul.

Some respondents in Nangarhar, including those who were interviewed repeatedly over the course of the research, were from the rural elite and participated in both formal and informal political institutions involved in conflict resolution at local and provincial levels. Other respondents were farmers, both landed and land-poor, who offered their accounts of some of these same processes (or their understanding of the decisions made) from a different perspective. These contrasting experiences became a further element in the maximum variation sampling that shaped my fieldwork.

Ultimately the number of respondents within each embedded unit, the diverse socio-economic groups interviewed and repeated visits to the same areas painted a more complex picture of the local political economy. These factors allowed data to be cross-checked across the different groups within a community and between opposing sides in some of the disputes that came to dominate the political landscape over the course of this research. The longitudinal nature of the research also allowed the shifting alliances among different local, sub-national and national elites to be mapped.

The findings of each round of fieldwork were also discussed with key informants, both national and international, all with long-term experience in Nangarhar and Helmand. Some of these individuals were researchers who had conducted research primarily with elite groups, offering a contrasting source of data with which to cross-check the results of my fieldwork. Other key informants resided in Nangarhar and Helmand over a number of years. This group of individuals proved an invaluable source of secondary data.

Adapting to the Security Environment: Methodological and Ethical Considerations

Adapting the Methodology

There is a wide body of literature documenting the challenges associated with conducting research in war and conflict zones (Kovats Bernat, 2002; Helbardt et al., 2010; Vlassenroot, 2006; Wood, 2006; Goodhand, 2000). Much of this literature refers to the problems of access and the reliability of the data collected. Helbardt et al. (2011: 356) go so far as to suggest that: '[a]ny kind of systematic data collection is close to impossible, because it depends fully on the current security situation, which determines where one can go and whom one can talk to.' It is certainly the case that data collection in rural Afghanistan has been increasingly shaped by the prevailing security situation. Helmand has been a challenging security environment since the fall of the Taliban regime, particularly from 2005 onwards. Parts of Nangarhar became increasingly insecure and some areas were inaccessible to Afghan researchers in 2013. Experience shows that formal surveys are treated with suspicion; those conducting surveys are seen to be working for the Afghan government and/or international community and can be subject to punishment (Pinney, 2010).

Fieldwork in Helmand was conducted by Afghan colleagues throughout the study period. However, as the security situation deteriorated, I found it increasingly difficult to conduct fieldwork, even in Nangarhar. As with other researchers, my presence sometimes led respondents to accuse me of working for law enforcement or intelligence agencies—a misconception which I successfully rebutted (Sascha Helbardt et al., 2011: 358; Rawlinson, 2008: 19). With the increase in criminality, including kidnapping, and incursions by insurgent groups, some respondents warned me not to travel to visit them even in more accessible parts of Nangarhar and offered to come to Jalalabad for more detailed discussions in 'neutral space' (Kovats-Bernat, 2002: 212).

The worsening security situation in rural Afghanistan raised concerns not only for my personal safety but for that of my colleagues, as well as community members (Helbardt et al., 2011: 357). Due to the threats against local researchers working with foreign nationals and communities in some of the more remote parts of Nangarhar, I did not travel to areas where local researchers and respondents were uncomfortable with my presence.

The security situation and the sensitive nature of the subject matter prevented the same households from being visited for each round of the fieldwork, even by Afghan researchers. Even in Nangarhar, repeated visits to the same households in each research site every six months aroused suspicions and placed fieldworkers and respondents at risk. However, it was possible to build a small core of respondents in each of the districts over a number of years that allowed for some longitudinal studies with individual households.

A further response to the worsening security situation was the closer integration of photography and remote sensing data into the project design. In part, photography and remote sensing data provided a mechanism for cross-verifying the results of fieldwork once the bulk of the data collection was delegated to local researchers. This was a valuable management tool. However, imagery of the research sites derived from both satellite sensors and helicopter reconnaissance trips was also a useful medium for further investigating primary data and informing both subsequent rounds of fieldwork and the collection of remote sensing data.

Ethical Implications

> By the very fact that we are participating in research that investigates, considers or at least is engaged amid violence or terror or the threat thereof, we are inviting the possibility of victimization on ourselves and on our informants. (Kovats-Bernat, 20002: 214)

The prevailing security situation in rural Afghanistan presents a number of ethical challenges, not just for respondents but also for the Afghan researchers who have taken on the burden of much of the data collection since 2009.

In practice, the security risks to respondents have been negligible. During the early stages of the research, particularly following the implementation of the opium ban in Nangarhar, there were concerns that crop eradication might be targeted against those involved in the research. In practice, this was never an issue. However, to mitigate the risk that respondents might be arrested or have their crops destroyed if field notes were examined by the local authorities, the names of those interviewed were not recorded. Even those who became part of the group for which longitudinal data was collected remained anonymous and were written up under aliases.

In this context, informed consent meant that respondents understood the objective of the research and were aware of the consequences of providing information (Wood, 2006: 379). The consent procedure was oral; given the prevalence of opium poppy cultivation among many of those interviewed, requesting written consent could have exposed respondents to the risk of arrest or crop eradication.

The research was presented to respondents as a study of the change in the lives and livelihoods of rural households over the preceding agricultural season. The focus on the household, the assets at their disposal, details of the portfolio of activities they pursued as part of their livelihood, and the shocks they experienced meant that many respondents were willing to talk at length about their experiences (Wood, 2006: 378). Most respondents welcomed the opportunity to be heard, particularly those who were in more inaccessible locations or were more marginalised members of communities, such as daily wage labourers and the land-poor, who complained that foreign visitors and national representatives from NGOs typically restricted their dialogue to community elites (Helbardt et al., 2011: 364).

Local researchers face the dual threat of being blamed if law enforcement efforts, including interdiction, to target either the crop or the trade in a community in which fieldwork has taken place, as well as the risk of kidnap or violence from criminals and anti-government elements. The security of those conducting fieldwork has been paramount. Indeed, the discussions with the team before every round of fieldwork have always included a conversation about security and the need to abandon research in areas where the local researcher might be at risk. This conversation was repeated so often that the local researchers would inform me that I had told them this many times before and would thank me for my concern for their safety. I would assure them that this request not to put themselves in danger for the purpose of the research was repeated because it was a priority.

In practice, local researchers were well aware of the prevailing security conditions. They had established procedures for determining whether a particular area was safe and typically had contacts in the area (Kovats-Bernat, 2002: 214). Any travel I made to more distant research sites was contingent on my local colleagues' approval and their prior visit to be sure that long-term contacts in the area were willing to meet me. It was concern for the security of my local researchers, contacts and respondents that led me to reduce my travel in later rounds of fieldwork.

As the security situation deteriorated, some research sites in the most remote upper valleys of Nangarhar were abandoned on the advice of the local researchers. Guides were also recruited from specific valleys in both upper Khogiani and Achin so as to facilitate access and ensure safety.

Further measures were also adopted to reduce local researchers' exposure to risk. For example, it was vital that researchers understand when not to pursue a particular line of inquiry. In some cases respondents in the field offered information on the processing of heroin, such as the location and ownership of what are referred to locally as 'factories'. Showing an interest in this information and soliciting further details could have aroused suspicions, particularly if law enforcement subsequently targeted these facilities. When presented with this kind of information in the field, I too changed the subject and returned to more mundane conversations about rural livelihoods. It is only with long-term trusted contacts that this kind of line of inquiry was pursued.

Conclusion

This chapter has charted the challenges of conducting primary research in a sensitive area of inquiry, which increased as the security situation in eastern and southern Afghanistan deteriorated. It has provided an account of the different component parts of my research, and how they have intertwined, building over many years to cross-verify the findings of previous iterations of research, as well as examine new lines of inquiry as they emerge. It has been particularly important to chart this process and the methodological developments given the amount of literature on drug crop cultivation in Afghanistan that is not grounded in long-term empirical inquiry or is not transparent in its methodology, yet has been so instrumental in shaping drugs policy within the country.

This chapter has shown how my research evolved, building on an exploratory phase of fieldwork in the 1990s, when the environment was far more conducive to fieldwork even for internationals, to one where primary research in some parts of rural Afghanistan was not possible even for local researchers. The chapter has shown how I adapted data collection to address the methodological and ethical issues that this growing insecurity presented, including the introduction of remote sensing technology for the selection of research sites and the verification of findings.

This chapter has also shown the conceptual developments in my research as I have moved from an inquiry that primarily focused on the livelihood portfolios of rural households to one that placed politics and power at the centre of the analysis. This integration has required widening my field inquiries in rural Nangarhar and Helmand in order to understand local political structures, conflicts and the political settlements that link local, sub-national and national elites in what are often fragile and fluid arrangements. It has also required me to draw on my direct experience in the policy process: 'the real events, struggles and dramas' (Burawoy, 1998: 5) that have resulted in individuals and institutions pressing for a ban or coalescing behind Afghan and international protagonists who have called for rapid and dramatic reductions in opium production in a specific area.

5

AN HISTORICAL OVERVIEW

STATEBUILDING AND DRUG PRODUCTION
IN AFGHANISTAN

Introduction

This chapter provides a broad historical overview of statebuilding and the emergence and consolidation of the drugs economy in Afghanistan. It highlights the diverse patterns of production that can be seen across the country and the different approaches to drug control that that have been pursued over time, and by different donors in different regions. It examines some of the major points of divergence in the policy debate on drug control post-2001, as a prelude to the empirical studies detailed in Chapters 6–10.

This chapter is divided into two sections and a conclusion. The first section examines the history of state formation and statebuilding in Afghanistan, highlighting its uneven and contested nature. Particular emphasis is given to the statebuilding project pursued by the international community following the collapse of the Taliban regime. The second section positions the evolution of the drugs economy within this historical statebuilding process and the rural livelihoods framework discussed in Chapter 3. It analyses the different phases in the emergence of the drug economy, the structural environment and the bottom-up pressures that led to its consolidation, the various actors and networks involved, and how drugs are inseparable from the dynamics of statebuilding and conflict in Afghanistan.

Statebuilding in Afghanistan

Subjugating the Periphery: The Foundation of the Afghan State

As Goodhand (2012: 5) notes, Afghanistan represents 'an unpromising site for statebuilding'. As leaders of a tribal confederacy founded in the eighteenth century, Afghan rulers relied upon tribute and booty generated by raiding the wealthier Iranian and Indian territories. The expanding Russian and British empires closed off this option of conquest in the nineteenth century, denying the state access to the capital it required to concentrate successfully the means of coercion. This created a buffer state dependent upon foreign subsidies and unable to control or administer effectively the sparsely populated and mountainous tribal zone located on the eastern and southern borders (Barfield, 2004).

It was Amir Abdur Rahman Khan (1880–1901) who turned the Pashtun-led Durrani Kingdom of Kabul into the centralised nation state of Afghanistan. He drew on Islam to legitimise his rule and took control over the clergy by nationalising the Islamic endowments, which had traditionally been independent of the state. He also centralised the judiciary, making himself responsible for the appointment of all judges, rendering all decisions of the court subject to his approval, and positioning himself as the final arbiter in capital cases (Gregorian, 1969: 130, 137; Barfield, 2010: 1747).

Most importantly, with the financial and military support of British India, the Amir established a central army that set about subjugating the autonomous and warring fiefdoms that he had inherited (Gregorian, 1969: 131; Barfield, 2010: 147). These were bloody battles that succeeded in eliminating those who resisted central rule. He deployed a divide-and-rule policy, splitting the regions into smaller administrative units and appointing governors from the centre. To prevent challenges to his rule, he also undermined the power bases of the elders, the tribal *khans* and *maliks*, who had traditionally acted as interlocutors between the state and the countryside. Where possible, deals were brokered, marital alliances were formed and financial subsidies were paid. Those elders who defied him were brutally suppressed, provoking numerous rebellions that were put down with military force (Sharani, 1979: 63).

Once the rebellions were pacified, a new order was established in the countryside. This tied the rural elite to the central state through patronage, the payment of allowances and pledges of fealty to the Amir (Barfield, 2010: 174). Elders were accountable only to the centre. They were charged with educating the rural population as to their duties and responsibilities, and they were also responsible for securing the countryside. By the end of his rule in 1901, Abdur

Rahman had unified Afghanistan politically, established a civil administration and placed state representatives in the provinces and in some of the most remote parts of the country (Kakar, 1979: 62). He imposed 'standardized taxes, laws, currency, conscription, and administrative structures that put all Afghans in a single system' (Barfield 2010: 159). In doing so, he had killed more than 100,000 of his own population (Barfield, 2010: 174).

Yet, beneath this tale of absolute rule was a fault line—the Durand Line—that marked the border between British India and Afghanistan. Forced through by the British in 1893, after they imposed an economic embargo on the country in the middle of Abdur Rahman's campaign in the Hazarajat, this border became a source of continuing instability for the Afghan state. Indeed, according to Gregorian (1969: 159):

> ... the Durand agreement resulted in the strengthening of the political position of the tribes of Afghanistan. The policies of the Afghan rulers became more sensitive to the wishes of the major tribes, on which they were dependent for the defence of the country. The stance of these tribes on any given issue became an important consideration in the successful implementation of domestic policies, especially those affecting eastern Afghanistan, the tribal homelands.

Barfield (2010) goes further and argues that, independent of the demarcation of Afghanistan's borders by the Imperial powers of Europe, Abdur Rahman's centralised rule of Afghanistan was unstable. With a long history of competing dynasties residing over territories that maintained a degree of economic and political independence through their links with neighbouring states, the kind of autocratic rule that Abdur Rahman established over the Afghan polity was sure to fail; it was only a question of when.

Shifting Politics in the Centre

Some of the rulers who followed Abdur Rahman Khan tried to emulate his rule; the wiser ones left the population in areas of limited statehood to their own devices. Abdur Rahman's grandson, Aminullah (1919–29), was a reformer. He pressed through a modernisation programme that proved unpopular in the countryside. It included universal conscription and formal education for women and it restricted polygamy, child marriage and Pashtun customs related to the treatment of women, including bride wealth and the settling of disputes through the exchange of women (Barfield, 2010: 183; 185).

Aminullah's radical programme followed Afghan independence from Britain in 1919, which ended the subsidies from British India that had supported his grandfather, Abdur Rahman, and his father, Habibullah (1901–19). Without foreign funds to push through his programme of government, Aminullah raised taxes on the rural population and cut both military spending and stipends to religious leaders and the Muhammedzai elite that dominated the administration and the political class. These new taxes were payable in cash rather than agricultural produce and proved easy for local administrators to pocket. The corruption that ensued, when combined with both conscription and the attempt to fast-track modernisation, culminated in a rural rebellion that began in the peripheral areas of Shinwar, Khogiani and Kohistan, but ended in a direct attack on Jalalabad and then Kabul. By 1929 Aminullah was forced to abdicate.

The era of the Musahiban dynasty that followed (1929–78) was more cautious in its approach to those at the periphery. Nadir Shah (1929–33) immediately looked to distance himself from Aminullah's programme of reform and the absolute rule associated with Abdur Rahman Khan and his descendants. He established a conservative political settlement between the royal family, the clerics and the land-owning elite in the countryside. He proclaimed himself 'the servant of the tribes and the people' (Barfield, 2010: 196) and looked to a *jirga* of elders to legitimate his rule.

Following his assassination in November 1933, Nadir was succeeded by Zahir Shah, who ruled Afghanistan for four decades. Cautious of the forces of conservatism in the countryside, Zahir Shah's prime ministers—Hashim Khan (1933–46), his brother Shah Mahmud (1946–53) and their nephew Daud Khan (1953–63)—adopted a slow and iterative approach to reform that mainly impacted on the urban elite (Barfield, 2010: 202). The burden of taxes was shifted onto the commercial sector, including a small but growing export sector. Unable to meet the costs of growing public finances and a programme of modernisation—including the development of the military, establishment of agricultural industries and land resettlement projects—the Musahiban dynasty turned to foreign powers for financial support, including Germany, the US and the Soviet Union.

However, modernisation created a new source of tension within the Afghan political system during the 1960s and 1970s. A new class of malcontents could be found in the urban areas: disaffected youth, alienated by the lack of opportunities available to them after they completed their university studies. On one side there were the Islamists at Kabul University under the leadership of Burhanuddin Rabbani, Ghulam Rasul Sayyaf and Gulbuddin Hekmatyar. On the other side were the communists: the People's Democratic Party of Afghanistan (PDPA) led by Nur Muhhammed Taraki and Babrak Kamal.

In 1973, with the support of the PDPA, Daud Khan staged a coup against his cousin Zahir Shah which ended the Afghan monarchy. In rural Afghanistan, the change of power was largely irrelevant. The Musahiban dynasty continued. It was simply one cousin deposing another—an Afghan tradition. However, in Kabul and other urban centres, Daud set about consolidating his rule, removing the communists who had backed him from positions of power and driving the Islamists into exile.

The War Years: Empowering the Periphery

The Saur revolution in 1978 marked the end of the Daud's rule and the rise of the PDPA. Dominated by the Khalqi faction within the PDPA, the new government set about a radical programme of reform that once again looked to challenge the forces of conservatism in the regions. As Barfield (2010: 225) notes: '[the Khalqis] were not just interested in ruling Afghanistan but also in transforming the countryside though revolutionary policies of land reform, education, and changes in family law'.

Under the leadership of Nur Mohammed Taraki, the Khalqi faction of the PDPA made no attempt to mediate between the dichotomous forces that successive Afghan governments had sought to reconcile. Religious symbolism was discarded and replaced by the language of revolution and atheism. The interests of the feudal establishment were rejected in the push for modernisation, and the country's traditional position of neutrality on the international stage was abandoned in favour of an alliance with the Soviet Union. Those who opposed the new government were brutally suppressed, including President Daud, his family and prominent Islamist leaders from the Mujahaddi family, all of whom were killed. Internal purges within the PDPA were bloody and led to the marginalisation of the Parcham faction of the PDPA and the exile of their leader Babrak Karmal.

The reform agenda in rural areas was particularly ill-considered and poorly implemented. Land distribution, female literacy and changes to marriage law were an affront to conservative rural values. They challenged the social fabric, positioning the local rural elite against their land-poor neighbours and relatives, and both groups against new migrants who were settled on redistributed land. The policies were met with rural resistance, largely unorganised and local but nevertheless resulting in a significant loss of government influence over the countryside (Barfield, 2010: 230). In February 1979, Taraki was deposed by Hafizullah Amin, and was murdered a month later.

In December 1979, fearing the growing unrest in the country and the collapse of the increasingly unpopular Khalqi faction of the PDPA, Soviet President Brezhnev sent troops across the border. Installing Babrak Karmal as President, the new government set about repealing some of the more unpopular social reforms that the Khalqi regime had pursued, including land reform, women's rights and rural debt (Barfield, 2010: 237). The strategy failed, and the presence of Soviet troops proved a rallying cry for rural resistance.

In fact, the Soviet invasion marked a shift from localised and more spontaneous revolt to a more structured resistance couched in the language of *jihad* against infidel invaders. Political parties were formed and subsequently supported by the US and Pakistani governments. These largely Sunni Islamist parties formed the conduit for financial subsidies from foreign powers, not just for the refugees who had fled the fighting in Afghanistan and had to be registered with a political party in Pakistan to receive assistance, but also for the weapons and military training provided with US and Saudi help.

Over time, the resistance proved effective and the PDPA government made little headway in the countryside despite the Soviets' significant military force. A stalemate was reached, with the Afghan resistance in control of the countryside and the Soviet-backed PDPA dominating the urban areas and main transport routes. In some cases the Afghan military and the resistance formalised the deadlock and agreed not to fight each other.

In March 1985, incoming Russian President Gorbachev gave the Afghan leadership twelve months to make decisive progress. The human and financial costs of the war to the Soviets were proving to be too great a burden. Following a particularly bloody year with little to show for it, the Soviets announced in November 1986 that they would be withdrawing their forces from Afghanistan by the end of 1988. As part of the transition, and in an attempt to promote reconciliation with the resistance, Karmal was exiled in November 1987 and Najibullah, former head of the Secret Police (KhAD), took over as President.

Encouraged by the Soviet leadership, who were keen to see a stable Afghanistan when they left, Najibullah used Soviet aid to make arrangements with local resistance groups and to establish ceasefires. He renamed the PDPA the *Hizb-i-watan* (Homeland Party) and approached key members of the resistance, inviting them to form a coalition. Islam was once again embraced. Much to the surprise of many, the Najibullah government survived the withdrawal of the Soviet military and persisted for three more years.

The longevity of the Najibullah government was aided by the schisms within the resistance. The unifying themes of nationalism and Islam could not be relied on to elicit popular support once the Soviet military departed. Ethnic rivalries and personal animosity between factional leaders offered few opportunities for a more stable coalition from which an effective military campaign could be launched to depose the government from its urban strongholds. Moreover, party leaders and commanders did not have effective command and control over their local forces. Indeed, Barfield (2010: 240) suggests that they were:

> ... more like chieftains who had to cajole their followers into taking action rather than rules who could command them. Subordinate commanders could and did defect to another resistance party or even the PDPA if they felt abused or were attracted by a better deal.

Given the rivalries between the resistance leaders, weak party structures and fluid local loyalties, it is no surprise that when Najibullah was brought down in 1992—following the collapse of the Soviet Union and the loss of the aid that had propped up his government—the country descended into civil war. As none of the *mujahidin* parties had the coercive capacity to extend their power beyond their regional base, and all continued to benefit significantly from the war economy that thrived in their borderlands, there was little interest in unity and the formation of a coalition government in Kabul. Turf wars erupted as factions fought over control of resources and rents from cross-border smuggling, military and financial support from neighbouring powers and development assistance from NGOs and the UN.

The Taliban Government: Re-emergence of the Centre

In 1994 the Taliban movement, under the leadership of Mullah Omar, descended on Spin Boldak in Kandahar province with the aim of securing the area from fractious and predatory local commanders. With Pakistani support, they moved on to Kandahar city and started to absorb increasing amounts of territory. By January 1995 they had ousted the Akhundzada clan from Helmand and occupied Uruzgan and Ghazni, all without a major battle. By September 1996 the Taliban had taken Kabul and by August 1998 they had also absorbed Mazar i Sharif and most of the northern provinces. Only the north-eastern province of Badakhshan lay beyond their reach and continued to do so until the end of their rule in October 2001.

Once in Kabul, the Taliban set about establishing the structures of government. They began to rebuild ministries and issued a raft of policy positions. However, their administration was dysfunctional; policies decided in Kabul would be overruled a few days later by the real centre of government in Kandahar, where Mullah Omar was based. Efforts to strengthen the regime's relations with foreign nations and gain recognition for their government came to little as increasingly radical policies were adopted. With no sources of foreign support beyond the limited aid that Pakistan could offer, the Taliban put increasing pressure on the UN and NGOs to deliver social services and infrastructure. The relationship became increasingly strained as Taliban policies on gender, human rights and the intimidation of UN staff became intolerable. Assistance continued but aid flows diminished, despite a worsening drought and deteriorating humanitarian conditions as a consequence of the Taliban's treatment of the populations in the Shomali and Hazarajat.

In many rural areas of the south and east, Taliban rule was far less visible. While tribal and military elites acquiesced to Taliban rule, they were given varying degrees of autonomy (Johnson and Leslie, 2004: 145; Sinno, 2008; Crews and Tarzi, 2008: 111–12). Even the claims that the population had been disarmed were overstated; many rural communities—particularly those in the mountainous areas—retained their weapons but consented to withdraw them from public space as long as the Taliban maintained security. Maley (2002: 217) notes: 'The claim that the Taliban "controlled" large tracts of Afghanistan was misleading, since the Taliban presence in rural areas was light.'

In reality, the Taliban regime, like its predecessors, ruled through a combination of coercion and negotiation. In the lower areas of 'consolidated statehood', located along the main trading routes and river valleys, the Taliban regime could easily impose its will on a population that was more accessible and that consists of numerous tribes settled over many years. In the more mountainous areas where the population is more cohesive, there was little evidence of Taliban presence beyond a few armed militia located in the district governor's office. In these areas of limited statehood, the Taliban regime, like its predecessors, adopted a strategy of containment working with the rural elite to neutralise dissent.

By 2000, there were signs that the regime was under strain. There was evidence of growing rural dissent even in the southern provinces of Helmand and Kandahar (Rashid, 2001; Crews and Tarzi, 2008: 259–68). Conscription was proving unpopular (Vendrell, personal communication, 24 April 2001; Crews and Tarzi, 2008: 262, 265) and the Taliban's inability to bring economic growth frustrated the population. As discussed in Chapter 6, the ban on opium imposed during the 2000/1 growing season—an act designed to gain recognition and attract financial assistance—proved a step too far in light of al-Qaeda's attack on the US on 11 September 2001.

Statebuilding Post-2001

In some senses, the statebuilding project undertaken by the international community in Afghanistan since 2001 faced the same challenges as previous regimes of trying to balance the interests of the different centres of political power. However, the task was far more difficult as a result of the protracted war in which greater economic, political and military power was devolved to the regions (Goodhand, 2013). The war not only led to closer links between the military and political institutions of neighbouring states and a new class of 'military entrepreneurs' (Giustozzi, 2009) in Afghanistan; it also strengthened cross-border connections for the rural population who could maintain family members, jobs and business interests in Afghanistan while linking with refugee communities and the cities of Pakistan or Iran. The smuggling of licit goods as well as opiates provided remunerative and reliable economic opportunities on both sides of the borders, further weakening the role of Kabul as a source of patronage.

While masquerading as an effort to build a modern democratic state, the internationally led statebuilding project more often than not gave preference to centres of power in the regions (Goodhand, 2013). The Bonn Agreement, signed in December 2001 after the fall of the Taliban, reflected these underlying contradictions and tensions. On the one hand, Bonn set out an ambitious programme aimed at establishing a liberal democracy in Afghanistan, calling for 'the establishment of a broad-based, gender-sensitive, multi-ethnic and fully representative government' (cited in Mukhopadhyay, 2014). On the other hand, it distributed ministerial portfolios to those who had helped the US and its allies, neglecting the interests of those on the losing side—the Pashtuns and Pakistan—in what Goodhand (2012) has referred to as an 'exclusive elite pact'. On top of this, it placed Hamid Karzai, a leader with no military constituency, at the helm.

The inclusion of these 'violence entrepreneurs' (Giustozzi, 2009) in Bonn and in subsequent political processes such as the Constitution *Loya Jirga* was seen to be part of the 'big-tent strategy' aimed at co-opting those who had the potential to spoil the statebuilding project. These individuals and their armed factions were also bolstered in the regions with military support and security and logistics contracts, with the goal of mopping up the remnants of the Taliban and al-Qaeda as part of the 'war on terror'. There was a further tension between the initial 'light footprint' advocated by UN Special Representative of the Secretary General (UNSRSG) Brahimi, that conformed with the minimalist model preferred by USG and its allies, and the principles laid out at

Bonn under which security was delegated to regional warlords, and entire military groups were incorporated into the police force and army.

At the same time, Western donors supported Afghan technocrats who favoured a more centralised regime and set about building the structure of the central state in Kabul. Priority was given to the institutions of central government, a new constitution was written, central ministries were built and public- and security-sector reforms were initiated. During these first years there was little development activity in the provinces. Even some of the flagship National Priority Programmes, such as the National Solidarity Programme—a 'project in every village'—and national programmes for education and health were criticised for being geared towards shoring up electoral support for the 2004 election of Karzai and gaining legitimacy for the international state-building project.

By 2004, the international military effort, led by the North Atlantic Treaty Organisation's (NATO) International Security Assistance Force (ISAF), became increasingly focused on the regions, driven by concerns over the growing strength of the insurgency particularly in the south and east. ISAF began to locate soldiers and civilians in Provincial Reconstruction Teams (PRTs), which were, in effect, military bases, even if some were described as 'civilian-led'. Therefore perceived failures in 'shock therapy' centralisation or top-down statebuilding led to a growing focus on local governance and building the state from below.

By 2011, at the peak of the military and civilian buildup under the Obama administration, there were twenty-six PRTs, and almost 900 ISAF bases and installations in districts across the country (Turse, 2012). There was a further proliferation of local initiatives, including Focus District Development, Community Development Volunteers and, latterly, the Afghan Local Police, designed in theory to improve security for the rural population.

The PRTs were at the forefront of internationally supported statebuilding efforts in the regions. Although designed to assist the Government of the Islamic Republic of Afghanistan (GIRoA) to extend its authority, they increased the tensions between the formal statebuilding project pursued in Kabul and what Western nations considered more pressing operational requirements at the periphery. Rather than strengthening the central state and supporting its efforts to determine government policy and position itself as arbiter in the allocation of funds and political patronage, the move to the provinces exacerbated the fragmented and regionalised political economy that emerged during the war years.

Karzai became increasingly frustrated by the establishment of PRTs, as they undermined his efforts to centralise patronage through the allocation of funds. He referred to the PRTs as 'parallel structures'—referring to his efforts to build rival informal power bases in the regions to governors and warlords whom he opposed or wished to keep in check (Giustozzi and Orsini, 2009). Provinces with a US-led PRT, in particular, received large amounts of aid that bypassed the Afghan government entirely. For example the Commanders Emergency Response Programmes (CERPs), the Afghan Infrastructure Fund (AIF) and the Afghan Security Forces Fund (ASFF)—all of which were outside the purview of the Afghan government—each disbursed hundreds of millions of dollars per year. And it was not just bilateral programmes that skewed the amount of assistance available to provinces. Once Western nations were in the lead in particular provinces, the National Priority Programmes also tended to favour those provinces where the military forces of major development donors led the PRT.

Government programmes also became increasingly regionalised as provincial governors, often empowered by their Western patrons, challenged the primacy of the centre, pursuing strategies that were out of line with the policy papers and positions found in Kabul. Poorly monitored funding which circumscribed the central state had the effect of strengthening the position of regional strongmen who actively resisted the extension of state authority in the provinces. Western nations interfered with government appointments in the provinces where they were in the lead, frustrating the President's desire to use government posts to strengthen his influence over the regions. In the districts, this kind of patronage, which often entailed political, military and financial support, bolstered the position of local elite groups, and on occasion exacerbated political and military rivalries that led to growing unrest.

Ultimately the proliferation of contracts in the security, construction and transportation sectors that accompanied the initial military campaign, the establishment of the PRTs and the subsequent increase in military and civilian presence in the districts after 2010 strengthened regional and local strongmen, exacerbating centrifugal forces that had gained strength during the war years.

Two key themes emerge from the literature on Afghan statebuilding and are salient to subsequent discussions on drugs and counternarcotics policies. The first is the ongoing struggle between power holders at the political centre in Kabul and alternative sources of authority at the rural periphery. This struggle for military and political ascendancy, underpinned by competing notions of justice and governance, has periodically led to violent struggles and political upheavals. And often the incubators of rural revolt have been the unruly borderlands or areas of limited statehood. Second, the Afghan state's weak economic base and geopolitical vulnerability have perpetually rendered its leaders dependent on foreign patronage for survival. A fragile rentier state is vulnerable to collapse, as happened after the withdrawal of the British subsidy to Aminullah in 1919, and with the end of Soviet support for the Najibullah government in 1992 following the dissolution of the Soviet Union.

These two themes highlight the challenges inherent in pursuing aggressive counternarcotics policies in tandem with, or as part of, a statebuilding agenda in modern Afghanistan. The desire to see dramatic reductions in opium production positions the Afghan state in the unenviable position of extending its writ into areas where it has not traditionally had direct rule. By failing to pursue a ban, the state risks a loss of legitimacy on the international stage, thereby jeopardising the funding that it so desperately needs for its political survival. However, by banning opium it also risks the opprobrium of the population at the periphery; a population that has proved to be adept at challenging the authority of the state and even deposing the existing political order.

Opium Production, Policy and Efforts at Control

The Emergence and Consolidation of the Opium Economy

The opium economy has undergone significant changes over the last thirty years which have been shaped by the war years and by recent efforts at statebuilding. Overall levels of cultivation have followed an upward trend since the 1980s when the USG first began to produce estimates. However, there are also some significant fluctuations in cultivation over this period. This section outlines the evolution of the opium economy in Afghanistan, the structural environment and the bottom-up pressures that have led to its consolidation, the various actors and networks involved and the links between drugs, statebuilding and conflict in Afghanistan.

Emergence During the War Against the Soviets

Although opium poppy cultivation in Afghanistan is thought to date back to the times of Alexander the Great, it was not until the 1980s that there were evidence of the scale of illicit production for which Afghanistan has now become known (Macdonald, 2007: 59). In fact throughout much of the first half of the nineteenth century, cultivation was contained within a limited number of areas in a minority of provinces. During the 1930s and early 1940s the crop was produced under government licence, and legal opium sales represented an important source of foreign revenue for the Musahiban government who had exploited the disruption to the traditional suppliers of opiates, such as Turkey and Iran, caused by World War II (Bradford, 2013: 67; Collins, 2015).

As the demand for Afghan raw opiates expanded and prices rose, opium production also increased in areas outside the government regulated system. By the early 1940s the US government—one of the primary purchasers of Afghan opiates—expressed growing concerns about illicit opiate production in Afghanistan and, in an effort to get the Afghan state to curb illegal production, made it increasingly difficult for the Afghan government both to export opium to the US and to import much needed pharmaceuticals. According to Bradford (2013: 86), the pressure to maintain the flow of revenue and drugs, as well as the desire to attract US foreign assistance following the war, prompted the Afghan government to ban opium altogether in 1945.

As Bradford (2013) documents, this first ban (a ban in all but name), as well as the subsequent prohibition of opium production in the north-eastern province of Badakhshan in 1958, was an early attempt by the Afghan government to project the appearance of power on the international stage and thereby elicit foreign support. As later chapters will show, this is a motivation that has shaped subsequent drug control campaigns in Afghanistan, including the Taliban prohibition of 2000/1, and provincial based bans in Nangarhar and Helmand under the Karzai regime.

By the late 1960s and 1970s it was the International Narcotics Control Board (INCB) that censured the Afghan government for its inability to control the production and trade of opium within its own borders. However, even then production was limited to a small number of provinces, with particular concern over rising production in the north-eastern province of Badakhshan.

However, this changed in the late 1970s with the convergence of the Iranian Revolution, the proclamation of the Hadd ordinance banning opium production in Pakistan and the outbreak of civil war in Afghanistan, creating the ideal conditions for opium production to flourish. During the war years, Afghanistan emerged as the global leader in opium production based on what Goodhand (2012) has referred to as a 'triple comparative advantage of favourable physical, political and economic conditions'.

It is very difficult to assess the scale and location of cultivation accurately during the 1980s and 1990s, given the problems of accessing remote and insecure rural areas and the cost and accuracy of remote sensing imagery at the time.[1] However, the general trajectory of the growth in cultivation and the factors behind it is clear.

Much of the growth in cultivation in the 1980s can be linked to the political and economic interests of regional and local warlords who through the taxation of cultivation and trade, and in some cases direct involvement in the trade, built patronage networks. However, the degree of market control and regulation that these actors offered can be overstated. As discussed in Chapter 2, the lootable characteristics of drug crops make regulation difficult for either state or non-state actors. This was particularly true in a political environment where the means of violence were fragmented among local commanders with strong links to neighbouring powers and cross-border economies (Goodhand, 2009).

Opium production became an ideal agricultural commodity for the rural population in the war years, in the absence of a functioning state that could either support growth in the legal rural economy, or constrain the cultivation of opium poppy through law enforcement efforts. Opium production had several obvious advantages for farmers under these conditions. As a relatively drought-resistant crop, a yield could be obtained where conflict had led to inconsistent water supply or where irrigation systems were damaged. Further, as a high-value/low-weight commodity, opium could be easily transported on poor roads or even across difficult but porous borders, thereby allowing farmers and small traders to exploit differentials in market prices. As an annual agricultural crop, opium produced additional gains in income for farmers who could afford to wait until later in the agricultural cycle, after the main harvest in the spring, when market prices typically rise.

Figure 2: Levels of Opium Poppy Cultivation in Afghanistan, 1987–2014

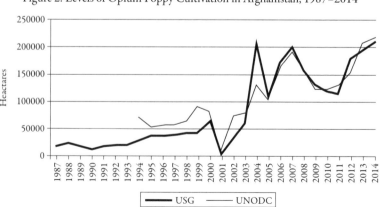

Another advantage was that, although opium was a labour-intensive crop, the skills involved in cultivation were easily learned and the tools required for harvesting could be produced by local craftsmen or even by farmers themselves. There was still another advantage in market support from local traders and opportunists within the community who would offer to purchase the crop before harvest as a form of loan, at harvest time, or later in the year. As this purchase would take place on the farm or within the village, farmers did not incur the transport and transaction costs, or incur the post-harvest losses associated with travelling on damaged and insecure roads that were controlled by armed factions looking to tax passing trade. Finally, it was also during the war years that the use of opium increased significantly in Afghanistan and among the Afghan diaspora in Pakistan and Iran, thereby increasing the demand for opium production in the region (Macdonald, 2007).

As opium cultivation expanded beyond the upper valleys and border areas where it was historically grown and moved down into the lower valleys of provinces like Helmand, Nangarhar and Badakhshan, its role in the livelihoods of the rural population and its significance in the overall economy began to grow. It not only provided income to those who cultivated the crop on their own land; as a labour-intensive crop, it also provided income opportunities for a growing body of land-poor and underemployed males who knew how to produce it. The expansion of the crop from the higher valleys into larger landholdings in the lower areas meant that many landowning households could not meet the labour requirements of the opium crop, particularly during the harvest season. Land in the lower valleys would therefore be offered to sharecroppers who were willing to cultivate opium poppy, developing a symbiotic relationship between the landed and the land-poor, and fuelling socio-economic differentiation between and within rural areas.

Critically, opium played a multifunctional role in the livelihoods of the land-poor, providing access to land on which they could grow a high-value cash crop and also cultivate food crops such as wheat and maize, which both their family and their livestock could consume. This provided some insurance against market failure for food items—a growing risk in a country increasingly riven by conflict—and also provided other sources of revenue if the opium crop failed. The system of advance purchases on opium—known locally as *salaam*—also provided liquidity for households during periods of food scarcity, family illness or life-cycle events such as births, marriages or deaths. The expansion of opium poppy across a wider geographic area also provided a source of wage labour for the land-poor who were willing to travel to neighbouring districts or provinces, or even further afield, to work during the harvest period. Further economic opportunities were created by the multiplier effect: the service industries associated with the cultivation, trade and processing of opiates, as well as the disposable income it generated, some of which was reinvested in the local economy.

For those with capital and access to the means of violence, the expansion in opium production during this period provided increasing opportunities for asset accumulation and political and military influence. Within rural communities, the landed could accrue the surplus value of labour of those cultivating opium on their land, as well as absorbing the bulk of the crop through the provision of advances. They could sell the opium later in the growing season when prices rose. Some moved into trading at the local level and, through the establishment of patronage networks, extended their reach over a larger area, engaging in cross-border trade and—with the right know-how and contacts—processing the crop into morphine base and heroin. Often linked with the rural elite and commanders within the *mujahidin*, this expansion of the opium economy during the war years resulted in 'a recalibration of centre–periphery relations in which borderlands were empowered politically and economically' (Goodhand et al., 2012: 252).

During this period it appears that lack of agricultural know-how, poor market linkages, relatively low prices and low yields in areas that had little experience with the crop, kept cultivation concentrated within a limited number of provinces.

The opium economy provided economic and social benefits for a large part of the rural population, and there was little that could be done to contain it during the 1980s and 1990s. Drug control efforts were particularly rare at this time and were largely for show, aimed at building political links to foreign sponsors and encouraging an increase in the flow of development assistance (Mansfield, 2002b). In many cases—such as with Nasim Akhundzada in Helmand in 1990/1 and Hajji Qadir in Nangahar in 1994/5—there is considerable doubt as to the effectiveness of these campaigns due to the challenges associated with estimating levels of cultivation at the time, and questions over the degree of territorial control that these commanders had. As Martin notes:

> [Nasim] was certainly not the governor of northern Helmand, in the sense that a Western observer would understand—he did not have control over all the territory that he 'owned' for example.... Some areas like Baghran, he was never able to influence at all, and others he could only influence by proxy. (Martin, 2013:105–6)

These earlier efforts at drug control proved short-lived. They offered only temporary lulls in production within limited geographic areas. They unsettled political settlements with local commanders, possibly drugs traders and processors as well, and appear to have generated little of the donor assistance and patronage that regional commanders were looking for from Western donors and the UN.

Consolidation Under the Taliban

The Taliban's arrival in the south in the mid-1990s did nothing to stop the growth in opium poppy cultivation. Indeed, claims that they had banned production when they arrived in 1994 (Felbab Brown, 2010: 125; Strick Van Linschoten and Kuehn, 2012: 185) seem misplaced given that they did not rout the Akhundzadas from Helmand until the middle of January 1995, one month after the end of the planting season (Davis, 1998: 50–1; Dorronsoro, 1979: 246; Rashid, 2000: 33). In fact, under their rule cultivation expanded significantly, facilitated by the removal of checkpoints and militias along the major roads and driven by limited economic opportunities in the legal rural economy (UNDCP, 1998b). By 1999, UNODC estimated that the level of cultivation had reached 91,000 hectares, a significant rise from the 18,500 hectares reported by the USG in 1987 (US Department of State, 1997).[2]

During the 1990s there was a further expansion in cultivation as it moved beyond its traditional centres of production in the south, east and north-east to parts of the northern and central regions and in a growing number of districts in the eastern region (UNDCP, 1998b). Although there are some claims that this expansion was driven by traders offering seeds and agricultural services, as well as by commanders and then the Taliban instructing farmers to grow (Felbab Brown 2006: 137), much of the extension into new areas was attributed to patterns of labour migration as itinerant harvesters took what they had learned by working on the crop in provinces like Helmand, Nangarhar and Kandahar back to their own land in nearby districts and provinces (UNDCP, 1998b). Households with insufficient land in the core areas of opium production also sent family members to other provinces in which they had ethnic or familial ties, where they leased or sharecropped land and cultivated opium poppy, sharing their skills of opium production with the local population (UNDCP, 1998b; UNDCP, 1999c).

There was evidence of growing experimentation by farmers less familiar with the opium crop as they attempted to cultivate it for the first time, limiting production to small plots of land situated among other crops like wheat and onion in case their poppy should fail (UNDCP, 1998b). The proactive role of the rural population in facilitating the expansion in cultivation, and what Byrd (2008:17) has subsequently referred to as the 'footloose' nature of the drugs economy, point to the autonomy that existed in rural areas and the economic opportunities that opium offered to a wide range of actors.

During the Taliban's rule, the opium trade became consolidated within the Afghan economy (Goodhand, 2005). Certainly before the Taliban imposed a comprehensive ban in July 2000, they did little to hamper production or trade beyond a few flurries of activity—closing a number of laboratories in Nangarhar, small-scale eradication, and the production of a raft of proclamations prohibiting opium production—at the behest of UNDCP (Mansfield, personal communication). At the same time, opium was both dried and traded on the streets of accessible district bazaars, no distance from the main highway in places like Kishk e Nakod in Maiwand, Garmsir in Helmand and Markoh and Ghani Khel in Nangarhar. The main marketing hubs in the east and south, where cross-border traders would visit to purchase opium in person or by phone, also proliferated and moved closer to the main arterial roads (UNDCP, 1998c). More established opium traders welcomed the removal of the checkpoints and the insecurity that had hampered their business during the *mujahidin* years, while new entrants to the trade reported that under the Taliban there were no barriers to market entry (ibid.). Finally, heroin processing facilities were also found in the main valleys, sometimes no distance from the district centre and the Taliban soldiers located there (Mansfield, personal communication).

While some viewed this expansion of trade coinciding with the Taliban's territorial gains as evidence of the Taliban's control of the trade, the relationship was more complex. It reflected the local political settlements and bargains that were made when the Taliban movement extended its influence across a wider geographic area. In some cases the local Taliban leadership simply tolerated drug production and trade, being unwilling to challenge powerful local interests. In others, Taliban commanders were, or became, more actively involved in trading opiates and taxing production, processing and transport, as detailed in Chapter 6.

These local arrangements came undone with the imposition of the Taliban ban in July 2000. With cultivation continuing to rise in the late 1990s, and after numerous requests by the UN and international donors to act against the drugs trade, the Taliban finally imposed an effective ban on opium production in the 2000/1 growing season. This single act reduced cultivation from 82,000 hectares in 2000 to 8,000 hectares in 2001. Although billed as 'one of the most remarkable [drug control] successes ever' by United Nations officials at the time (cited in Jelsma, 2005: 1), it was an event that many would come to regret. For the Taliban, the ban imposed considerable hardship on the rural population, making it easier for Western military forces to persuade rural elites and the population to rebel against the regime in the fall of 2001 (UNODC, 2003; Mansfield, 2004c). For the Interim Administration, established in 2002, and its successor, the GIRoA, the complete cessation of opium in 2001 led to a rapid rise in the price of opium that made cultivation profitable in even the most marginal of areas. Combined with the return of many members of the *mujahidin* leadership to the provinces they had presided over in the 1980s and 1990s, opium production became one of the mainstays of the Afghan economy during the initial years of the Afghan statebuilding project and subsequently a metric by which both GIRoA and the international project in Afghanistan came to be judged.

Expansion and Fluctuations in Production During the Karzai Years

Giustozzi (2007: 9) argues that for political entrepreneurs the drugs economy became a means of accumulating power during the initial years of the Karzai regime. Members of Parliament, government ministers, regional power brokers—many with close links to the new government and to US-supported efforts to pursue the remnants of the Taliban and al-Qaeda—as well as elements of the security apparatus were all thought to be directly involved in the drugs trade or to receive payments for their role as 'security providers' (Mankin, 2009). Byrd and Jonglez (2006) reported growing market integration, while others claimed that trafficking had become concentrated in the hands of a few key traffickers and their entourages, many with connections to the Ministry of Interior (Buddenberg and Byrd, 2006: 201).

Evidence of market concentration was less obvious in the provinces following the Taliban's collapse. In fact, cultivation expanded significantly between 2002 and 2004, including in areas where there were few signs of pre-existing market linkages. Cultivation first moved into areas where agricultural conditions had not been conducive for opium poppy cultivation, and experience of production was limited, such as in Ghor, Wardak and Kunduz (Mansfield, 2006b). This was prompted by the tenfold increase in price following the Taliban ban and the fact that high prices were sustained following the collapse of the ban and the launch of counternarcotics efforts. Increases were next seen in the more fertile traditional areas of production, such as the lower valleys of Helmand, Kandahar and

Nangarhar, as farmers took advantage of high prices and the absence of government control to make up for the loss of income and, in many cases, the rising debts they had incurred as a result of the Taliban ban (UNODC, 2003; Mansfield, 2004c). Cultivation also began to move to the desert land in the south, fuelled by drought, better access to affordable deep-well technology, high opium prices and a shortage of land in the irrigated valleys (Mansfield and Fishstein, 2013). By 2004, opium poppy could be found in 194 districts out of 364 and was present in all 34 provinces, compared to only fifty-four districts in eight provinces in 1994 (UNODC/MCN, 2004).

After 2005, opium poppy cultivation fluctuated widely, following a downward trajectory between 2008 and 2010, only to rise again in 2011. However, aggregate levels mask regional, provincial and district-level variations. Some of the dramatic falls in cultivation seen in the aggregate data since 2005 can be attributed to the pursuit of provincial counternarcotics efforts in provinces where opium production has been centred. For example, as detailed in Chapters 7 and 8, cultivation fell significantly in Nangarhar in 2005 following the imposition of a ban by the then Governor Hajji Din Muhammad, as well as in 2007/8 under the Governorship of Gul Aga Shirzai, effectively removing a province that had been a major producer of opium, second only to Helmand in the south.

Similar efforts to ban opium in Balkh in 2007—after a brief boom in opium production between 2004 and 2006—resulted in cultivation falling to negligible levels and remaining there (Pain, 2007a). Finally, dramatic reductions were achieved in Helmand in 2009, when cultivation fell to 69,833 hectares from 103,590 the year before, following the introduction of the Helmand Food Zone[3] and the increase in international and national military forces in the province. Given the large amounts of opium cultivated in Helmand and Nangarhar over the years, reductions in these provinces had a significant impact on the aggregate statistics. This fact was recognised by both the UK and US governments and contributed to their demands to see a dramatic fall in production from the governors in both provinces.

Along with these counternarcotics efforts, a second factor in opium reduction was a shift in the terms of trade between wheat and opium (Mansfield et al., 2011; Mansfield and Pain, 2008) which also contributed substantially to the downward trend in cultivation in Helmand in the 2008/9 growing season, as well as in more marginal areas of production in the central and northern regions. The rapid rise in world cereal prices in late 2007, combined with growing insecurity in Pakistan following the assassination of Benazir Bhutto, restricted cross-border trade in Pakistani wheat flour and led to wheat prices in Afghanistan reaching as high as US$1.00 per kilogram. At the same time, high levels of opium production between 2002 and 2007 led to opium prices dropping significantly from as high as US$700 per kilogram following 11 September 2001 to less than $60 per kilogram in the 2007/8 growing season (Mansfield and Pain, 2008: 14). Farmers across Afghanistan became increasingly concerned about food security, opting to cultivate more of their staple, wheat, rather than cash crops. In the less fertile and drier areas where opium production had little tradition, and farmers did not possess the requisite skills, there was a move out of opium poppy entirely as farmers realised that they could obtain more wheat by producing it on their own land rather than growing opium and using it to purchase wheat (ibid.). Under these agricultural and economic conditions, farmers did not need to be coerced to abandon opium production, although this did not stop the political leadership in Kabul, in some provinces, and in the counternarcotics community from taking credit for the reductions in cultivation (Mansfield and Pain, 2008; UNODC/MCN, 2008: 2).

A third and related explanation for the reductions during this period was the growth in opportunities in the legal economy, particularly in areas of consolidated statehood where most of the investments in development assistance had been made. The World Bank estimated that between 2002 and 2012, US$55 billion of aid had been given to Afghanistan, and the average rate of annual growth in gross domestic product was 9% (cited in Goodhand, 2012). By 2008, the areas around provincial centres in most opium-growing provinces showed increasing signs of agricultural diversification and a movement into more complex cropping systems that included the production of high-value, short-season horticultural crops and the cultivation of several different crops on a single unit of land. This allowed farmers to manage the risk of crop failure better and to increase their farm income (Mansfield and Pain, 2008; Mansfield, 2008a). Households in these areas were also found to exploit the growing wage labour opportunities that could be found in the service sector and construction industry, further diversifying their income base (ibid.).

A fourth reason for falling levels of cultivation was the rollout of national and international security forces to the regions, which was particularly significant in explaining the variance in patterns of cultivation between and within provinces. After 2004, the international military and civilian effort began to mobilise in the provinces through the establishment of PRTs. By 2008, the perceived failures of centralised statebuilding, the growing insurgency and the new counterinsurgency doctrine all drove the shift towards bottom-up state-building with greater devolution to districts and local initiatives. A typical trajectory for cultivation in provinces with increased Afghan government and international military forces was for cultivation to decline in areas around the provincial centre where the state had a history of encapsulation. In provinces like Helmand and Nangarhar where military presence extended into the districts—even those where cultivation had been centred—production was also deterred. These reductions in cultivation could be seen in the northern and eastern provinces, as well as in the southern region in districts like Arghandab, Dand and Daman in Kandahar; in the district of Farah; and also in Helmand following the deployment of national and international troops and the establishment of permanent security infrastructure in the rural areas of Nawa Barakzai, Nad e Ali, and Marjeh in 2009 and 2010 (Mansfield et al., 2011; UNODC/MCN, 2012).

In some provinces these reductions were in part offset by striking increases in production in more remote areas where insurgent groups were located. For example in Helmand, cultivation in the former desert area north of the Nahre Boghra increased in parallel with reductions in the canal command area, rising from 16,036 hectares in 2008 when the Food Zone initiative began to 34,720 hectares in 2012. In Bakwa, a former desert area at the intersection of the provinces of Farah, Nimroz and Helmand, cultivation rose from 6,581 hectares in 2009 to 14,721 hectares in 2012, with little sign since then of abating (Mansfield, forthcoming). While much of the policy discussion attributed the rise in cultivation in these remote areas to the funding which the Taliban were alleged to derive from a tax on cultivation, fieldwork suggested a more complex picture where cultivation was driven by wider socio-economic and political forces and where the insurgency encouraged production to gain political support from the rural population and highlight the weakness of the Karzai government (Mansfield and Fishstein, 2013). After 2011, these increases in cultivation began to supersede any reductions that were achieved in areas of consolidated statehood. As we shall see in Chapter 8, cultivation also began to return to provinces that had previously been declared 'poppy free', including Nangarhar, which had been considered a model for counternarcotics efforts.

Overview of Counternarcotics Policies and Interventions since 2001

The structures for drug control policy were established by the Group of Eight (G8) Security Sector Reform (SSR) programme for Afghanistan in Geneva in

2002. Under this initiative, the security sector was divided into five pillars, each headed by a lead nation which was responsible for overseeing and supporting reforms. The UK took the lead for the counternarcotics pillar, Germany for the police, the US for the military and the Italians for judicial reform. Until 2004, much of the counternarcotics effort focused on institution-building in Kabul. In October 2002, the Afghan government established the Counter Narcotics Directorate (CND) under the auspices of the National Security Council, with support from the UK. Modelled on the Office of Narcotics Control Board (ONCB) in Thailand, the CND was responsible for counternarcotics strategy and coordination; meanwhile implementation sat with line ministries. In 2005, as an indicator of growing donor concern over the direction of counternarcotics, CND was elevated to become the Ministry of Counter Narcotics (MCN).

On paper there was a broad consensus on the need for a wide range of efforts to reduce cultivation and counter the trade in opiates in Afghanistan. Indeed, much of the policy discussion on counternarcotics was framed by the need for a comprehensive approach that included law enforcement, demand reduction, cross-border cooperation and rural development. All of these elements were reflected in policy documents by both Western donors and the Afghan government, including the various incarnations of the Afghan National Drug Control Strategy (AIA, 2003; MCN, 2006).

In particular, there was broad support for measures designed to deter planting, such as information operations; crop destruction both in the fall after planting, and during the spring before the harvest; and a variety of rural development initiatives that either stated reductions in opium poppy cultivation as a specific goal ('alternative development' or 'alternative livelihoods' programmes) or indirectly dissuaded opium production by promoting growth in the legal economy.

A priority element of the counternarcotics effort from the beginning was to encourage greater engagement by the large development donors in what came to be referred to as 'counternarcotics mainstreaming'—the inclusion of an analysis of the causes of cultivation and measures to address them in planning and implementing development programmes (CND, 2004). However, as will be seen in Chapter 7, the interest of development donors typically waxed and waned according to the political priority they gave to reducing levels of production in the aftermath of dramatic increases in production. Nevertheless, over the last decade, donors such as the United States Agency for International Development (USAID), the European Commission, DFID and the World Bank all supported rural development programmes that funded an array of activities from single-sector interventions, such as roads and credit, to more comprehensive efforts with explicit reference to counternarcotics objectives.

Eradication was also featured as a component of the counternarcotics strategy after 2001. In its initial form, the Afghan National Drug Control Strategy (ANDCS), drafted with the support of the UK in its role as lead nation, stated that eradication was only to be undertaken 'in areas where alternative livelihoods existed' (AIA, 2003). As time progressed and cultivation rose, this position became increasingly untenable. By 2007, following further rises in cultivation and the claim that drugs were the primary source of funding for the Taliban, the demands for more aggressive eradication reached a crescendo, with some advocates within the US administration looking to introduce aerial spraying (Semple and Golden, 2007; US Department of State, 2007: 51; Schweich, 2008).

While the Afghan government rejected the calls for any form of chemical eradication, crop destruction remained a major focus of the counternarcotics effort. Even with the Obama administration's call for a shift in focus and the disbandment of the US-sponsored Afghan Eradication Force (AEF) in 2010, the US continued to support Governor-Led Eradication (GLE), focusing on the seven major poppy-producing provinces. In fact, in 2012, over 10,000 hectares of opium were destroyed by GLE—considerably more than during the years of the AEF (UNODC/MCN, 2012).

Law enforcement efforts were also an integral element of the counternarcotics strategy after 2001. They were, however, much slower to start. In policy discussions, those advocating a more robust interdiction strategy were reluctant to arrest significant traffickers, or High Value Targets, in the absence of a robust judicial system. It was often felt that arresting an important trafficker, only to have him released due to corruption and political pressure, would do more harm than good. While investments were made in the Counter Narcotics Police, the judicial system (in particular the Criminal Justice Task Force) and the improvements to Pul e Chawki prison, to ensure that those convicted were held, the US also targeted individual traffickers whom they believed to be supporting the Taliban. With continuing criticism that the interdiction effort should primarily prosecute local dealers and traffickers as a more legitimate target for drug control efforts than farmers, the Obama administration made the targeting of 'drugs kingpins' and trafficking networks a priority in 2009. To support this effort, the Drugs Enforcement Agency (DEA) was strengthened and a new intelligence cell was established at Bagram airfield. A target list of 367 named individuals, including fifty 'nexus targets', was also identified for 'kill or capture'.

In contrast with the policy rhetoric and the recognition that enduring reductions in cultivation would take a 'generation or more', the operational environment for counternarcotics was heavily shaped by the political imperatives of counteracting rising levels of cultivation. Indeed, as early as 2001, the UK government supported the Afghan Interim Administration to implement a compensated eradication scheme in Nangarhar, Helmand and Badakhshan in an attempt to reduce the headline opium production figures.

Subsequent upticks in counternarcotics efforts in the provinces of Nangarhar, Balkh and Helmand can also be associated with the coverage given to rising cultivation found in the headlines.

As detailed in Chapter 7, the rhetoric that accompanied rising levels of cultivation gave little space to more gradual and longer-term efforts advocated by some development donors. In particular, the association between the increasing concentration of opium production in the south in 2008 and the territorial gains of the Taliban bolstered calls for a more aggressive eradication campaign from many actors and institutions within the international community and the Afghan government (UNODC/MCN, 2007; Schweich, 2008).

In terms of policy, the primary area of disagreement among some Western nations, as well as Afghan leaders in Kabul and in the provinces, was the pace of reduction in drug crop cultivation and how low levels of production could be achieved and maintained. A crude characterisation might distinguish between those who saw cultivation as a function of weak and corrupt government institutions and those who positioned drug crop cultivation within the wider development challenges facing Afghanistan, which included the vulnerability of many farmers in areas where cultivation was concentrated.

Those who viewed cultivation as a function of the failings of government institutions often lamented the lack of commitment of state actors to counternarcotics efforts. This view was shaped by the idea that counternarcotics efforts are a useful tool in extending the writ of the state over rural areas. Those who saw the drugs problem as an issue of the lack of strong leadership largely sat within a body of national and international organisations charged with delivering on counternarcotics objectives, such as MCN, UNODC and INL.

These divisions persist today. At perhaps its most basic level, the counternarcotics community sees its task as finding advocates for drug control within the administration and encouraging them to bring about rapid reductions in drug crop cultivation. This is a model that is heavily shaped by often inaccurate descriptions of past drug control efforts, such as those pursued by Nasim Akhundzada in 1989/90 and the Taliban in 2000/1. As the former head of INL, Bobby Charles, argued in his push for aerial spraying in 2004, 'All I need is one strong Governor' (personal communication, 2004).

This group has often found advocates for rapid reductions outside the counternarcotics community, particularly among the international military forces who tend to view widespread cultivation as reflecting the poor performance of Afghan civilian and security institutions and, thereby, reflecting on their own efforts at statebuilding. The pressure to deliver rapid and substantial reduction is intimately tied to the idea that a strong state does not have large-scale illicit drug crop cultivation and that an absence of opium poppy implies strong leadership.

For the proponents of this position, counternarcotics interventions can be targeted at encouraging and supporting the political elite to act against drug crop production. They consider development resources a mechanism for soliciting the support of national and provincial elites to reduce cultivation in the countryside. This is an instrumentalist view of development shaped by the belief that those cultivating opium are relatively wealthy and will be largely unaffected by reductions in cultivation, even by rapid reductions (UNODC/MCN, 2007; Schweich, 2008).

This view shapes the more contractual development programmes seen in Afghanistan, where development assistance is made contingent on reductions in cultivation (a 'conditionality' model). A recent example is the Good Performers Initiative, where development monies are distributed through the Governor's office to provinces that rapidly reduce cultivation or maintain low levels of cultivation. Under this model, development outcomes—improvements in the lives and livelihoods of rural households and communities—are largely irrelevant.

From this perspective, imposing and sustaining a ban require building a critical mass of those who are perceived to have sufficient influence and power to coerce the rural population into abandoning opium poppy cultivation. This requires the provision of largesse and the threat that development assistance and political support will be withdrawn if there is a resurgence. Coercion is a further critical component of this approach. Support is given for crop destruction at the provincial level in order to create a 'credible threat'. To achieve this, and to bring about the rapid reductions in cultivation required, eradication needs to be comprehensive and not limited to specific areas or groups. Here we see a further departure from the call for more targeted crop destruction as advocated under the initial NDCS.

This is a more proactive approach to drug control, driven in part by the demand for greater progress in achieving counternarcotics objectives, but also by the growing international presence in the provinces since 2004. It is an approach that can be seen to be linked to the priorities of the US and UK and their leads in Nangarhar and Helmand respectively. It is also an approach that is intimately tied to our understanding of past efforts in drug control and the role that politico-military actors, particularly the Taliban, have played in determining levels of production.

This narrative of the strong leader has a real resonance in Afghanistan. It is not uncommon to hear rural Afghans lament the loss of the days of strong government and the stories they have heard about the draconian rule of Abdur Rahman Khan. As security has worsened since 2008, there are even nostalgic references among rural Pashtuns to the order imposed by the Taliban regime. As earlier sections of this chapter have shown, the reality is quite different; there is a history of rural Afghanistan resisting the centre's attempts to impose control, particularly when it has involved taxation, conscription and efforts to change culture and traditions. Resistance has often been accompanied by accusations that the Afghan leadership has fallen under the influence of foreign powers and their ideas. The call for a *jihad* against an apostate leadership, be it Aminullah Khan or the PDPA, has been a common mantra of those looking to mobilise the rural population against efforts to centralise political power.

We hear the same call for strong leadership in the discussion around opium production and its control. Stories of regional and local commanders encouraging—or even instructing—farmers to cultivate opium poppy, as well as banning opium production altogether, pervade the literature and policy discourse, creating the impression of centralised economic and political power in rural Afghanistan. Yet opium production is both symptomatic of the dispersion of power and a major contributor to the growing autonomy of those at the periphery. As an illegal and easily lootable good opium has been both a source of revenue for the rural population and a means to political power for local and regional elites.

In contrast, drug control is representative of the centralisation that the periphery has been so keen to avoid. In theory it is an act of repression that brings the security apparatus of the state, or its representatives, into the rural areas where opium is grown. By preventing cultivation it threatens the financial and political autonomy of the population and their leadership, rendering them dependent on the rigours of the market or the largesse of the state or foreign patrons. As such, engaging in efforts to ban drug crop cultivation in Afghanistan is a political process that pits those in power against the interests of the rural population and their representatives, an act that has proved to be provocative through much of Afghan history.

As Chapters 6–10 will show, those who have engaged in drug control in Afghanistan have looked to foreign patrons to bolster their political position in precisely the same way that various Afghan national leaders have attempted to centralise political power over the last two hundred years. In doing so, they have presented themselves to their foreign donors as having greater political power than they actually possessed, and sought to conceal the process of negotiation and bargaining with rural communities that allowed them to prohibit opium in the first place.

Conclusion

Many important points can be drawn from the evolution of the opium economy in the context of the shifting centres of power in Afghanistan, in particular the dispersal of economic, political and military power to the regions. The first is that the factors driving opium production are highly localised, shaped in part by political and economic structures and patterns of trade. They are also shaped by the capacity of rural communities to adapt to price fluctuations and also to use their experience as migrant labourers and their knowledge of agricultural techniques and markets to relocate opium production to new areas or expand cultivation in existing ones. In practice, the claims that traders, armed factions and those in positions of state power have encouraged cultivation have often been overstated.

A rural livelihoods perspective illustrates that farmers cultivate opium poppy because it can offer a number of benefits. They do not need to be coerced into cultivation, or even encouraged by outside actors; they only need those who wield power locally to see the mutual advantages of opium production and trade and not to try to prevent it. Similarly, farmers may move out of production driven by falling prices, low yields or better economic opportunities within the area or in neighbouring areas or even other countries. We should be careful not simply to attribute these reductions to regional or local powerbrokers, and their claimed success in counternarcotics.

This raises a second important point: the challenge that imposing an effective ban presents not just to those who cultivate the crop, but also to those who have imposed controls on opium production. This is particularly true in areas where the crop has become concentrated and where a growing proportion of the population has become dependent on it for their livelihood. Over the last thirty years there have been many attempts to restrict cultivation. Most have proved to be short-lived, in part because those who have imposed them appear to have gained little political patronage and financial support from an international community which requests that the Afghan state conform with international drug control conventions. Those who have coerced the population to reduce or abandon cultivation have also experienced resistance among the rural population and other vested interests. As we shall see in the following chapters, this resistance has typically begun in areas where those in positions of state power in either Kabul or in the provincial centre do not have direct control.

The third and final point returns to the economic viability of the Afghan state highlighted in the first section of this chapter. The opium economy has proved to be a valuable source of income for varied groups within Afghanistan. Far from being the antithesis of development and a source of instability as some of the literature on drugs suggests (UNODC/MCN, 2007), opium has provided employment, liquidity and rural income, and has been a driver of rural transformation (Goodhand, 2008). Efforts to ban it can interfere with these processes, foster corruption and increase rural antipathy towards the state. At the same time, counternarcotics can attract development funds and political patronage from both international and national institutions; a failure to act against prolific production can result in the loss of position or international criticism for national and sub-national leaders. This dilemma positions efforts to ban opium within a complex and crowded institutional terrain, where multiple and often competing interests are at work.

6

REPOSITIONING A PARIAH REGIME

THE TALIBAN BAN OF 2000/1

Introduction

This chapter draws on primary research undertaken before, during and after the Taliban ban. It is divided into four sections and a conclusion. The first section explores the international political context that influenced the Taliban leadership's decision to ban opium, placing prohibition within the regime's wider efforts to obtain international recognition. The second section examines how the Taliban exploited the opium ban's impact on the rural population as a way of extracting development assistance from the international community. It discusses the role of the United Nations, and in particular UNDCP in supporting these efforts. The third section looks at the image of state authority that the Taliban sought to project through its implementation of the opium ban and how this was subsequently perceived by the international community when the regime failed to act against the opium trade. The fourth section examines the domestic political environment and highlights the fragility of the ban, particularly in the more remote parts of the country, where even the Taliban regime found its authority challenged.

The Taliban prohibition of the 2000/1 growing season is the best known attempt at the cessation of opium production in Afghanistan, and it is the only ban to have been implemented effectively nationwide. At the time it was called 'one of the most remarkable successes ever' by UN officials, and since then it has often been used as a benchmark against which to judge subsequent narcotics efforts (Jelsma, 2005: 1). Announced by decree on 27 July 2000, the Taliban ban ordered the complete cessation of opium poppy cultivation in Afghanistan. By August 2001, UNDCP[1] reported that cultivation in Afghanistan as a whole had fallen from 82,000 hectares to 8,000 hectares between 2000 and 2001, and in Taliban-held areas had fallen from 78,885 hectares to 1,220 hectares.

Since the fall of the Taliban in late 2001, interpretations of the Taliban ban on opium production have been influenced by the narrative on the 'war on terror' and the subsequent 'demonisation' of the Taliban regime (Donini et al., 2004: 130; Johnson and Leslie, 2004: 89–98). Most accounts of the prohibition have been written by academics and journalists who were not acquainted with the regime at the time and have relied heavily on secondary sources, in particular UNDCP (Shanty, 2011; Farrell and Thorne, 2005; Peters, 2009a and 2009b). Even some who were critical of the Taliban at the time have sounded like apologists for the regime in their description of the dramatic reduction in opium poppy cultivation achieved under their rule and the subsequent upswing in cultivation that followed their fall. Implicit within this narrative is a critique of the failure of the post-2001 administration and the international community—most notably the governments of the US and UK—to control the level of opium poppy cultivation to the same extent.

Many critics of the Taliban regime of the 1990s have cited the regime's human rights record and implied that the opium ban was implemented with greater repression than was actually found to have occurred at the time (Windle, 2011: 150).[2] They have countered any criticism of the ineffectiveness of counternarcotics efforts under the Karzai administration by arguing that, were such a ban to be implemented now, it would require an authoritarian regime inconsistent with current statebuilding efforts.

The most common explanation of the Taliban ban, however, has been based on the view that prohibition was motivated by a desire to raise the farmgate price of opium and increase the value of inventory held by senior Taliban or their associates (Perl, 2001: 1–5; United States Senate, Committee on Foreign Relations, 2009: 4; UNODC/MCN, 2007: iv).[3] Evidence to support this price manipulation by the Taliban has, to date, been largely circumstantial. It has typically been informed by UN assertions that significant stockpiles of opium were present in Afghanistan in the late 1990s (Peters, 2009b: 94; Felbab Brown, 2010: 131) despite the lack of supporting evidence in either the opium bazaars or the market behaviour of traders at the time (Donor Mission, 2001: 13–14; Gannon, 2008: 55). This market manipulation thesis also overlooks the persistence of high opium prices into 2003, long after the collapse of the Taliban regime (Paoli et al., 2009: 70). Those who press this view tend to see the financial gains made by opium traders closely associated with the senior Taliban leadership as the primary reason for implementing the ban, rather than as an externality of it (UNODC/MCN, 2007; Peters, 2009b: 94).

For a full understanding of the Taliban's prohibition of opium in the 2000/1 growing season and its likely sustainability at the time, it is necessary to move beyond the simplistic explanations that have been offered since the regime's collapse, and to contextualise the ban within the international and domestic political challenges that the Taliban faced. It is also important to examine the multiple interests of the different stakeholders involved in the promulgation of the ban, including the role of the UN.

Taking the Moral High Ground

The Taliban's decision to ban opium production during the 2000/1 growing season has to be considered within the context of the regime's isolation at the time and its broader efforts to improve its political and economic position, both regionally and internationally.

Although many considered the regime isolationist, with little regard for what other member states thought of it and its policies, recognition had long been an objective of more moderate parts of the leadership since the mid-1990s (Nojumi et al., 2002: 172–4; Johnson and Leslie, 2004: 147; Crews and Tarzi, 2008: 49; Fergusson, 2011: 130). Despite the Taliban's presence across as much as 90 per cent of Afghanistan, the only countries to recognise it as the legitimate government of the country were Pakistan, Saudi Arabia and the United Arab Emirates (Barfield, 2010: 264; Fergusson, 2011: 112). At the UN, Burhanadin Rabbani remained the formal head of state for Afghanistan, and the United Front had permanent representation in 2000 when the ban on opium was announced (Gannon, 2005: 55). The UN Security Council imposed sanctions on the Taliban in November 1999 (Resolution 1267) for its support of Bin Laden. Additional restrictions in December 2000 (Resolution 1333) further increased the regime's sense of isolation before and during the opium ban (Barfield, 2010: 265; Crews and Tarzi, 2008: 268).

International sanctions and lack of recognition not only had political ramifications for the regime but also made it ineligible for financial support from international financial institutions such as the World Bank, and from the private sector. The Taliban's policies—particularly those regarding women—

had already rendered it unpopular with international development donors who might otherwise have responded more positively to the fact that Afghanistan was one of the poorest countries in the world. These policies and the ongoing conflict resulted in the failure of numerous efforts to attract private investment in the late 1990s, culminating in the collapse of what had proved to be rather productive negotiations with the Union Oil Company of California (Nojumi et al., 2002: 176, 199, 201) and the cessation of Saudi donations in 1998 (Rubin, 2000: 1767; Sinno, 2008: 233).

A protracted drought, with some parts of the south exposed to a fourth consecutive year in the 2000/1 growing season, increased the vulnerability of the rural population but did little to increase aid flows (Fergusson, 2011: 132; Donini, 2004: 133; Rashid, 2001: 127; Marsden, 2009: 86). Even UNDCP's efforts to raise development funds for countering drug crop cultivation remained only partially funded despite the fact that such programmes were often seen as catering to the interests of European consumer nations (Marsden, 2009: 121; Mullah Hassan Rahmani, personal communication, 2 May 2001;[4] Mullah Kabir, personal communication, 26 April 2001;[5] Rashid, 2001: 124).

Within this context, the Taliban's cessation of opium poppy cultivation can be seen as an attempt to recast the dialogue with the international community, a dialogue that had become dominated in the late 1990s and 2000 by discussions about the movement's relationship with Osama Bin Laden, its poor record on women's and other human rights and latterly the destruction of the Buddhas in Bamian (Zaeef, 2010; Barfield, 2011: 266; Fergusson, 2011: 138). The ban followed previous efforts in the late 1990s to draw attention away from criticism of these social policies (Mansfield, 1999).[6] It was also part of a broader diplomatic effort in 2000 and 2001 aimed at improving the Taliban's international reputation in the run-up to the meeting of the Credentials Committee at the UN General Assembly in October 2001. This effort included citing the Taliban's role in mediating the release of hostages in Kandahar from a hijacked plane from Kathmandu (Jaggia and Shukla, 2000), as well as the arrest and subsequent trial of international staff of a Christian NGO (Shelter Now International), who were accused of proselytising, contrary to Afghan law at the time (Zaeef, 2010: 132; Gannon, 2008: 83–4; Maley, 2001: vii).

As with the hijacking and the trial of the Christian missionaries, the prohibition of opium provoked the international community to engage more proactively with the Taliban as legitimate interlocutors and potentially to offer the regime technical and financial support (Crews and Tarzi, 20008: 254).

The ban offered advantages over these other events in that few governments in the international community could argue—particularly given their treaty commitments—that the complete cessation of opium was undesirable.

In his discussions with the donors, Mullah Mohammed Hassan Rahmani, the Regional Governor for the South Western Region, presented the ban as a 'humanitarian issue' and argued that the international community should treat the prohibition of opium as distinct from any political differences with the Taliban movement (personal communication, 2 May 2001). As Hassan explained at the time:

> The Taliban has done its bit and the international community should not mix politics with drugs—this is a humanitarian issue. If the international community wants drug control in Afghanistan it needs to separate the issues of politics and drugs. Neither short term nor long term assistance [in response to the ban] should be related to politics. (Mullah Mohammed Hassan Rahmani, personal communication, 2 May 2001)

With the imposition of the ban on opium, the Taliban authorities found themselves in the rare position of occupying the moral high ground on the international stage. It provided an opportunity to counter the image of Afghanistan as a pariah state and allowed the leadership to present the ban as the conduct of a responsible member of the international community: an act of self-sacrifice where the interests of consumer nations were given priority over the economic needs of the rural population of Afghanistan. During the donors' mission to Afghanistan to explore the sustainability of the opium ban, Taliban leaders emphasised their altruism, citing their objective of reducing the impact of drug use in neighbouring countries and in Europe (Donor Mission, 2001: 10).

The State High Commissioner for Drug Control, Akhundzada, framed the prohibition as an 'obligation under the international treaties' (personal communication, 29 April 2001) and suggested that it was always the intention of the Islamic Emirate of Afghanistan to prohibit opium production across the country and that the ban in 2000/1 was the culmination of efforts that had begun in 1997 with Mullah Omar's original edict outlawing opium production (UNDCP, 1998a: 6).[7] The religious sanctity of the ban, as one of many edicts against opium promulgated by Mullah Omar, was mentioned only in passing by Taliban leaders and was featured far more in conversations with internationals.[8]

The Taliban leaders were particularly keen to juxtapose their concerted efforts to control opium in the 2000/1 growing season with continued cultivation in those areas controlled by the United Front. A permanent and nation-wide ban was presented to the donors as a benefit of a Taliban victory in the north-east of the country and a vision of what the country could look like once the regime achieved its political and military goals (Haqqani, personal communication, 15 April 2001). To the Taliban leadership, prohibition did not just serve to place the regime on the moral high ground internationally; it also highlighted the inconsistency of the way the international community favoured the United Front (Nojumi et al., 2002: 140).

The Ball is in Your Court: Negotiating with the International Community

While the Taliban leaders were adamant that the prohibition of opium poppy cultivation was permanent and unconditional, it was clear that they had put nothing in place to mitigate the severe loss of welfare that farmers experienced due to the ban (Donor Mission, 2001: 4,10). The Taliban leadership expected that development assistance would follow in response to the ban, and references were made to the obligation of the European countries that consumed Afghan opiates to respond accordingly and prevent farmers from returning to opium poppy cultivation (Mullah Kabir, personal communication, 26 April 2001).

Maulavi Amir Mohammed Haqqani, head of the Nangarhar Drug Control and Coordination Unit, referred to an impending 'disaster' due to the opium poppy ban and argued that the '[Taliban] may not be able to sustain the ban unless the international community provides assistance' (personal communication, 25 April 2001). He warned that 'if a disaster happens, then it is the responsibility of the international community'. Mullah Mohammed Hassan Rahmani claimed that a second year of the ban would be pursued, but implementation would require 'many people to be killed and others to face starvation' (personal communication, 2 May 2001). Were this to happen, the 'responsibility would lie directly with the international community if it failed to deliver sufficient development assistance to the people of Afghanistan' (ibid.). Haqqani expressed concerns about the potential for an increase in crime as a consequence of the ban, and in central Helmand there were claims that the rise in the price of opium had already led to an increase in household robberies (Haqqani, personal communication, 15 April 2001; Helmandi resident, personal communication, 23 April 2001).

The ban caused notable hardships for the rural population, including reducing the quality and quantity of food consumed, postponing health expenditures and having to sell long-term productive assets such as livestock and land. The rise in opium prices, from around US$100 to US$500 between September 2000 and July 2001, led to an exponential rise in the level of opium-denominated debt. Faced with the ban, farmers were unable to repay in opium the advance payments that they had received on their crop. Traders swiftly converted these opium-denominated debts into cash at the prevailing market price. For these farmers, an advance payment of just US$50 per kilogram of opium, agreed prior to the planting season of 2000/1, had risen to a debt of US$500 per kilogram at harvest time (Mansfield and Pain, 2008: 8–9). This increase led to the mortgaging of land and the exchange of daughters as payment on outstanding loans (UNODC, 2004).

The ban also affected the wider economy, leading to higher levels of rural unemployment. Groups of young men lost their work as itinerant harvesters at a time when there were few wage labour opportunities. Migration to Pakistan was a common response to the imposition of the ban in both the southern and eastern provinces. The Donor Mission (2001: 9) concluded that 'in the coming winter season [2001/2] it is expected that many former opium poppy households will be unable to meet their basic needs' and raised concerns that 'without alternatives there would be a growing resistance to the ban amongst the rural population' (Donor Mission, 2001: 11).

Requests from the Taliban leadership for development assistance in response to the ban were reiterated by rural communities. For example, meetings arranged by the Taliban authorities and UNDCP between the donors' mission and representatives of different tribal groups in the eastern and southern provinces typically involved detailed requests for development assistance involving exhaustive lists of projects. The orchestrated nature of these events meant that the discussions of assistance were invariably accompanied by requests from tribal elders that the international community recognise the Taliban as the legitimate government of Afghanistan (elders from Rodat and Shinwar, personal communication, 26 April 2001). Conversations with individual farmers on their land in the absence of Taliban soldiers took a different direction; the farmers expressed considerable anxiety over their economic predicament and directed their anger at the decision of the Taliban to ban opium (Gannon, 2008: 59; personal communication with farmers during Taliban ban mission, 2001).

During the Taliban's efforts to attract development aid from the international community in response to the prohibition, they found advocates within the UN. Barfield (2010: 256) refers to a 'co-dependency' between the Taliban and the UN in the late 1990s: a situation in which they tolerated each other in order to ensure the flow of humanitarian assistance into the country. With regard to the prohibition of opium production, for once the UN was not in dispute with the Taliban. Instead, they found themselves working in partnership to respond to the regime's delivery of what was viewed as a global public good and to address the humanitarian crisis that was developing due to the successful implementation of the ban.

Rather than being neutral observers and facilitators of the donors' mission investigating the Taliban ban, some in the UN in Afghanistan welcomed the ban as an opportunity for a more constructive dialogue and to improve the flow of aid to the country (Donini et al., 2004: 129–30; Johnson and Leslie, 2004). The donors' mission was confronted with an unusually unified UN effort, involving agencies that had seldom been advocates of drug control in the past. The UN coordinator at the time, Erick de Mul, stressed the importance of the donors responding to the ban by 'doing something, and doing it quickly' (personal communication, 23 April 2001).

UNDCP, in particular, anticipated that it would be at the forefront of the response to the ban and would benefit as the main interlocutor between the Taliban and the international community, as well as the recipient of renewed funding at a time when the country programme had closed due to inadequate funds (Farrell and Thorne, 2005: 84–5; Mansfield, 2002b: 7). Pino Arlacchi, the Executive Director of UNODC at the time, had already sought to elicit a ban from the Taliban leadership in return for a ten-year programme valued at US$250 million (Steele, 2011: 196–8; UN Office of Internal Oversight Services, 2001: 5). Mullah Mohammed Hassan Rahmani (personal communication, 2 May 2001) highlighted the shared interests of the Taliban and UNDCP for the donors' mission, stating that, 'UNDCP told the Taliban that they should take this important step and ban poppy and then [the Taliban] would get assistance'. The UN coordinator also referred to UNDCP's role in encouraging the Taliban's prohibition (Erick de Mul, personal communication, 23 April 2001).[9]

In fact, during the late 1990s UNDCP had worked more closely with the Taliban authorities than many other UN agencies (Farrell and Thorne, 2005: 84).[10] UNDCP had facilitated meetings between the Taliban leadership and the international donors and provided financial and technical support to the Islamic Emirate's State High Commission for Drug Control (SHCDC) in Kabul as well as to the regional Drug Control and Coordination Units (DCCUs), which were implementing partners for UNDCP's demand reduction and rural development efforts in the country (Farrell and Thorne, 2005:

84). The relationship prompted criticism from the donors in 1997 during a review of UNDCP's country programme in Afghanistan. Of particular concern to the donors were UNDCP's capacity-building work with Taliban institutions,[11] the technical and financial assistance it provided to the Taliban's efforts to electrify Kandahar,[12] and the Executive Director's efforts to launch a ten-year national programme[13] which would undoubtedly have led to further support being channelled to the Taliban (UNDCP, 1997: 15, 17).

While the close relationship was in part a function of UNDCP's drug control mandate and its need for a partner with coercive capability, it was also a consequence of UNDCP's contractual approach to development assistance in the 1990s. Much of UNDCP's dialogue with the Taliban was structured around signed agreements known as Drug Control Action Plans (DCAP); these plans outlined development interventions to be undertaken in specific districts and a corresponding timetable for reductions in opium poppy cultivation (Mansfield, 2001b: 5–6). Although these plans, and their predecessor, 'the opium clause', had been assessed as unrealistic and counterproductive by a series of reviews in the 1990s and in 2000, they continued to inform UNDCP's understanding of how to address the drugs issue in Afghanistan into the 21st century (Brailsford, 1989a: 22–4; UNDCP, 1995c: 24; Gebert, 2000; Mackrell, 1999; UNDCP, 1999: 10; UN OIOS, 201: 5).[14] The Taliban's prohibition was based on a similar model of conditional development, in which reductions in cultivation would result in the inflow of development assistance (Farrell and Thorne, 2005: 85).[15]

The creation of a humanitarian crisis through an opium ban that had been welcomed by the international community placed strong pressure on donors to respond with development assistance. The Taliban leadership likely calculated that the international political support gained by prohibiting opium outweighed the unpopularity the ban would engender among the rural population. This perception was reinforced in conversations between UNDCP and Taliban leaders. It was calculated that if the international community kept their part of the deal, the economic impact of the ban on the rural population would be short-lived, while if the international actors failed to deliver, the ban could simply be rescinded. In April 2001, the USG announced that it would provide an extra US$43 million to Afghanistan, and Secretary of State Colin Powell stated that there was a need to 'continue to look for ways to provide assistance the Afghans, including those farmers who have felt the ban on poppy cultivation—a decision by the Taliban that we welcome' (cited in Bearak, 2001).

Damned if You Do, Damned if You Don't

By prohibiting opium production in 2000, the Taliban was not only interested in presenting itself as a credible interlocutor; it was also keen to confront the allegations that it benefited financially from the opium trade. Taliban leaders pointed to the ban as evidence that they were not dependent on opium as a source of finance (Mullah Mohammed Hassan Rahmani, personal communication, 2 May 2001; Zaeef, 2010: 132; Fergusson, 2011: 105–7), refuting the prevailing opinion that the ban was imposed to increase the price of opium and the movement's revenues (Saikal, 2004: 222; Stepanova, 2011: 295).

The prohibition of opium certainly succeeded in conveying the image of state authority that the Taliban wished to project to the international community. It was, after all, the only edict that was implemented consistently across the entire occupied area. Ironically the Taliban's success in implementing the ban only increased the expectations of the international community (Gannon, 2005: 55; Johnson and Leslie, 2004: 127). If the Taliban could deliver a complete cessation of cultivation, why were its leaders reluctant to impose an immediate ban on the opium trade, particularly given concerns that 'over-production' in Afghanistan during the 1990s had led to significant stockpiles? The Taliban's failure to act against these alleged stockpiles provoked criticism that the regime was benefiting from the rise in opium prices, indirectly through the taxation of opium and directly through involvement in the trade (UN Security Council, 2001: para 58).[16]

Senior leaders unsurprisingly denied the presence of stockpiles, arguing that the dramatic increase in farmgate prices which accompanied the ban was evidence that there was no such inventory (Haqqani, personal communication, 25 April 2001). They also dismissed as 'propaganda' the claims that the Taliban had appropriated the agricultural tithe known as *ushr*, payable on all crops including opium, and had imposed a tax on the drugs trade (Mullah Kabir, personal communication, 26 April 2001; Mullah Hassan Rahmani, personal communication, 2 May 2001). Mullah Hassan Rahmani further argued that, 'There is massive propaganda against the Taliban with regard to the use of poppy as a source of finance for the war; now there is a ban and no opium it shows we are not reliant on opium' (personal communication, 2 May 2001).

While these views are clearly partial, empirical evidence at the time presented a far more complex picture of Taliban finances than is often presented, particularly since the collapse of the regime in 2001 (Naqvi, 1999; Rubin, 2000: 1796; UNDCP, 1998c). Although there is little doubt that taxes were imposed on the production and trade of opium and that members of the

Taliban regime benefited from the business, the assertion that these revenue streams formed part of a regularised and national system of taxation is not consistent with the political realities of the time. For example, in considering the feasibility of a more coherent and centralised taxation system, it is important to recognise the degree of autonomy that local commanders were able to maintain, even under Taliban rule (Marsden, 2009: 91; Sinno, 2008). It is equally important to question the political wisdom of appropriating the agricultural tithe, which was essentially the salary of the village mullahs who were viewed as the bedrock of Taliban support.[17]

Fieldwork during the late 1990s showed the varied and localised nature of payments for both *ushr* and income tax (generically referred to as *zakat*), negating claims that the Taliban authorities were implementing a uniform system of rent extraction on the cultivation and trade of opium (UNDCP, 1998c: 21; UNDCP, 1999c: 26). Primary research with opium traders in Nangarhar, Kandahar and Helmand in the late 1990s revealed that the growth in the opium trade during the Taliban's rule had been fuelled by the improving security environment and the removal of both checkpoints and taxes that had been imposed under the *mujahidin* government (UNDCP, 1998c: 23, 25).

Typically opium traders reported that, apart from the initial capital required for investment, there were no barriers to entering the trade; they could travel freely between areas and did not incur taxes en route. Opium traders in Musa Qala claimed that before the Taliban captured the area, business had suffered and moved to Sangin due to the predation of the local *mujahidin* leader Mullah Ghulam Rasul Akhundzada. With the removal of the Akhundzadas by the Taliban, business had recovered in Musa Qala, and Balochi traders were once again travelling directly to the area to purchase opium in bulk. Only a small number of traders in the south reported making contributions to the local authorities. In some cases this was referred to as a 'gift', others paid *zakat* based on their overall wealth, including the money they generated from the opium trade (UNDCP, 1998c).[18]

Moreover, contrary to some of the historical revisionism following the 'war on terror', the drugs trade was not the 'regime's sole source of foreign exchange at the time' (UNODC, 2007: iv). The World Bank reported in 1999 that the taxation of the Afghan Transit Trade Agreement and the smuggling of licit goods into Pakistan were the Taliban's primary sources of income (Naqvi, 1999; Rashid, 2001: 124). This point was reiterated in 2001 when the Committee of Experts appointed by the UN Security Council to monitor Resolution 1333 (UN Security Council, 2001: para 68). Rubin (2000: 1796) concluded that 'Afghans, including the Taliban, earn relatively little from [the opium] crop' and 'less revenue from opium trade than the transit trade'.

This complex picture of the Taliban delivering a relatively secure environment in which the drugs trade prospered and local systems of taxation and payments prevailed is a more accurate reflection of the situation on the ground. In this environment, the tax revenues of local commanders as well as individuals with inventories of opium undoubtedly increased with the rise in opium prices as a consequence of the Taliban ban. It would be a surprise if some of these individuals were not close to the Taliban leadership and did not have prior knowledge of any plan to prohibit opium production; one example is Hajji Bashir Noorzai, who is reported to have funded the Taliban during the 1990s[19] and was subsequently imprisoned in the US on drugs charges.[20] However, the fact that some individuals gained by what might be called 'insider trading' does not explain the primary motivation for the ban, particularly when considered in relation to the international and national political context.

A Movement, Not a Monolith

The State High Commissioner for Drug Control stated that '... there was little that the Taliban could do on stockpiles'. He argued that '... if the Iranian government can't control traffickers [the international community] cannot expect the Taliban to control the drugs trade' (Akhundzada, personal communication, 24 April 2001). While the Taliban ban gave an impression of consolidated territorial control, informed accounts stress a different reality, arguing that the administration was dysfunctional and inconsistent (Rashid, 2001: 212; Johnson and Leslie, 2004: 152–3: Donini et al., 2004: 190; Marsden, 2009: 93). Ministries were largely a façade; they lacked budgets, policies and an effective bureaucracy. Instead, the regime largely relied on the development community to deliver social services and in many cases infrastructural projects.

Furthermore, policy positions adopted in Kabul would often be undermined by those in Kandahar with a far more conservative agenda. In the countryside there was considerable scope for pragmatism; non-governmental organisations and the UN continued to deliver education to women and girls in parts of the country where local leaders and communities were more supportive and pragmatic than the edicts of Mullah Omar would suggest. Even the claims that the population had been disarmed were overstated; rural communities, particularly those in the mountainous areas, retained their weapons but consented to withdraw them from public space as long as the Taliban maintained security. As Maley (2002: 217) notes: 'The claim that the Taliban "controlled" large tracts of Afghanistan was misleading, since the Taliban presence in rural areas was light.'

In reality, the Taliban regime—like Afghan governments before it—ruled through a combination of coercion and negotiation. In the lower areas located along the main trading routes and river valleys, the Taliban regime could easily impose its will on a population that was more accessible and consisted of different tribes settled over many years. This can be understood as the 'state space' that previous regimes had also governed with relative ease (Scott, 2009). However, in the more mountainous areas, the population was more cohesive, often consisting of a single tribal group, and had historically been given greater autonomy. In these hinterlands there was little evidence of Taliban presence beyond a few armed militiamen located in the district governor's office. In these areas the Taliban regime, like its predecessors, adopted a strategy of containment, working with the rural elite to co-opt and neutralise dissent (Scott, 2009; Barfield, 2010).

When the Taliban expanded their base from the south across the country they defeated some of their opponents militarily but reached political settlements with others. Tribal and military elites may have acquiesced to Taliban rule but they were given varying degrees of autonomy depending on the political and military capital at their disposal (Johnson and Leslie, 2004: 145; Sinno, 2008; Crews and Tarzi, 2008: 111–12). Moreover, these settlements were constantly evolving, particularly in the late 1990s when the Taliban faced growing dissent and increasing financial difficulties (Vendrell, personal communication, 24 April 2001; Crews and Tarzi, 2008: 262, 265).

The Taliban prohibition on opium was illustrative of the kind of negotiated settlements with which the leadership had to engage. For example, earlier attempts by Mullah Omar to impose a one-third reduction on opium poppy cultivation in the 1999/2000 growing season had been largely ignored. However, in the 2000/1 growing season there were reports that elders from the Shinwari tribe had received a direct payment of US$150,000 from the Taliban to comply with the ban. They were also given preferential access to the donors' mission to make direct appeals for development assistance (Donor Mission, 2001: 6). Even when the donors' mission was investigating the prohibition, the Taliban leadership in the east had to negotiate safe passage for the mission to visit the Mahmand and Pekhar valleys in Achin. This was an area where the mix of civil disobedience in protest against the ban, the presence of traders and drug processing facilities, and reports of the inflow of weapons raised major security concerns for the Taliban, given the seniority of some of the diplomats on the donors' mission.

In the southern provinces of Helmand and Kandahar, the population largely accepted the ban in the 2000/1 growing season. There were reports of a delegation of tribal elders from Nade Ali visiting Mullah Omar to present their case against the ban, but these did not yield a change in position. However, fieldwork during the period that would in a normal year have been the opium poppy harvest season revealed an underlying resentment of the authorities that had imposed the ban. Implicit threats were common. As one farmer in Musa Qala recounted (personal communication, April 2001), when asked about the sustainability of the ban: 'There have been many Amirs in my lifetime, I am sure there will be many more!'[21]

It is also important to acknowledge that the ban was implemented amidst a backdrop of growing resentment and dissent against Taliban rule even in Pashtun areas (Rashid, 2001; Crews and Tarzi, 2008: 259–68). As with their predecessors, conscription made the Taliban increasingly unpopular, particularly as many conscripted fighters were dying in battles in the north (Vendrell, personal communication, 24 April 2001; Crews and Tarzi, 2008: 262, 265). The Taliban's inability to bring economic stability, despite improvements in physical security, led to growing frustration among the population. Incidences of corruption became more widespread and there were a number of armed rebellions throughout their rule, even in districts that were considered to be the heart of Taliban territory, including Arghandab in the province of Kandahar, and Kajaki in Helmand (Crews and Tarzi, 2008: 262).[22]

There were also tensions within the Taliban's leadership, which had evolved from a core of Kandahari conservatives in the mid-1990s to include a variety groups (including former communists from the Khalqi party) who did not necessarily share the same moral and social vision for the country (Goodson, 2001: 107). There were reports of disputes between the 'conservatives' in Kandahar, headed by Mullah Mohammed Omar, and the 'moderates' under the Mullah Rabbani, who was based in Kabul (Crews and Tarzi, 2008: 238–73; Nojumi et al., 2002: 179–81; Gannon, 2005: 51–65; Johnson and Leslie, 2004; Donini et al.: 2004: 190). The divisions were such that Rashid (2001: 212) saw the potential for the moderates to stage a coup against Mullah Omar.

As late as 1999, UNDCP recognised the limitations of the verbal and written agreements that it had reached with the Taliban and expressed doubts as to whether the authorities would comply. A note to file stated:

> The fluid nature of the conflict in Afghanistan would certainly call into question the ability of the authorities to comply with the written and verbal agreements they have reached with UNDCP. The shifting alliances and the absorption of different

factions and parties of the *mujahidin* into the Taliban movement pose particular problems for centralising decision making. Institutionally the Taliban would appear to be a loose coalition of factions, many of which are regionally based and pre-exist the Taliban. Consequently policies and attitudes differ from region to region as is evident by the differing stances of the southern and eastern authorities to the gender issue. With this fluid political environment, compromises and agreements are made to ensure that the alliance holds together, and in some cases this may include the acceptance of some factions involvement in the drugs trade. (UNDCP, unpublished note)

While projecting the image of state control, the Taliban's authority in the country was more tenuous than it appeared. At the time there were considerable doubts about whether the Taliban could sustain the ban into a second consecutive year (Donor Mission, 2001). Pressing the rural population to abandon opium poppy cultivation during the 2000/1 growing season was a political gamble, given the number of farmers involved in cultivation and the rural origins of the movement. But there was the potential to mitigate some risks if they succeeded in extracting development assistance from the international community. There is no doubt that pressing for the cessation of the opium trade risked confronting more powerful elements within the country, and possibly within the Taliban itself, and could have proved to be political suicide.

Conclusion

It is widely believed that the prohibition of opium in the 2000/1 growing season demonstrated the Taliban's capacity to extend its rule over remote rural peripheries. However, a closer examination of the motives behind the ban—as well as the highly localised and rather fragile political processes involved in negotiating compliance with rural communities—suggests that the ban was a political gamble designed to reposition the Taliban on the international stage and attract development assistance at a time when the regime was facing increasing isolation, growing fissures within the leadership and experiencing signs of rural unrest (Crews and Tarzi, 2008: 263; Rashid, 2002: 103–4).

Through historical revisionism, the Taliban ban has been dismissed as an act of market manipulation by a rogue regime that sought to increase its revenue stream. This view fails to take into consideration the unregulated structure of the drugs trade, as well as the negotiated and fluid nature of the Taliban's authority over the regions. While members of the Taliban and their associates may have engaged in 'insider trading', simply dismissing the ban as a cynical attempt to manipulate prices ignores the wider geopolitical goals served by the prohibition of opium and the political context in Afghanistan at the time.

Caricaturing the Taliban ban as simply an attempt to increase market prices does not help us understand the efficacy of this and more recent drug control efforts under the Karzai government. At the time, the ban succeeded in its purpose. It gave the Taliban regime the appearance of having the moral high ground with the international community, when in the past it had been censured for its poor record on human rights and for the sanctuary it gave to Osama Bin Laden. The ban also served to embarrass the United Front and challenge their legitimacy as the internationally recognised head of state with an official seat at the United Nations. The prohibition of opium production also forced Western nations to engage with the Taliban as a credible interlocutor, as seen in the seniority of many members of the donors' mission sent to Afghanistan to investigate the impact and sustainability of the ban.

Finally, the prohibition compelled Western donors to provide short-term development assistance in response to the humanitarian impact of the ban, and to consider how they might engage with the regime regarding medium- to long-term development support (Donor Mission, 2001: 5). In fact, were it not for the tragic events of 11 September 2001 and the subsequent international intervention in Afghanistan, the Taliban's success in prohibiting opium production might have changed the way in which the international community engaged with the regime, leading to an increase in development assistance for a rural population that increasingly saw the Taliban as failing to deliver improvements in their economic welfare.

In terms of domestic politics, the ban was far less successful. When the Taliban banned opium there were few other economic opportunities in Afghanistan. Consequently, when the donors' mission visited districts such as Achin and Khogiani in Nangarhar and Musa Qala and Kajaki in Helmand, it found itself surrounded by young men with little to do. These were areas where only twelve months earlier farmers would be willing to spend time talking with researchers in the field only while harvesting their opium crop. With the cessation of opium poppy cultivation across the entire area and the widespread cultivation of wheat, farmers had not only lost the opportunity to cultivate opium on their own land but they had lost the daily wages they earned from working as itinerant harvesters in a neighbouring district or further afield.

At the time the income from opium production had become an important part of the overall income of numerous farmers, not only in those areas where opium poppy was cultivated but in areas where there was no tradition of cultivation. For example, many seasonal workers employed in Helmand during the harvest came from the province of Ghor, which did not have a history of intensive opium poppy cultivation (UNDCP, 1999a: 9). The experience of some of these workers was such that they were preferred by landowners who were looking to maximise the amount of opium extracted from the plant during the harvest. For example, the Taimani, a tribe from southern Ghor, were referred to as 'surgeons' for their harvesting skills, which enabled them to collect more opium than others.

The loss of both on-farm and off-farm income from opium production during the Taliban ban was significant. The crowds of men surrounding the donors' mission were not violent, but they resented the economic impact of the Taliban's ban and blamed Western nations as much as they did the Taliban. Most reported that, in the absence of opium production, they would travel to Pakistan in search of employment; there were already reports of growing numbers of families leaving the country. A few of those interviewed threatened to look for opportunities to join armed groups in Afghanistan and in other countries, where at least they would be fed regularly.

The economic consequences of the ban had not yet been fully realised at the time of the donors' mission. The loans that many had taken on their opium crop before the planting season were not yet due until June 2001. As these had been monetised at the new inflated price of US$500 per kilogram, the prospects of repaying were bleak and there were already reports of people absconding to Pakistan to avoid repayment. Furthermore, food shortages in rural Afghanistan are typically most acute in the winter. Even with the widespread cultivation of wheat in the 2000/1 growing season, many farmers would have faced the winter of 2001/2 without either wheat flour or cash with which to purchase it and other basic necessities. Despite the debate on stockpiles that prevailed amongst policy-makers and in the Western media, there was little evidence of these being held by farmers or farmgate traders in rural Afghanistan.

Maintaining order in the face of the widespread economic dislocation that the ban had caused would have been a challenge, particularly in areas where the Taliban did not have a strong presence. The imposition of the ban changed the nature of the relationship between rural communities, the Taliban and those in the rural elite who had played a part in imposing prohibition. While coercion had been an important element of the bargaining process with rural elites and the local population, it was largely what Kalyvas (2006: 12) would call an act of 'selective violence', used judiciously to encourage compliance. A far more critical element in gaining consent in these more autonomous areas was the potential for patronage and rent from future development assistance. As this chapter has shown, the expectation that development assistance would be forthcoming was high at all levels of society, but particularly among the rural population and key tribes like the Shinwari who had been instrumental in the imposition of the ban in the eastern region.

Ultimately the ban on opium shifted the political settlement that had been reached between the Taliban and much of rural Afghanistan during their rule. If it had been sustained, prohibition had the potential to challenge the political and financial autonomy of the periphery, making them reliant on the patronage of the centre. Without the concentration of violence and the development funds needed to shore up the support of local elites and lessen the impact of the ban on large swathes of the rural population, there was little prospect of prohibition being pursued for another year. It is important to recognise that in Afghanistan every leader has both his constituents as well as political and military adversaries who are adept at capitalising on their opponent's failure to deliver patronage. The fragile deals that were struck at the periphery would have been hard to maintain without some evidence that the rural population's economic prospects would not continue on a downward trajectory. It is highly likely that, if development assistance were not delivered, the Taliban would have come under considerable political pressure from key tribal groups to abandon the ban. It is equally likely that the leadership would have capitulated, particularly given the availability of weaponry within Afghanistan and throughout the region, the ongoing conflict, and the Taliban movement's own internal struggles.

Negotiating a second year of a ban under these conditions would have presented a major challenge for the rural elite as well as the Taliban leadership. Considerable political capital had been expended by the Taliban leadership, tribal leaders and local elders in the process of implementing prohibition. The resistance that was seen in the upper parts of Achin during the spring of 2001 could easily have turned into a widespread rural rebellion, challenging the image of sovereignty that the Taliban looked to project internationally and domestically. In fact, in April 2001 there were already reports that Hajji Qadir was moving weapons across the border into eastern Afghanistan, and the potential for dissent in other parts of the country was extremely high. As Francesco Vendrell noted at the time of the ban, while reflecting on what he saw as the 'rebellious mood amongst the rural population, the Taliban will not put religious purism ahead of their military ambitions' (personal communication, 24 April 2001).

NANGARHAR

A MODEL PROVINCE

Introduction

Chapter 7 offers a detailed account of two efforts to ban opium production in the province of Nangarhar following the fall of the Taliban. In contrast to the Taliban prohibition, these more recent events took place at a time when Western nations were directly engaged in Afghanistan and were increasingly seeing the level of drug crop cultivation as a litmus test for the overall state-building project.

In 2008 and 2009, the province of Nangarhar was being lauded as the success story of reconstruction and statebuilding efforts in Afghanistan, following the prohibition of opium poppy cultivation from 2007/8 to 2009/10 under the governorship of Gul Aga Shirzai. This accolade was not undeserved. Measures of security suggested that it was one of the border provinces least affected by the insurgency between 2007 and 2009 (Radin and Roggio, 2008; Mukhopadhyay, 2014). Rapid reconstruction efforts, including infrastructural development, earned the governor Gul Aga Shirzai the nickname 'the bull-dozer'. In particular, the completed reconstruction of the Kabul to Torkham road and arterial roads to the district centres greatly reduced travel times between rural areas and the cities of Peshawar, the provincial centre, Jalalabad and Kabul, thereby improving livelihood opportunities and building confidence in the government's capacity both to deliver development assistance and to penetrate rural space (Mukhopadhyay, 2014; Mansfield, 2008a). The province was also contributing a greater proportion of customs revenue from the Torkham border crossing, rising from 17 per cent to 23 per cent between 2007 and 2009, as well as absorbing increasing amounts of aid from the USG, European Commission and World Bank (Mukhopadhyay, 2014).

In 2008, Nangarhar was found to have less than 100 hectares of land dedicated to opium poppy, resulting in UNODC declaring the province 'opium poppy free'. This was an even more impressive achievement given that the province had been one of the top two opium producers during much of the 1990s. The pace of reduction compared to other provinces, and the fact that low levels of cultivation were sustained into 2009 and 2010, enhanced Nangarhar's reputation as a 'model province' for counternarcotics efforts. This sense of achievement was reinforced by the fact that a previous ban imposed by then Governor Hajji Din Muhammad in 2004/5 had not penetrated the upper reaches of the Spinghar piedmont and had collapsed in 2007.

There was so much optimism about the future of the province in 2009 that parts of the international community, including US Ambassador William Wood, began touting Nangarhar as a 'model of success' (David Spencer, cited in Mukhopadhyay, 2014). Officials from the USG would often cite Nangarhar as an example of how things should be done. PRTs from other provinces and the staffs of Western embassies in Kabul made numerous visits to Jalalabad to find ways to replicate these achievements elsewhere, including in the troubled Helmand province.

The governor himself received many accolades for his efforts, from being voted 'Person of the Year' in a radio poll of the Afghan population to being extolled for his 'effective provincial leadership' by UNODC (UNODC/MCN, 2008: 9). The visit by the prospective US presidential candidate, Senator Barack Obama, to Jalalabad in July 2008, and the subsequent invitation to Governor Gul Aga Shirzai to attend the president-elect's inauguration in January 2009, reinforced the governor's image as a strong and credible Afghan political leader and boosted his reputation as a potential presidential candidate in 2009. It is clear that the reputations of both the province and the governor in 2008 and 2009 were intimately associated with Nangarhar's achievement of poppy-free status. Indeed, Mukhopadhyay (2014: 139) describes the initial ban as a 'watershed moment for the Americans', leading to a significant rise in the amount of aid that the province received.

This chapter examines how the province of Nangarhar went from being one of the most significant producers of opium poppy in Afghanistan to one that achieved 'poppy-free status' and maintained low levels of cultivation for three consecutive years. It looks at the political context in which the demand for low levels of cultivation in Afghanistan became a priority in Afghanistan and why Nangarhar was at the forefront of counternarcotic efforts by imposing bans on two occasions. It examines the different international and national protagonists that supported prohibition; the formal and informal institutions that aligned with the demands for a ban; and the practicalities of how each ban was enforced.

This chapter is divided into two sections. The first offers background information on the province: its strategic significance within Afghanistan, the importance of its border location to the USG and Pakistan and its role as one of the main producers of opium in the country. The second section focuses on the bans imposed by Governor Hajji Din Muhammad in 2004/5 and his successor, Gul Aga Shirzai, in 2007/8. The conclusion offers a comparative analysis of both bans.

The Provincial Context

The province of Nangarhar is located on Afghanistan's eastern border with Pakistan. Together with its neighbouring provinces of Laghman and Kunar, it forms a geographically enclosed basin of interlocking valleys drained by the Kabul and Kunar rivers and their subsidiary streams. To the south of Nangarhar lie the Spinghar mountains, to the north the massif of the eastern Hindu Kush and Nuristan.

Nangarhar is one of the most densely populated provinces in the country. The estimated population of 1.4 million consists mainly of Pashtuns, although in the northern districts around Dar-e-Nur the Pashai people dominate. The provincial centre, Jalalabad, is located at the confluence of the Kabul and Kunar rivers. The Kabul River runs in an easterly direction, flowing into Pakistan. The Nangarhar canal, built in the 1960s, flows from the Kabul River and irrigates over 35,000 hectares within the province. The dam at Darunta, built by the Soviets in 1964, provides electricity to Jalalabad and the surrounding districts.

The climate is considered sub-tropical, with mild winters (except in the mountains) and hot summers. A broad range of agricultural crops cultivated in the main river basin includes citrus and olive trees. Double cropping can be achieved in areas irrigated by the Kabul and Kunar rivers, but in areas reliant on seasonal flood streams or on the underground irrigation systems (known as *karez*)[1] water shortages are more common and cropping patterns more limited. Drought had a significant effect on these areas during the late 1990s and early in the twenty-first century.

Nangarhar province has long been an economic hub of the eastern region. Throughout the 1980s and 1990s, it was a major recipient of development assistance from aid agencies located across the border in Peshawar, Pakistan. Peshawar still dominates the province economically, with considerable trade between Afghanistan and Pakistan, passing though the official border crossing at Torkham and through a variety of unofficial border crossings throughout the province. Even as late as the spring of 2014, the Pakistani rupee (PR) was the main currency used in the province.

Nangarhar's role as an economic hub and transit route for goods to and from Pakistan is reflected in the fact that in 2008/9 the province officially earned $66 million in taxes from imports and exports, second only to Herat province. It also generated US$101 million in government revenue—one-fifth of the central government's total revenue (GIRoA, Central Statistics Organisation, 2009: 228). Taxes on the movement of goods through the province have long been an important source of revenue for those in positions of power in Nangarhar. Control over the border crossing at Torkham provided a source of rent for consecutive governors and their patronage networks. Governor Gul Aga Shirzai extended his capacity to extract rent by taxing vehicular traffic passing through the province under a scheme known as the Nangarhar Reconstruction Fund. The governor claimed he had a dispensation from the Office of the President to use this source of revenue at his own discretion (Mukhopadhyay, 2014; Rosenberg, 2009).

As a border province and a major transit route for North Atlantic Treaty Organisation (NATO) supplies to Afghanistan, Nangarhar has strategic significance to both Pakistan and the USG. Pakistan has maintained business and political interests in Nangarhar; in 2008/9, Pakistan exported US$489 million of goods to Afghanistan and received US$264 million of imports. While Nangarhar was not the sole transit point for these goods, 'Herat and Jalalabad ... ha[d] become the main cities through which most of the external trade takes place' (GIRoA, Central Statistics Organisation, 2009: 203). The Pakistani government maintained a consulate in Jalalabad and the Pakistani military were contracted to improve the Jalalabad to Torkham road between 2006 and 2009, at a value of US$55 million (Kiani, 2006). Pakistani political interests permeate the border, and there is a long history of migration between Nangarhar and the Pakistani province of Khyber Pakhtunwa, with ethnic groups that straddle both sides of the border. Many of the former *jihadi* elite who took up positions of power in Nangarhar—including Gul Aga Shirzai—resided in Pakistan during the war with the Soviets and allegedly maintained strong links there (Mukhopadhyay, 2014).

From 2001 on, the US military had a considerable presence and interest in Nangarhar province, resulting in large investments in the province's infrastructure, with a number of interventions aimed at penetrating the remote border areas neighbouring Pakistan. Development funds from the USG included US$118 million between 2005 and 2009 for the Alternative Development Programme—aimed at supporting farmers' shift from opium poppy to legal livelihoods—as well as interventions aimed at promoting stability, such as the Local Governance and Community Development Programme (LGCD) and the Commanders Emergency Response Programme (CERP). The European Union also funded rural development efforts, road reconstruction and work in the health sector in the province. GIRoA's National Priority Programmes (NPPs)—the National Solidarity Programme (NSP), Micro Finance Investment Support Facility for Afghanistan (MISFA) and, in 2010, the Comprehensive Rural Agricultural Development Facility (CARD-F)—were implemented in the districts around Jalalabad.

Nangarhar also has a history as a significant producer of opium. Before and during the Taliban regime, the province typically cultivated between 15,000 and 20,000 hectares per year, making it one of the most significant opium producers after the province of Helmand. With the collapse of the Taliban in 2001, the ban that they had imposed in July 2000 was lifted, and the rural population reverted to widespread opium poppy cultivation in the 2000/1 growing season. From an estimated 19,780 hectares of opium poppy in the 2000/1 growing season, levels of cultivation in Nangarhar continued to rise until 2003/4, when cultivation reached an unprecedented 28,213 hectares (see Figure 3).

In addition to cultivation, Nangarhar was also involved in trading and processing opiates. In the 1990s, the bazaar in Ghani Khel in Shinwar district, only 6.5 kilometres from the main Torkham road, was a market hub of the opium trade in the eastern region (UNDCP, 1998c). Traders would come to the area to purchase opium in bulk and ship it for processing in the various 'laboratories' within the district and in the more mountainous parts of the province. The price ripple that these large purchases created would prompt local traders and farmers to travel to outlying districts and provinces to purchase opium in an attempt to exploit price differentials. Following the collapse of the Taliban regime and subsequent efforts by the international community

Figure 3: Levels of Opium Poppy Cultivation in Nangarhar Province, 1987–2014

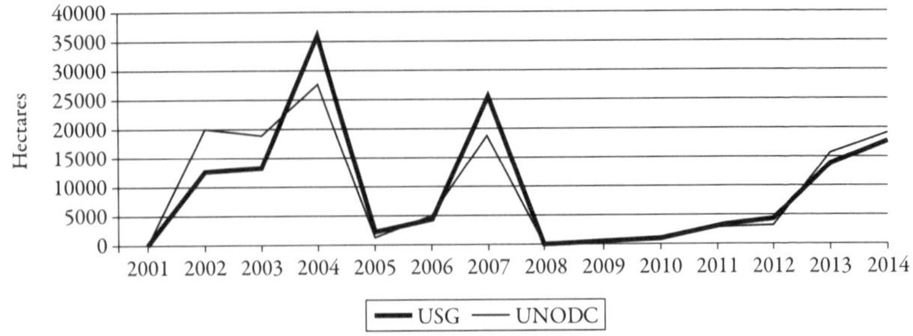

and Afghan special counternarcotics forces, the trade moved farther up the valleys, first to Kahi in Achin district, then to Shadal Bazaar in the upper parts of Spinghar, before finally moving to individual houses in 2009 and 2010.

There was also a history of heroin processing in Nangarhar, in facilities that typically consisted of no more than a rural dwelling. They were located in the upper reaches of the Spinghar piedmont where both national and international forces had found them harder to interdict. However, during the Taliban regime in the 1990s, heroin processing was also found in the more accessible lower areas, perhaps reflecting the more laissez-faire attitude of the authorities at the time (Felbab Brown, 2010).

Power holders in Nangahar are also alleged to have been involved in the drugs trade. The late Hajji Qadir—governor until he was murdered in 2002—and his son Hajji Zahir are thought to have been major protagonists in the drugs trade (Filipov, 2002; Blair and Morgan Edwards, 2002). Widespread cultivation in their ancestral lands in Surkhrud during the 1990s supports the view that the family was directly engaged in drug production, even if their land was largely managed by tenant farmers and sharecroppers.

Aside from these more obvious protagonists in the Nangarhar elite, allegations of trading in opium have been made against Hazrat Ali, Pashai commander, former head of the Provincial Police and Member of Parliament (Baldauf, 2003; Harris, 2001), as well as Mirwais Yasini, former head of the Counter Narcotics Department (the predecessor to the Ministry of Counter Narcotics) and First Deputy Speaker in the Parliament.[2] By spring 2012, members of the Taliban were allegedly taxing and trading in opium in the upper reaches of Achin and Khogiani, as well as in some of the lower districts.

Indeed, it would be hard to find anyone in the political elite of the province who is not suspected of involvement in the drugs trade, with a great deal of anecdotal evidence to support the suspicion. Given the opportunity, it would be irrational for someone to reject the chance to accumulate income, political support and patronage. At the same time, finding robust evidence to support such claims is difficult. These allegations are easily made by political adversaries as a way of discrediting opponents. Such claims are often circumstantial; they link individuals to wealth accumulation and neglect the wider business interests of the political elite, as well as the rent that they have recently extracted from the legal sectors of the Afghan economy in transport, security and construction.

We need to be wary of over-emphasising the importance of the drugs economy in the motivations of the political elite and assuming that failure to act against drugs production is an indicator of some kind of involvement in the drugs trade. To simply allege that a ban is not sustained or action is not taken against a major trader due to involvement in the drugs trade is drugs fetishism. There is a need to be wary of reducing any action—be it efforts to control illicit drugs or a failure to pursue counternarcotics efforts—to a function of the vested commercial interests of those whom we perceive as having the power to act against drugs if they so chose. This is not to be naïve or dismissive of accusations and claims; it is just recognising the wider economic and political context in which the drugs trade and actions against it take place.

Banning Opium in Nangarhar

In any society, there are trade-offs to make between different policy priorities. In a patrimonial system such as Afghanistan, where the state has not concentrated the means of violence, people need to build political and military coalitions in support of a particular course of action. This is true with regard to efforts to ban opium, given the concentration of production in areas of limited statehood. It is useful to examine the conditions under which coalitions were built around bans on opium production in Nangarhar in both the 2004/5 and 2006/07 growing seasons; why such disparate actors and institutions coalesced around the calls for a ban; and how these bans were subsequently enforced across different economic, political and geographic terrains within the province.

Nangarhar has been at the forefront of drug control efforts in Afghanistan since the 1990s, and has been subject to a number of efforts to reduce levels of cultivation. In 1995, then Governor Hajji Qadir conducted an eradication campaign that was estimated to have destroyed 5,433 hectares, with a 49 per cent reduction in levels of cultivation compared to the previous growing season (UNDCP, 1995b: 17). In 2000/1, Nangarhar, like the rest of Afghanistan, was subject to the Taliban prohibition, and, as shown in Chapter 6, was one of the only provinces to show signs of resistance, albeit rather limited.

Even in the 2001/2 growing season, after the Taliban's collapse and following signs of resurgent cultivation, Nangarhar, along with Helmand and then Badakhshan, was targeted by the Interim Administration for counternarcotics efforts supported by the British government. In Nangarhar this initiative consisted of compensating for eradication along with a one-off interdiction in Ghani Khel Bazaar; it was undertaken between February and April 2002, long after the crop had been planted. Implementation involved prominent provincial leaders such as Hajji Qadir, the newly appointed governor; his son, Hajji Zahir; and Hazarat Ali, the Pashai commander and Chief of the Provincial Police (Morgan Edwards, 2011: 113–31).

These bans on opium have much in common. None led to a reduction in cultivation in Nangarhar for more than a single season, and all broke down with considerable acrimony. Each ban was followed by a return to cultivation which—depending on whether we listen to members of the international community or Afghans—was attributed to a lack of commitment, corruption and involvement in the drugs trade levelled at the Afghan protagonists, or to a failure by the international community to deliver on the promise of development assistance.

Since the 2004/5 growing season, counternarcotics efforts in the province have proved to be more enduring. Not only have dramatic reductions in cultivation been achieved, but they have continued over consecutive growing seasons in some of the remote areas where the Afghan state has traditionally had limited presence. Efforts to counter drugs production in Afghanistan began with the ban imposed by Hajji Din Muhammad during the 2004/5 growing season, which reduced cultivation from 28,213 hectares to 1,093 hectares in a single season. After resurgent cultivation in 2007, a further ban was imposed by his successor, Governor Gul Aga Shirzai, which culminated in Nangarhar being declared 'poppy free' by UNODC in 2008, with negligible levels of cultivation continuing even in the Spinghar piedmont until 2010.

As with the Taliban prohibition, both bans in Nangarhar can be viewed through a series of lenses in order to map the different institutions and actors involved in imposing a ban and their multiple and often competing objectives. The first lens is the wider policy debates of the time. These debates addressed the extent to which the priority given to counternarcotics efforts was recalibrated due to worsening metrics and a growing international narrative around the failure of the Afghan project. The second lens is the role that sub-national actors play in enforcing a ban and the advantages that they look to gain by pursuing counternarcotics objectives. This lens helps clarify the motivations of different provincial institutions and actors in Nangarhar to engage in counternarcotics efforts at that moment in time. The final lens is the role of local actors: how bans are imposed on rural communities; the role of local elites; and how the balance between coercion and persuasion differs according to the political topography of the province.

The Drive to Ban Opium in 2004/5: Prohibition under Hajji Din Muhammad

By the end of the 2004/5 growing season, cultivation in Nangarhar had fallen to an estimated 1,093 hectares from 28,213 hectares the year before. This reduction was achieved despite the fact that the official eradication campaign conducted in the spring destroyed only 1,860 hectares (UNODC/MCN, 2005: 53). As in the case of the Taliban ban before it, farmers had simply chosen not to plant. The only crop that remained was found in the hinterlands of upper Achin, where the provincial authorities' strategy of patronage, promises and targeted coercion had limited effect. These achievements were all the more remarkable when compared with the Taliban prohibition four years earlier. In 2005, Governor Hajji Din Muhammad and the provincial authorities had neither the presence nor the coercive capacity of the Taliban. Despite this, the governor managed to co-opt the rural elite into supporting his efforts to prevent opium poppy cultivation across much of the province and to achieve dramatic reductions in cultivation.

The International Context: a Coalition around Bad Metrics to Save the Afghan Project

The government of the UK had been given the role of G8 lead on counternarcotics in Afghanistan in 2002, tasked with coordinating the efforts of international donors and the Afghan government. The UK approached counternarcotics as a cross-cutting issue and recognised how long it had taken countries like Thailand and Pakistan to reduce opium poppy cultivation to negligible levels. Building on the experience of these countries, as well as illicit drug-producing countries in Latin America, the UK advocated an approach in which crop destruction was only undertaken once farmers had a viable alternative—a position that was adopted by the initial Afghan National Drug Strategy of 2003 (Transitional Islamic State of Afghanistan, 2003: 19) and reiterated in 2006 (GIRoA, 2006).

To begin with, there was broad support for this position across the international community. Even those leading global counternarcotics efforts within the US administration—who had long been advocates of aggressive eradication in other parts of the world, including the use of aerial spraying—realised that the situation in Afghanistan was qualitatively different from other drug-producing nations. For example, Rand Beers, the head of INL, argued that the scale of cultivation within the country, the formidable challenges the population faced following the civil war, drought, the collapse of state institutions and the amount of reconstruction and development assistance that was to be made available all meant that responses to drug production in Afghanistan needed to be different from those in other source countries (R. Beers, personal communication, December 2001). As such, neither INL nor USAID pressed for rural development programmes specifically aimed at reducing opium poppy cultivation or for conditionality, where continued development assistance is contingent on the population abandoning opium production. Instead, the emphasis in these initial years was on designing a wide range of interventions that would meet the immediate needs of the Afghan population and, in part, address the causes of opium poppy cultivation (Ross Wherry, USAID, personal communication, 2002).

This was all to change in 2004 when UNODC estimated that opium poppy cultivation reached the unprecedented level of 131,000 hectares: an increase of 64 per cent compared to 2003. Cultivation had spread to all the provinces of the country for the first time (UNODC, 2004: 3). According to Risen (2006: 152), this news ran contrary to the headline figures that were often used to describe statebuilding efforts in Afghanistan—particularly the success of the Afghan elections in October 2004, cited by the Executive Director of UNODC in the preface to the Annual Opium Survey (UNODC, 2004). Indeed, in 2004 there was still considerable optimism about what could be achieved in Afghanistan. In contrast to the negative news generated by the war in Iraq, the international media coverage remained broadly favourable towards statebuilding efforts in the country (Jones, 2010: 148). Performance indicators in health and education had shown considerable progress since the collapse of the Taliban, and efforts to build the Afghan National Army were progressing (US Government Accountability Office, 2005).

At the time, it was felt that the rise in cultivation since the fall of the Taliban undermined wider achievements in Afghanistan (Risen, 2006). The scale of the increase in cultivation in Afghanistan in 2004 and the media's continued comparison with the 8,000 hectares grown during the last year of the Taliban regime compounded the problem and shifted the debate on narcotics in Afghanistan. It provoked a reassessment in the US administration, aided by the new head of INL, Bobby Charles—a vocal supporter of aerial eradication, who stated that the US position on counternarcotics would be 'to lead from the back' (personal communication, 2004).

A growing sense of urgency developed in the US as politicians from both sides of Congress and USG officials raised concerns over the trajectory of the statebuilding project in Afghanistan and pronouncements that illegal drugs were 'the biggest threat to Afghanistan's future' (Lancaster, 2004; Koehler, 2005: 67, 83). Amidst calls for a heavier international footprint in Afghanistan (Suhrke, 2011), the counternarcotics rhetoric grew more strident, and the threat of a 'narco-state' was used repeatedly by UNODC and USG officials to galvanise international action (Risen, 2006: 156, 161). In Congress there was increasing pressure on the US administration to take a more proactive role in counternarcotics policy in Afghanistan. The UK was openly criticised for its position on targeted eradication, with advocates in Congress and INL pressing for a more aggressive eradication policy (US Committee on Government Reform, 2004: 25). Those favouring aerial spraying and biological methods of crop eradication also began to voice their support for the pursuit of far more ambitious targets for crop destruction (Risen, 2006: 152, 159–61).

While support for aerial eradication increased within parts of the US administration and in Congress in the latter part of 2004, a number of factors prevented its adoption. The first was the lack of consensus within the international community and within the US administration itself. At the time, spraying was opposed; it was viewed as counterproductive in Europe—including by the UK, the counternarcotics lead in Afghanistan—as well as within parts of the US administration. The Department of Defense and the US Ambassador to Afghanistan, Zalmei Khalizad, both opposed spraying, and President Karzai also rejected it (Smith, 2010: 81; US Government Accountability Office, 2007: 10; Risen, 2006: 160, 162). The opposition also recognised that there was neither funding nor time to bring in aerial-spraying aircraft in the 2004/5 growing season (Blanchard, 2009: 29).

To head off the threat of aerial eradication and to address genuine concerns about the growing problem of opium production, officials in the US administration, the Afghan government and the wider international community rec-ognised a need for demonstrable progress in reducing cultivation in the 2004/5 growing season. By late 2004, the USG had made counternarcotics a top prior-ity in Afghanistan and had developed a five-pillar strategy to reduce the cultiva-tion, production and trafficking of illicit drugs (US Government Accountability Office, 2006: 9). This strategy was broadly in line with the structure of the Afghan National Drug Control Strategy. It encompassed (i) alternative liveli-hoods, (ii) elimination and eradication, (iii) interdiction, (iv) law enforcement and justice reform and (v) public information. In Kabul the US Embassy was restructured with the appointment of a 'US Drugs Tsar' in-country, who reported directly to the US ambassador, and the establishment of a permanent Narcotics Affairs Section (US Government Accountability Office, 2005: 27). Funding for counternarcotics efforts in Afghanistan was also greatly increased, from US$380 million between 2002 and 2004 to US$782 million for 2005 (US Government Accountability Office, 2006: 2, 8).

GIRoA also raised its profile in counternarcotics in the 2004/5 growing season. With the help of the international community it established a Ministry of Counter Narcotics[3] to lead the effort, a Cabinet Sub-Committee on Counter Narcotics and a Counter Narcotics Trust Fund. A Deputy Minister for Counter Narcotics was also created in the Ministry of Interior with respon-sibilities for counternarcotics law enforcement, including eradication. Several implementation plans were drafted, covering law enforcement, eradication, information and alternative livelihoods. Perhaps most importantly, on 9 December 2004, two days after his inauguration, the President declared a *jihad* against opium poppy cultivation at a two-day conference in Kabul. In his statement to an audience of Afghan politicians, governors and tribal elders, as well as representatives of the international community, he called for significant reductions in opium production and threatened provincial governors with dismissal if they did not act to eliminate cultivation that season.

The development community, which had been wary of directly engaging in anything that could be construed as counternarcotics, also responded to the increase in drug crop cultivation in Afghanistan. Their reservations about becoming involved were largely sidelined as development organisations like the World Bank began to recognise the risks that drug production, corruption and insecurity posed to Afghanistan's development, as well as the problems of being seen to channel development inputs into areas that used these inputs to increase opium poppy cultivation (World Bank, 2005: 111–30; Ward and Byrd, 2004: 98). There were concerns that a failure to support efforts to reduce opium poppy cultivation would lead to the adoption of an eradication approach that could jeopardise ongoing rural development efforts (Ward and Byrd, 2004: 76–8). Consequently, in late 2004, drug control objectives were integrated into some of the National Development Programs by the World Bank and other donors (Ward and Byrd, 2004:114–26). By 2005, increasing amounts of rural development assistance were being labelled as 'alternative livelihoods' by development donors in an attempt to be seen as engaged in counternarcotics efforts (Mansfield and Pain, 2005: 8–9).

GIRoA, however, was not interested in relabelling or redesigning existing development programmes, particularly when the war in Iraq was absorbing more and more international funding, with the associated fear that this would reduce Afghanistan's flow of development assistance. Consequently, not unlike the Taliban before it, GIRoA proved adept at presenting its counternarcotics efforts as working in the interests of the international community, with expensive price tags attached to its endeavours (Koehler, 2005: 76). According to Koehler (2005: 76), the Deputy Minister for the Interior, Daud Daud, pressed for annual investments of US$3.5 billion; the Minister for Rural Reconstruction and Development, Hanif Atmar, anticipated that around US$2–3 billion would be required to 'counter the macro-economic effects of a successful eradication of the opium poppy economy'. As such, while members of the Afghan government talked of their commitment to eliminate opium poppy, they recognised that by doing so they risked impoverishing and antagonising sections of the rural population. As the Taliban had done in 2000/1, the Afghan administration began to refer to the consequences of banning opium poppy as a humanitarian concern and the responsibility of the international community to resolve (Koehler, 2005: 71–2).

The Provincial Context: the Importance of Nangarhar

The pressure to prevent a further rise in cultivation in the 2004/5 growing season was felt particularly acutely in Nangarhar for two reasons. First, the province had experienced substantial increases in the amount of opium poppy cultivated in 2004, rising to 28,213 hectares from an estimated 18,904 hectares in 2003 (UNODC/MCN, 2004). In addition, Nangarhar had been an area of strategic interest for the US military from the beginning of the invasion in 2001, due to its location on a major transit route for fuel supplies and reconstruction material from Pakistan. The US had established a significant military presence in the province, accompanied by large investments in the infrastructure and the establishment of a US-led PRT in late 2003.

In its desire to see a fall in cultivation nationally, the international community also supported the drive to reduce levels of cultivation in Nangarhar. Senior UK officials, including the Ambassador, visited the province and called for restraint. Even the European Commission—which had taken a more development-oriented approach to drug control—expressed its concerns that if cultivation were to continue its upward trajectory in the province, Brussels would have to reconsider its development funding (Fitzherbert, 2004).

The political negotiations around the imposition of a ban in Nangarhar took on a familiar form, with attempts to use reductions in cultivation to extract development assistance from the central government and international community. As the senior patron in the province, Governor Hajji Din Muhammad made sure he was seen soliciting development assistance for his rural constituents with both the central government and the international community. He took every opportunity, either in person or indirectly through the media, to press the international community to respond to the ban by increasing the amount of development assistance available to the province. In November 2004, in front of tribal elders from the province, he presented donors in Kabul with a list of development projects required for the 'donors to honour their pledges' (Fitzherbert, 2004). He often berated the donor community in the media for not 'solving the farmers' problems' (Goudsouzouzian, 2004; IRIN, 2004a).

At this time, the economic and political conditions were relatively conducive to the implementation of a ban on opium poppy in Nangarhar. Politically there was significant support for the statebuilding efforts of the government and the international community. President Karzai had been recently elected, drawing on support from the governor, tribal elders and rural population of Nangarhar. Development assistance had also begun to flow into the province, with promises of much more to follow. Major infrastructural development had begun, including the rehabilitation of the Kabul to Torkham road. National Priority Programs in health and education, as well as community-based efforts such as the National Solidarity Program, were being implemented in most districts, albeit in a limited number of villages. Along with the vibrant cross-border trade with Pakistan, there was every reason for the population to a share a sense of optimism about the future development of the province.

GIRoA was quick to draw on the political capital that it had generated in the province. President Karzai's declaration of a *jihad* against opium poppy cultivation gained widespread coverage in the media. His threat to dismiss governors who did not act against the crop was taken seriously by Hajji Din Muhammad (Koehler, 2005: 65). In fact, in subsequent discussions with district governors and security commanders, many of whom owed their positions to the patronage of Hajji Din Muhammad and the Arsala family, the governor informed them that if he were dismissed from his post, they too would lose their jobs. The rural elite were presented with a dilemma: if they ignored the president's call for a ban on opium poppy they would be undermining the very leadership for which they had solicited votes only two months before, which would damage their standing with their rural constituents.

The economic situation also favoured a reduction in cultivation in the 2004/5 growing season. The price of wheat increased by as much as 49 per cent in Nangarhar between October and November 2004, raising concerns over food security among the local population (Mansfield, 2005a). There were fears that wheat prices would rise even further due to the Government of Pakistan's decision to limit the diversion of Pakistani wheat flour into Afghanistan and to restrict the trade between Punjab and the Khyber Pakhtunwha. Previous research had shown that in just such conditions, households that fear they will not be able to purchase wheat on the open market often increase their wheat cultivation at the expense of their opium crop, even where the financial returns on opium are higher (UNDCP, 1995c).

Uncertainty over the future opium crop also supported the government's efforts to ban opium poppy in the 2004/5 growing season. Opium prices in Nangarhar had fallen from the equivalent of US$320 per kilogram at harvest time in May 2003 to US$136 in May 2004 (UNODC, 2004: 81; Mansfield, 2005a: 11). Yields had also dropped, and there were reports of crop failure in the districts of Achin and Khogiani in 2004. While some farmers attributed these low yields to a spraying campaign by the USG—which was later dismissed as a 'dummy run'—poor crop rotation is generally thought to be a more logical explanation, given the proportion of agricultural land allocated to the crop in these areas over the previous three growing seasons (Landay, 2007; Mansfield, 2004c: 22; Shuljgin, 1953: 1–8; Fist, 2001). Either way, the risk of crop failure was heightened in the minds of farmers, favouring an increase in wheat production in the 2004/5 growing season.

The Local Context: Co-opting the Rural Elite and Minimising Rural Dissent

With international, national and provincial institutions aligned behind a ban in Nangarhar, the governor and his administration set about enforcing it. The process of enacting the ban drew heavily on the Taliban's experience in the 2000/1 growing season, co-opting both formal and informal institutions into the process. Negotiation and political bargaining were at the forefront of Hajji Din Muhammad's strategy to reduce opium production; the reward of increased development assistance formed an integral part of the dialogue between the governor and the rural population (Koehler, 2005; Mansfield, 2005a).

As with the Taliban ban, the focus was on dissuading farmers from planting the crop in the first place. Eradication had a role but it was used sparingly and only targeted against isolated and recalcitrant groups when negotiations had already minimised opposition to the ban. The strategy to prevent planting consisted of two parallel approaches. The first approach involved charging the district governor and security commander with inviting tribal elders and *shura* members from each village to the district centre at the start of the planting season. At these meetings, the invited guests were informed that opium poppy should not be cultivated in their village. Once the planting season began, if there was evidence of opium production, village elders and *shura* members from each village were again summoned to the district centre and told that villagers should eradicate their opium poppy or face arrest by the security commander.

The second element of the strategy required the engagement and support of local elites. By persuading this group to refrain from cultivation and to advocate drug control within their tribes and communities, the governor created division. If the rural elite gave the impression that they expected their own crop to be eradicated, the ordinary farmer would perceive that there was a much greater probability that his crop would be destroyed and would think it unlikely that the community would mount an effective collective response to a government ban. Soliciting the support of the rural elite to advocate and enforce the ban required patronage. Direct payments and hospitality were the crudest methods of gaining their support. More important was the provincial authorities' recognition and support for the rural elites' status as credible interlocutors. In particular, priority was given to enabling the rural elite to solicit development assistance from the central government and the international community through meetings in Kabul and Jalalabad.

The governor facilitated access to members of the Afghan cabinet and to donors in Kabul and Jalalabad so that the rural elite could request development assistance for their communities (Fitzherbert, 2004; Koehler, 2005). These fora gave the rural elite the opportunity to show constituents that, in the face of the ban, they were negotiating with the highest levels of government for additional development assistance. Along with the governor's requests to the central government and donors for aid, an emphasis on the transactional nature of the ban made it clear that continued support was contingent on the future delivery of development assistance (Koehler, 2005: 72–3; Mansfield, 2005a).

A further element in the governor's strategy was to target specific geographic areas for strategic effect. For example, compliance with the ban in Surkhrud, the district where the governor and his extended family resided, was seen as essential. A failure to enforce the ban here, in a low-lying district where the governor had land and influence, would have undermined the ban immediately. Consequently, Hajji Zahir, the governor's nephew, played a personal role in preventing cultivation in the district of Surkhrud.

Success in a more remote area of limited statehood where the authority of the state was negotiated rather than absolute was also seen as pivotal. A reduction in this kind of terrain would have an effect on other parts of the province. To this end, Hajji Din Muhammad targeted Khogiani district and drew on the support of the district administrator. As a former *jihadi* commander who had resisted eradication campaigns in previous seasons, the administrator's active involvement in implementing the ban in the 2004/5 growing season had a demonstrable effect in neighbouring districts in the Spinghar piedmont and in lower-lying areas (Mansfield, 2005a: 24).

As with the implementation of the Taliban ban in Nangarhar, authorities used coercion sparingly to maximise the effect while minimising the risk of provoking widespread resistance or violent confrontation. In some areas, such as Khogiani, farmers were arrested for refusing to destroy their own crop. However, typically these farmers were quickly released once their families verified that their opium crop had been destroyed.

One approach was to delegate eradication to farmers themselves, tasking them to destroy their own crop. This eliminated the need for a major logistical exercise with large numbers of tractors and police, a practice that has often proved to be provocative to rural communities. Eradication was also conducted early in the planting season, just after germination, so that farmers could replace their opium crop with another winter crop, typically wheat. Most important, conducting eradication in the fall reduced the need for eradication later in the growing season. Later-season eradication has often found farmers more willing to protest, partly to delay eradication and allow them to harvest their crop, but also to express their anger at the accumulated time and costs they have invested, as well as the psychological effect of losing the crop so close to harvest (Mansfield, 2004c: 21; Salmon, 2009: 61).

The role that negotiation played in reducing cultivation, bolstered by the careful use of eradication linked to the threat of coercion and targeted violence, can be seen in the fact that the authorities did not press into areas where they had not gained sufficient leverage and support. Where there was a hostile reaction to eradication, the authorities typically withdrew. For example, earlier in the growing season, eradication had proved to be possible in the lower parts of Achin district around Kahi and even in more remote parts such as the Pekhar valley (Mansfield, 2005a: 20). However, by the spring an eradication campaign in upper Achin provoked an angry reaction from the population that led to the death of one farmer and the Afghan National Police (ANP) curtailing their campaign (Mansfield, 2005b). While the ANP did not withdraw immediately, they did not seek a prolonged confrontation that might escalate and lead to further violence.

In sum, the dramatic reduction in cultivation in one season was significant, all the more so for the low level of eradication and the fact that Hajji Din Muhammad lacked the coercive means with which to impose a ban if he had faced widespread rural opposition. The political imperative, however, was clear in 2004: a reduction in cultivation was essential if the Afghan project was not to be seen as faltering on the international stage. In Nangarhar it was possible to form a coalition of international, national, provincial and local actors, all temporarily aligned—for quite different reasons—behind efforts to reduce cultivation that year. It was a remarkable feat and it is likely that the governor would have received more kudos for his efforts if it had not been for his handling of the Jalalabad riots in May 2005, and his subsequent transfer to serve as governor of Kabul (Mukhopadhyay, 2014).

Achieving Poppy-Free Status: Banning Opium Poppy Under
Gul Aga Shirzai

Gul Aga Shirzai replaced Hajji Din Muhammad as governor in July 2005. He came to Nangarhar after serving as governor of Kandahar three times and as Minister for Public Works. During his last year in Kandahar, opium poppy cultivation was estimated to have increased from 4,969 hectares in the 2003/4 growing season to 12,990 hectares in 2004/5 (UNODC/MCN, 2005). He arrived in Nangarhar province at a disadvantage. He had no prior history there, and he inherited district officials who were loyal to his predecessor. Moreover, Hajji Din Muhammad's strategy of extending promises of development assistance amidst threats of eradication had started to unravel in the southern districts bordering Pakistan (Mansfield, 2006b).

As an outsider, Governor Gul Aga Shirzai had few levers to pull during his first two years in the province. In 2006, cultivation rose to 4,871 hectares and was found across the Spinghar piedmont. Unsuccessful attempts by the provincial authorities to stage the eradication process and negotiate levels of crop destruction in the southern districts created the impression that rural communities could manage the threat of eradication and that the provincial authority did not have the means to impose a ban for a further year.

By late 2006, the counternarcotics effort in the province was in disarray and faced widespread dissent (Mansfield, 2007a: 33). Eradication efforts, although limited to areas alongside arterial roads, provoked demonstrations and violence. Moreover, contrary to the 2004/5 growing season when farmers destroyed their own crops and planted wheat, in the 2006/7 growing season many farmers irrigated and fertilised their damaged opium crop so as to assist recovery and prompt the growth of ungerminated seed (Mansfield, 2007b: 33).

In a desperate attempt to save face, the governor reportedly drew on the threat of NATO bombing to try to contain the threat of armed resistance to the eradication campaign (Mansfield, 2007a: 32, 90). By the end of the season UNODC estimated that 18,739 hectares of opium were grown and the crop was once again found across the province. Only the low-lying districts of Kama, Behsud and Surkhrud refrained from cultivation. At a time when the absence of opium poppy was taken to signify state power, the writ of the government in Nangarhar was limited to the districts that lay adjacent to Jalalabad and the provincial capital itself.

This was all to change, however, in 2008, when the province would again be declared 'poppy free' and Governor Gul Aga Shirzai would be celebrated for his counternarcotics efforts. This was all the more remarkable given that low levels of cultivation persisted across much of the Spinghar piedmont for three consecutive seasons, and have continued in the Kabul River basin until the present day. Paradoxically, the push for the re-imposition of a ban in Nangahar was shaped by many of the same political imperatives that led to the dramatic reductions in cultivation under Hajji Din Muhammad, and Gul Aga Shirzai engaged in many of the same political processes. But the latter governor mobilised support from a proactive US military and civilian presence in the province.

The International Context: Another Bad Year

In 2007, UNODC reported that cultivation had reached an unprecedented 193,000 hectares, up from 165,000 hectares in 2006. In the preface to the

Annual Survey, Antonio Maria Costa, the executive director of UNODC, denied any relationship between drug crop cultivation and poverty—a point that was subsequently refuted by his own office in Vienna, as well as by UNODC's Independent Evaluation Unit, and by researchers in the field (Kemp cited in Rubin and Sherman, 2008: 56; UNODC, 2008b: 11–12, 52; Mansfield and Pain, 2007: 14). Costa also tied opium production intimately to the Taliban, citing as evidence the coexistence of opium poppy cultivation and the insurgency in the south, and claiming a history in which opium was 'the regime's sole source of foreign exchange' (UNODC/MCN, 2007: iv).

In making these claims, the executive director pressed for a more aggressive eradication campaign in the southern region. He argued that such a campaign would not risk pauperising farmers in the south, given their relative wealth; nor would it alienate the rural population, given that they already supported the Taliban (UNODC/MCN, 2007; Kilkullen, 2009: 63; Schweich, 2008: 30). Indeed, in a later meeting at NATO in September 2007, he appeared to back calls for aerial spraying by the Afghan Vice President Ahmed Zia Massoud—although many commentators doubted the wisdom of supporting a political leader from the Panshir in his efforts to press the President to spray the Pashtun south (Reuters, 2007; Mayne, 2007).

Despite the absence of empirical evidence to support Costa's arguments, the increase in cultivation in 2007 and the escalation in the rhetoric of state failure led to renewed pressure from those who instinctively believed that eradication—specifically aerial eradication—was the way forward in Afghanistan (Neumann, 2009: 147). This included US President George W. Bush, who had often been described as a 'spraying kinda guy', a comment frequently cited by US interlocutors as a veiled threat to push through a more aggressive eradication policy (Cowper-Coles, 2011: 84; Schweich, 2008).

It became clear that, although the pressure to introduce spraying had previously dissipated—due to the reductions at the national level in the 2004/5 growing season and progress in specific provinces such as Nangarhar—the issue remained alive in parts of Washington, DC. The southern region of Afghanistan still posed a significant problem for both the US and UK governments, given that estimates of cultivation continued to increase unabated, particularly in Helmand province, where the UK had established a PRT in mid-2006. UNODC's estimate that cultivation had trebled in Helmand in the 2005/6 growing season, and increased by as much as 59 per cent for the country as a whole, fuelled calls for aerial eradication by advocates in the US Department of State (UNODC/MCN, 2006).

Among politicians and senior officials, eradication had increasingly become the metric by which counternarcotics efforts were judged, and there was considerable pressure from policy-makers in Washington to show progress (Neumann, 2009: 10, 61, 137, 187, 193). The Afghan Eradication Force (AEF), a centrally planned paramilitary group funded by the USG and located within the Ministry of Interior, was tasked with increasing crop destruction. As in the 2004/5 growing season, support for an increase in manual eradication came from a diverse collection of civilian and military organisations that recognised how a failed effort would reinvigorate those pressing for aerial eradication. US Ambassador to Afghanistan Ronald Neumann (2009: 10) describes a strategy of 'eradicat[ing] enough to keep Washington happy while buying time for other elements of the strategy to begin taking hold'. The pressure to eradicate more of the crop produced growing evidence of over-reporting by both the AEF and Governor Led Eradication in Helmand (Cranfield, 2007). Fields that were reported as having been completely destroyed were found to contain large amounts of unscathed crop.

By the 2006/7 growing, season, faced with predictions of another bumper crop and recognising the limitations of efforts to destroy the crop manually in a non-permissive environment, a cabal of US officials pressed once again for spraying. These included two former US ambassadors to Colombia: Anne Patterson, Assistant Secretary of State for the Bureau of Narcotics and Law Enforcement, and William Wood,[4] who was appointed US Ambassador to Afghanistan in April 2007, as well as Tom Schweich,[5] Coordinator for Counternarcotics and Justice Reform in Afghanistan (Schweich, 2008). Despite the Afghan cabinet's rejection of a proposal for a pilot ground-based spraying initiative in January 2007 (Neumann, 2009: 148), Ambassadors Schweich and Wood persisted with their demands for aerial spraying following UNODC's announcement of the rise in cultivation in Helmand province (Cowper-Coles, 2011: 19; Schweich, 2007: 52). It was this persistence and his offer to be sprayed with the herbicide himself that earned the US ambassador to Kabul the nickname 'Chemical Bill' (Cowper-Coles, 2011: 19).

While the US Department of Defense and the UK government, among others, continued to oppose aerial spraying, many officials recognised that it would become harder to resist the political pressure being applied if cultivation continued to increase in the 2007/8 growing season (Cowper-Coles, 2011: 51; Schweich, 2008; Neumann, 2009). In fact, there were already signs that the UK government, as lead nation, was being pressed by Downing Street to accept a more limited spraying programme; hence its support for ground-based spraying in early 2007 (Cowper-Coles, 2011: 84). Further increases in cultivation would have fundamentally changed the nature of the policy debate. Once again, unfavourable metrics and the narrative surrounding them pushed drug control up the priority list, as a variety of national and international institutions sought to avert the prospect of aerial spraying and the deleterious effect that many believed it would have on statebuilding efforts.

The Provincial Context: in the Firing Line Again

For precisely the same reasons as in the 2004/5 growing season, Nangarhar was going to feature prominently in any reinvigorated effort to reduce opium poppy cultivation by the Afghan government and the international community. The US lead in Nangarhar, the strategic importance of the province as a conduit for supplies to Kabul and the scale of development meant there were growing concerns over the resurgence in cultivation and its implications. The achievements in reducing cultivation in 2005 added to the pressure to enforce a ban in the province in the 2007/8 growing season.

In 2007, however, the conditions were in place for a more comprehensive opium ban. For one, the governor's political ambitions, with a possible eye on running for president in 2009, made him an enthusiastic advocate for counternarcotics efforts that would win him support among the international community. In fact, his ambition was such that there were rumours that he himself advocated aerial spraying and was willing to support efforts to introduce it into the province.

Also, by the fall of 2007, Governor Shirzai had consolidated his political position in the province with both formal and informal institutions, as well as with successive leaders of the PRT (Mukhopadhyay, 2009a). With regard to formal institutions, by 2007 he had built strong relationships with many former *mujahidin* commanders who were employed in the district authorities and who previously had been allied with the Arsala family, but now relied on Shirzai for patronage. He had also succeeded in dominating the security agencies within the province, subordinating them to his own ad hoc structures, including the establishment of a Military Commission of military, police and intelligence officers (Mukhopadhyay, 2014).

In terms of informal institutions, the governor had invested heavily with tribal elders, sometimes appointing them to official positions, and built relationships with local entrepreneurs. Ad hoc payments from these local businessmen, taxes such as the Nangarhar Reconstruction Fund and a share of the duties imposed on the cross-border trade at Torkham also allowed the governor to offer the largesse needed to build patronage and extend his reach into the rural areas (Mukhopadhyay, 2014; Rosenberg, 2009; Goodhand and Mansfield, 2010: 12).

The significant increase in the presence of US military assets in the province as part of the counterinsurgency effort in the east also paved the way for an effective ban during the 2007/8 growing season (Kemp, 2010: 39). These assets, along with Afghan National Security Forces (ANSF), were increasingly deployed in the districts bordering Pakistan, where the insurgency had been gaining ground in 2007 and where the resistance to the previous opium ban had been most pronounced (Kemp, 2010: 34). Forward Operating Bases (FOBs) were established in Chapahar, Khogiani and in Achin in 2007. There was an increase in the number of checkpoints in the southern districts in mid-2007, and house searches became a more regular feature in the bazaars and villages in the remote rural areas where state presence had previously been limited. In the spring of 2008, the 101st Airborne Division provided a battalion air wing offering greater mobility for US and Afghan forces in the southern districts (Kemp, 2010: 36, 39).

Development investments in the province were also having an effect by the fall of 2007. Infrastructural projects (particularly roads), started under the governorship of Hajji Din Muhammad, were finished, facilitating the transport of goods to the major markets in Peshawar and Kabul. The increase in US military assets in the province was matched by the growth in development funds available to the military (Mukhopadhyay, 2014), as well as USAID-administered programmes aimed at delivering on both development and COIN objectives. By fiscal year 2009, it was estimated that the province was receiving US$100 million in US development activities (SIGAR, 2010: ii). The National Priority Programs had also extended their reach across the province with the National Solidarity Program and the National Emergency Employment Program expanding into southern districts. A comprehensive long-term plan for the province known as 'Nangarhar Inc' was being developed, budgeted at US$1.1 billion (Nangarhar PRT, 2007: 62).

Finally, although of much less significance in Nangarhar than the influx of US resources and the governor's success in bolstering his political position, the economic conditions in the province also favoured a reduction in opium production. High world food prices and growing insecurity in Pakistan had led to a 183 per cent rise in the price of bread and cereals between May 2007 and

April 2008. At the same time, the farmgate price of opium fell to levels that had not been observed since before the Taliban declared their prohibition in July 2000. Such was the decline in the terms of trade between opium and wheat that in parts of the country where opium yields were more marginal, farmers were able to obtain more wheat by growing it on their own land than by producing opium and exchanging it for wheat (Mansfield, 2009a). Consequently, as with the Taliban prohibition and the ban imposed in the 2004/5 growing season, Governor Gul Aga Shirzai was able to draw on the farmers' genuine concerns about food security and their natural preference for wheat production to press for further reductions in opium poppy cultivation.

The Local Context: Conflating Counterinsurgency and Counternarcotics Objectives

With international, national and provincial institutions aligned behind a renewed opium ban and political, military and economic conditions favouring implementation, Governor Shirzai was well placed to deliver significant reductions in cultivation in 2008. As his predecessor had done in the 2004/5 growing season and the Taliban before that, he prioritised deterring planting through patronage and the threat of eradication and arrest. District authorities and tribal elders were co-opted into persuading the farmers in their area of the risks of engaging in opium poppy cultivation through a combination of direct payments and offers of largesse (Mukhopadhyay, 2014; Mansfield, 2009b:12).

The governor himself mounted a proactive campaign, visiting many of the district centres, as well as the more remote parts of the province, such as Shadal Bazaar in upper Achin, to inform the rural population of the government's decision to ban opium. Promises of development assistance were a consistent part of the discussion during these visits, as were the demands of Western countries that opium production should stop. As with the ban imposed by Hajji Din Muhammad, the arrest of farmers who ignored the government's warnings and persisted with planting proved catalytic in deterring cultivation in the lower-lying districts in the 2007/8 growing season.

In contrast to the ban imposed in the 2004/5 growing season, Governor Shirzai's counternarcotics efforts led to the complete cessation of opium poppy across Nangarhar, including the more remote parts of Achin and Khogiani. Like the Taliban, Governor Shirzai succeeded in projecting state power into even the most peripheral parts of the province. In fact, the arrests during the planting season, designed to deter cultivation in other districts, were in the Mahmand valley of upper Achin—an area that did not abandon cultivation in the 2004/5 growing season due to the resistance of the local population, and where even the Taliban's ban had been challenged in 2000/1. The pre-planting campaign was so successful in deterring cultivation that in the spring of 2008 there were few signs of opium poppy anywhere, and only 26 hectares of opium poppy needed to be destroyed (UNODC/MCN, 2008: 72).

What made the ban so much more effective than the one imposed by Hajji Din Muhammad was the population's increased fear of violence. In particular, the backdrop of a significant increase in the number of US military forces on the ground allowed the governor to conflate the counterinsurgency campaign with counternarcotics efforts in the minds of many farmers. The establishment of Forward Operating Bases, increases in road checkpoints and raids on household compounds all helped to raise the rural population's perception of the capacity to enforce a ban within the province (Mansfield, 2008a: 25).

While the security measures pursued by the US military were ostensibly aimed at the presence of insurgents in the southern districts, farmers did not see them as such. Rumours that US soldiers were directly involved in delivering counternarcotics messages in the districts led to a perception that the US military's primary goal in the province was drug control. When opium was discovered in household compounds and farmers arrested by US forces, who were actually in search of insurgents, it reinforced this view.[6] The governor was also alleged to have played upon this impression, informing the residents of Achin during a meeting in November 2007: 'You should not grow poppy! I don't have the power to protect you and your land from US forces' (Mansfield, 2008b).

In October 2007, tribal elders from Achin complained to the governor about the security measures imposed in the southern districts. The rural elite pledged to the governor that they would not cultivate opium poppy on condition that there would be no permanent presence of US military forces in Achin. Part of this agreement also stipulated that the elders would not give the Taliban access through the district as they travelled between Pakistan and Afghanistan.

Co-opting the rural elite of Achin into supporting the ban proved critical to the compliance of other parts of Loya Shinwar, as well as other tribes within the province. The cooperation of a number of influential elders, in particular Malik Niaz, a Sepai tribesman from the Mahmand valley in upper Achin, was of particular significance, given his reputation within the greater Shinwari tribe and in Hezbi Islami Khales (HIK). The fact that the population in the

Mahmand valley supported the ban in 2007/8, but had not complied with Hajji Din Muhammad's earlier counternarcotics efforts, lent further support to the credibility of the campaign (Mansfield, 2008b).

By the end of the season, Gul Aga Shirzai had succeeded in projecting state power into the furthermost valleys of the province and Nangarhar was declared 'poppy free' (UNODC/MCN, 2008: 8). Even the Taliban had not achieved such low levels of production and had faced some resistance in the upper reaches of Achin.[7] While Gul Aga Shirzai deployed many of the tools that both Hajji Din Muhammad and the Taliban had used, it was ultimately the coercive power of the US military forces that the governor drew upon to negotiate a comprehensive ban with local elites and the rural population.

The governor's conflation of the US counterinsurgency effort in the southern districts with counternarcotics proved effective in maintaining low levels of cultivation for two more seasons. In the 2008/9 growing season, raids on household compounds reinforced the perception amongst farmers that the governor and US forces were determined to prevent a return to opium poppy cultivation in the province.

Although the province was not declared 'poppy free' for a second year, only 294 hectares of cultivation were found in the hinterlands of the southern districts of Nangarhar in 2009. Moreover, the rural elite across the southern districts largely maintained support for the ban, playing the role that they had the year before in persuading farmers not to cultivate and informing against those who contravened their instructions. Once again eradication was deployed strategically and was required only in 226 hectares. In the Kabul River valley where the government maintained a significant presence and where increasing levels of development assistance were rolling out, there were few signs of dissent, even in districts like Shinwar where there had been a long tradition of cultivating and trading opium poppy.

Even in the 2009/10 growing season, low levels of opium poppy cultivation were maintained. Three consecutive years of negligible cultivation had never been achieved before in Nangarhar, especially not in the Spinghar piedmont. By the end of the season, only 719 hectares of opium were found, primarily in the upper areas of Sherzad, as well as small amounts in the more remote border areas of Khogiani, Achin and Lalpoor. This time, however, eradication was much more significant than in 2008 and 2009; less in terms of the amount of crop destroyed than with regard to the way that the campaign was conducted in the district of Sherzad—an area of limited statehood (Dalrymple, 2013: 434–5).

Chapter 8 will describe the governor's failure to engage in a process that recognised the negotiated nature of state power in this area, and his decision to push through with an aggressive eradication campaign in Sherzad that proved catalytic. When combined with the constantly changing economic and political terrain in the country, the growing competition for power and patronage among the provincial political elite and the realisation that US military forces would be withdrawing, this act came to symbolise the vulnerability of the state and the potential for rural dissent and rebellion to shift the balance of political power in the province.

Conclusion

This chapter has taken a close look at the imposition of two bans in the province of Nangarhar after the fall of the Taliban regime. Both the ban on opium production imposed by Hajji Din Muhammad and the more enduring prohibition enforced by Gul Aga Shirzai show common features and differences that are worth considering. The first is the role that a variety of international actors and institutions played in implementing each ban. Some—primarily those focused on counternarcotics—helped build the political momentum behind each prohibition, drawing on the impetus of bad metrics and the accompanying discourse on the failure of the Afghan project to provide the incentives for a range of international and national institutions to fall in behind efforts to reduce cultivation.

Other international institutions—typically those more at the periphery of counternarcotics efforts in-country—provided the resources and the unity of purpose with which to press the Afghan authorities to act. Within the development community, this was less a question of political imperatives in the wake of increasing levels of cultivation and more a desire to avoid what they considered 'bad policy': aerial spraying. This motivation has had implications for maintaining a quorum for counternarcotics efforts in Nangarhar and elsewhere. Development institutions have typically been only temporary partners, returning to their 'day jobs' when levels of cultivation have fallen and when the threat of more aggressive eradication efforts has faded.

The second similarity is the way Afghan interlocutors at national, provincial and local levels use reductions in cultivation to bargain with other institutions in the political marketplace—particularly international development donors—for an increase in the flow of development assistance. While in part this appears a genuine effort on behalf of Afghan elites to extract more funds and present themselves as credible interlocutors and patrons to their constituents, it is also used by elites to distance themselves from bans on opium in the eyes of the rural population. By blaming the ban on those higher up the chain, elites in areas of limited statehood can deny their own role in prohibition and, for their political survival, acknowledge the view among rural populations that the continuation of the ban is conditional on development assistance from outside. This display often contradicts the proactive role that many of these actors have played in imposing the ban and the political and financial advantages they have gained from doing so. This strategy of brokerage, where local intermediaries mediate between different audiences and sets of interests, renders any agreement inherently unstable.

The third similarity is the way that both of these bans were imposed: the focus on persuasion and promises of development assistance rather than coercion and violence. Common features of both bans—and indeed the Taliban ban before them—are the drive to dissuade farmers from planting in the first place; the co-option of local elites in the process; and the strategic use of eradication, largely in areas of potential dissent in the southern districts of Nangarhar, as a form of selective/targeted violence (Kalyvas, 2006: 12). This process of negotiation stands in stark contrast to the narrative of state power and control that is often associated with successful efforts to ban drug crop cultivation in Nangarhar and in Afghanistan more generally.

A significant difference between the two bans is the role of foreign coercion. Indeed it is Gul Aga Shirzai's success in drawing on the coercive power of the US military that distinguished his efforts from those of Hajji Din Muhammad, and allowed a ban to be successfully imposed in the southern districts of Nangarhar for three consecutive seasons.

Hajji Din Muhammad's ban can be seen to be built around a more endogenous political bargain, where sub-national and local elites gained the compliance of the rural population in an attempt to obtain patronage and financial support from both foreign and national institutions. The threat of violence was part of this political process but was more implied than real and, being reliant on Afghan politico-military actors, was perceived by the rural population to be regulated by local norms, including the role of negotiation. By contrast, the ban imposed by Gul Aga Shirzai can be viewed as exogenous in nature: a function of the heavier footprint of the international effort at the time and what Suhrke (2011: 9) has referred to as 'the systemic bias towards deeper and deeper involvement in response to the emerging signs of problems'. Here we see the role that foreign actors have played in 'distorting the political marketplace', particularly in what was perceived by the rural population as the USG's unconditional support for the governor and his efforts to ban opium.

While Gul Aga Shirzai's close association with the US military allowed him to establish the appearance of state power in areas of limited statehood and set a precedent in drug control in the province, it also inflated his sense of his own power and ultimately denigrated his standing with the rural population. Over time, drawing on the coercive power of US military forces undermined the legitimacy of Shirzai in the eyes of those in the Spinghar piedmont, in the same way that the authority of the PDPA was challenged by its reliance on the Soviet army. The governor's inability to travel to the southern districts without US military support, the threat of US military action against villages that did not comply with Shirzai's demands, his aggressive pursuit of eradication in Sherzad, and ultimately the duration of the opium ban in these upper areas were all viewed as the acts of someone who did not fully understand his rural constituency and how to engage in politics in areas of limited statehood.

8

THE BAN UNRAVELS

Introduction

To map the reasons for the collapse of the opium ban in Nangarhar between 2010 and 2013, this chapter draws on the political economy and rural livelihoods frameworks detailed in Chapters 2 and 3. It situates the collapse of the ban within an analysis of the shifting political alliances within the province and between the governor and the administration in Kabul, with a concurrent deterioration in the welfare of the rural population in areas of limited statehood on the borders with Pakistan.

The chapter is divided into two sections and a conclusion. The first section discusses developments at the political centre of the province—the networks and rivalries within the provincial political elite—and the relationships between the provincial elite and the rural constituents from whom they drew political legitimacy and military power. The second section examines the effect of the second opium ban on rural areas, with an emphasis on the bargains reached between the provincial and rural elites and rural communities. It documents the economic opportunities that were made available or denied to different groups within the rural population, tracing the livelihood trajectories of the population during the 2011/12 growing season (Risse et al., 2011). The conclusion differentiates between the areas in which the ban has been largely maintained and those in which opium poppy has returned.

Chapter 7 described the period between 2005 and 2010 during which Governor Gul Aga Shirzai presided over Nangarhar as a 'model' province, extending the writ of the state into some of the most remote parts of the province. However, after four years of relative stability, the security situation began to deteriorate in late 2009. There was a growing sense that Shirzai was no longer the dominant force in provincial politics. Among the rural population there was growing disquiet about his close relationship with the US military presence, the deteriorating security situation in the southern districts, and Shirzai's unwillingness to travel much beyond the city of Jalalabad without logistical support from his foreign backers.

By 2010, the governor was isolated and relied heavily on support from the USG. Karzai increasingly kept Shirzai at a distance. Within Nangarhar, disputes over the distribution of rents and government positions and patronage, as well as personal acrimony, had led to the regrouping of old *jihadi* alliances and the formation of new coalitions against the governor. The competition for control over state institutions had become increasingly intense with the resurgence of prominent former *jihadi* commanders who were elected to national and provincial representative bodies in 2009 and 2010. Growing discontent in the countryside allowed insurgents to consolidate their position in the southern districts, particularly in the district of Sherzad after a poorly managed eradication campaign in April 2010.

Opium production and efforts to control it played a critical role in the political crisis in Nangarhar. By 2011, the province-wide ban on opium production imposed by Governor Shirzai in the 2007/8 growing season was showing signs of stress. A return of opium production in the southern districts of Achin, Khogiani, Nazian, Pachir wa Agam, Chapahar, Sherzad and Deh Bala in the 2011/12 growing season was followed by widespread cultivation in 2013. Discontent over the impact of the opium ban on the rural economy of the southern districts manifested itself in violent resistance. State institutions, including the ANA, were unable to impose another year of prohibition on large parts of the rural population. The rural elite that had once facilitated the state's imposition of the ban in these areas was increasingly marginalised in the face of growing rural discontent and rising insurgency. In the face of the growing political crisis in the province, there were concerns that cultivation would return to the low-lying districts of Shinwar and Bati Kot in 2014, with Nangarhar again becoming one of the major opium-producing provinces in Afghanistan.

But how did this happen? How did a province that was once viewed as a model of Afghan counternarcotics efforts return to widespread cultivation, following such a rapid reduction in the amount of poppy grown and three successive years of negligible opium production? Why did some of the main advocates for prohibiting opium production abandon their drug control efforts? What fuelled the growing hostility to the provincial authorities and the support for the insurgency, and how did it take hold in the upper areas of Achin, where rural leaders had taken such a firm position against both the Taliban and opium production? Finally, why did cultivation remain negligible in some districts, while in others opium poppy was almost the only crop to be seen? Would the ban hold in areas with a history of state encapsulation and finally where negligible levels of cultivation were accompanied by a sustained period of economic growth and improvements in the lives and livelihoods of much of the rural population?

Politics at the Centre: The Return of the Nangarhari Elite

Governor Shirzai had used his backing by the USG and the Afghan government to dominate the institutions of power in the province and either to subdue or to reach an accommodation with many of those in the Nangarhari political elite who had previously held power. The successful ban on opium production was seen as an indicator of his capacity to project state power and gain the acquiescence of the population in even the most remote parts of the province where his predecessor, Hajji Din Mumhammed, had failed.

There were suggestions that the governor would run against Karzai in the presidential elections of 2009 (Radio Free Europe, 2008). A visit by Senator Barack Obama to Jalalabad in July 2008 and Shirzai's attendance at President Obama's inauguration in January 2009 spawned speculation that the USG would support the governor's candidacy (Rosenberg, 2009). In Kabul, the concerns over Shirzai's popularity led to rumours that President Karzai had made a number of personal appeals to the governor to withdraw his candidacy.

In May 2009, Shirzai announced that he would not run for president and would back the incumbent. Significantly, the announcement of his withdrawal was accompanied by a visit to Jalalabad by his old adversary in Kandahar, Ahmed Wali Karzai, the brother of the president. This event was interpreted locally as a sign that Shirzai would be rewarded with a senior cabinet post in return for his decision not to run (Wafa and Gall, 2009).

In hindsight, Shirzai's decision to propose himself (or allow others to suggest his candidacy) for president and then to withdraw was not a wise one. Once he had decided not to run, he lost much of his political leverage over President Karzai. The president failed to promote him to a cabinet post in

2010—specifically the desirable position of Minister of the Interior—and there were rumours that he might be transferred to another governorship in 2011. These events exposed how little political capital Shirzai had in Kabul and suggested that he was largely relying on US support to retain his position as governor. Despite growing concerns for his safety and numerous reports of his request to be transferred, the governor was seen to languish in Nangarhar, making him vulnerable to his political opponents in the province who, by the close of 2009, were growing in number and strength.

Encircling the 'Bulldozer'

The elections for the Nangarhar Provincial Council in 2009 and the parliamentary election in 2010 further weakened Shirzai and tilted political power in the province back towards the *jihadi* commanders and the ruling elite that had gained prominence during the anti-Soviet resistance. The old guard of *jihadist* commanders had been manoeuvred out of office in the province in the early years of the Karzai administration and, in many cases, had 'retired' to Parliament. They joined with a new generation of politicians from the influential Arsala family in an attempt to oust the governor from office and regain control of the province's political institutions.

Unlike his political opponents, the governor could claim no popular mandate. In fact, he was in a more precarious position; he owed his position to a president who was increasingly perceived as weak and who, as we have seen, showed little favour to Shirzai. His other patrons were the US military forces whom the rural population was increasingly blaming for civilian casualties and for the imposition of the poppy ban (Mansfield, 2009a, 2009b).

Of particular importance was the fact that the Provincial Council and parliamentary elections delivered political office to the next generation of leaders from the Arsala family, including two of Hajji Qadir's sons—Hajji Zahir and Hajji Jamal—as well as their cousin Nasratullah, the son of Hajji Din Muhammad. Hajji Zahir was elected to the Wolesi Jirga; Hajji Jamal and Nasratullah to the Provincial Council. Events since 2009 indicate that the election of this new generation of the Arsala family was catalytic. It provided the vehicle for the former *jihadists* and their families to plot against the governor, using both formal state institutions and the informal power they had generated through local patronage networks and the threat of violence (Mukhopadhyay, 2014; Mansfield, 2011b).

The Arsala family has been a powerful force in Nangarhar and national politics for generations. Originally from the district of Hesarak, the family settled in Surkhrud where they maintained significant landholdings. During the *jihad* against the Soviets, the brothers Abdul Haq and Hajji Qadir were prominent commanders in HIK, the Hezbe Islami party of Yunous Khales, while a third brother, Hajji Din Muhammad, was the political deputy to Khales himself. Following the *mujahidin* capture of Nangarhar, Hajji Qadir[1] took up the position of head of the Eastern Council in 1991, before being finally expelled by the Taliban in 1996. After the fall of the Taliban, the family returned to its traditional role with senior positions in government: Hajji Qadir became Governor of Nangarhar as well as Minister of Interior until his assassination in July 2002, after which Hajji Din Muhammad was appointed governor. When Hajji Din Muhammad was removed from his post in Nangarhar in 2005, he was transferred to the governorship in Kabul. With the removal of Hajji Din Muhammad, a generation of the Arsala family that had fought against the Soviets and occupied the most senior positions of power in Jalalabad subsequently graduated to national politics, and a new generation took centre stage in Nangarhar: Hajji Zahir, Hajji Jamal and Nasratullah.

Since Hajji Zahir's election to the Wolesi Jirga in 2010, and after his appointment as deputy speaker in early 2012, he actively worked against Gul Aga Shirzai, accusing him of corruption and of responsibility for the deterioration of the security situation in the province. He was joined in his efforts to remove the governor by his brother Hajji Jamal, who was elected to the Nangarhar Provincial Council in 2009, despite his legendary reputation for violent and predatory behaviour (Mansfield, 2012). Their cousin Nasratullah was also elected to the Provincial Council in 2009 (Foschino, 2011b). Despite some differences with Hajji Jamal over the leadership of the Council, Nasratullah aligned himself with his cousins to try to oust Shirzai in 2011. Other members of the alliance to remove Shirzai were Fraidoon Mohmand, a member of the Wolesi Jirga and former HIK commander, as well as an old opponent of the Arsalas, Hazrat Ali, the Pashai commander who had been provincial police chief until 2004 before becoming a Member of Parliament. This group also drew on the support of influential rural *maliks* and former comrades from HIK, such as Malik Niaz from the Mahmand valley in Achin, to press for the removal of Shirzai, both directly and through President Karzai (Jawad, 2011; Foschini, 2011a).

Among the contending theories about what provoked the attempt to unseat the governor, the most prevalent focuses on a breakdown in the arrangement between Shirzai and members of the alliance over the division of unofficial payments at the Torkham border crossing (Jawad, 2011). Complaints also circulated that the governor monopolised reconstruction contracts and did not share the revenues generated from the Nangarhar Reconstruction Fund. Locally, most people simply believed that the old *jihadi* elite wished to regain control over the key positions of power that they had held in the initial years of the Karzai administration.

While unsuccessful in its bid to remove Governor Shirzai in 2011, the alliance between the Arsala family and the other *jihadi* commanders persisted. Although they became more restrained in their efforts to oust the governor, attempts to curtail their worst excesses proved ineffective. For example, in March 2012 Hajji Jamal was arrested following allegations that he was behind a series of robberies and kidnappings of local businessmen (Hashmi, 2012a). He was released from captivity in mid-April 2012, after which he immediately staged a parade through the streets of Jalalabad, bringing traffic to a standstill. This act showed the population that he could act with impunity and that it was only a question of time before the next generation of the Arsala family took over the reins of office in Nangarhar.

Making Friends with Other People's Enemies

Although Shirzai retained his position as governor during the president's removal of a number of governors in September 2012, he became increasingly marginalised within the province (Hodge and Sultani, 2012). The population and officials typically referred to the governor as a spent force, in power only because President Karzai did not know what to do with him. By keeping him in Nangarhar, the president prevented Shirzai from returning to his home province of Kandahar, where his influence within the Barakzai tribe, his ambitions and his wealth would unsettle the political order that continued to favour the Karzai family and their Popalzai tribe.

Recognising how politically vulnerable he was in Nangarhar, Shirzai built relationships with those who opposed the Arsala family and their old *jihadi* allies. In particular, he drew on the support of the surviving family members of another *jihadi* commander and bitter opponent of the Arsalas, Hajji Zaman Ghamsharik, as well as other members of the rural elite who feared a return to the old political order.

The reasons for the rift between the Arsala family and Hajji Zaman were well known. Hajji Zaman left Afghanistan for Pakistan (and then France) in 2002 after being accused of planning the assassination of Hajji Qadir. His repeated attempts to return to Afghanistan—on some occasions at the invitation of President Karzai—were reportedly blocked by Hajji Zahir. In 2007, Hajji Zaman's brother, Aman Khairi, was arrested and imprisoned in Afghanistan, accused of being involved in the murder of Hajji Qadir, as well as of being an informant for the DEA with information on Ahmed Wali Karzai, the president's brother (Risen, 2006). In 2009, following the media-tion of the president's adviser, Aman Khairi was released from prison in time to run an unsuccessful campaign for the Wolesi Jirga. At the same time, Hajji Zaman Ghamsharik's exile was lifted, and he returned to Kabul (Nordland, 2010a). However, in February 2010 Hajji Zaman was killed in a suicide attack, along with fourteen others, while visiting the Chemtala refugee camp on the border of Khogiani and Surkhrud (ibid.).

Locally, many believed that Hajji Zahir was behind the attack and that Hajji Zaman was killed in revenge for the murder of Hajji Qadir in July 2002. While both sides denied involvement in the murder of each other's fathers, there remained considerable suspicion that the families agreed on a truce from the desire to avoid a protracted violent conflict that would have imposed signifi-cant losses of lives and capital and disrupted their business interests in the area.

While the murder of Hajji Zaman Ghamsharik did not lead to an outbreak of violence between his family and the Arsalas, it did herald new entrants into the political order in the form of an alliance between Gul Aga Shirzai; Hajji Zaman's brother, Aman Khairi; and Hajji Zaman's son, Jawed Zaman (Jawad, 2010). Other allies of Gul Aga Shirzai in 2011 included those who also opposed the return of the old *jihadi* political order. For instance, following the attempt to unseat the governor in February 2011, a number of tribal elders sent a delegation to Kabul to request that the president keep the governor in his post. This group resented their exclusion from the original alliance to oust Shirzai, but were also concerned about the potential return of a dominant clique of *jihadi* commanders to positions of power in the province. At the time, some of the elders who attended the meeting with the president and requested that the governor stay on in Nangarhar claimed that they were motivated not by support for Shirzai but by defiance towards the Arsala fam-ily and their allies (Hewad, 2011; Mansfield, 2011b).

However, by 2012 even this group showed signs of abandoning the gover-nor, and there were indications that the multiple alliances and business deals that Shirzai had entered into since moving to the province were further under-mining his political base. In particular, the numerous land grabs that had taken place with his explicit or implicit consent became an increasing source of tension in the province. For example, in April 2012 prominent Mohmandi elders who had advocated retaining the governor in 2011 spoke out publicly against Shirzai's alleged involvement in a land grab in Rodat (Zaher, 2012). The land dispute between the Alisherkhel and Sepai in Achin also created a fissure between the governor and Malik Niaz of the Shinwari tribe in upper Achin, who had been an important ally in the implementation of the poppy ban and a protagonist in tribal efforts to exclude the Taliban from the Spinghar piedmont.

It became increasingly clear that Shirzai's multiple—and often conflicting—bargains with elites in Kabul and in Nangarhar were fragile and showing signs of strain. Maintaining political order became increasingly difficult. In part this was simply a function of the years that the governor had been in office and the cumulative exposure the population and elites had to agreements that were reneged upon, promises that were not met and political alliances that were highly unstable. The governor also saw his authority challenged by a further round of provincial and parliamentary elections that delivered government posts in Kabul and in Jalalabad to the old *jihadi* commanders and their families. The insurgency began to gain ground in the southern districts, limiting the physical space in which the state could operate, as described in the next section. This served as yet another reminder of the governor's growing weakness.

Most importantly, time revealed that Gul Aga Shirzai lacked the backing of Kabul and was only tolerated by the central government. This made him all the more vulnerable to an indigenous political elite that believed it had a right to rule the province. With what was believed to be his closest ally—the US military—showing increasing signs of impatience with the governor's performance in 2012, the growing number of allegations of corruption against him (Hodge and Sultani, 2012) and the announcement of US troop withdrawal in 2014, the governor knew that he had few powerful allies left in the province. His alleged business interests in construction and land development, as well as his control over the Nangarhar Reconstruction Fund—none of which he could transfer to another province—made his removal from office all the more appealing to an indigenous political elite keen to regain its control over state power and the governor's 'commercial interests'.

Beyond the Politics of Personalities: An Analysis of the Changing Political and Economic Circumstances of Rural Constituents

Having experienced the loss of power in 1996 when the Taliban took Jalalabad, the political elite in Nangarhar were acutely aware of how quickly existing political settlements could collapse and new ones form, and how today's political allies can quickly become tomorrow's adversaries (and vice versa). However, the fight for power in Nangarhar should not just be seen solely through the prism of the interests and bargains of the provincial political elite. This group is not autonomous; it derives part of its power from its capacity to draw political and, if necessary, military support from its rural constituents.

In addition to the political backing of Kabul and the military and financial backing of the USG, Gul Aga Shirzai enjoyed considerable support from the rural population. This was largely due to his ability to deliver development assistance (Mukhopadhyay, 2014) and the relationships he had developed with influential tribal elders such as Malik Usman and Malik Niaz of the Shinwaris.

There are tiers of 'mini-bargains' and conflicts that tie the interests of those in outlying districts of Nangarhar to elite groups in Jalalabad and Kabul. A failure by either local or provincial elites to promote the interests of rural constituents can lead to the withdrawal of support, if not direct opposition, from what is typically an armed rural population—one that has historically drawn on the support of neighbouring countries if it feels the need to re-arm. The precarious position of an elite that often stands only as 'first among equals' is made all the more difficult by the presence of political and military adversaries within the elite who are adept at capitalising on the failure of their rivals to respond to the interests of the rural population. Consequently, elite groups, be they in Jalalabad or in the more peripheral districts, need to be perceived as serving the interests of their various rural constituents if they are not to find themselves outmanoeuvred by an opponent and rejected by the very people they claim to represent.

The challenges of appearing to meet the demands of rural constituents are all the more problematic in Nangarhar where there are multiple and often conflicting interests at play, and where the resources for largesse are largely derived from external agents: donors, the military, the centre in Kabul and the rents generated by the cross-border trade. There is, of course, also the presence of armed insurgents whom the elite cannot simply reject, particularly in the border districts where there is heavy support for populist messages that include the argument for opium production. Although members of the rural elite may be tied to the state in Jalalabad, they need to find ways to accommodate insurgents if they are to minimise the risk of violence directed at themselves, and maintain their privileged position if there were to be a change in the political order.

This relationship and bargaining tradition between provincial and local elites and the rural population is a function of the history and political economy of specific space and territory. The rural population in some of this space has better resource endowments than others, is less exposed to shocks and crises, and has greater opportunities for diversification between on-farm, off-farm and non-farm income. It is in this highly varied environment that the opium ban imposed by the governor beginning in the 2007/8 growing season played out, affecting the economic position of different sections of the rural population, as well as the life cycles of political alliances. Empirical evidence of these complex factors is found in fieldwork in the districts of Kama, Surkhrud, Shinwar, Achin and Khogiani. These districts can be divided into areas of consolidated statehood in the valley plains and areas of limited statehood in the hills.

Absorbing Areas of Consolidated Statehood

The History of the Valley Plains

The districts of Kama and Surkhrud offer an example of the areas in Nangarhar that have traditionally had strong bonds with those holding state power in Jalalabad, Kabul and Peshawar. Located in the irrigated plains and close to the provincial centre and the arterial road that runs from Torkham to Kabul, these areas have been encapsulated by the state. They belong to what Ahmed (1977: 21) referred to as the 'qalang'-type Pashtun areas, where agricultural surplus has provided a tax base for the Afghan state and supported the development of landed 'khans'.

Positioned in the Kabul River basin in the districts of Kama, Goshta and Lalpura, the Mohmandi tribe in particular has been known for its 'distinct hereditary leaders', who according to Merk (1984: 17) have had 'intimate relations with the Kabul government'. Noelle (1997: 224) suggests that by the nineteenth century a tribal aristocracy had become entrenched in the Mohmand tribe, shaped by court patronage and with privileged access to economic resources that the ruling elite brought to specific Mohmandi families. Successive Afghan leaders appear to have favoured the Mohmand elite due to the tribe's strategic location and its role as guardians of the Khyber Pass, straddling both sides of the border after the Durand agreement. The Mohmand were so important to Kabul that even Abdul Rahman Khan offered concessions to one of their most important leaders, the Khan of Lalpur, at a time when most tribes were being subjugated (Kakar, 1971).

The alignment of the interests of the Mohmand leadership and the state have induced respective governors in Jalalabad—and on occasion the

British—to call upon the Mohmandi to punish recalcitrant tribes like the Shinwaris when they acted against state interests (Merk, 1984). The enduring and almost symbiotic nature of the relationship between the Afghan state and the Mohmandi tribal elite also led the PDPA to find some of its first allies among the Mohmand tribe when it began a policy of rapprochement in 1981 (Giustozzi, 2000: 150; Hyman, 1982; Roy, 1990).

The same social hierarchy and alliance between the landed elite and the state can be observed in the district of Surkhrud to the south-west of the city of Jalalabad, where the Jabbarkhel division of the Ahmedzai tribe dominates. The adopted home of the Arsala family—a chiefly clan with historical links to the Afghan state—it owns large tracts of land in the district, which it rents out to tenant farmers and sharecroppers from other areas. The Arsala family views the district as their domain, perhaps best highlighted by the fact that in both the 1994/5 and 2002/3 growing seasons the district was a primary target for the counternarcotics efforts of Governor Hajji Qadir.

There is further evidence of the enduring bond between the state and the rural elite in the districts of Kama and Surkhrud. Kama, for example, has been a major recipient of development aid and is one of the few areas in the province where farmers have consistently reported increased project activity; and a burgeoning cross-border trade in smuggled goods passing through Kama from Gandau in the neighbouring district of Goshta has continued unabated in full sight of the authorities in Jalalabad.

In the district of Surkhrud, the state has either allowed land grabs by the provincial elite or recognised that there is little it could do to prevent them. For example, in 2009 Hajji Jamal purchased land south of Kheyrabad and built a township, 'Hajji Qadir Mina', selling the equivalent of 400 square metres for 100,000–200,000 PR. To the east, further desert land was taken by Hajji Zahir and his cousin Sar Malim Akhtar.

The political reality in Surkhrud and Kama is that the interests of those in state power and the rural elite are often synonymous, so much so that the landed elite from these districts have often occupied government posts in Jalalabad. Moreover, the hierarchical social structure in these areas has led to a more compliant population, fearful of both state coercion and the potential for the landed elite to restrict their access to patronage and resources. The state's encapsulation of these areas has allowed it to subjugate the population when required. This includes its efforts to ban opium poppy.

These are also areas where security has been largely left to the ANSF. US military forces could be seen passing through both districts en route to more peripheral and problematic areas along the border with Pakistan—in the case of Kama to their base in Goshta, and in Khogiani to numerous FOBs. The close relationship between the rural elite and those within the administration in Jalalabad also meant that the international community, both civilian and military, was less involved in political patronage and the delivery of development assistance in this area than in areas of limited statehood such as the southern districts bordering Pakistan.

An Area of Economic Surplus

The Kabul River basin in Nangarhar is not an area of consolidated statehood solely because its physical terrain and effective elites facilitate the process of encapsulation, but also because of the economic benefit from the agricultural surplus and trade carried out in the area. This economic activity provides a tax base that has proved to be economically rewarding to the political elite in Nangarhar and Kabul and has led to improvements in income and well-being despite the loss of opium poppy in the 2004/5 growing season.

Located in the Kabul River basin, much of the land in both Surkhrud and Kama is well irrigated and can yield two to three crops per year. Since 2008 there has been a dramatic shift in cropping patterns in these districts. The initial response to the ban in the 2004/5 growing season was to replace opium poppy with a single cash crop, such as green bean in Kama and onion in Surkhrud. In the short term this proved remunerative as traders from Jalalabad and Kabul flowed into the area to purchase these crops in advance at the farm-gate, for onward sale to a burgeoning market in Kabul.

However, following over-production and a dramatic fall in farmgate prices in 2007, it became apparent that this simple single-crop substitution model was not viable. In 2008 and 2009, intercropping and off-season vegetable production, which had initially been seen only in the areas nearest to Jalalabad, began to expand across both Surkhrud and Kama. Farmers began to adopt complex cropping patterns that incorporated a wide range of fall, spring and summer vegetables. Farmers also became more aware of the agricultural prices in different markets and could exploit them due to better access to transportation. Road improvements reduced journey times as well as the amount of rent-seeking en route from the districts to Jalalabad and Kabul. More farmers began transporting vegetables to Jalalabad, Kabul and Peshawar directly, as well as selling them to farmgate traders. Farmers were seen to pool both their crops and the costs of transportation to take goods to Kabul and fully exploit price differentials (Mansfield, 2010).

A good example of crop diversification was described by a farmer in Surkhrud who has been a respondent for this research since 2005. Following the ban on opium production in the 2004/5 growing season, he repeatedly cultivated a combination of wheat and onion on his land in the fall, as well as some maize in the summer. This persisted for many years (but only during the years when there was sufficient irrigation). However, in the 2011/12 growing season, this farmer had grown fresh onion and coriander (sold for 70,000 Pakistani rupees per *jerib*), spinach (7,500 PR per *jerib*), wheat (not harvested), onion (not harvested), as well as tomato and marrow in the spring. Due to flood protection in the river bed in upper Surkhrud, he also cultivated paddy rice in the summer, which he had not been able to do in the past. His two sons also reached working age over the course of the research; they were sent to Kabul to work in the construction industry during the summer months, providing a further source of income diversification. In 2012 other such examples could be seen across both districts and further down the Kabul River valley in Jani Khel in Bati Kot and in parts of lower Shinwar.[2]

Agricultural incomes in the districts of Kama and Surkhrud were further supplemented by the sale of livestock and their by-products. Livestock sales, locally or through cross-border smuggling, earned farmers between 70,000 and 100,000 PR per year. The sale of yogurt, cheese and milk in Jalalabad was also increasingly popular, purchased at the farmgate by traders or sold locally in the bazaar. In Kama one farmer reported selling milk from his three cows in the bazaar in Sray and earning 300–400 PR every day for seven months each year. This was in addition to producing sufficient milk for his family to consume. In Kama and Surkhrud, farmers could earn 2,000–2,500 PR a week in the spring of 2012 processing milk from the same number of cows and selling it as cheese. In both districts farmers reported that there had been assistance from NGOs to support the handling, processing and sale of dairy products.

Kama also saw an increase in local non-farm income opportunities that mitigated the need for family members to join the ANSF permanently, as was common in the more mountainous districts of southern Nangarhar. Local development projects provided an important source of income, and there were increasing opportunities for employment in the private sector, where workers in 2012 were paid 300–400 PR per day for unskilled labour, and up to 800 PR per day for skilled work. Infrastructural projects in both districts and on seized land to the south and east of Surkhrud created short- and medium-term employment opportunities. In 2011 and 2012, a growing number of people in the area were working as guards, cooks and other service providers. In addition, there was a notable increase in the number of local households that had purchased cars and tractors to lease.

Employment in Jalalabad was also far easier from Kama and Surkhrud due to proximity, improved roads and reduced travel times. Male family members could work in Jalalabad and return to their families at night, thus conforming to cultural and personal preferences and minimising accommodation costs. Rural households in these areas became adept at exploiting the wage differentials in Jalalabad and Kabul, sending male family members to work in the provincial centre in the winter and spring, where they were paid in Pakistani rupees, and then to Kabul in the summer where they were paid at a higher wage rate in Afghanis. Moreover, wage labour rates in Jalalabad and Kabul continued to rise between 2011 and 2012, increasing from 400–450 PR a day to 500 PR per day for unskilled work; and from around 900–1,000 PR to 1,100–1,300 PR per day for skilled work, such as masonry.

The loss of opium poppy was not compounded by co-variate shocks in either district. Improvements to prevent flooding from the river in upper Surkhrud and work on the intake in Kama improved access to irrigation in areas that were previously vulnerable to drought. The security situation in both districts was also more permissive than any other district in the province, facilitating the trade in vegetable production and the provision of development assistance.

While individual households experienced idiosyncratic shocks, usually due to the death of a family member or a protracted illness, the availability of on-farm, off-farm and non-farm income opportunities made it easier for them to manage these shocks without selling long-term productive assets or mortgaging or selling land. There was a loss of employment opportunities in Peshawar following the expulsion of Afghans without Pakistani identity cards in 2007, and then due to growing insecurity along the border in 2008 after Benazir Bhutto's death. But this was more than compensated for by the growth in wage labour opportunities in Kabul and Jalalabad.

In fact, such was the economic growth in these area that rents in Kama rose from around 80–100 *seer* per *jerib*[3] between 2010 and 2012, inflated by a growing demand for land. Farmers in the district referred to the income opportunities that vegetable production had brought.[4] Those who migrated from other districts to Kama and Surkhrud also talked of the greater income opportunities available to them compared with at their point of origin, as well as the lower levels of violence and conflict in Kama.[5]

In sum, the districts of Kama and Surkhrud were favoured, benefitting from their strategic position along the Kabul River basin and spanning the transit route to Peshawar. This geographic advantage—combined with the economic potential of the area and the clear benefits of improved access to public goods over the last decade—helped strengthen the government's position in the Kabul River valley. In these districts opium poppy had all but been forgotten. The ban on opium was not only met with compliance in these areas when it was initially imposed by Hajji Din Muhammad during the 2004/5 growing season; there was no resurgence in 2007 or in 2013 when the rest of Nangarhar returned to widespread opium poppy cultivation.

Managing Areas of Limited Statehood

The southern districts of Nangarhar stand in stark contrast to the irrigated plains of Kama and Surkhrud in the Kabul River valley. Historically the Afghan state failed to concentrate the means of violence in these districts on the border of Pakistan, and has only been able to make its presence felt intermittently. Even when the state benefited from the military and financial backing of foreign powers—the British and the Soviet Union, and, following the collapse of the Taliban regime, the US—it only obtained the temporary acquiescence of the population in the Spinghar piedmont.

This border area is dominated by the Shinwari and Khogiani tribes, each of which is divided into sub-tribes known as *khels*. Loya, or Greater, Shinwar covers the five administrative districts of Achin, Deh Bala, Dur Baba, Nazian and Shinwar (also known as Ghani Khel).[6] With a population that spans a contiguous area from the Pakistan border in the south to the main arterial road between Torkham and Kabul in the north, the Shinwari tribe has been a dominant force in provincial politics for almost four centuries. It has a long history of resisting state interference, including leading the rebellion against Amanullah in 1928. It straddles the international border and has strong links with Pakistan.

The Khogiani tribe has a traditional enmity with the Shinwaris, exacerbated by British and successive Afghan leaders drawing on tribal militias or levies to quell rebellious rival tribes (Kakar, 1971: 95; 1979: 11). In the districts of Pachir Wa Agam, Sherzad and Khogiani in south-western Nangarhar, bordering Pakistan, the Khogiani tribe has opposed state intrusion in their affairs. In the twentieth century, the tribe produced one of the most prominent anti-Soviet leaders, Mawlawi Mohammed Younis Khales (1919–2006), leader of HIK, the Khales faction of Hezb-e Islami (Dorronsoro, 2005: 152n23). Following the death of Younis Khales in 2006, his son, Anwar al

Haq Mujahid, became a prominent figure in the insurgency against the Karzai government. He formed the Tora Bora Military Front from elements of HIK, and aligned its members with the Taliban insurgency.

Both the Shinwari and Khogiani tribes are what Scott (2010) refers to as 'the self-governing peoples' at the periphery of the state. Akbar would define them as '*nang*' Pashtuns—those who live with honour, free from the domination of others—and would contrast them with the '*qalang*' Pashtuns of the irrigated valleys, in areas such as Kama and Surkhrud, who have been subjugated by the state and submitted to taxation (Ahmed, 1977: 20). The Shinwari and Khogiani tribes inhabit more hostile terrain, where arable land is scarce and agricultural surpluses are limited (Barfield, 2000: 7). Both tribes have mounted a number of armed rebellions against state interference and have on occasion fled to even more remote territory to prevent state capture (Gregorian, 1969: 132; Noelle, 1997: 48; Kakar, 1997: 177–8).

As with Pashtun groups in the lower areas, the political order amongst the Shinwari and Khogiani tribes is one of segmentary allegiance based on multiple and dynamic relational bonds (Marsden and Hopkins, 2011). However, as opposed to the Mohmandi and Ahmedzai tribes in the Kabul River basin, no permanent elite has emerged from the Shinwari and Khogiani tribes. While there are tribal elders with whom the state can engage and construct a dialogue, the highly developed sense of equality among these tribes means that the support that the elites receive from their rural constituents is conditional, localised and largely derived from the capacity to extract patronage from the central authorities while at the same time resisting outside interference—particularly policies that do not conform to local values (Barfield, 2000). Intratribal rivalries and a multiplicity of small landowners further constrain the development of a stable political leadership with which the state might foster more permanent bonds (Goodhand and Cramer, 2002).

Given the challenges of the physical and political terrains and the absence of obvious resources for rent extraction, the Afghan state has seen little benefit in looking to conquer the areas inhabited by the Shinwari and Khogiani tribes. It has instead sought to manage better the threat that these populations might present to the interests of the state and what Scott (2009) refers to as the 'state-governed peoples' in the valleys. These tribes have often been allowed to avoid state taxes and conscription and have succeeded in resisting the interference of the provincial authorities in Jalalabad (Noelle, 1997: 172, 194; Barfield, 2000). In fact, rather than pay taxes to the central state like those in the lower districts of Nangarhar, the tribal elite in these southern districts typically received allowances during much of the eighteenth and nineteenth centuries (Kakar, 1971: 93–4). Furthermore, they were granted the authority to impose levies on those transiting through their territories (Hopkins, 2008: 29; Gregorian, 1969: 32; Noelle, 1997: 171–4).

The state has accepted its inability to regulate individual and economic behaviour in these border areas (Marsden and Hopkins, 2011: 216). Smuggling has been a mainstay of their economies, linking the population to transnational organisations—including criminal groups—involved in the trafficking of drugs. The state has had little choice but to accept the cultivation of opium poppy and cannabis. Moreover, the state has had to negotiate access to these areas with the tribal leaders. When order has broken down, the state has mounted punitive raids, but when violence has been threatened, the state has usually retreated back to the valleys and rarely sought to occupy these peripheral areas.

The reign of Abdur Rahman Khan (1880–1901)—the 'Iron Amir'—is one of the only periods in Afghan history in which the state sought to govern the remote upper valleys of Nangarhar. However, he achieved dominance, which often proved short-lived, only through brutal suppression of the tribes (Kakar, 1971: 93–101). While Abdur Rahman Khan is credited with establishing the 'first thoroughly centralised regime' and eliminating tribal resistance across Afghanistan by the end of his reign in 1901, the subjugation of the tribes in the southern districts of Nangarhar was hard won (Gregorian,1969: 133–4). It was only in 1892, after a ten-year campaign, that the Shinwari tribe was finally subdued; even then, the 'Iron Amir' found his rule of the territory challenged by Mullah Haddah until 1897 (Edwards, 1996: 64; Nawid, 1997: 592; Kakar, 1971:132).

It is important to differentiate the subdivisions within the Shinwari tribe, the geographical terrain they inhabited and the degree of autonomy they maintained during this period. In his description of the campaign against the Shinwaris, Kakar (1971: 88–100) identifies four sub-groups: the Sangu Khel, the Ali Sher Khel, the Sipah and the Mandozai. The Sangu Khels are described as the most resistant to any rapprochement with Abdur Rahman Khan, even after the other sub-tribes capitulated. The Sangu Khel themselves subsequently divided in 1889, when 'those who lived in the lower parts of the valleys, north of the Nazian glen, accepted terms, while those in the upper parts still asserted their independence' (Kakar, 1971: 99). For three more years this sub-group mounted raids against Abdur Rahman Khan's government, despite repeated attacks that forced them further into the mountains of Spinghar.

During the twentieth century, the Shinwari and Khogiani tribes progressively loosened the grip of Abdur Rahman Khan's successors and exposed the state's inability to impose its policies across their tribal territories. With the end of British subsidy following full independence, the Afghan state had to raise taxes to finance its armed forces. This proved calamitous for Amir Amanullah Khan, the ruler of the country; in 1928 a Shinwari rebellion, joined by the Khogianis, led to the fall of the regime (Edwards, 2002; Saikal, 2006: 87). Since then, successive regimes have recognised the limits of their coercive power in these upper areas. According to Marsden, as early as 1981 the PDPA was seeking to engage with tribal leaders in these areas, offering them greater autonomy (Marsden, 2009: 52). Deals were reached with parts of the Shinwari tribe that fractured their resistance to the communist government but ultimately led to the PDPA having little control over the southern districts of Nangarhar.

As with its predecessors, the Taliban—despite claims of having centralised the means of violence—had an uneasy relationship with the population in these peripheral border districts. Visits to the area during the Taliban regime revealed that state presence was limited to a small number of militiamen located in the district administrator's office. The population argued that it had not been disarmed per se but had consented to refrain from carrying their weapons in public as long as order was maintained. The Taliban prohibition of opium illustrates the negotiated settlements that the leadership had to enter into in these areas. Earlier attempts by Mullah Omar to impose a one-third reduction in opium poppy cultivation in the 1999/2000 growing season were ignored in Nangarhar. As discussed in Chapter 6, while there was compliance with the Taliban ban in the 2000/1 growing season, it was reported that Shinwari tribal elders received direct payments from the Taliban to comply with the ban. The Shinwari were also given preferential access to the donors' mission to appeal for development assistance (Donor Mission, 2001: 6).

After the fall of the Taliban, Hajji Din Muhammad failed to deliver an opium ban in the upper parts of Khogiani and Shinwar during the 2004/5 growing season; these areas actually increased levels of cultivation the following year when the ban continued to be effectively enforced in the lower parts of Nangarhar. In fact, as Chapter 7 shows, it was only the US military presence, along with Governor Shirzai's successful conflation of counterinsurgency and counternarcotics in the minds of the population, that allowed a ban to be imposed in these areas in the 2007/8 growing season. Even then, promises of development assistance were made to communities along with threats for non-compliance (Mansfield, 2008a). Moreover, as seen in subsequent growing seasons, this ban has not endured in the southern districts in the wake of a growing insurgency and the breakdown in the political settlement between the governor, the rural elite and the local population (ibid.).

Pulling Back the Curtain on State Policies in the Southern Districts

Research in the southern districts highlights that elements of the Achin population were again resisting government interference. Foreign occupation and civilian casualties mobilised resistance and added to the resentment the Sepai tribe felt over the provincial government's mishandling of a violent land dispute. These events enhanced the cumulative effect of the ban on opium, imposed since the 2007/8 growing season.

Those members of the rural elite who had acted as principal interlocutors with the state and had supported the government's imposition of the opium ban, and had led both the land grab in the desert north of Sra Kala and the subsequent negotiations with the government, found their position weakened within the tribe. Rivals among the elite took advantage of the growing unpopularity of elders such as Malik Usman (Haiderkhel) and Malik Niaz (Rahimdakhel). By 2012, the state was engaging with interlocutors who were seen as unrepresentative and whose relationship with the state had undermined their support from the rural population. In the eyes of the population, the state was pursuing a foreign-led plan to eliminate opium production. This undermined its legitimacy and that of the tribal elite that supported it.

In Khogiani, the situation was even worse. Here the governor found himself without a rural elite that could marshal the population. Moreover, the eradication campaign of 2012 was met with higher levels of violence than had been seen in Nangarhar for some years: a total of forty-eight dead, of whom forty-five were killed in the district of Khogiani alone. Indicative of the state's diminishing coercive power in Nangarhar, the 2012 eradication campaign did not even attempt to destroy the opium crop in the upper valleys of Khogiani, or in Sherzad, despite increasing levels of cultivation.

My research demonstrates that the breakdown in the political bargain between the rural population and the local and provincial elite should not be seen solely as a reaction to the violent outcome of the land dispute in Achin (described below) and the growing resentment towards the state's coercive policies on opium production in the Spinghar piedmont. The return to opium poppy cultivation was not just an act of political defiance by a disgruntled population; indeed, there was a significant economic component to the growing unrest in these areas that led to farmers transitioning from everyday resistance to open rebellion (Scott, 2009).

The reality is that the majority of households in Achin and Khogiani did not have a viable alternative to opium production and experienced a steady decline in their quality of life due to the imposition of a ban. While enlistment in the ANSF offered some respite for many families, the production of relatively high-value crops such as opium poppy and cannabis enabled rural households to meet their basic needs and potentially accumulate assets so that they could manage risk better (Mansfield, 2011b). The loss of income and the depletion of assets associated with the cumulative impact of the opium ban undermined support for the state and those involved in the implementation of the prohibition.

The Karzai administration, pressed by international military forces, repeated the mistakes of many of its predecessors. It over-extended its reach into the political and economic domains of tribal areas with a history of resisting encapsulation and foreign interference. It drew on the coercive power of foreign military forces to impose a ban on opium poppy and then to counter an attack by tribesmen over a local land dispute. As with past encounters in these areas, by April 2013 the state faced violent resistance and the threat of being pushed back into the Kabul River basin, where it has a longer history of domination.

Evicting the State from Achin: the Shinwari Land Dispute

The land dispute between the Sepai and the Alisherkhel presented a formidable challenge to the central and provincial governments. What began as a conflict between two sub-groups of the Shinwari tribe ended up drawing in political figures from across the province and Kabul. It led to delegations to and from the president and culminated in a firefight with ISAF forces in October 2011, resulting in the death of eighteen Sepai tribesmen and injuries to sixty more.[7]

While foreign forces were involved in the dispute—arming the main protagonists, the Sepai, in October 2009 and during the violent clashes in October 2011—the local population blamed the provincial government and the tribal elite for the conflict. The governor was singled out for opprobrium, on one hand for failing to act as an independent arbiter in the dispute, while on the other for becoming too involved in a 'tribal matter'. Others, including the provincial administration, politicians and the rural elite, were also blamed by the rural population for provoking the dispute in order to serve their own political agendas. In particular, the Sepai tribesmen believed that they incurred the physical, economic and political costs of the land dispute while the tribal elite sought their own economic and political advantage through their relationship with the government. This belief ultimately undermined rural support for both the state and parts of the tribal elite, and—along with the impact of the opium ban—provided an entry point for insurgents in what had once been a bastion of support for the Karzai government in Nangarhar.

The Cause of the Dispute

For many, the Shinwari land dispute finds its roots in the arming of Sepai tribesmen in November 2009. There are various views on who decided to provide weapons to the Sepai following an attack by Afridi Taliban on Malik Niaz's nephews in Achin the month before.[8] Locally there were rumours that it was the PRT that distributed around 400 weapons to Malik Niaz and his men. The Alisherkhel, however, blamed Governor Shirzai, accusing him of favouring the tribe due to his close links with the Sepai Maliks, particularly Malik Usman (Mansfield, 2012).

In public, the governor distanced himself from the decision to provide weapons and the PRT's negotiation of a tribal agreement, known as 'the Shinwari pact' of February 2010. At the time, Shirzai concurred with President Karzai in criticising any intervention that attempted to work directly with the tribes rather than through the central government (Partlow and Jaffe, 2010). The US Embassy in Kabul also distanced itself from the effort to engage directly with the tribe and instructed its diplomats not to meet to discuss the issue (George and Paradiso, 2011).

Regardless of who exactly provided the weapons, it was perceived locally that the USG favoured the Sepai; this unsettled relations both within the tribe and among rivals. One international development worker described the growing confidence of Niaz during their conversations over the years and cited the Malik's claim of having 'US backing'.[9] In mid-February, only a few weeks after signing the Shinwari Pact, Sepai tribesmen occupied the desert land along the main road between Ghani Khel and Sra Kala, opposite established Alisherkhel villages. It remains unclear why the Sepai elders chose to lead a land grab at this juncture. At the time some Sepai farmers reflected on the potential value of the land and how relocating could offer better access to government services such as education, health and water (Mansfield, 2011). Most cited what they believed was a traditional claim on the land, given its location down-stream from the Mahmand valley in Achin in which the Sepai village of Syachob in Shinwar district was located.

At the time the Alisherkhel blamed Governor Shirzai for the land dispute. They claimed that the formation of an armed militia, known as an *arbaki*, under the leadership of Malik Niaz had bolstered the elder's income, confidence and ambitions. They accused Sherzai of providing the Sepai with the tents used to occupy the land, and alleged that the ANP had protected the Sepai while the foundation stones for houses were laid in the desert. The Alisherkhel also claimed that their attempts to meet the governor during the early stages of the dispute were spurned. On 27 February 2010, the Alisherkhel attacked the Sepai tribesmen in the desert, killing fourteen and injuring a number of others.

After these initial deaths, all subsequent efforts to resolve the dispute failed. An early attempt at resolution involved the formation of a *jirga* from all twenty-two districts of Nangarhar, including members from the Mohmandi, Khogiani and Shinwari tribes. This *jirga* met with both Sepai and Alisherkhel elders and took 40,000,000 PR from both sides as *machalgha*, a deposit, to guarantee peace for twelve months.

In April 2010, the *jirga* decided that the desert land west of the road between Ghani Khel and Kahi would be given to the Sepai, while land in the Gurukoh area near the Torkham Bazaar (where the Sepai and Alisherkhel were also in dispute) would be allocated to the Alisherkhel, provided both sides introduced thirty elders who would swear on the holy Koran (*qasam*) that the land was theirs. The Sepai accepted the *jirga's* decision but the Alisherkhel did not, believing both pieces of land belonged to them. Arguing that the decision had been influenced by the governor, the Alisherkhel mounted a delegation of fifty elders to travel to Kabul and requested that the president remove Shirzai from his post.

After this decision, there were a number of further efforts to end the conflict. Numerous Provincial Council members and Members of Parliament from Nangarhar became embroiled. Far from looking to resolve the conflict, most became involved as a way of gaining support from the local population and, more importantly, of either highlighting the failings of Governor Shirzai or coming to his support.

By April 2011, there were reports of more weapons flowing into Achin, and armed men were visible throughout the district of Achin and parts of Upper Shinwar. Vehicle checkpoints were established in both Alisherkhel and Sepai

Photo 1: 'White flower' opium poppy (known locally in the eastern region as spin guli) opening to reveal its capsule, Khogiani district, Nangarhar.

Photo 2: A farmer fertilising his opium crop at the flowering stage, Chaghcharan district, Ghor.

Photo 3: A young boy, no older than eight, helping with the final irrigation of the opium poppy growing season, Dawlat Yar district, Ghor.

Photo 4: A family—including sons and daughters—harvesting opium poppy together, Argo district, Badakhshan.

Photo 5: Itinerant harvesters from Tirinkot, Oruzgan collecting opium gum, Nahre Seraj, Helmand.

Photo 6: An opium capsule lanced using a tool (known locally as a neshtar) typical of the eastern region, Behsud district, Nangarhar.

Photo 7: An opium poppy capsule immediately after being lanced with fresh opium oozing from the fine cuts made by the *neshtar*. This type of *neshtar* made from sharpened metal, cloth and twine was common in Badakhshan in the 1990s but has since been replaced by tools made of wood and razor blades not unlike those found in the southern and eastern regions.

Photo 8: Raw opium gum after it has turned brown, ready for collection, Shinwar district, Nangarhar.

Photo 9: Opium gum being collected using a crude collection tool, known locally as a *rambey*, Mehtarlam district, Laghman.

Photo 10: A small *rambey* typical of the southern and central region, Sharak district, Ghor.

Photo 11: Farmer harvesting opium in Chaghcharan district, Ghor in 2007 where the crop is rarely taller than 50 cm.

Photo 12: A particularly healthy opium crop in Shinwar district, Nangarhar, in 2007 which stood at over 150 cm. This crop was aided by soils that were rested for two years due to a government imposed ban on opium poppy cultivation in both 2005 and 2006.

Photo 13: A young girl collecting opium gum in Darayem district, Badakhshan.

Photo 14: Once full of opium each rambey is emptied into a common pot and then wrapped in poppy leaves and stored, Shinwar district, Nangarhar.

Photo 15: A trader testing opium for its quality and adulterants by drying it on a hot plate, Maiwand district, Kandahar.

Photo 16: The inside of an opium trader's store, complete with two man (the equivalent of 9kg) bags of fresh 'black' opium, dried opium stored in metal pots, scales, and lock-boxes, Kajaki district, Helmand.

Photo 17: A farmer and his opium after harvest, Kajaki district, Helmand. In contrast to eastern Afghanistan, opium is typically stored in polythene bags in quantities of one or two man (the equivalent of 4.5 or 9 kg) in the southern provinces.

Photo 18: A dried cake (chakai) of high quality black (tor) opium. Wrapped in poppy leaves, this chakai would have been the equivalent of one seer (1.2 kg) when fresh, Achin district, Nangarhar.

Photo 19: Children clearing the dried poppy plants from the field, Faizabad district, Badakhshan.

Photo 20; Dried opium capsules at a roadside pharmacist, Faizabad district Badakhshan.

Photo 21: Children holding the dried remnants of opium crops which have been fashioned into toys with the capsules acting as wheels, Shinwar district, Nangarhar.

Photo 22: A crowd of young men surrounding the donors mission that was tasked to investigate the Taliban prohibition of opium poppy in 2001, Kajaki bazaar, Helmand.

Photo 23: A convoy of UN cars en route to Achin district, Nangarhar, during the donors mission examining the Taliban ban, April 2001.

Photo 24: One of the Taliban guard assigned to accompany the donors mission to the Spinghar piedmont, Achin district, Nangarhar.

Photo 25: A shopkeeper in the district bazaar in Baharak, Badakhshan alongside a counter narcotics poster distributed as part of an eradication campaign, December 2006.

territory and manned by armed tribesmen. The conflict also led to the closure of Kahi Bazaar, the administrative centre of Achin, and the relocation of the Alisherkhel students to the high school in Kogha Khel in the lower part of the district. In October 2011, the dispute took a further turn for the worse. In a show of force, the governor went to Ghani Khel with the provincial security commander and demanded that the tribes disarm and leave the desert. He met with elders from both tribes and informed them that if they did not leave within twenty-four hours they would be forcibly disarmed and arrested. They were also instructed by the governor to make a truce (*tigha*) for three years and told that a heavy fine (as much as 10 billion Afghanis) would be imposed on whichever side instigated any fighting.

The tribal elders accepted the governor's terms, but in the confusion of the withdrawal a firefight broke out between the ANP and armed men from the Sepai tribe. The Sepai are alleged to have fired on the ANP using rocket-propelled grenades and automatic weapons, killing one police officer, injuring two others, and destroying two vehicles. In response, the authorities called in ISAF air support, culminating in the deaths of eighteen Sepai and injuries to sixty.

An Unstable Peace

In January 2012, a presidential delegation headed by the president's adviser, Asadullah Wafa, obtained a written commitment from elders of the Sepai and Alisherkhel tribes not to take up arms against each other for three years while the government decided what to do with the land. Locally this agreement was seen to belie the continuing conflict between the Sepai and the Alisherkhel, the Sepai and the provincial authorities—particularly Governor Shirzai—and the deepening tension between the rural population and the rural elite in both tribes.

While most of the Alisherkhel and Sepai elders signed the agreement, there was little sense that the 'peace' would endure. The Sepai argued that, while they accepted the authority of the government to settle the land dispute, the authorities had no jurisdiction to resolve the conflict over the thirty or more Sepai tribesmen who had been killed since February 2010. In fact, the Sepai held the Alisherkhel responsible for these deaths—even those killed by the ISAF—and there were repeated calls to avenge those who had lost family members.

The fragility of the peace was perhaps best illustrated by the fact that even in April 2013 the vast majority of shops remained closed in Kahi, the administrative centre of Achin and Spinghar, and the high school remained divided, as it was in February 2010. Governor Shirzai also stood out as a target of the ire of the Sepai. Such was the hostility towards the provincial authorities that by April 2012 the insurgency had gained a firm foothold in the Mahmand valley to the south of Asadkhel. Here the population increasingly 'opposed the government' and identified themselves as Taliban. Incursions by US forces into the area were repeatedly repelled by armed men, and local researchers were warned not to travel beyond Asadkhel due to the presence of armed insurgents.[10]

In Asadkhel itself there were reports that the Taliban were present during the night, looking for support from the population. It was argued that those Taliban soliciting support in the village were not 'Pakistani' Taliban, but local villagers. There were also claims that the rural elite had reached an accommodation with insurgents in the area[11]—an irony, given that it was the firm stand of these same *maliks* against the Taliban in October 2009, and the subsequent financial and military support they received, that served as a catalyst for the land dispute and ultimately the violent conflict with the government and ISAF.

By 2013, the situation had worsened even more and insurgents had moved farther north. During fieldwork in April 2013, it was the white flag of the Taliban that flew over Shadal Bazaar, the district centre of Spinghar. Opium was once again openly traded in the shops, for the first time since 2008. The political situation in the Mahmand valley had also become more complex with the arrival of Mangal Bagh, a Pakistani militant who many in the area believed was supported in his cross-border operations into Pakistan by the NDS and India. Moreover, rural households seemed to be no longer required to take sides in what was naively seen as a dispute between the state and insurgents. Instead, farmers in these upper areas appeared to transcend this dualistic notion of conflict. Many claimed to have family members in the ANSF, as well as relatives in the Taliban; they took advantage of government services in the form of education and health facilities, which had not been closed by insurgents, yet paid 'taxes' to the Taliban both on their opium production and at the mosque in the form of cash payments known as '*chanda*'.

Those who were most disadvantaged by the loss of the state's capacity to subjugate the population and the withdrawal of US military forces were the local elite who had been so instrumental in extending state power (or at least the appearance of it) into this remote terrain. In fact, the tribal elite that had attempted to maintain a relationship with the government and its unpopular policies were now more ambivalent. They began to reach out to different factions among the insurgents in Mahmand, along with Mangal Bagh, a potential new source of patronage and power. The rural population increasingly viewed the local elite with disdain. They were no longer seen as patrons who could draw on the close ties with the governor and the US military, but as servile to the village. As one respondent put it, 'They are *charrasey* [guard or cleaner]. If our village has work to do with the government or others, we should send them to do the work.'

Yet it was through these tribal interlocutors, and with the backing of US military forces, that the Afghan state had firmly established its presence in these remote areas. With international support, the Karzai administration had extended education and health services in these areas, established the infrastructure for a resident district administration and created an effective security presence. And with the support of local elites and US operational assistance, the government had enforced an effective opium ban in the most remote parts of Achin over three consecutive years, and even longer in some of the more accessible lower valleys. This era came to a resounding climax in Achin in the spring of 2013, as a larger area became out of reach of the state due to rural unrest and direct attacks on state infrastructure and the security forces. The government was also unable to counter resurgent opium poppy cultivation, revealing state weakness again and setting the stage for further cultivation in subsequent growing seasons.

Resisting State Interference: the Opium Ban

As the discussion on the land dispute shows, there has been a steady increase in the rural population's antipathy towards both the state and the rural elite in Achin. However, the land dispute is only part of the picture. The opium ban imposed since the 2007/8 growing season also undermined local support for the provincial government and the rural elite that played its role in the effective prohibition of the crop.

The rural population's condemnation of the tribal elite for its involvement in the opium ban was not instantaneous. In fact, in late 2007, support for the ban by the rural elite was seen as understandable in light of the combined coercive power of the Afghan state and the US military. Given the repeated assurances of the donors and the Afghan government, it could even be argued that engaging with the government's counternarcotics effort offered an opportunity for the rural elite—and thereby the population—to access development assistance and the patronage of national and international sponsors more easily. In fact, the potential for increased patronage was demonstrated by the numerous opportunities for meetings of tribal elders with foreign dignitaries and cabinet ministers in Jalalabad, and through the governor's repeated visits to the area.

Growing Economic Distress

Once the farmers in the mountains experienced the cumulative effect of the opium ban over a number of consecutive years and came to recognise that their economic position would continue a downward trajectory, their support for the tribal elite and the government began to shift. Initially there were repeated complaints that some of the *maliks* had received cash payments, gifts, lavish meals and favours from the provincial authorities for their role in helping impose the ban. The *maliks* were accused of serving the interests of the government and not responding to the priorities of the rural population. During previous rounds of research in these areas, increasing numbers of threats against the *maliks* were evident; some were even subject to verbal abuse in the bazaar (Mansfield, 2007c, 2008a).

The economic impact of the opium ban in the upper valleys of Achin cannot be ignored. Small landholdings, high population density and poor soil have the effect of limiting agricultural potential. In Achin, cultivating wheat in the winter and maize in the summer—the crops that occupy the majority of land in the absence of opium poppy and marijuana—on such small parcels of land would not allow a typical household of ten family members to meet its basic food requirements. Households that experienced sickness, injury or death found it difficult to meet the costs of healthcare without borrowing money and would often delay treatment even for serious conditions.

Even the movement into higher-value crops such as onion, bean and garlic for those with better irrigation and access to local markets offered little respite, given the small landholdings and large number of dependants in each household. Livestock holdings were also small, and any sizable income generated from sales tended to be due to distress sales which were not sustainable. Faced with an effective ban on illicit drug crop production, non-farm income became an increasingly important part of local livelihood strategies for those with enough active male family members. In the upper part of the Mahmand valley, a marble mine provided daily wage opportunities, with many earning around 500 PR per day. However, the work was arduous; many respondents reported that it was difficult to work for longer than six months under such trying conditions.

Development interventions did not fill the income gap left by opium production. Outside assistance was not extensive, and little of it was invested in income generation. Much development assistance focused on construction, which farmers complained offered employment opportunities for only a limited period of time, rarely exceeding twenty days per household. Access was typically a function of patronage, and there were repeated complaints that the most vulnerable members of the community, such as the land-poor, were neglected by these schemes.

Investments in infrastructure such as roads had little resonance with the local population; many challenged the utility of a road in the absence of legal crops to trade, when they did not have an income and were experiencing food shortages. A classic response from farmers in this position was that they 'can't eat asphalt!' For others, when road construction was accompanied by a ban on opium production and lacked a viable alternative, it took on a more sinister form—far more about enforcement and state penetration than about rural development. As one farmer in lower Achin put it, after the Ghani Khel to Kahi road was metalled: 'The road is not so good; now the American solders can come to my house in 30 minutes.' In recent years the asphalting of the roads has been seen primarily for protecting US military forces and the ANSF from attack, on the basis that it is harder for insurgents to conceal IEDs once the surface is metalled.

Other sources of cash income typically required people to travel farther afield. For example, during 2007 and 2008 when opium production was at its peak in the south, the demand for labour was such that an increasing number of recruiters could be found in Bajazai Chawk in Jalalabad and in Markoh Bazaar in Shinwar, recruiting people to work in Helmand. These 'guarantors' often resided in Helmand but had family connections in Nangarhar. They guaranteed employment at agreed rates of up to 800 PR per day and transported labourers directly to Helmand province to work in the poppy fields.

By late 2008, working in the harvest in Helmand was problematic. Falling opium prices, a reduction in the amount of land planted in the 2008/9 growing season, and deterioration in the security situation meant that fewer households were willing to risk travelling south to work for lower rates of pay (500 PR per day). Some did persist with the journey, but typically only to work for their extended family or with long-established contacts. With restrictions on working in Pakistan imposed at the same time, off-farm and non-farm income opportunities became all the more restricted in 2009 when the impact of the ban took firm hold.

In the absence of suitable local employment opportunities or wage labour opportunities in Pakistan or the poppy fields of the southern provinces, households were compelled to send young men to enlist in the ANA and ANP. In fact, many of those interviewed in Achin had sons in the ANSF, serving in Kabul, Kunar, Khost, Uruzgan, Nimroz and Wardak, and earning between 21,700 and 24,400 PR per month. Some had more than one household member serving in the ANSF. Without this source of income, households typically earned a gross income of much less than one US$ per person per day (Mansfield, 2013). However, even a relatively generous salary from the ANSF was spread thin in the context of the average size of households, the large number of dependants in each and the limited on-farm, off-farm and non-farm income opportunities available in Achin.

It is also noteworthy that enlistment in the ANSF was not without risk, and there were regular reminders of the dangers. A few days before fieldwork in April 2012, in the village of Maidanak, the body of a young man who had been serving in the ANA in Helmand was brought back for burial. In May 2012, the bodies of four men serving in the ANSF arrived in Marko Bazaar before being returned to their villages. Key informants reported that a common response to this tragedy in the tea houses and bazaars was that these young men would not have been in the ANSF and subsequently killed were it not for the opium ban. In the minds of many farmers in the southern districts of Nangarhar, a successful return to opium poppy cultivation offered young men the economic means with which to leave the ANSF and reside with their families on a more permanent basis.

Resurgent Opium Poppy Cultivation in 2011–12

Poppy cultivation returned to the upper parts of the Mahmand valley during the 2010/11 growing season (Mansfield, 2013). However, farmers were cautious, and cultivation was limited to the area of Batan and the valley further south. Apart from the upper reaches of the Mahmand valley where opium poppy was more densely cultivated, fields were often small and cultivation was at a distance from the main road.

By the 2011/12 growing season, levels of cultivation doubled in the Mahmand valley. Those who had cultivated opium poppy the previous year increased the amount of land they allocated to the crop in 2011/12, and there were new entrants with land near the main road and lower down the valley beyond Sra Kala. A number of farmers cultivated opium poppy in Maidanak in lower Achin, where it had not been visible in the 2010/11 growing season. There were even traces of cultivation in upper and lower parts of Shinwar district, where it had not been seen since 2007.

The government responded to the expansion of opium poppy cultivation by mounting a limited eradication campaign in April 2012. Consequently, many of those interviewed in Maidanak and in the northern parts of Batan at the time had lost their crop only a few days earlier or actually on the day that fieldwork was conducted. In the *manteqa* of Batan, local elders had instructed the population not to cooperate with the eradication campaign. Many farmers were found in their household compounds in protest, but there were no reports of violence. There were signs of some damage to other licit crops in the area due to the eradication. One respondent complained that the campaign had not only destroyed his opium crop but had also irreparably damaged the pomegranate saplings in which he had intercropped opium poppy. In Maidanak, respondents stated that the government had exaggerated claims of the extent of eradication.

In the areas south of Batan, where insurgents dominated, much of the land was used to cultivate poppy in the 2011/2012 growing season. Near the road in Asadkhel, where the land was more vulnerable to the threat of eradication, about 30 per cent of the land was growing poppy, while across the river it was nearer to 60 per cent. The crops of respondents with land on the far side of the river remained unscathed at the time of fieldwork, while small amounts of the crop had been destroyed near the road. South of Asadkhel, there were reports of extensive opium poppy, and farmers commented that there was very little wheat to be seen in these higher valleys.[12] As cited above, there were reports of anti-government activity and the local population warned researchers not to go to the area even during the day time. During the harvest season, the government's eradication campaign had not attempted to enter the area, and there was little expectation that a robust campaign would be conducted.

For many who had lost their crop, there was a difference between their priorities and those articulated by the government and the tribal elite. The act of crop destruction was often compared with what was seen as a lack of development activity in the area over the previous two years, and with the perception that the government lacked sufficient coercive power either to prevent the incursion of insurgents or to conduct an eradication campaign south of Asadkhel in the upper part of the Mahmand valley. By the end of the growing season, UNODC reported that cultivation had increased from 254 hectares in 2011 to 580 in 2012; still a relatively small amount of opium poppy compared with the concentrated levels of cultivation prevalent in the 1990s and the early part of the twenty-first century.

Monocropping in 2012/13

This was to change by the 2012/13 growing season, when the ban completely collapsed in the upper reaches of Achin and the state security infrastructure was pushed out of the area. By 2013, opium poppy was widespread and all but monocropped across the upper valleys of Mahmand and Pekhar. Furthermore, opium had strayed down the valley around the district centre in Kahi, and even into Marouf Chinar in upper Shinwar. Advance sales on opium, not seen in the area since 2008, had also returned, with a growing number of respondents receiving loans on their opium crop at the beginning of the season—a sign of growing confidence among farmers that the government was not in a position to destroy their crop.

Indeed, the government seemed powerless to respond in these upper areas. Eradication was cosmetic and often consisted of the authorities appealing to the local population to allow some of the crop to be destroyed 'for the camera'.[13] There were no signs of a local elite willing to align with the government's policy and press for an opium ban—a significant departure from the years of effective enforcement between 2008 and 2010. Indeed there were rumours that some *maliks* were actively encouraging cultivation. By the end of the harvest, insurgents were also found to be taxing opium, a sign that they were consolidating their position and were increasingly seen as a source of protection for the crop by the local population.

As had occurred in upper Achin in 2010 and 2011, there was a cautious return to opium cultivation by farmers in the more accessible lower valleys of Achin and upper Shinwar in 2013, including Syachob and Marouf Chinar. In these areas opium poppy occupied between 15 and 20 per cent of agricultural production. However, even in these relatively accessible areas, eradication was conducted judiciously in the spring of 2013 for fear of alienating the local population and provoking widespread dissent. This response was notably different from the robust efforts seen in these areas in 2007, 2008 and 2009, aimed at compelling farmers to desist from cultivation.

It remains to be seen whether the population in these lower areas will look to reconfigure their political leadership towards one that is less amenable to the central government and less favourable to a prohibition on opium and marijuana production. While much of the cultivation remains concentrated in the upper reaches of Loya Shinwar in Achin, Nazian, Deh Bala and Dur Baba in the 2013/14 growing season, only small amounts are found in the more accessible areas—although not the canal irrigated areas of Shinwar district itself. However, the growing presence of anti-government elements in Shinwar and the increasing reluctance of the ANSF to leave their bases suggest that it may only be a matter of time before opium poppy can once again be seen from the Jalalabad to Torkham road.

Khogiani: Insurgency and Opium Poppy

Khogiani is another district where the Afghan state has historically had to negotiate access. It has also been plagued by insecurity throughout the Karzai administration, stemming partly from the enmity between competing *mujahidin* commanders that pre-dates the Taliban's capture of Nangarhar. There is little evidence of a cohesive leadership amongst the Khogiani. Four of its most prominent commanders during the time of the Eastern Shura and the *mujahidin* government are now dead: Engineer Mahmood from Hakimabad, a commander in HIK, was killed in 1996 during the Taliban's capture of Jalalabad; Hajji Khair Mohammed, a leading elder from Zawah and commander for Hezb-e Islami—Gulbuddin Hekmatyar (HIG), died in 2004; Mawlawi Younis Khales died in 2006 after siding with the Taliban in 2003; and, as noted earlier, Hajji Zaman Ghamsharik, nephew and rival of Khair Mohammed and opponent of Hajji Zahir and the Arsala family, was killed in a suicide attack in Khogiani in February 2010, only months after his reconciliation with the Karzai administration.

Among these commanders, only Mawlawi Younis Khales was followed by a successor who could mobilise wider military support. Following the death of his father, Anwar al Haq Mujahid split from HIK and formed the Tora Bora Military Front in 2007. He aligned the movement with the Taliban, concentrating their efforts against US and Afghan government forces in the upper valleys of the Khogiani districts of Pachir wa Agam, Sherzad, parts of Chapahar and Khogiani itself. In the Khogiani districts, Mujahid successfully built on the growing opposition to civilian casualties and the divisions within the rural elite—often manifested in revenge killings and accusations of collaboration with the insurgency—and moved further down the valleys towards Kargha, the district centre of Khogiani.

However, within the Khogiani tribe itself, the eradication campaign in the district of Sherzad in April 2010 was a catalyst for the growing popularity of the insurgency. In particular, Shirzai's antagonistic position to the tribal elders during the campaign was seen as provocative and led to the Taliban being invited into the area to protect the crop (Dalrymple, 2013; Hashimi, 2010). For many farmers in Khogiani this single act highlighted the disconnection between the governor and the rural population. The governor's insults to the local elite (and allegedly their wives) and his disregard of the tradition of the state negotiating access to the area offended social mores and suggested that he 'had forgotten [he too was] Afghan'. In addition, his decision to press on with the operation, and the subsequent loss of ANP lives, reflected the vulnerability of the state in the absence of US military support.

By April 2011, the upper valleys in the south of Khogiani had a significant Taliban presence. The valleys of Zawah and Pirakhel in particular had become a challenging environment for the government. Insurgents were known to patrol these valleys after dark, and it was alleged that government access had to be negotiated through local elders and insurgents (Mansfield, 2011). Opium poppy cultivation was estimated to occupy as much as 70 percent of the land in parts of the Pirakhel valley in the 2010/11 growing season and the government was not in a position to mount an eradication campaign.

A year later, local farmers and key informants reported that the valleys of Pirakhel and Zawah were firmly under the control of insurgents. Taliban fighters openly patrolled these valleys during the day and night, and local farmers advised those not from the area against travelling south of Ahmedkhel. As in Achin, farmers reported that these Taliban were typically local villagers and that the small number of 'Waziris' from Pakistan present in Pirakhel were constantly on the move, fearing detection by US forces.

There were also reports of a growing Taliban influence in Ahmedkhel to the north in 2012. Locals alleged that the Taliban regularly patrolled the area at night and were present during the day, but more circumspect. It was claimed that these Taliban were local and did not 'push the people' or 'demand money'. Farmers did, however, report that organisations that had been providing development assistance were warned to leave the area, and that there had been announcements in the mosque that 'people should not send their sons and brothers to join the ANA and ANP'. There was also a genuine fear about going out after dusk, even when it was a household's turn to irrigate, for fear of being stopped by either Taliban or US military patrols.

By the winter of 2012/13, this would all change again, with significant ANSF operations across the district, particularly in the upper areas of Zawah and Pirakhel. What is of interest is how this counterinsurgency effort came to be intimately tied to resurgent opium production across the district, including the lower areas bordering Surkhrud, and what this tells us about the kind of arrangements ANSF are likely to make with the local population in areas of limited statehood in a post-2014 environment.

The Return to Extensive Poppy Cultivation

In tandem with the deterioration in security, opium poppy cultivation was a lot more apparent in Khogiani in April 2012 than it had been during the 2010/11 growing season. Respondents in Ahmedkhel, Hakimabad and Khelago cultivated opium poppy in the 2011/12 growing season, whereas they had not grown it the previous year. In many areas, opium poppy could be seen only 200 to 300 metres from the roadside, even in areas where the government maintained some semblance of control. In the Pirakhel valley, up to 95 per cent of the land was dedicated to opium poppy in the 2011/12 growing season.

As in Achin, the rural population in Khogiani typically found their economic prospects constrained by small landholdings, high dependency ratios and limited non-farm income opportunities. While there were increasing signs of agricultural diversification compared to the monocropping of wheat that accompanied the earlier ban, landholdings were rarely greater than six *jeribs*, presenting a major challenge to a household of ten people that needed to meet its food requirements through a combination of wheat production and the sale of cash crops. Even high-value cash crops such as cabbage and cauliflower, which earned a gross income of 90,000 PR and 70,000 PR per *jerib* respectively, rarely yielded more than one US$ per person per day for households entirely dependent on agricultural production.

Those who sharecropped land and/or did not have access to non-farm income were particularly vulnerable. The situation was even more acute in the drier areas where yields were considerably lower than in the upper valleys and there was persistence of a low-yielding maize and groundnut during the summer months.

Given these economic and political conditions, the government's decision to launch an eradication campaign in the spring of 2012 could only be seen as destabilising. Initial forays by the authorities into Khogiani during the research in 2012 were met with resistance. For example, an eradication campaign in Memla in lower Khogiani on 4 April 2012 led to a protracted gun battle and the deaths of one member of the ANP and a local farmer. As the season progressed, levels of violence in the district increased so dramatically that on a single day—17 April 2012—eleven people were killed. By the end of the eradication season in 2012, UNODC and the MCN reported a total of forty-five dead and thirty-six injured in the district of Khogiani alone.

Most of these incidents occurred in lower Khogiani, concentrated around Memla. If the government had mounted a robust eradication campaign in the upper valleys of Khogiani, there would have been many more casualties. It is noteworthy that, as opposed to April 2010, there were no reports of eradication in the district of Sherzad, despite reports of increasing levels of cultivation in the 2011/12 growing season.

By April 2013, Khogiani was awash with opium poppy, even in the lower areas around Khelago, where the crop had not been seen since 2007. The situation in Khogiani offered a good example of the multiple and competing objectives that the state was trying to balance as US military forces withdrew from the province. During research in April 2013, it became clear that the provincial authorities were unwilling to experience the kinds of casualties that had occurred during the eradication season the previous year. More importantly, the Afghan security forces were unwilling to lose the gains they had made in three counterinsurgency operations during the winter. In fact in Khogiani, farmers were under the impression that the ANA commander who had led these operations—appreciative that villagers had asked the Taliban to leave the area and grateful that farmers did not take up arms themselves—had announced to the district's elders that their opium crop would not be destroyed in the spring of 2013.

The governor's reaction to this announcement further signalled his impotence to the rural population in the area. No longer able or willing to travel to the district centres to impose a ban as he did in the 2007/8 and 2008/9 growing seasons, he was alleged to have written to district officials requesting that they eradicate the crop. Aware of the limits of their territorial control and the late stage in the season, the district governor of Khogiani looked to negotiate a specified amount of eradication for each *manteqa*—to which elders and communities were unwilling to agree. Reports suggested that farmers were not even willing to sacrifice their weakest crops 'just for photos for the foreigners', even though it was proposed that they would be compensated by their neighbours.

Events around the eradication campaign in Khogiani in the spring of 2013 offer a fitting conclusion. They reflect the state's complete retreat from the upper districts back to its historical position in the lower valleys, a process that was likely to continue in the run-up to transition in 2014. In these areas of limited statehood, where there were no viable alternatives, the opium ban had exacted a toll. It had entailed brokerage between the governor and elements of the fractured rural elite whose authority over the rural population is constantly challenged, particularly when it fails to deliver patronage. To achieve his aims, the governor had promised development assistance to the wider population and threatened force with the implied involvement of foreign military power, doing little to aid state legitimacy.

Ultimately, the cumulative effect of the ban in these areas led to a deterioration in the economic welfare of large sections of the population and the adoption of coping strategies that placed family members at risk. With such a delicate hold on power in the southern districts, and no history of state encapsulation, it was inevitable that a policy that expended so much political capital would ultimately unravel. In the advent of other crises and shocks—the land dispute in Achin and the subsequent violence that followed, as well as the intra-tribal enmities in Khogiani—the ban on opium poppy presented a further reason for farmers to resist state penetration and engage in active rebellion.

Conclusion

By spring of 2013, much of Nangarhar was in disarray. Most notably, the insurgency had gained a firm foothold within the province. No longer hemmed in along the Pakistani border, the insurgency could be found throughout Sherzad and Hesarak, the Shinwari tribal areas, and in the lower districts of Chapahar and Bati Kot. There were also signs of a growing insurgent presence in the main Kabul River valley along the Jalalabad to Torkham road.

At the political centre of Nangarhar, there was growing conflict as a result of the breakdown in the political settlement between the provincial ruling elite, Governor Shirzai and different political factions in Kabul. Disputes over rent extraction, the distribution of government positions and patronage, as well as personal acrimony, had led to the regrouping of old *jihadi* alliances and the formation of new political coalitions in opposition to Shirzai. The contest for control over state institutions in the province became intense with the resurgence of prominent former *jihadi* commanders and their families following their election to national and provincial representative bodies in 2009 and 2010. The withdrawal of US forces, the closure of the PRT in April 2013 and the presidential elections in 2014—with uncertainty over how the potential candidates and their respective networks would align—further fractured the body politic.

It would be wrong, however, to assume that political order in Nangarhar was determined solely by the manoeuvrings of the provincial political and military elite, many of whom have had their control over state power wrested from them on many occasions over the last two decades. In part, these provincial leaders derived their power from the local elite and the rural population that they claimed to represent, and from the political and military support these communities could provide. Events in the rural districts of Nangarhar, given the significance of the provincial economy, also had a significant influence on the dynamics of power sharing and rent distribution in Kabul. As Coburn notes (2013: 2), in Afghanistan 'national figures have for a good part remained relevant because they continue to convince enough local leaders at the district level that it is in their best interests to support them'.

Opium production and efforts to control it were also an essential element in the dynamics of Nangarhari politics. Over the last two decades, opium production and counternarcotics policies have played pivotal roles in the bargains between the rural population, local elites and those vying for power in Jalalabad. Cultivation and efforts to control it have shaped political relations and patronage with the political centre in Kabul, as well as with the international community—most notably the USG—in Washington, DC, Kabul and within the province itself.

As with the previous opium ban, enforced in the 2004/5 growing season, the province-wide prohibition imposed by Governor Shirzai in 2007 had largely unravelled by spring 2013. This ban, which drew considerable praise from the international community in 2008 when the province was declared 'poppy free', had shown signs of stress since the 2009/10 growing season. The resurgence in opium production witnessed in the upper reaches of the southern districts in the 2011/12 growing season was eclipsed by much greater levels of cultivation in 2013, as well as by evidence of widespread opium poppy cultivation in the lower valleys of the Spinghar piedmont and in the district of Chapahar.

By the 2012/13 growing season, the Afghan state was unable to enforce a ban in many poppy growing districts of Nangarhar. The outbreak of violence which began with resistance to eradication in the district of Sherzad in April 2010 had escalated, culminating in the deaths of forty-eight people during the eradication campaign in 2012, despite the government avoiding Sherzad, Achin and Khogiani where insurgent groups were more deeply entrenched. The deterioration in the state's hold over the countryside was so great that by the spring of 2013 the government had all but abandoned any effort to eradicate the crop. There were growing reports of district security commanders, and even elements of the ANA, brokering deals that offered the authorities displays of crop destruction 'for the cameras' but avoided provoking widespread dissent.

While there were some reports of corruption associated with eradication in 2013, the situation was very different from previous efforts to ban opium in the province. Low levels of eradication and protracted negotiations between government officials and the rural elite did not foster the threat of eradication to leverage payments out of the rural population, as they had in the past. It was more a case of officials asking for the 'assistance' of rural communities and local elites in agreeing to quotas for eradication, so as not to expose the state's inability to act.

Indeed, by 2013 counternarcotics objectives had largely been abandoned by both national and international institutions. The international community in Western capitals, Kabul and Jalalabad were largely silent. The PRT closed in April 2013 and along with it any possibility of a proactive campaign like the one in late 2007 that conjoined counternarcotics and counterinsurgency objectives in the eyes of the rural population. In particular, many of the provincial political elite who had been behind previous efforts to ban opium were disengaged. The governor rarely strayed from his palace in Jalalabad, unlike his active role in the planting seasons of 2007/8 and 2008/9 when he travelled through the southern districts persuading farmers to abandon opium poppy cultivation. Others who had been instrumental in enforcing previous bans, including Hajji Zahir, had little interest in continuing a ban that would reflect well on the governor, their main political rival in the province. Besides, they had more pressing interest in their collaboration to oust Shirzai.

At the local level, the elites that had brokered the state's imposition of the ban in the Spinghar piedmont during Shirzai's governorship and had been instrumental in keeping the Taliban presence to a minimum found themselves increasingly marginalised in the face of growing rural discontent and a rising insurgency. Those elders who wished to maintain some influence among the rural population in the upper valleys were conscious of the political capital they had expended supporting the ban in its initial years. They were now advocates of a return to cultivation in the face of growing rural opposition to the provincial authorities, and were aware of the more complex and divided political terrain.

It was only in the lower areas around the provincial centre that the ban remained intact, as it had been since 2005. In these areas a dominant political elite, favourable resource endowments and strong investments in public goods—including improved security—supported a transition out of opium poppy that did not have a deleterious effect on the welfare of the population. Indeed, as opposed to areas of limited statehood in the Spinghar piedmont, the population in Kama and Surkhrud succeeded in diversifying both their income and their cropping patterns. The absence of co-variate and idiosyncratic shocks in these areas favoured a relatively smooth transition out of opium poppy without resistance and subsequent rural rebellion seen in the upper valleys of Nangarhar.

The unravelling of the ban in Nangarhar raises a number of salient points with regard to my hypothesis that the dynamics and sustainability of opium bans will be fundamentally different in areas of consolidated statehood, compared to areas of limited statehood. The first is the fragility of the political coalition behind a ban on opium, given the number of institutions and actors involved, their different interests and motivations and the constantly evolving political terrain that they all inhabit. The shifting priorities of international and domestic actors—particularly the USG and Karzai—were instrumental in shaping the rural population's and political elite's perception of Shirzai and how much coercion and capital he could draw upon in his pursuit of low levels of cultivation and, more broadly, his control over formal and informal institutions in the province. Once the support of Karzai and the USG was seen to be ambivalent, Shirzai's position became increasingly untenable. In particular, he lacked a rural constituency with which to mobilise mass support, especially in the wake of a prolonged and sometimes violently imposed opium ban. He also found himself encircled by a political elite that felt excluded and resented the rent Shirzai was extracting from public-sector institutions and his growing business interests within the province.

The second point is the much greater instability of the political coalition behind the ban in areas of limited statehood, where local political structures render the rural elite more responsive to the rural population. In these areas, with limited resources and low levels of investment, the opium ban created what Scott (1976: 205) refers to as 'patterns of collective insecurity' that undermined political support for the rural elite. Along with other co-variate shocks, this led to growing antipathy and then rebellion against the state. What began as 'acts of everyday resistance' in an attempt to limit crop destruction and negotiate better access to public investment became violent resistance to the state and its foreign backers, drawing on limited support from cross-border networks in Pakistan.

Areas of limited statehood like Achin and Khogiani had their own distinct histories of resistance against the state, but both were shaped by a narrative of a state that had overreached itself, taken on the priorities of its foreign patrons and did not understand the needs of a rural population. Unable to realise meaningful development outcomes in such challenging terrain, it was only a question of time before the rural population and the rural leadership used violence to expel the ANSF and return to opium production as a means of securing their livelihoods. Moreover, the rebellion in each area grew in strength in part as a function of the success of acts of resistance in other areas. As the limits of state power were revealed for all to see and poppy returned to the periphery, the collapse of the ban accelerated dramatically, culminating in an increase from 3,151 hectares in 2012 to 15,719 hectares in 2013 and then 18,227 hectares in 2014 (UNODC/MCN, 2013: 8).

The third point is the role that international actors have played in distorting and destabilising the political marketplace, particularly in the pursuit of an opium ban in areas of limited statehood. Governor Shirzai's threat of the use of foreign force to enforce a ban in Achin in 2007/8 and his eradication campaign in Sherzad in 2010 were indicative of campaigns that became increasingly disconnected from the Afghan state's engagement with the population on its borders, as well as the coercive capacities of the ANSF. The same disconnect can be seen in the handling of the land dispute in Achin.

Bolstered by the patronage of the USG and, to a lesser extent, Karzai, Shirzai made short-term decisions shaped by his career ambitions in Kabul rather than his need to shore up political support and gain legitimacy with the population in Nangarhar. At the local level, foreign support for rural leaders such as Malik Niaz and Usman, through initiatives such as the Shinwari Pact, also fostered unstable 'spot bargains'. These events would inevitably motivate leaders who had not been favoured, to look for their own patrons, perhaps across the border in Pakistan, but more logically from the rural population who had borne the cumulative costs of the opium ban. It was almost inevitable that sub-national and local leaders who had been so active in supporting the ban would find themselves increasingly marginalised once market conditions changed, particularly when international priorities shifted away from counternarcotics, the US military forces announced their withdrawal from the province, and the political leadership sensed reduced opportunities for patronage from development budgets.

These points suggest that the reasons for the resurgence in cultivation in Nangarhar are more prosaic and endogenous than the explanations that are often offered: increases in opium prices associated with an effective prohibition that prompts farmers to return to cultivation, encouraged by insurgents and their desire for political support and the opportunity to tax production. Instead we see the collapse of the ban in what were already fragile political coalitions that had little chance of enduring in areas where the state has not concentrated the means of violence, where the population is more likely to experience a loss in welfare due to a ban, and where there is a history of violent rebellion where the loss of welfare is state-imposed.

9

THE HELMAND FOOD ZONE

A TECHNOCRATIC RESPONSE
TO A COMPLEX PHENOMENON

Introduction

Chapter 7 examined the political processes that underpinned two distinct bans on opium production in Nangarhar. The first ban, imposed in the 2004/5 growing season, was largely an Afghan-led effort; it failed to eliminate opium poppy completely from the province and ultimately proved short-lived. In contrast, the second ban, imposed in the 2007/8 growing season, resulted in the province being 'declared poppy free'; it maintained low levels of cultivation even in more remote and inaccessible southern districts until 2010 and in the lower valleys until as late as 2013. Chapter 8 charted how this second ban impacted on the livelihoods of different population groups within the province and how prohibition, in parallel with other events, undermined the political settlements that had supported prohibition in areas of limited statehood, ultimately creating a 'butterfly' effect that began to threaten the authority of the state even in the Kabul River valley.

Chapters 9 and 10 describe efforts to ban opium poppy in central Helmand in southern Afghanistan. Any analysis of opium production and efforts to control it needs to consider this province, which has for many become synonymous with opium poppy cultivation. Chapter 9 examines the different institutions behind the effort to ban opium production in central Helmand between 2008 and 2013 and the initiative that came to be known as the

'Helmand Food Zone'. In contrast to earlier bans, this chapter describes a more technocratic and contractual model of drug control, not based on indigenous forms of negotiation and deal-making as witnessed in Nangarhar, but anchored in Western understandings of state power, and driven by foreign advisers and a heavy international military presence. It examines why different international, national, sub-national and local actors mobilised behind the calls to ban opium, and it documents how the ban was imposed.

The chapter is divided into two sections and a conclusion. The first section offers a brief background on Helmand—its strategic significance within Afghanistan and its role as a main producer of opium in the country. The second section examines the profoundly political processes that underpinned the ban on opium production in the canal command area in the 2007/8 growing season. It explores why different institutions within the international community and GIRoA sought to prioritise counternarcotics at that time and how the ban was subsequently imposed. The conclusion reflects on the cognitive dissonance associated with the Food Zone and its perceived impact on levels of opium poppy cultivation in Helmand.

During the 1990s, Helmand was one of Afghanistan's primary opium-producing provinces, typically cultivating between 30,000 and 40,000 hectares of opium poppy annually. With the fall of the Taliban regime and the collapse of the ban on opium production, levels of cultivation increased in Helmand province, reaching a peak of 103,590 hectares in the 2007/8 growing season. As the primary producer of Afghan opium, Helmand was a focal point in the debate on counternarcotics policy and a target of international support for drug control efforts in the country. In contrast to Nangarhar, where the strategy was largely based on agreements with communities to desist from planting, drug control efforts in Helmand have often focused on the greater levels of crop destruction. Over the years substantial investments were made with the goal of increasing eradication in Helmand province, including the establishment of a centrally funded eradication force between 2005 and 2010 that operated almost exclusively in Helmand and cost an estimated US$992 million (Government of the United States Government Accountability Office, 2010: 4).[1]

Eradication efforts were also supported by significant investments in rural development in the province; in 2007, US State Department officials stated: '... if Helmand were a country, it would be the fifth largest recipient of USAID funding in the world' (Schweich, 2007: 47; Wood, 2007). Yet, despite these investments, cultivation remained persistently high and showed few signs of abating prior to 2008. Moreover, throughout 2006 and 2007 the security situation in the province deteriorated significantly, resulting in the curtailment of development aid in the north and a growing concentration of aid in the area around the cities of Lashkar Gah and Gereshk. Eradication efforts each spring were also subject to repeated violent attacks, hampering efforts to reduce levels of cultivation (UNODC/MCN, 2008: 87; UNODC/MCN, 2009: 52).

However, in late 2008, counternarcotics efforts in Helmand province were recast. The arrival of the new governor, Mohammed Gulab Mangal, was clearly a catalyst, particularly after what were seen as lacklustre performances in counternarcotics by his immediate predecessors, Mohammed Daoud (2005–6) and Asadullah Wafa (2006–8), and the enduring influence of the former governor, Sher Mohammed Akhundzada (2002–5). By the fall of 2008, the Governor's Office had, along with advisers in the PRT and the Poppy Elimination Programme (PEP), developed the 'Helmand Food Zone Programme', consisting of an integrated plan to reduce opium poppy cultivation within the canal command area in the central part of the province. The programme explicitly linked the provision of development inputs—primarily wheat seed and fertiliser—through a signed agreement with farmers not to cultivate opium poppy. It was backed with the threat of eradication.

In the 2008/9 growing season, levels of opium poppy cultivation in the Food Zone fell by 37 per cent, and further reductions were seen in both 2010 and 2011. In fact, by the spring of 2011 there had been a 40 per cent reduction in cultivation in Helmand compared to the 2007/8 growing season, especially in the districts of Nad e Ali and Marjeh. These reductions were automatically attributed to the Food Zone Programme and the perceived commitment of Governor Mangal to the counternarcotics agenda.

While the new governor was clearly a more proactive advocate of counternarcotics efforts in Helmand than his predecessors and a valuable focal point for the Food Zone, the actions of Gulab Mangal were not solely responsible for the reductions in cultivation. This assumption ignored the fact that the Food Zone Programme was implemented when many other factors also favoured falling levels of opium production. These included the shift in the terms of trade between wheat and opium following the dramatic rise in food prices between mid-2007 and late 2008, alongside a drop in opium prices over the same period, and the substantial increase in the presence of international and Afghan military forces in central Helmand beginning in June 2009 in the districts of Nawa Barakzai and Garmsir, culminating in the inflow of troops to Marjeh and Nad e Ali under operation Moshtarak I and II in spring 2010

(Mansfield et al., 2011). Simply attributing the reductions to the former governor also tends to neglect the central role that international actors played in the counternarcotics effort in central Helmand at the time.

The Provincial Context

Helmand is the largest province in Afghanistan, occupying approximately 62,000 square kilometres. It has an estimated population of 1.4 million people (Central Statistics Office, 2006), comprising mainly Pashtuns with some Baloch and Hazaras. The province is located in the south-west of the country and neighbours the provinces of Kandahar, Dai Kundi, Uruzgan, Nimroz, Farah and Ghor. It shares a 160 kilometre border with Baluchistan, Pakistan. The terrain is mostly clay or sand desert in the south, and dry rocky mountains in the north. Only 4 per cent of the land is cultivable and only 2.5 per cent is irrigated. Rainfall varies from 2 to 9 inches per year. Summers are hot and dry, and winters are mild with average temperatures above freezing, but the number of sub-freezing days hampers the growth of tropical crops and fruit.

Much of the most productive agricultural land, as well as the population, straddles the Helmand River and the irrigation systems it feeds. However, the desert areas brought under cultivation in the 1950s and 1960s though the Helmand Valley Authority—later the Helmand and Arghandab River Authority—suffer from flat gradients, poor soils, high evaporation rates and poor water management, resulting in drainage and salination problems. Alluvial or old river terrace soils of moderate to low fertility predominate in the Helmand area (Shairzai et al., 1975: 3). Subsoils are frequently underlain by an impermeable conglomerate, and waterlogging has created a persistent weed problem, particularly in Nad e Ali and Marjeh (Cullather, 2002). Despite this, 'the hot days and relatively cool nights in summer, the mild climate of winter with good light intensity are all favourable factors for plant growth in Helmand' (Cullather, 2002: 3).

Beyond the areas irrigated by the river and the canal system in central Helmand are desert communities that began to take root in the 1980s. This process of settlement began in the interstices of the canal command area: desert areas in the districts of Marjeh, Nad e Ali and Lashkar Gah that were not brought under agricultural production by the USG-funded canal project. By 2004, encroachment into former desert areas—and what is still regarded as government land—gathered apace, absorbing large tracts of land north of the Boghra Canal. By 2013, a belt of almost contiguous agricultural land stretched up to 8 kilometres from the Boghra Canal, from as far west as Marjeh to the area south-west of Gereshk in Nahre Seraj. Further settlements and new agricultural land could also be found on the perimeter wall of the US/UK military base at Camp Bastion/Leatherneck, as well as north of Highway One in Nahre Seraj and Nawzad. Irrigated at first by shallow wells and later by deep wells between 60 and 90 metres deep, much of this desert land was initially grabbed by powerful military commanders linked with the *mujahidin*. These commanders typically distributed the land to their extended families and military subordinates before parcelling it and selling it to those from tribal groups considered indigenous to the province. As will be discussed in Chapter 10, this process of settlement has had a profound effect on both the physical and political terrain in central Helmand.

Economically the province of Helmand is dependent on agriculture. There are few non-farm income opportunities and small industry is largely absent (Gordon, 2010: 9). In 2008/9, wheat occupied the greatest amount of active agricultural land during the winter: an estimated 85,493 hectares. Opium poppy was the second most prolific crop, with 75,076 hectares under cultivation (Cranfield, 2009: 24). Other winter crops include fodder crops such as alfalfa as well as seasonal vegetables grown primarily for household consumption in most areas beyond the environs of the urban centres of Lashkar Gah and Gereshk. In the spring and summer there is greater agricultural diversity, including premium-quality watermelon. Cotton production also persists despite the relatively low prices offered by the state gin. In the former desert areas, opium poppy dominates the landscape in the winter, with only a small proportion of land allocated to wheat. In this area, spring and summer crops are largely limited because the recurrent costs of irrigation are so high.

While the province has agricultural potential, there are many constraints on its realisation. Traditionally Helmand has been a peripheral economic player. The centre of economic growth lies in Kandahar; the main agricultural market is not in the capital city of Lashkar Gah, with a population of only around 200,000, but in Kandahar city, with onward destinations to Kabul and Quetta, Pakistan (Gordon, 2010: 6). Between 2005 and 2009, insecurity along the main highway between Gereshk and Kandahar city—particularly in the district of Zahre—hampered the movement of goods along this road. Due to the risks of violence or robbery, transportation costs were also particularly high in the south, with nuisance taxes considerably higher in the provinces of Helmand and Kandahar than anywhere else in the country (Mansfield, 2008b: 45–6; Mansfield, 2009b: 63–4). There is no official border crossing with Pakistan located in Helmand, so government revenues from imports and exports are zero. Crossing these borders unofficially are guns, drugs and people—some of whom are armed and belonging to anti-government elements. The border areas lie beyond the control of the provincial authorities, and any rents generated here do not flow to the government.

Politically the province is deeply divided. The rise of the former *jihadi* commanders who were ejected under the Taliban—Sher Mohammed Akhundzada (Alizai), Abdul Rahman Jan (Noorzai), Dad Mohammed Khan (Alikozai) and his brothers Mohammad Daoud and Gul Mohammad, Hajji Abdul 'Koka' Wali (Alizai) and Mir Wali (Barakzai)—to formal positions of authority within the provincial administration in 2001 alienated much of the rural population. These were names that were already associated with corruption, violence and involvement in the drugs trade (Coghlan, 2009: 121–2 and 126). Their return to power in Helmand after the fall of the Taliban was a surprise to the population who remembered the role the commanders had played in the collapse of the *mujahidin* government and why the Taliban had swept into the south in the mid-1990s with the support of the rural population. Key tribes such as the Ishaqzai who were prominent in the Taliban regime, along with many other smaller tribes such as the Dawtani and Kakar, found themselves marginalised and largely ignored in the allocation of government jobs and patronage that made up the spoils of war.

The lack of progress made across many key development indicators in the province reinforced the view among the rural population that those in government had little interest in the provision of public goods and were more concerned with increasing their private wealth (Giustozzi, 2007: 215). These sentiments and growing tribal grievances gave the Taliban entry points into rural areas, particularly in the north and in areas bordering Pakistan. Counter-narcotics efforts that have often been criticised for targeting the poor and the powerless (in the case of eradication) and competitors (in the case of interdiction) were also blamed for undermining support for the provincial authorities (Gordon, 2011; Giustozzi, 2007).

Interventions by Western nations have had a profound effect on the physical and political geography of the province. In the twentieth century the Helmand Valley Project—in particular the construction of the Nahre Seraj and Boghra Canals—changed the face of central Helmand, bringing thousands of hectares of former desert land under agriculture and more than 5,000 new families into the area, primarily from other provinces (Dupree, 1997: 499–507). These new residents were located alongside the original settlers of central and southern Helmand, most notably the Barakazai. Their apparent advantages over the indigenous tribes to the north—the Ishaqzai, Noorzai, Alizai and Alkozai—fuelled friction and resentment. With the irrigation and land settlement programme came significant investments in agricultural development. These included improved seeds, fertiliser, mechanisation, roads and transportation, as well as a substantial Western presence in Lashkar Gah, which became known as 'Little America' (Chandrasekaran, 2012).

In the twenty-first century, Western interventions in Helmand have been just as pervasive, and the province has become a major focus of both the military campaign and international development assistance in Afghanistan. This did not happen right away. Immediately after the collapse of the Taliban regime, Western interests in Helmand were limited, reflecting the province's rather peripheral role in the political economy of the southern region and the importance of the regional hub in Kandahar. In fact, between 2004 and 2006, when the US was in charge of the Helmand PRT, they maintained only around 200 soldiers and the PRT spent only US$9.5 million on reconstruction projects (Gordon, 2011: 31). While USAID mounted a much larger rural development programme aimed at reducing opium poppy cultivation, with a budget of US$130 million for the southern region as whole, this programme was largely abandoned in Helmand in May 2005, following the murder of several staff working in Babaji alongside the Boghra Canal (Hafvenstein, 2007).

The situation changed in May 2006, when the UK government took the lead at the PRT. Anxious to maintain influence with the US and make up for what Farrell and Gordon (2009: 65) refer to as 'the long shadow' cast by the British campaign in Iraq, Prime Minister Tony Blair agreed to take the lead in Helmand, one of the most challenging provinces in the country. The focus of the UK effort was to secure what appeared to be areas of consolidated statehood—the area irrigated by the Helmand River between Gereshk and Lashkar Gah and that brought under cultivation by the Boghra Canal. Securing these areas was intended to allow sufficient investments in reconstruction and development.

The UK effort in Helmand was plagued by problems from the start. The first problem was historical, the baggage of three Anglo-Afghan wars, and in particular the Battle of Maiwand, used by the insurgency to agitate the rural population against the British intervention (Ledwidge, 2011: 62–3; Mackenzie, 2010: 5). The second problem was the removal of then-Governor Sher Mohammed Akhunzada at the insistence of the British, who believed that their role as lead nation on counternarcotics under the Security Sector Reform process would be compromised by a governor who was widely assumed to be involved in the drugs trade (Ledwidge, 2011: 66). Once removed, the governor did his best to destabilise the province, openly admitting that his supporters in the north shifted their allegiances to the Taliban.

These first two problems served to exacerbate the third: that the UK had too few soldiers for the scale of the task. The initial military deployment consisted of a task force of only 3,500 troops, of which only 650 were combat soldiers. Faced with growing agitation in northern Helmand and under pressure from the new Governor Daoud and President Karzai to ensure that none of the districts was seen to fall to the Taliban, these solders were soon deployed to the district centres of Nawzad, Sangin and Musa Qala. This decision proved costly; with insufficient ground forces, an aggressive military campaign was mounted that relied heavily on air power (Egnell, 2011: 305). This provided evidence to the local population that the British military had returned to southern Afghanistan to take revenge for their defeat at Maiwand, and were in league with elements of a provincial and district administration that was widely viewed as predatory and corrupt (Farrell and Gordon, 2009: 671; Ledwidge, 2011: 83). The fourth problem the British military forces faced was rapid turnover. With six-month rotations, each brigade felt compelled to make its mark; to take on the enemy and defeat them in battle. But territory was rarely held and the Taliban soon returned, leading one task force commander to comment that military operations 'were mowing the grass' (King, 2012: 30).

Farrell and Gordon (2009: 762) have referred to the period from the arrival of UK forces in May 2006 until early 2008 as 'eighteen months of strategic drift'. The level of fighting and the dispersal of UK military assets greatly weakened the original UK plan: to invest around US$9 million in small-scale reconstruction and development projects and almost US$45 million through a large-scale rural livelihoods programme, Helmand Agriculture and Rural Development Project, as well as USAID's Alternative Development Programme–South (ADP-S). These projects had to be scaled back and focused on the areas closest to Lashkar Gah. In this kinetic environment there was little space for development activity (Gordon, 2011: 34).

After 2008, there was a marked increase in the attention given to Helmand by the international community and in the resources committed to the province. This was largely because at that time Helmand came to represent the perceived failure of statebuilding in Afghanistan. The virulence of the insurgency, its presence in a number of district centres—not just in the north but also in the settled area of Marjeh—and the unprecedented levels of opium poppy cultivation all fuelled the image of the failure of both the Afghan state and the UK military. For the UK there was the added embarrassment of what appeared to be the success of the effort in the eastern region and constant comparisons with the US-led PRT in Nangarhar, where there were much lower levels of violence, negligible opium poppy cultivation and significant investments by the USG in economic development and security.

Reputational risk for both the UK effort in Helmand and the overall state-building project in Afghanistan prompted the uptick in UK investments in the province. By 2008, there were over 8,500 British troops in Helmand provided with an additional 500 armoured patrol and support vehicles (Farrell and Gordon, 2009: 677). The civilian presence also increased from twenty-five in 2007 to eighty in 2009, headed by a senior Foreign Office diplomat (Egnell, 2011: 308). In April 2008, the USG also provided reinforcements with a 1,200 man battalion of US Marines, who, along with UK soldiers, mounted an assault on the southern district of Garmsir, engaging the Taliban in a protracted battle and cutting off a vital supply route from Pakistan (Malkesian, 2013: 119).

Once the USG turned its attention to Helmand, the situation on the ground began to change. In 2009 and 2010, a series of military operations were launched that began not only to 'clear' the insurgents from central Helmand, but also to 'hold' some of the territory. Operations Panther's Claw and Khanjar in the summer of 2009 sought to push the Taliban out of central and southern Helmand and to establish the conditions for the rural population to vote in the presidential elections in October 2009. Operation Khanjar alone deployed over 4,000 Marines and 600 ANA and ANP simultaneously in Nawa Barakzai, Khanishin and the southern part of Garmsir; Panther's Claw deployed over 3,000 British soldiers, 700 Danes, 130 Estonians and 650 ANA into Nad e Ali. This campaign of military operations culminated in Operation Moshtarak in February 2010, which involved over 15,000 ISAF and Afghan soldiers. Phase 1 of this campaign, led by the British, targeted Nad e Ali; Phase 2 was a major offensive led by the US Marine Corps into Marjeh (Dressler, 2010).

Alongside these military operations came concerted investment in the governance, security and development of Helmand: part of the 'build' element of the counterinsurgency effort. Funding for rural development witnessed a substantial uplift. For instance in 2009, USAID enhanced an existing US$60 million national programme distributing agricultural inputs—the Afghanistan Voucher for Increased Production in Agriculture (AVIPA-Plus), implemented by International Relief and Development (IRD)—to include Helmand and Kandahar, adding another US$250 million over two years for these two provinces alone (USAID, 2010: 4). The Afghan Stability Initiative (ASI), implemented by Chemonics, was also expanded to include the southern region with a further US$159.6 million over three years (USAID, 2011: 1). There was also further funding from DFID in the form of a US$45 million programme of investments in infrastructure and private-sector development, aimed at promoting economic growth: the Helmand Growth Programme, and the Commanders Emergency Response Programme (DFID, 2009).

Investments in the security sector were also significant, with training and support for the ANA and ANP in Helmand and the establishment of units of the Afghan Local Police (ALP). The physical infrastructure—the FOBs and the checkpoints—that accompanied the Afghan and international military forces located in Helmand was such that one British officer described the district of Nad e Ali as having 'a checkpoint on every junction in some areas' (Mike Martin, personal communication, May 2014). These investments created a permanent presence that changed rural perceptions of the state (Mansfield et al., 2011: 3).

It is not the purpose of this section to assess the success of the counterinsurgency campaign in Helmand. Rather, the intent is to show how the security environment in central Helmand changed since 2008, when it became clear that Helmand was being viewed as 'mission critical' not just for the province and southern region but for the Afghan statebuilding project as a whole. Against this backdrop, efforts to address the burgeoning levels of opium poppy cultivation in the province can be assessed and we can understand more clearly why different institutions and actors with diverse mandates and interests began to see counternarcotics as a priority—one that was entirely consistent with the statebuilding agenda.

Banning Opium in the Canal Command Area: The Establishment of the Helmand Food Zone

There were two major attempts to reduce opium poppy cultivation in Helmand after 2000. As with the bans in Nangarhar, both focused on dissuading farmers from planting the crop rather than destroying it once it was already in the ground, and both combined promises of development assistance with the threat of eradication and coercion. The most comprehensive was the Taliban prohibition of the 2000/1 growing season discussed in Chapter 6. In Helmand, the result of this ban was that cultivation fell from an estimated 42,853 hectares in June 2000 to negligible levels of opium poppy cultivation twelve months later. However, it also had a significant effect on the rural economy and, consequently, on support for the Taliban regime. For example, between September 2000 and July 2001, the price of opium increased from around US$100 to US$500. The ban also led to a significant rise in opium-denominated debt and a striking increase in rural unemployment. The senior leadership of the Taliban hoped that the ban would result in a massive inflow of development assistance to mitigate these risks, but it ultimately established the conditions for a dramatic rise in the price and level of cultivation, not just in areas where opium poppy had been entrenched for years, but also where cultivation had been rather marginal until 2001. The ban did little to bolster support for the Taliban among the rural population in the strategic Pashtun provinces once the events of 11 September 2001 unfolded.

After the Taliban's collapse, an estimated 29,950 hectares of opium poppy were cultivated in Helmand in the 2001/2 growing season despite attempts to implement a scheme of compensated eradication in the central districts of Nad e Ali, Marjeh and Lashkar Gah by the Afghan government, with the support of the UK. In the 2002/3 growing season, Governor Sher Mohammed Akhundzada launched his own counternarcotics effort. This did not reduce cultivation as significantly as the Taliban prohibition, but it did succeed in reducing cultivation by an estimated 50 per cent between 2002 and 2003 (Hafvenstein, 2007: 193). Over that year, reductions were concentrated in the central districts of Nad e Ali, Nawa Barakzai, Sarban Qala and Musa Qala, with total cultivation falling from an estimated 29,950 hectares in 2001/2 to 15,371 hectares in 2002/3. Even greater reductions would have occurred if it were not for increases in cultivation in the northern districts of Kajaki and Baghran.

While many accused Governor Sher Mohammed Akhundzada of targeting his drug control efforts at his competitors in the drugs trade and at those who did not belong to his tribe, evidence for this accusation is far from clear from district-level data. By late 2003, the governor argued that the failure to deliver on the promises of development assistance led to a loss of political capital, and that he was unable to push for lower levels of cultivation in the 2003/4 growing season (Sher Mohammed Akhundzada, personal communication, November 2003). There seems little doubt that the pending presidential election in 2004 also deterred the governor from pressing for continued reductions in cultivation, given that he was charged with soliciting votes for the incumbent. By the 2003/4 growing season, cultivation had rebounded to an estimated 29,353 hectares and continued to climb (Goodhand and Mansfield, 2010).

After 2005, levels of opium poppy cultivation increased dramatically in Helmand from an estimated 26,500 hectares in 2004/5 to an unprecedented

103,590 hectares in 2007/8. These rises occurred under Governor Sher Mohammed Akundzada's successors, Governor Daud (2006–7) and Governor Wafa (2007–8), and coincided with a significant deterioration in the security situation in the province. For the international community, rising levels of cultivation in Helmand had become a major source of embarrassment, thrusting the province, along with Nangarhar, on to the centre stage in the policy debate on counternarcotics and the strategic and operational discussions on using drug control efforts to deliver on wider counterinsurgency and state-building objectives.

The drug control effort known as the Helmand Food Zone began in the 2008/9 growing season. With mounting pressure for an aggressive eradication campaign from some quarters in Washington, DC, Helmand became the focus of the call for aerial spraying and, when this failed, an invigorated counternarcotics effort. This section examines the different institutional interests that the counternarcotics agenda served and the catalytic role that the new governor, Mohammed Gulab Mangal, played in establishing and continuing the Helmand Food Zone Programme. The section considers the component parts of the Helmand Food Zone, their implementation and the different interpretations of what led to such significant reductions in the level of opium poppy cultivation in Helmand between 2008 and 2011.

A Last Push for Aerial Eradication

Chapter 7 described the international political pressure directed at stemming the increases in cultivation in Afghanistan, including Helmand, following the 2003/4 growing season. It highlighted how the calls for aerial eradication became particularly loud when aggregate levels of cultivation rose by 17 per cent between 2006 and 2007 (Neumann, 2009; Cowper-Coles, 2011). And it detailed the growing challenges associated with a narrative of successful statebuilding in Afghanistan at a time when levels of opium poppy cultivation had reached an unprecedented level.

In fact, it could be argued that the persistence of high levels of production in central Helmand created a particular presentational challenge for both past and ongoing efforts at statebuilding in Afghanistan. After all, cultivation was concentrated in the parts of Helmand that many considered areas of consolidated statehood and that received considerable financial assistance from the USG in the 1950s and 1960s, including the districts of Nawa Barakzai, Nad e Ali and Nahre Seraj.

More importantly, such high levels of cultivation in this settled area only a short distance from the provincial centre were seen by many to represent the failure of contemporary efforts at both statebuilding and counternarcotics. If opium production could not be stopped in this area, what was the likelihood of success in more isolated parts of the country, and how would failure be viewed by others? For the government of the UK there was an added challenge: it had the unenviable task of being the 'lead' (and then 'partner') nation in counternarcotics while also being responsible for the PRT in the province with by far the greatest amount of opium poppy cultivation in the country (Walsh, 2007). With the British Army feeling that its reputation with the US had been damaged by its withdrawal from Basra in Iraq (King, 2012: 27; Ledwidge, 2011: 104), there was increasing pressure for a more aggressive and successful military campaign in Helmand, which over time came to include calls for much lower levels of cultivation in central Helmand.[2]

Advocates of an aggressive eradication effort in Afghanistan were quick to jump on Helmand as a *cause célèbre*, particularly in their calls for aerial spraying. They drew on three arguments in their push for a programme of widespread crop destruction in the province.

The first was basic arithmetic. As the primary opium-growing province, responsible for over half of the total area cultivated in the country, success in Helmand could deliver an important reduction in the national data and turn around media criticism of a failed counternarcotics effort. On the surface, the fact that the bulk of production was located in the more accessible canal-irrigated areas of the province—in particular the districts of Nad e Ali and Marjeh west of the city of Lashkar Gah—provided the impetus for a more concentrated eradication effort. If eradication were to succeed in eliminating a large part of the crop in these two districts, it would have a big effect on the amount of opium grown both in the province and in the country as a whole. Photographs of opium production in central Helmand were featured in the campaign to convince others of the logic of the argument for eradication (UNODC/MCN, 2008: 10).[3] The flat terrain, the regular shape of the plots and the organised nature of the canals gave a sense of modernity and order; an environment in which formal rules could be applied. Moreover, UNODC claimed that the destruction of 25 per cent of the standing opium crop would have an impact on levels of cultivation in subsequent growing seasons.[4] Although this claim had no empirical basis, it contributed to making central Helmand the ideal target for a renewed eradication effort.

The second argument for a more aggressive campaign of crop destruction in central Helmand was that the population there appeared to be relatively resource-wealthy compared to other parts of the province and of the country (UNODC/MCN, 2007; Schweich, 2007). Advocates pointed to the fact that landholdings in the canal command area were relatively generous, that the steady source of irrigation allowed crops to be grown year round, and that, due to the concentration of opium production for well over a decade, there was little evidence of the deprivation seen in other parts of the country. Given relatively large landholdings and extensive cultivation over the years, it was assumed that farmers had accumulated stocks of opium that they could draw upon and could therefore experience an aggressive eradication policy without major losses in welfare and potential destitution.

Such claims ignored the complex land tenure arrangements in place in Helmand, and the important role that opium plays in providing the land-poor with income through sharecropping arrangements, tenancy and work as labourers during both the weeding and harvesting seasons. Furthermore, relative wealth with opium poppy does not necessarily mean that a farmer will not endure absolute poverty once he has been compelled to abandon the crop, as evidenced by the large number of land-poor households leaving the canal command area to take up residence in the former desert areas north of the Boghra Canal, following the implementation of the Helmand Food Zone (see Chapter 10).

The final argument used to support a more aggressive eradication policy—and perhaps the one that gained the most resonance with those beyond the counternarcotics community—was the growing claim that the Taliban, now deeply embedded in the province, derived the bulk of its funding from taxing the production and trade of opiates (UNODC/MCN, 2007; Semple and Golden, 2007; United States Department of State, 2007: 51; Schweich, 2008). At the time, estimates of the revenue generated by the Taliban (although it was often unclear which insurgent groups were included under this heading) ranged from US$70 million to US$500 million per year (Peters, 2009). Despite this huge variation in the estimates and the resulting uncertainty over the scale of funding, UNODC (2008: 3) and authors like Peters (2009) went further, arguing that the Taliban were directly involved in producing and processing opiates and had become no more than 'criminal organisations', discarding their political or religious doctrines in favour of the pursuit of profit and market share (Peters, 2009; UNODC, 2008: 3). By late 2008, UNODC went so far as to suggest that the Taliban were actively engaged in market manipulation, retaining stocks of opium so as to prevent further reductions in price and looking to impose a further ban on opium poppy cultivation to increase the value of their inventories (UNODC/MCN, 2008: 2–3; Costa, 2007).

The argument that the Taliban were synonymous with drug trafficking organisations gained support among many policy-makers and academics (United States Congress, 2009: 10; United States Senate Caucus on International Narcotics Control, 2010: 2l; Kilcullen, 2009: 64–6) and was often used to justify an eradication policy in Helmand that would not only eliminate a large proportion of the standing crop, but would also reduce the funds that flowed to the insurgency.

The Executive Director of UNODC elaborated on what he considered a symbiotic relationship between the Taliban and avaricious farmers. He claimed: 'The Taliban today control vast swathes of land in Helmand, Kandahar and along the Pakistani border. By preventing the national authorities and international agencies from working, insurgents have allowed greed and corruption to turn orchards, wheat and vegetable fields into poppy fields' (UNODC/MCN, 2007: iii). Some officials such as David Kilcullen (2009: 63), at the time a counter-terrorism adviser to the US Department of State and a frequent visitor to the PRTs in Helmand and Kandahar, argued that a campaign of crop destruction would not only limit the Taliban's funds but counter their claim that they could protect the rural population, further undermining support for the insurgency. In his support for aerial eradication, Kilcullen (2009: 63) went further, claiming that 'even the harshest of efforts to eradicate the poppy would be unlikely to alienate anything like the majority of the population, except in the areas that already firmly support the Taliban and are therefore already alienated anyway'.[5]

Those highlighting the links between drug traffickers and the Taliban typically cited Hajji Bashir Noorzai and Hajji Juma Khan as evidence of the depth of the relationship (Peters, 2009). They referred to allegations that Hajji Bashir Noorzai, a trafficker currently incarcerated in the United States, served on the inner Shura during the Taliban regime in the mid to late 1990s. Yet earlier chapters on Nangarhar and Mike Martin's (2014) detailed history of Helmand have shown that allegiances in Afghanistan are fluid and political ideologies adaptable to changing events. Hajji Bashir Noorzai, for example is the cousin of Mohammed Arif Noorzai, who represents Kandahar province in the Wolsei Jirga and was also first deputy speaker until 2009, when he was given the government post in charge of the Community Defence Initiative (Naval Postgraduate School, 2010). Following the fall of the Taliban regime, Hajji Bashir Noorzai handed over Taliban weapons to US forces in 2002; he is alleged to have acted as an informant for the USG, and maintained close relationships with the provincial leadership of the Afghan government in Kandahar (Risen, 2007).

While senior US officials such as Tom Schweich, US Coordinator for Counternarcotics and Justice Reform in Afghanistan, and Ambassador William Wood continued to press the argument that the Taliban were synonymous with the drugs trade as justification for an aggressive eradication policy, interviews in rural areas of the south suggested that these claims did not resonate with the wider population (Mansfield, 2008b: 48). In fact, it was a common perception that those working for the government were more actively involved in the narcotics trade than the Taliban (Mansfield, 2010b: 22–3). These allegations were reported in the international media, including accounts that linked the former Deputy Minister Daud[6] and the head of the border police, Colonel Razik,[7] to drugs traders in the south (Smith, 2009; Watson, 2005; Aikins, 2009; Chandresekaran, 2010). Arif Noorzai's father, Hajji Musa Jan Noorzai, was alleged to have acquired a fortune from his involvement in the drugs trade in the 1960s, and Arif Noorzai himself is related by marriage to both Ahmed Wali Karzai and Sher Mohammed Akhundzada (former governor of Helmand), both of whom have been accused of involvement in the drugs business (Forsberg, 2010: 34–5; Giustozzi and Ullah, 2006: 13).

In Helmand, direct links between the drugs trade and those in government were often far more apparent to the local population (Ruttig, 2009b). For example, Sher Mohammed Akhundzada, governor between 2002 and 2006 and now senator in the Afghan parliament, was found with 9 metric tonnes of opium in his residence in 2005 and was subsequently replaced (Gopal, 2010). Dad Mohammed Khan, known locally as 'Amir Dado', Helmand Chief of Intelligence between 2001 and 2005 and then Member of Parliament, also stood accused of being a major protagonist in the drugs trade until his death in March 2009 (Coghlan, 2009: 119; Hafvenstein, 2007: 130–31, 313). Abdul Rahman Jan, former chief of police, is also thought to be a significant opium trader in the province, responsible for a number of violent attacks against his rival traffickers, some of which have been blamed on the Taliban (Hafvenstein, 2007: 244; Coghlan, 2009: 122). He was even thought to have obtained protection for his opium crop in Marjeh from the Taliban following attempts to destroy it (Gopal, 2010; McChrystal, 2013: 320). Mir Wali, former commander of the 93rd Division in Helmand—disarmed in 2004 by the DDR process and a member of the *wolsei Jirga*—is still a major powerbroker in

Helmand's Gereshk district, and widely considered a rogue commander with influence over an illegal armed group involved in the narcotics business.[8]

Drug control organisations like UNODC recognised the limits of portraying the drugs trade as the preserve of the Taliban, given the links that Afghan government officials had to the industry. To justify a more aggressive eradication policy, they pointed to reports that the Taliban generated as much as 10 per cent of the opium crop as tax (UNODC/MCN, 2007: iv).[9] As with the relationship between the insurgency and the drugs trade, empirical evidence presented a more complex picture of the role that opium played in funding the Taliban. For example, farmers in Helmand reported much lower levels of payment to the insurgency that were not simply a function of the opium yield and that fluctuated according to prevailing economic conditions. And in Nad e Ali in 2008, when opium poppy was grown extensively, farmers reported paying a land tax of 12,000 PR per unit of land known as a *forma*,[10] as well as a tax on their opium crop of two *khord* per *jerib* (the equivalent of 225 grams per *jerib* and 2.25 per cent of the final yield) at a time when UNODC was reporting yields of around 10 kilograms per *jerib*. Later fieldwork revealed that as levels of opium poppy cultivation fell in the canal command area of Nad e Ali, so did the land tax, from 8,000 PR per *forma* in 2009, to 6,000 PR in 2010 and only 2,000 PR in 2011 (Mansfield, 2011: 31). This suggested an insurgency that could not only be more responsive to community needs than often presented by policy-makers, but that was also less reliant on the income generated from taxing opium production than claimed.[11]

Ultimately, despite the policy rhetoric that linked winning the war against the Taliban with eliminating opium production in the south, and in particular in the province of Helmand, those advocating aerial spraying within the USG remained a vocal minority. Other elements within the USG—most notably the Department of Defense and the intelligence community—argued against spraying, fearful that it would fuel rural support for the insurgency. The UK and the European Commission, along with member states of the European Union and NATO, all opposed the call to spray the opium crop from the air. And although the UK bowed to US pressure and supported a proposal to pilot a ground-based spraying operation in 'permissive areas', the Afghan government quashed this idea in January 2007 (Neumann, 2009: 146–9; Cowper-Coles, 2011: 84). This left the counternarcotics community with little choice; with the failure to get a consensus on aerial spraying the options on eradication were limited to supporting more effective Governor-Led Eradication and bolstering the central eradication force so that it could later be the vehicle for a more robust campaign once circumstances allowed (US GAO, 2010: 15).[12]

A Governor in Need of Friends in the Right Places: The Arrival of Gulab Mangal

For the first time since 2005, aggregate levels of opium poppy cultivation fell in Afghanistan in 2008, at the same time that UNODC declared Nangarhar 'poppy free' (UNODC/MCN, 2008: 8). To a large extent, the reversal of the upward trend in the national figures for cultivation, and in particular the emergence of a 'successful model' for counternarcotics in Nangarhar, disarmed those advocating aerial eradication in Afghanistan, at least for another season. Despite these successes, the growing concentration of opium poppy cultivation in the southern region continued to present a problem that had to be addressed. The UK effort in Helmand continued to be lambasted in the media for rising levels of cultivation at a time when it was the partner nation on counternarcotics and when British soldiers were losing their lives.

In March 2008, Mohammed Gulab Mangal was appointed Governor of Helmand. He arrived with a solid reputation as an administrator from his time as Governor of Paktika (2004–6) and Laghman (2006–8), and was instantly lauded by the international community (Leithead, 2008). Gulab Mangal was a notable contrast to his predecessors, particularly Governors Wafa and Akhundzada, both of whom were close to President Karzai. The British remained hopeful, given the new governor's talk of government reform and Taliban reconciliation and his active community engagement from the start.

Mangal immediately showed himself keen to act against drugs production (Gall, 2008). Both publicly and privately he linked the counternarcotics effort with counterinsurgency and the rule of law. He talked of traffickers living with impunity in Lashkar Gah and the need to act against corruption and illegality. He also encouraged the British and the US to increase their interdiction efforts (Hall, 2008; *Guardian*, 2009). As early as July 2008, 'a short term provincial counter narcotics strategy' emerged from the governor's office, drafted by a member of the Poppy Elimination Programme (PEP) and a military officer appointed to the counternarcotics team in the PRT. This strategy outlined a combination of initiatives aimed at reducing the level of opium poppy cultivation in Helmand during the 2008/9 growing season, including a pre-planting public information campaign, a programme of alternative livelihoods and an invigorated law enforcement and eradication effort (Office of the

Governor of Helmand, 2008: 5). The strategy argued that it came at a time when 'successful models for counternarcotics had been developed in Nangarhar and Laghman, making it possible for these models to be adapted for application in Helmand' (ibid.: 4).

In reality, this strategy—which came to be known as the 'Helmand Food Zone'—appeared to have little to do with the complex socio-economic and political processes that had led to such a striking reduction in Nangarhar during the 2007/8 growing season. Instead, the Helmand counternarcotics strategy appeared to have much more in common with the alternative development programmes undertaken by UNDCP in the 1990s, where development assistance was directly tied to reductions in cultivation. Furthermore, the focus on wheat as an alternative to opium poppy was reminiscent of the crop substitution programmes that had been discredited in the 1980s. The limits of replacing a cash crop with a food crop seemed obvious to many, more so given the accumulating evidence of the role that opium poppy played in accessing credit, land and labour for the different socio-economic groups involved in its cultivation.

Despite these reservations, the programme proved popular with the PRT and with a drug control community that was searching for a response to the burgeoning levels of cultivation in the southern region. Most importantly, the Helmand Food Zone showed clear intent to reduce opium at a time when there was growing political pressure to do so. It was also simple, almost contractual in nature, and reflected the order and modernity that a casual observer might assume prevailed in the canal command area of Helmand. It had a clear logic and thereby a basis for attributing results: in return for the delivery of agricultural inputs, rural communities would stop cultivating opium; if they did not, their crop would be destroyed. It was a technical and logistical response that could be delivered by the different international agencies that were involved, regardless of any reservations by the development agencies about the efficacy of wheat seed and fertiliser distribution.[13] If successful, the Helmand Food Zone might also silence advocates for aerial spraying for another year.

Perhaps the greatest attraction was the fact that the governor was quick to take ownership and eager to become the public face of the Food Zone and the wider counternarcotics effort—the 'Afghan face' that had been noticeably absent in Helmand up to then.

Governor Mangal had many reasons to be enthusiastic about the Helmand Food Zone. The first reason was his genuine concern about the proliferation of opium poppy cultivation and its impact on the province, particularly given the linkages between the drugs trade and the insurgency, and corruption within the provincial and district authorities.

The second—and perhaps even more important—reason for Mangal's support for the Food Zone was the implication that a continued upward trajectory in cultivation would affect his tenure and likely prospects of promotion within the Afghan government. As with Governor Shirzai in Nangarhar and Mohammed Atta Noor in Balkh, Mangal felt assured that as long as cultivation fell he would retain the support of the US and UK governments and thereby his position as governor; and that they might even support him in his quest for higher office (Vistisen, 2011).[14]

Mangal was particularly vulnerable because of his position with the president. While popular with the international community, in particular the US and UK, Mangal was at best tolerated by President Karzai (Cowper-Coles, 2011: 191). Karzai openly blamed the increasing insecurity in Helmand on the removal of Sher Mohammed Akhundzada—a demand of the UK government when they took over the PRT in 2006 (McChrystal, 2013: 373). Within months of Mangal's appointment there were rumours that the president would dismiss him; and this continued throughout Mangal's tenure (Gall, 2008; *Guardian*, 2010a, 2010b, 2010c). Mangal found it hard to get an appointment with the president during his visits to Kabul and was often confronted with accusations that he was too close to the British.

Akhunzada campaigned against the new governor from the start and often approached Karzai requesting his position back or looking for his allies to be appointed to key positions in the province. Even in 2010, Governor Mangal faced the prospect of Abdul Raman Jan—former chief of the provincial police, and close ally of Sher Mohammed Akhundzada, with an appalling record of abuse, corruption and even complicity with the Taliban—being appointed district governor of Marjeh when the area was cleared by Operation Moshtarak. Mangal knew that without objections from the US and UK, President Karzai would have reappointed Akhundzada governor of Helmand (Malkesian, 2013: 269; Cowper-Coles, 2011: 191), particularly in the run-up to the 2009 presidential election when Karzai hoped that the former governor could repeat the successful campaign that he had run in 2004.

The third reason for Governor Gulab Mangal's support for the Food Zone was the level of resources that it brought to bear. In the 2008/9 growing season, the programme cost US$12 million (Office of Governor, 2009: 3). A further US$12.9 million was spent on the programme in the 2009/10 growing season, with a final contribution of US$18 million by the UK and US in the 2010/11 growing season. In all three years the vast bulk of the expenditure was on agricultural inputs, notably wheat seed and fertiliser. Aside from the distribution of these items—which came to be seen as a key element in district stabilisation following the military's efforts to clear armed opposition groups—the Helmand Food Zone Programme gave Governor Mangal access to other assets from which to build his own patronage networks within the province. The public information campaign, for example, provided him with access to military transport and the opportunity to project his leadership within the districts. GLE provided generous payments to compensate for the costs of crop destruction each year, and in 2009 the Good Performance Initiative—funded by INL and the UK and administered by MCN—allocated an additional US$10 million for development projects in Helmand on the basis of the reductions that had been achieved between 2008 and 2009 (US Department of State, INL, 2010: 1).

Governor Mangal's zeal in counternarcotics became an intrinsic part of his image as a good governor and strong leader with whom Western nations could 'do business' (US Department of State, 2010: 95–6; Wayne, 2009). The reductions achieved over such a short time frame contributed to the growing sense that Mangal could do no wrong. Concerns about the sustainability of the Food Zone Programme and the efficacy of wheat seed distribution, and even questions over whether the fall in opium production could be attributed to the Programme, did not deter funding for the programme or plaudits for the governor. The governor was so popular with the international community at this stage that, in the words of the former British ambassador Sherard Cowper-Coles, he became 'the mascot of successive commanders of Task Force Helmand and successive heads of the PRT, and a figure in the British as well as the Afghan media' (Cowper-Coles, 2011: 166). The international community's desire to see progress on counternarcotics in Helmand left little space to question either the programme or Governor Mangal, even when reports of corruption began to surface (MacKenzie, 2010).

Further reductions in levels of cultivation became an annual obsession. They were implicitly linked with the performances of individuals, institutions and the overall statebuilding project in Afghanistan. Neither the governor, successive heads of the PRT nor military commanders at the level of Task Force Helmand or the Regional Command wanted to preside over an increase in cultivation during their tenure. Even the US Marine Corps found itself taken to task in the midst of one of its largest military manoeuvres, Operation Moshtarak, in the spring of 2010 for not actively seeking to reduce the level of opium poppy cultivation in Marjeh. This was despite the fact that the crop had been planted four months before the USMC's arrival in Marjeh and a campaign to assure community leaders and members that their crops would not be destroyed (Chisholm, 2010; Nissenbaum, 2010).[15]

Governor Mangal himself pressed for year-on-year enlargement of the geographic area covered by the Food Zone within which eradication should be targeted, including encroachment into the former desert areas to both the south and north of the Boghra Canal. While these areas were formally recognised as government land, many had been appropriated by local commanders linked with the former Governor Akhundzada before being gifted to their solders and extended families or sold (Mansfield, 2011b). In this context, Mangal's support for eradication and counternarcotics could be seen as a device to promote the coercive power of the Afghan state across an ever-increasing geographic space, and a way of weakening the position of his political opponents within the province, most notably Sher Mohammed Akhundzada (Coffey, 2012: 32). Governor Mangal knew that he was placing parts of the international community in Helmand in a difficult position: either they could call for the governor to refrain from extending the ban into new areas, or they could succumb to his demands and live with the military, economic and political consequences of his desire to project state power through the ban on opium production.

The Helmand Food Zone

Implementation

The Helmand Food Zone Programme focused on three interlinked components: a pre-planting public awareness campaign, alternative livelihoods and finally interdiction and eradication.The pre-planting awareness campaign absorbed only a small part of the overall effort. Launched in late summer of each year, the campaign consisted of a range of activities that sought to raise the social costs of opium production. It highlighted the illegality of opium poppy cultivation, its forbidden status under Islam, and the impact of opium production on the user population within the country. The legal and practical implications of producing opium were emphasised with farmers, in particular the threat of eradication. The risk of arrest for those cultivating opium poppy was also a component part of this campaign; in some parts of Helmand it became a more credible threat as the programme entered its third year and the numbers of ANSF and international military forces increased.

Governor Mangal played a key part in outreach in the pre-planting campaign, travelling to different district centres within the Food Zone and holding meetings to persuade elders to convince their fellow villagers to accept the programme and desist from poppy cultivation. *Shura* meetings were reinforced with radio messages, posters and other initiatives to increase awareness of the Food Zone and the governor's position on opium poppy cultivation.

The effectiveness of the public awareness campaign during the early years of the Food Zone has to be seen in the context of the security situation at the time. Initially the governor's mobility was limited and he had to be transported to the district centres by the PRT. As was the case for Governor Shirzai in the southern districts of Nangarhar, the fact that Governor Mangal was required to travel with a foreign military escort reinforced local perceptions that the government had little control of the area. Moreover, in areas where the Taliban maintained influence, the messages warning farmers not to plant opium poppy were not cascaded down to the rural population, as the elders feared that they would be seen to be acting on behalf of the government and punished by the insurgents (Read and Ryder, 2009: Annex H). And while the PRT often cited attendance at these *shuras* as evidence of their success, farmers themselves were sceptical of the representation at these meetings in the 2008/9 and 2009/10 growing seasons, arguing that many of the *maliks* appointed to represent the community could not be found in the village but were instead residing in Lashkar Gah. But the perceptions of these meetings and of the overall counternarcotics effort were to change with delivery of other components of the Food Zone Programme in the 2010/11 growing season, following Operation Moshtarak I and II and the substantial increase in ANSF and international military forces in the area.

The second and largest component of the Helmand Food Zone Programme was alternative livelihoods. Although some of the development advisers involved in the design of the programme anticipated it evolving into a platform for wider development with a range of crops and assistance, the Food Zone as outlined by the governor's counternarcotics programme remained focused on the distribution of wheat seed and fertiliser. Other assistance, including packages of spring crops and wider rural development activities, did become available over time and came to be more closely associated with the counternarcotics effort, but these were not formally part of the Food Zone.[16]

The idea behind the provision of a package of wheat seed and fertiliser to eligible farmers was simple: it was a gesture of support to communities in return for their commitment to give up opium poppy, and was intended to improve wheat yields within central Helmand Food Zone (Malkesian, 2013: 141). It was not intended to replace the monetary value of opium production, although in 2008 the net returns on the two crops were comparable (Mansfield, 2009b; 48).

Given the resource and logistical constraints of the programme, not all farmers within the Food Zone were eligible to receive wheat seed and fertiliser; both areas and farmers had to be prioritised. The geographic focus was on the most fertile parts of the Helmand canal command area and subsequently areas that had undergone major military campaigns to clear them of the insurgency. As such, the geographic parameters of the Food Zone expanded over the three years from the original sites in the canal-irrigated areas of Nad e Ali, Nawa Barakzai, Garmsir and Nahre Seraj districts to include the river-irrigated parts of Musa Qala, Marjeh, Khanishin Sangin and Nawzad districts.

Distributing the agricultural inputs to eligible farmers in these areas proved the most challenging and resource-intensive part of the Food Zone Programme. For example, the task of getting 11,000 metric tonnes of wheat seed and fertiliser out to the different distribution sites in Helmand prior to the planting seasons was a major logistical challenge. In the first year, distribution was centred in Lashkar Gah and Gereshk due to the security conditions in many of the districts covered by the programme. However, in the fall of 2009, with security conditions improving in many district centres, it was possible to decentralise the distribution to all but the district of Marjeh, whose farmers were required to come to Lashkar Gah to receive their wheat seed and fertiliser. By the 2009/10 growing season, inputs were distributed in the ten districts covered by the programme, including from the Forward Operating Base in Marjeh. Security remained a concern throughout the life of the programme; even in the 2010/11 growing season, ISAF were deployed to protect the convoys of the contractor responsible for the procurement and distribution of the wheat seed and fertiliser.[17]

The distribution of the agricultural inputs to the actual farmers proved even more complex. From the start of the programme it was decided that only farmers who owned land would be eligible to receive the wheat seed and fertiliser; each farmer would receive a package of 100 kilograms of wheat seed, 100 kilograms of Diammonium Phosphate (DAP) and 200 kilograms of urea. However, given funding constraints, how was the programme to decide who received the wheat seed and fertiliser in a specific area and—perhaps more importantly—how was the programme to monitor the use of the seeds?

With regard to distribution, the programme fell back on traditional patterns of Afghan patronage: the local administration drew up beneficiary lists in conjunction with village elders. Those on the list were required to come to the distribution centre on a specific date and collect their wheat seed and fertiliser in return for a co-payment[18] and a signed commitment to desist from opium poppy cultivation. These beneficiary lists proved a major point of contention throughout the programme's life. It was generally accepted that the lists favoured the rural elite and that a disproportionate number of names on the list were relatives of elders and local officials.[19] However, even more serious allegations of corruption were levelled at elders and local officials, with claims that they conspired to enter false names on the list and to misappropriate inputs for their own advantage (Mansfield et al., 2011: 67; SIGAR, 2013: 4; USAID, 2010: 6).[20] While PRT officials wrestled with different ways to identify eligible farmers—including offering inputs in the spring of 2010 on a first come, first served basis—the central government (in the form of the Ministry of Agriculture, Irrigation and Livestock) and the provincial and district authorities were adamant that they should retain influence over which farmers would receive agricultural inputs.

During the course of the programme there was a litany of complaints from farmers in Helmand about the distribution of wheat seed and fertiliser. Some complaints related to logistics and the fact that wheat seed was not received until after the planting season; others were over the quality of the seed and continuing rumours that it was not improved,[21] which culminated in the arrest of a number of government officials in late 2009 (Mackenzie, 2010; Mansfield et al., 2011: 67). A further complaint related to what farmers saw as a disconnect between the provision of what was after all a small amount of development assistance and the pressing security and development problems that communities faced. The fact that this assistance was contingent on abandoning opium poppy only added to the farmers' frustrations with the provincial authorities.

There were also widespread complaints from farmers in more insecure areas that they could not transport the wheat seed that they received to their farms for fear of punishment from the Taliban. Some farmers reported repackaging their wheat, removing it from the bags that indicated distribution by the government or internationals, or selling it on. In fact, there were widespread reports of a thriving business in the resale of agricultural inputs which involved government officials, shopkeepers in Lashkar Gah and Gereshk, and prospective buyers working on commission who approached farmers as soon as they left the distribution sites. In November 2010, interviews with farmers revealed that, rather than use the wheat seed and fertiliser they had received, many had resold their agricultural inputs, receiving around US$120 for a package that had cost only US$40 (Mansfield et al., 2011: 67).

Despite the challenges that the programme faced—including direct attacks on one of the distribution centres in late 2009 and the ongoing concerns over corruption—distribution continued until the fall of the 2010/11 growing season. During the first year, the PRT reported that 33,000 households had received wheat seed and fertiliser, with a further 39,640 in 2009/10) and a final 48,200 in the fall of 2010 (Macpherson and Hannah, 2010: 43).

Formally, the final component of the Food Zone Programme was law enforcement and eradication. However, in reality this element only included crop destruction; the responsibility for interdiction sat with law enforcement officials within the Afghan government, the US and the UK, and was not tied to the other components of the Food Zone Programme. Eradication consistently proved to be the most controversial element of the Helmand Food Zone Programme, particularly given its history in the province. Indeed, an eradication campaign had been conducted in Helmand in one form or another every year since 2000. These included small amounts of crop destruction under the Taliban during the 2000/1 growing season, as well as the compensated eradication campaign supported by the British in early 2002. In Helmand, eradication had typically involved tractors and, with the establishment of the Afghan Eradication Force (AEF), All Terrain Vehicles (ATVs). Teams of men wielding sticks had also been used in the 2002/3 growing season and in 2003/4 when Sher Mohammed Akhundzada was governor.

After 2006, eradication in Helmand became more institutionalised. It was conducted through two distinct operations, both of which undertook their campaigns in the spring. The first operation, Governor-Led Eradication (GLE), used a large number of tractors. It was protected by the Afghan National Police and directed by the Governor of Helmand's Eradication Committee. The second operation, the AEF—later renamed the Poppy Eradication Force (PEF)—consisted of a mix of tractors and ATVs. It was backed by a sizable security force and logistical support. This later operation was funded by the USG to the tune of around US$60 million a year and implemented by a private contractor, Dyncorp, which was also the contractor for aerial spraying in Colombia (Anderson, 2007). The AEF/PEF operated between 2005 and 2009 until funding ceased under the Obama administration. Although it was deployed from Kabul and theoretically could operate anywhere in the country, this force spent much of its time in Helmand during the eradication season.[22]

Both GLE and the AEF/PEF were subject to many violent attacks over the years and had personnel killed. Numerous allegations of corruption were levelled at both forces, with reports that farmers could elude eradication in return for payments (Gordon, 2011: 28). Assessing the level of crop destruction by both operations was highly problematic, particularly given the prevailing levels of insecurity. Initially UNODC had been reluctant to engage in eradication verification, concerned about the security of their staff and the potential effect of verification assessments on the implementation of their annual survey. Despite UNODC's reservations, they were persuaded to conduct eradication verification[23] and given funds to do so by the UK and the US. UNODC adopted a method that initially relied on visits to rural areas after the eradication campaign had been completed, but growing concerns over exaggerated figures in 2006 and 2007 led to greater use of remote sensing imagery, drawing on technical support from Cranfield University.[24]

The methodological and security challenges associated with eradication verification were greatly exacerbated by the politics of eradication, most notably the fact that eradication was often used as a metric by which to judge performance against counternarcotics objectives related to statebuilding as well as to institutional and individual accomplishments (Neumann, 2009). This led to over-reporting by Afghan nationals and also resulted in a preference for inflated figures among internationals. It became particularly evident with the level of over-reporting by the AEF/PEF in the spring of 2007 that culminated in a review and subsequent reduction in the figures reported (Cranfield, 2007).[25]

GLE suffered from the same problems, not least because the US and UK governments provided generous compensation for each hectare destroyed,[26] creating further incentives for over-reporting. Due to the intense interest in higher eradication figures, the ground verifiers working for UNODC found themselves under considerable duress to exaggerate their reports of the amount of crop destroyed. The pressure placed on verifiers—coupled with the realisation that fields not eradicated properly could recover if irrigated and fertilised—meant that there was often a need for closer scrutiny of the eradication figures than took place.

In the final year of the Food Zone Programme, following the closure of the AEF, monitoring of GLE increased. Tractors were fitted with Global Position System (GPS) tracking devices allowing daily reviews of their movements

(Cowper-Coles, 2011: 86–7; US GAO, 2010: 11). With the Obama administration and the appointment of Richard Holbrooke, a vocal opponent of eradication, the USG agreed to a more targeted approach to eradication in Helmand, and crop destruction became concentrated in the more productive canal command area. Consequently, in contrast to the GLE campaign in the 2007/8 and 2008/9 growing seasons—when more marginal communities in less productive land were targeted for crop destruction and the AEF/PEF focused on the former desert areas to the north of the Boghra—95 per cent of the crop destruction in the 2009/10 growing season took place in the more productive agricultural land where wheat seed and fertiliser had been distributed. This accorded with the initial intention of the Food Zone Programme (Mansfield et al., 2011: 24–5).

Moreover, with the significant increase in the number of ANSF and international military forces in central Helmand, farmers found that there was less scope for bribing the eradication team and avoiding crop destruction. By the 2009/10 growing season, eradication was seen as more resolute in the canal command area; farmers claimed that crop destruction was more comprehensive than in earlier campaigns and that fewer fields were spared. Even attempts to bribe the eradication teams were reportedly spurned (Mansfield et al., 2011: 39–40) as the eradication team became conscious that it was under closer scrutiny.

The Results of the Helmand Food Zone Programme

From its inception, the Food Zone was considered a flagship intervention, credited with successfully reducing opium poppy cultivation in the central part of Helmand province. While there are challenges in comparing annual levels of cultivation within what appears to have been a constantly changing boundary, it is clear that opium poppy cultivation fell significantly in the Food Zone after the programme began in the fall of 2008. The USG reported that, in the area covered consistently throughout the Food Zone initiative, cultivation fell from 32,889 hectares in 2008 to 6,142 hectares in 2013 (see Figure 4).[27]

Advocates of the Food Zone Programme point to the fact that during implementation cultivation fell dramatically. However, explanations for the fall in cultivation in the Food Zone are confused by contrasting definitions of the actual operations of the Helmand programme; of the relationship of levels of cultivation to exogenous factors; and of the different interventions occurring in Helmand at the time.

Figure 4: Changes in Opium Poppy Cultivation in Helmand 2008–2014 (hectares)

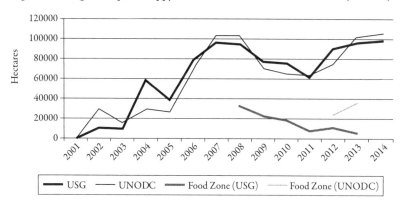

A minimalist interpretation, for example, would consider only the original design of the programme and its three component parts. It would argue that at a time when wheat seeds were being distributed and farmers were being threatened with eradication, opium poppy cultivation fell dramatically in the area designated as the Food Zone and wheat cultivation almost doubled in the same area (Cranfield, 2009).

Supporting evidence for the success of the Food Zone and Governor Mangal's critical role in reducing cultivation draws on the fact that, at the same time as cultivation in Helmand was falling, even larger amounts of opium poppy were being cultivated in the neighbouring province of Kandahar, where roughly the same conditions applied but the governor showed no commitment to counternarcotics. Geospatial analysis in Helmand conducted by the USG suggests that the act of eradication alone in 2009 deterred levels of opium poppy cultivation in 2010, with the most significant effect being felt 100 metres to 200 metres from where crop destruction was conducted the year before (USG, 2011).

However, there are several problems with this line of argument. The most obvious is that other factors influenced levels of cultivation during the period that the Food Zone was being implemented. Therefore a broader analysis of the Helmand Food Zone would not just consider the impact of these three interventions—the pre-planting campaign, the distribution of wheat seed and fertilizer, and eradication—but would also include the concurrent economic, social and political processes that impacted on levels of opium poppy cultivation at the time.

237

One of the most important economic factors is the notable shift in the terms of trade between opium poppy and wheat between October 2007 and April 2009, and how this affected farmers' concerns over food security both within and outside the Food Zone. For example, Cranfield University estimated that while opium poppy cultivation decreased in the Food Zone by 37 per cent between 2008 and 2009 and increased in the area outside the Food Zone by 8 per cent, both areas saw a doubling of the amount of land under wheat. This estimate strongly suggests that both those who were and were not directly affected by the programme made significant investments in wheat production. Inside the Food Zone, the increase in wheat production, stimulated by over-production of opium in 2008 and concerns over food security, took place at the expense of opium poppy cultivation due to the finite amount of land under the Helmand canal command area. Outside the Food Zone, in the former desert areas where no such barriers existed, the 98 per cent increase in wheat cultivation occurred by bringing new land under cultivation (Mansfield, Alcis and OSDR, 2011).

A broader analysis of the results of the Food Zone would also take into account the effect of the increased inflow of international military forces and the ANSF since 2009 and 2010, particularly with the military operations Panjai Palang, Khanjar and Moshtarak in central Helmand and the major expansion of security infrastructure and personnel until the end of the 'surge' in the summer of 2012. It is particularly hard to ignore the fact that the amount of land dedicated to opium poppy in Marjeh was almost 60 per cent in 2010 and fell to less than 5 per cent the season after Operation Moshtarak when almost 15,000 ANSF and USMC had taken up posts within the district (Mansfield, 2012: 3). Farmers across central Helmand referred to the prevalence of government and international forces within rural communities—concurring with Mike Martin's statement of 'a checkpoint on every junction'—and how this deterred future cultivation.

In fact, contrary to the geospatial imagery presented by the USG suggesting that eradication determined levels of cultivation in subsequent plantings, farmers argued that the ongoing presence of the state—in the form of security infrastructure and the delivery of public goods and services—determined the level of cultivation in central Helmand in subsequent growing seasons (Mansfield et al., 2011: 3, 38–43).[28] Where security conditions prevented the state from establishing a more permanent presence in an area, eradication was seen as a random act that could be managed by farmers through patronage and corruption. This perception led to increasing resentment; farmers described the government's eradication under these circumstances as acting like a 'thief in the night'. And contrary to some Western nations' claims that eradication extended the writ of the state in rural areas, many farmers argued that it was a sign of state weakness, particularly when undertaken with the support of foreign military forces such as the AEF (Read and Ryder, 2010: Annex H; Mansfield, 2010b: 1, 5, 7). This attitude prevailed in the area north of the Boghra Canal where the attempts of Governor Mangal and his successor, Naeem Baloch, to use eradication to extend their reach beyond the canal command area are seen as just another opportunity for government to engage in rent extraction (Mansfield, 2014).

It is also necessary to consider the notable increase in the amount of development assistance (not just counternarcotics support) that flowed into Helmand province from 2008 onwards. As early as 2007, Ambassador Wood talked of Helmand as the 'fifth largest recipient of USAID funding in the world' (Wood, 2007). Yet by 2009, even more development assistance was being distributed in Helmand by both USAID and DFID through development programmes such as AVIPA-Plus, HARDP, the Afghan Stability Initiative and the National Priority Programmes in health and education, as well as through increased amounts of money from the military in the form of CERPs and large-scale construction projects. There were even more increases in 2010 and 2011 accompanying the surge. By 2011, USAID estimated that it had spent US$489.9 million in Helmand, the vast majority of it since 2008 (USAID, 2011: 1). While there have been many questions regarding the value for money of this assistance and its sustainability, as well as broader questions about the extent to which aid delivers on stabilisation objectives, there is no doubt that with the inflow of aid money have come increases in available jobs, wage labour rates, agricultural diversification in areas near cities, and also an increase in market opportunities—a point to be pursued in Chapter 10.

Finally, this broader interpretation of the results of the Food Zone Programme would recognise the wider process of market penetration and globalisation that increased the rural population's exposure to improved technologies over the last decade, particularly mechanised transport. Helmand is no longer the isolated area that it once was. Investments in the main arterial and district roads, as well as improvements in the security situation along Highway 1 and within the canal command area in 2009 and 2010, created new opportunities for many rural households in Helmand. The falling cost of motor vehicles and the development of affordable technologies such as water pumps, generators, solar panels and herbicides all served to increase agricultural productivity and provided greater opportunities for employment in small businesses and trade (Mansfield, 2014).

Given the dramatic changes that were seen in Helmand after 2008—the significant uptick in the international effort by both the UK and the US, the investments of hundreds of millions of dollars in security and development, and the broader reach of economic growth and market development that could be seen in the province—it would seem misplaced to attribute the reductions in cultivation to Governor Mangal and the Helmand Food Zone alone. These factors also suggest that those who cite increasing levels of cultivation in Kandahar province as evidence of the success of the Helmand Food Zone are ill-informed. They fail to take into account at least two major factors: the inconsistency between UNODC's reports of falling levels of cultivation at the same time that the USG estimated a sizable increase in these levels (see Figure 3) and the fact that the primary opium poppy-growing areas of Kandahar lacked the inflow of foreign military forces securing the rural areas in Helmand from 2008 on and the massive amounts of development aid that accompanied them (Dressler, 2009: 47–54).

Finally, it would not be prudent to consider the reductions in cultivation within the boundaries of the Food Zone in isolation; there is a need to look beyond levels of opium poppy cultivation within the canal command area of central Helmand to consider the province as a whole. After falling from 103,693 hectares cultivated in 2008 before the Food Zone Programme began to 63,307 hectares in 2011, levels of cultivation were back up to 100,693 hectares by 2013 (see Figure 5).[29] This resurgence in cultivation occurred outside the canal command area of the central districts, in the newly settled former desert lands north of the Boghra Canal. This area saw a dramatic increase in agricultural land, concentration of opium poppy and numbers of settlers after the imposition of the opium ban in the canal command areas in the 2008/9 growing season. Chapter 10 will show that the divergent trends in cultivation in these quite different political and ecological terrains are directly related, and that many of the causes of the concentration of opium poppy and anti-government sentiment in the former desert space north of the Boghra Canal are found in the assumptions that underlie the design of the Food Zone initiative.

Conclusion

This chapter has explored the reasons why a fall in opium poppy cultivation in Helmand became such an important part of the statebuilding project in

Figure 5: A Comparison of Estimates of Opium Poppy Cultivation in Kandahar, 2001–2014 (hectares)

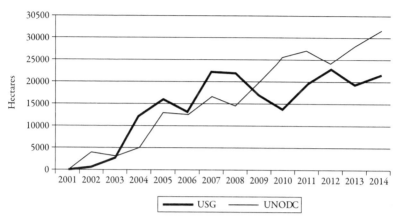

Afghanistan and how the origins of the Food Zone can be found in the desire of multiple institutions and actors in Helmand to be seen as acting against the burgeoning drugs problem at that particular moment in time. The chapter has also shown how the Helmand Food Zone Programme and Governor Mangal became so indistinguishable that neither could be seen to fail if the international effort in Helmand was to be deemed a success. This narrative and its underlying logic allowed little room for manoeuvre in any debate about the role of the Food Zone in reducing opium poppy cultivation in the canal command area of Helmand. Ultimately the rush to replicate the programme in other provinces (Feinstein, 2010) undermined the opportunity to identify how best to minimise the risk of what Scott (1976: 196) calls 'patterns of collective insecurity' that might result in the protests, violence and rural rebellion seen in the southern districts of Nangarhar, or the relocation of population groups and opium poppy cultivation into former desert land experienced in Helmand.

What is perhaps most notable in the genesis and implementation of the Helmand Food Zone is its legalistic and bureaucratic nature. While perceived as the product of the governor and his office, the initial document outlining the Food Zone was written by foreign advisers with no previous experience of the drugs issue or rural livelihoods in Afghanistan. The plan was presented to the governor and then emerged from his office with few noticeable changes. Far from learning from what had worked in Nangarhar or Laghman, the Food

Zone strategy re-introduced a crop substitution approach that had not been seen for years in Afghanistan, or indeed in other source countries, after it had become discredited in the 1980s. The emphasis on replacing opium poppy with a staple (wheat) rather than a cash crop was a further twist to the Food Zone initiative. The plan included conditionality clauses, asking farmers to sign commitments that they would not grow opium poppy in return for assistance—another element that had fallen into disrepute in the 1990s in Afghanistan.

Implementation lay with the PRT, district officials and contractors. Convoys of wheat seed and fertiliser were sent to district centres to be collected by farmers who had been identified by district officials and village representatives and who were willing to sign the letter of commitment. Even eradication had a bureaucratic veneer. Eradication targets were determined by a committee in the governor's office with support from the PRT, and until 2009, when the AEF was eventually disbanded, crop destruction was undertaken by a foreign-funded and staffed specialist eradication force. Furthermore, unlike the imposition of the bans in Nangarhar or under the Taliban, eradication in Helmand was conducted in the spring on the understanding that this was the most effective point at which to damage the crop and minimise the potential for recovery (Cranfield, 2007).

Despite the orderly construct that the Food Zone presented, political realities still prevailed. For the provincial administration and the governor the Food Zone Programme was a valuable source of patronage through the provision of development assistance to district officials and rural elites, and allegedly through the diversion of resources into their own pockets and networks (Mackenzie, 2010). At national and international levels the Food Zone's association with notable reductions in cultivation brought much acclaim. Like Gul Aga Shirzai in Nangarhar, Helmand's Governor Mangal was lauded for his efforts on counternarcotics, the province was awarded funds under the Good Performance Initiative, and his links to Western donors came to be far more important than the rather antagonistic relationship he had with the president in Kabul (Vistisen, 2011).

For the PRT and Taskforce Helmand, cultivation fell at a time when Governor Mangal had taken up the mantle of counternarcotics, distributed wheat seed and fertiliser and threatened the rural population with the destruction of their crops; causality was much less important than concurrent timing. However, the tendency to see the Food Zone in reductionist terms—seed and fertiliser provision, eradication and counternarcotics messaging—and to argue for replication in other provinces ignored the very conditions that led to the significant fall in the level of cultivation: the shift in the terms of trade between wheat and poppy and the considerable increase in the number of ANSF and international military forces on the ground in central Helmand.

While a number of internal reviews questioned the attribution of the reductions in opium poppy cultivation, the Food Zone came to be labelled as a good governance programme by some, and as a stabilisation programme by others (Read and Ryder, 2009; Zebedee, 2010: 5–6; Macpherson and Hannah, 2010: 30). Internally, the Food Zone was a programme looking for a purpose, while it was seen by the outside world as the cause of dramatic reductions in cultivation in one of the most concentrated areas of opium production in the world. This made it very hard to terminate, despite its detractors in DFID and USAID and the subsequent corruption charges against some of the governor's most senior staff.

Ultimately, the Helmand Food Zone stands in sharp contrast to the Taliban's nationwide prohibition and to Hajji Din Muhammad's and Gul Aga Shirzai's efforts to ban opium poppy cultivation in Nangarhar. Under the Taliban and in Nangarhar there was no quid pro quo arrangement around the distribution of agricultural inputs such as wheat seed and fertiliser, only the promise of more assistance to come. Nor was eradication left until the spring when farmers had already invested time and money into the crop; it was conducted just after the planting season in key locations, designed to maximise the demonstration effect, allow farmers to plant something else and reduce the threat of widespread resistance.

Moreover, the Taliban prohibition and the bans imposed in Nangarhar were all heavily shaped by local politics, by the need for divergent methods of engagement with rural communities in different economic and political terrains. Even the ban imposed by Gul Aga Shirzai in 2008, that depended on the coercive power of the US military, worked through informal power structures and sought accommodations with the rural elite.

In Helmand there was little evidence of the kinds of local political settlements seen in Nangarhar. The Food Zone was a largely a technocratic response to prevailing levels of opium poppy cultivation, shaped by a governor and Western advisers who had little understanding of the terrain they were operating in and who saw central Helmand as an area of consolidated statehood where the state has historically imposed taxes on land and agricultural sales— an area reminiscent of the Kabul River valley in Nangarhar and the canal-irrigated areas such as Rodat, lower Surkhrud and Upper Kama. Chapter 10 will demonstrate why this assumption does not hold; it will explain how the political geography of central Helmand has changed so critically over the last three decades; how the efforts to reduce opium poppy cultivation under Governor Mangal led to further shifts in demographics and state–societal relations and ultimately how these factors led to the concentration of opium poppy cultivation in the former desert areas north of the Boghra Canal, outweighing the fall in opium production within the Food Zone.

10

SHIFTING SANDS

MOVEMENTS IN POLITICAL GEOGRAPHY
AND POPPY CULTIVATION

Introduction

Chapter 9 examined the political factors that underpinned the establishment of the Helmand Food Zone—how the interests of multiple stakeholders were served by prioritising counternarcotics objectives in Helmand. It looked at how the components of the Helmand Food Zone Programme were implemented before examining the socio-economic and political processes that led to a dramatic fall in levels of cultivation in the canal command area and to the subsequent uptick in cultivation in the province that came to outweigh the reductions achieved in the Food Zone.

This chapter looks beyond the actions and interests of those responsible for the formal task of statebuilding in Helmand since the fall of the Taliban regime. It examines the diverse and complex socio-economic, political and ecological terrains in which the statebuilding project has taken place. It draws on political economy and rural livelihoods frameworks, as outlined in Chapters 2 and 3 and used in the empirical chapters on the Taliban prohibition and the collapse of the opium ban in the southern districts of Nangarhar (Chapters 6 and 8). As with those earlier empirical chapters, applying these analytical frameworks will foster a better understanding of the particular population groups in central Helmand that have been subject to prohibition; they will show how efforts to reduce opium poppy cultivation, as well as the wider statebuilding project, have reshaped the economic and political landscape. Particular attention will be given to the underlying socio-economic and political processes that led to the encroachment of the desert land north of the Boghra Canal and to the critical role played by the prohibition of opium poppy in the Food Zone.

The chapter is divided into two sections and a conclusion. The first section examines the changing political topography of central Helmand and the way that patterns of land settlement and conflict have altered state–societal relations in what should be considered an area of consolidated statehood. It looks at the settlement of the canal command area by tribal groups from northern Helmand with links to former leaders in the *mujahidin* and how the resettlement, and the conflict following the collapse of the Taliban regime, have recast the political order in the canal command area. The second section points to the impact of the statebuilding venture in central Helmand and how the costs and benefits have been distributed so unevenly across the rural population. It contrasts the experiences and livelihood trajectories of different population groups: those who have benefited from the international intervention, those who have suffered as a consequence of it, and those who have been driven out by the socio-economic processes that it created. The conclusion asserts that the political structure within the canal command area and the economic impact of the ban have facilitated a further shift in political geography, encouraging more people from the indigenous tribes of central Helmand to move and settle the former desert land in pursuit of the political and physical space to grow opium poppy. This process, combined with the potential return of opium poppy cultivation in the canal command area, poses a very real risk that production in Helmand will reach unprecedented levels after 2014.

The Changing Face of Central Helmand

On first appearance, the central districts of Helmand do not offer the divergent geographic and political terrain described in the earlier chapters on Nangarhar. In fact, all five of the central districts—Lashkar Gah, Nahre Seraj, Nad e Ali, Marjeh and Nawa Barakzai—would typically be considered well-irrigated, productive areas of consolidated statehood. Indeed, the bulk of the land in the districts of Marjeh and Nad e Ali would not be under agricultural production if it were not for a government-led process of land settlement that began in the 1950s. Earlier infrastructural works financed by the state and international donors also brought more land under agriculture in the districts of Nahre Seraj, Nawa Barakzai and Lashkar Gah.

Historically the 'self governing' (Scott, 2009) people of Helmand province, akin to the populations of Achin and Khogiani in Nangarhar, are found in the more mountainous northern districts—Baghran and parts of Nawzad, Musa Qala and Kajaki—as well as in the desert area of the south in Dishu and Khanishin. These are areas of limited statehood, where the rural population is more tribally homogenous and where there is greater resistance to state interference.

However, tribal groups and space are not as clearly delineated in central Helmand as they are in Nangarhar, and they have become more diffuse over time. The land settlement programmes in Marjeh and Nad e Ali between the 1950s and 1970s relocated an array of different tribal groups from across the country and settled them into former desert land in central Helmand. Since then there have been further informal settlements, or land grabs, many led by local *jihadi* commanders from tribes considered indigenous to Helmand. These settlements have further changed the tribal composition of the central districts, particularly in Nad e Ali and Marjeh, and have led to a rapid expansion in the amount of land under agriculture. This process has intensified over the last ten years with the encroachment into the desert north of the Boghra Canal and the settlement of around 35,000 hectares of land largely by the Ishaqzai, Noorzai, Alizai, Alikozai, Barakzai and Kakar.

The reconfiguration of central Helmand during the war, and later after the fall of the Taliban, has resulted in a rural elite that is fragmented, competitive and limited in its geographic sphere of influence. Such are the structural divisions in the canal command area that disputes over land and resources can lead to communities, and even sub-groups within them, constantly shifting their political and military alliances in an attempt to gain sufficient patronage and favour to protect themselves against their local adversaries. Within this setting, the Afghan government, the Taliban and international military forces have brokered deals with political and military actors in order to gain territorial influence. These pacts have been short-lived and ultimately divisive; supporting one local group or community has only succeeded in driving others to the opposing force as they look to maintain or regain control over territory.

Introducing New Blood: the Naqel and the Canal

A crude typology of the geographic distribution of the indigenous tribes of Helmand would suggest that in the north the Alizai dominate the districts of Baghran Musa Qala and Kajaki; the Noorzai rule in Nawzad and Washir; and the Alikozai and Ishaqzai tribes contest control over the Sangin in upper Nahre Seraj. In the south, in Dishu and in Reg, the Baloch are the dominant tribal group, while the Noorzai preside in Garmsir. Reflecting their preferred status, the Barakzai are found across the better irrigated plains of central Helmand, including in Gereshk in lower Nahre Seraj, along the Helmand River in the district of Lashkar Gah and in the district of Nawa Barakzai (Martin, 2011: 12–14).

When the districts of Marjeh and Nad e Ali were first settled in the 1950s, they constituted primarily Kuchi herders and farmers from outside Helmand, including the provinces of Nangarhar, Laghman, Wardak, Ghazni and Farah. The land that they were given was former desert, irrigated by the newly built Boghra Canal. In Nad e Ali, groups of 50–100 households typically formed villages either with a common tribal identity or with a mixture of tribes. They lived at some distance from their respective agricultural land (Dupree, 1997: 499–507; Scott, 1980: 7; Martin, 2011: 27). By the end of the settlement process in the early 1970s, as many as 3,000 households had been given between 10 and 30 *jeribs* of land in the district of Nad e Ali. By contrast, In Marjeh, villages were smaller (20–40 households) than in Nad e Ali and located closer to their land. Each village was composed of members of one common tribal group. Scott (1980: 9) cites as many as nineteen different tribal groups in Marjeh among the estimated 2,500 households (Dupree, 1997: 504–5).

Some of the initial soil surveys conducted in the 1950s classified the majority of the land under the canal command areas in these two districts to be of 'marginal and restricted suitability, requiring careful management for even fair to good yields of adapted crops'; much of the remaining land was considered 'of limited use for common tilled crops'. During the early period of the settlement of Nad e Ali and Marjeh, the combination of salinisation, poor soils and high ground water led to an overall drop in wheat yields (Cullather, 2002: 33). Although yields recovered in the 1960s and 1970s with the introduction of fertiliser and improved seed, the land brought under cultivation by the Helmand Valley Project remained plagued by environmental problems. These only increased with the onset of the war in 1979 and the subsequent loss of the investment and institutional capacity needed to tackle them (Cullather, 2002).

Even before the war, farmers in Nad e Ali and Marjeh used tractors and fertiliser to improve the productivity of the land. Surveys in the 1970s revealed that a large proportion of farmers in Nad e Ali used tractors since the hard clay soils in the area made it difficult to till the land with oxen (Scott, 1980: 8). During the same period, rates of fertiliser use in the district were among the highest in the country (Shairzai et al., 1975: 75). In fact, the costs of farming in the area were so high that farmers' net incomes were similar to those in the upper, drier parts of Helmand, and lower than those farming under the Shamalan and Darwishan Canals (Scott, 1980: 8; Owens, 1971: 59; Clapp-Wincek and Baldwin, 1983: 4).

The settler communities, known locally as *naqel* or 'chosen', still talk of the reluctance of the indigenous tribal groups in the north and south of the province to take lands in the former desert areas of Nad e Ali and Marjeh when they were first offered. The initial years of settlement were difficult, and many settlers left the area (Scott, 1980: 7). The position of the settlers was further challenged by their low status compared to the indigenous Helmandis, which led to problems accessing services and support from the provincial authorities:

> ... an ethnically homogenous area of long standing is able to present a unified position to proposed developments defined as disadvantageous by the farmers. In the same manner, such a group can petition government offices more effectively to receive early project benefits and services. The antithesis of this is the political impotence of a recently settled community of mixed tribal and ethnic origins. (Scott, 1980: 1)

By settling tribal groups from outside the province, the canal project was initially seen as an opportunity to weaken the indigenous tribes of Helmand. It was anticipated that establishing an area in central Helmand with ethnic and tribal heterogeneity would dissipate the influence of the Ishaqzai, Alizai and Noorzai. But in reality the *naqel* were never in a position to challenge the dominant position of indigenous Helmandi tribal groups which have, over time, increased in numbers in the canal command area and undermined the government's influence over central Helmand.

The Penetration of Areas of Consolidated Statehood
by the *Jihadi* Commanders

The balance of power in central Helmand changed briefly following the coup by the PDPA in April 1978. The reforms brought in by the PDPA sought to erode the power base of the indigenous landed elite, particularly the Barakzai, targeting landholdings of more than 30 *jeribs* for redistribution (Martin, 2011: 37). The *naqel*, who had received a maximum of 30 *jeribs* of land—and many substantially less—during the settlement of Marjeh and Nad e Ali were therefore not the target of these land reforms. In fact, Giustozzi (2000: 255, 289) notes that the PDPA found considerable support within the Helmand canal command area, with wide-scale party membership among the settler community.

The local *khans* established armed resistance groups to fight against the PDPA's efforts to redistribute their land. The fighting that ensued in the late 1970s led to the death and imprisonment of many of the landed elite (Giustozzi and Noor Ullah, 2006: 10). In their place arose what Giustozzi and Noor Ullah (2006: 5) have referred to as 'tribal entrepreneurs'—individuals who obtained tribal leadership not through lineage (although some were tribal *khans*) but through their role as effective *jihadi* commanders and their capacity for violence.

Three prominent *jihadi* leaders were from the Alizai tribe in northern Helmand: Mullah Mohammed Nasim Akhundzada of Harakat e Inqilab e Islami, the leading political party in Helmand; Abdul Rahman Khan, from a prominent landowning family in Kajaki and member of Hizbe Islami (Hekmatayar); and Rais Baghrani Abdul Wahid (Hizb e Islami), who became a tribal commander in the Helmand district of Baghran. Another commander, Dad Mohammed Khan, an Alikozai, commanded the area around Sangin and was known as 'Amir Dado'. Moallem Mir Wali, a Barakzai, initially aligned to Abdul Rahman Khan and Hezbe Islami, was a *jihadi* leader around the city of Gereshk. Among these *jihadi* commanders Mullah Nasim Akhundzada rose to the fore, attacking Abdul Rahman Khan deep in his territory in Kajaki and absorbing much of the central and southern districts of the province (Giustozzi, 2006: 12).[1]

By 1981, there was little evidence of the government having any control outside the urban centres of Lashkar Gah and Gereshk (Martin, 2011: 42). The Soviet invasion did little to change this; their strategy was to keep the main highway from Kandahar to Herat open, maintaining a battalion in Gereshk to do so, along with further military presence in Lashkar Gah, Kajaki and Chanjir to maintain supply routes. According to Martin (2011: 43), these Soviet military units were backed up by Afghan army units under Soviet command and subsequently by militias.

In the countryside the different *jihadi* leaders fought for supremacy, control over territory and important trade routes, and opportunities for rent extraction. Their conflicts included the increasingly dominant drugs trade. Political parties meant little to these men; some *jihadi* commanders, such as Rais Baghrani Abdul Wahid, shifted their loyalties from Hezbi Islami to Jamiat, and ultimately to the Taliban in the 1990s before finally siding with the Karzai administration in 2005 (Giustozzi, 2006: 14). Over more than a decade, numerous commanders were killed in intra- and inter-tribal battles that took place in Helmand, Peshawar and Quetta. By 1990, the rivalry between these *jihadi* commanders led to the assassination of Mullah Nasim Akhundzada in Quetta, with speculation that he had been killed by Hizbe Islami for his decision to ban opium poppy in the areas that he controlled.[2]

Given more pressing priorities in Afghanistan, as well as the factionalism and fighting between the *jihadi* commanders, the Soviets saw little point in taking the fight to the countryside. They did, however, attempt to shore up support in the central districts of Helmand, establishing militias that could help in the defence of Gereshk and Lashkar Gah. This initiative also led to the rise of charismatic armed leaders, such as Khan Mohammed (nicknamed 'Khano'). Originally from Farah province, Khano was recognised as a good fighter, recruited from among the youth and paid generously (ibid.: 15). Another prominent militia leader was Allah Noor, a Barakzai from Nawa Barakzai who began his career as a driver for the provincial governor before rising to head a militia and holding Lashkar Gah during the reign of President Najibullah. When the government of Najibullah fell in 1992, Allah Noor and Khano looked for allies to prevent the Akhundzadas from sweeping through Lashkar Gah. They found support in a local Barakzai commander from Jamiat Islami, and managed to hold the city until 1993 when they fell to an attack led by Ismail Khan from Herat, who helped install Rasoul Akunzade (brother of Nasim) as governor of Helmand.

During this prolonged period of fighting, central Helmand went through significant change. For one, the population in the districts of Marjeh and Nad e Ali came under considerable stress due to damage to the irrigation systems and the lack of maintenance. In addition, the Soviets are alleged to have drained some of the canals to punish the rural population, resulting in large numbers of farmers leaving the area altogether. Finally, the rise of armed 'tribal entrepreneurs' led to the settlement of abandoned land and former desert land by indigenous tribal groups (Martin, 2011: 43).

In Marjeh, for example, much of the land to the west and north of areas originally settled by *naqel* was taken by Ishaqzai and Noorzai commanders in the 1990s. In Nad e Ali, a local Ishaqzai commander, Haji Rakhmattiar from Hezbi Islami, captured forest land between Shin Kalay and Khoshal Kalay and distributed it to his men. (This land was cleared for agriculture and in some cases is now going through a second generation of sales.) Just south of the Boghra Canal between Gereshk and Naqilabad, a number of former commanders and men of influence from the Barakzai, Alikozai and Noorzai tribes absorbed land that had not been brought under cultivation during the initial settlement process. In Nawa Barakzai, former desert areas such as Dashte Shesherak and Dashte Aynak went through similar processes in the early 1990s, with land initially being captured by local commanders and their supporters before being sold to other farmers. Through these land grabs, the area under cultivation in central Helmand increased from an estimated 57,452 hectares to 91,663 hectares between 1975 and 1990. In Marjeh and a Nad e Ali, around 3,546 hectares of forest land were lost and turned over to agriculture over the same period (Mansfield, 2012).

Consolidating Power in Central Helmand

Ultimately the incursions by *mujahidin* commanders from the more influential and cohesive Noorzai, Ishaqzai, Alikozai and Alizai tribes in northern Helmand—as well as land grabs by the Barakzai who have traditionally dominated the prime irrigated land in the Helmand River valley—have changed the political geography of the canal command area and weakened government control. In fact, by 2010, there were 129,581 hectares of land under agriculture, a 125% increase compared to 1975 when the Afghan state had some semblance of control over central Helmand.

In central Helmand, land grabs appear to be a manifestation of how weak the government is in relation to the powerful individuals and families, most of whom are former *jihadi* commanders who are now part of the state infrastructure, or whom the state does not wish to confront. In the late 1990s, the Taliban limited the scale of the incursions into the desert land, which was considered 'government land'. Some sites north of the Boghra Canal were cultivated with water pumps during the Taliban regime, and a few similar incidences occurred elsewhere, but the number of land grabs was relatively low. Moreover, many of the *jihadi* commanders from Helmand went into exile in Balochistan. Some, such as Rasul Akhundzada, were subsequently murdered in Quetta, allegedly by the Taliban.

Land incursions did, however, increase after the fall of the Taliban, particularly with the settlement into the former desert area north of the Boghra Canal. Many of these incursions were supported by powerful individuals within the provincial government or by those associated with it, and reflected the return to power of the *jihadi* commanders. Most of these land grabs have involved the indigenous tribes and not the settler communities that arrived in central Helmand in the 1950s and 1960s. In fact, it is claimed that it is difficult for the *naqel* to obtain land north of the Boghra Canal permanently, even in areas where settlement has been more opportunistic and has not involved an initial land grab by commanders (Mansfield, 2011).[3]

After the collapse of the Taliban, many *jihadi* commanders, or their descendants, returned to Afghanistan in the 1980s and 1990s and reclaimed the power that they had lost. For example, Sher Mohammed Akhundzada, nephew of Mullah Nasim Akhundzade, was governor between 2002 and 2005; his brother became district governor of Musa Qala. Dad Mohammed Khan became Helmand Chief of Intelligence and his brother, Juma Gul, became the district governor of Sangin. Abdul Rahman Jan, a Noorzai, was appointed provincial chief of police; and Moallem Wali was made commander of the 93rd Division in Gereshk after the fall of the Taliban.

These individuals allegedly 'ran their departments as self-interested patronage networks, siphoning off government and, increasingly, PRT funding' (Gordon, 2011: 11). They used their positions to pursue adversaries and settle old scores (Martin, 2011: 61), particularly among the Ishaqzai who were accused of siding with the Taliban. It is widely alleged that the predatory behaviour of these commanders and their involvement in the drugs trade alienated the rural population, further fuelling support for an embryonic insurgency.

After Sher Mohammed Akhundzada and his allies were removed from office in 2005 at the insistence of the British (Gopal, 2010), their loss of *de jure* power caused many of these individuals to maintain their links to Helmand while strengthening their hand with Kabul. For example, Sher Mohammed Akhundzade became a senator in the Afghan parliament at the same time that his brother, Amir Mohammed Akundzade, was made deputy governor and charged with protecting family interests in the province. Dad Mohammed Khan became a Member of Parliament before being killed in March 2009 (Coghlan, 2009: 119; Hafvenstein, 2007: 130–31, 313); while Moallem Wali, a rival of Sher Mohammed Akundzade, was disarmed in 2004 by the disarmament, demobilisation and reintegration (DDR) process and then successfully ran for the first parliamentary elections. His son, Hekmattullah Khan, served as chief of police in Garmsir, and then Gereshk.

Abdul Rahman Jan also left office as provincial chief of police in 2005. He did not take up an official position in Kabul, although he did make a number of attempts to regain office in Marjeh following the military operations in the area in February 2010 (Chandresekaran, 2012: 81, 143). Abdul Rahman Jan, his son Wali Jan, a parliamentarian, and Sher Mohammed Akhundzade were reported to have campaigned for President Karzai in Helmand during his bid for re-election in 2009, while Moallem Wali remains a major powerbroker in Helmand's Gereshk district, with links to Gul Aga Shirzai.

After the departure of Sher Mohammed Akhundzada and his allies, Helmand had three more governors—Mohammed Daud, Asadullah Wafa and Gulab Mangal—who were all from outside the province. Then Naeem Baloch, a Helmandi, was appointed in September 2012. None of them succeeded in countering the influence of the *jihadi* commanders who came to prominence in the 1980s and took office during the Karzai administration. Each governor was undermined by the continuing influence of Sher Mohammed Akhundzada and his allies over local politics and posts within the administration, aided by their links to Kabul and the president's wish to see Akhundzada reinstated (Chandresekaran, 2012: 82, 140; Goodhand and Mansfield, 2010: 22). Government land continued to be taken by the most powerful amongst the indigenous tribes, gifted to others as part of a patronage system, or sold as a commodity. Corruption in the distribution of aid became rife and appears to have been part of the administration's political bargain with the local elite, fearful that without largesse these elite groups might support the Taliban.

As shown in Chapter 9, Western nations considered Gulab Mangal the most effective governor. Drawing on the coercive power of foreign military forces and a growing ANSF presence, he projected the appearance of state power in Helmand, improving physical security and delivering substantial reductions in the level of opium poppy cultivation. Yet, despite these achievements, the government remains without the credible and stable interlocutors that it needs to establish resilient relationships with the rural population.

Amongst the powerful, many of whom are from the northern part of the province, personal and family interests and the thirst for local power appear to be the primary factors that drive their choices of political and military affiliations. Tribes can contain groups that work within the government and its patronage system, as well as those that that oppose it and have links with the Taliban (Gordon, 2011: 25). A group that feels slighted because its rivals are gaining more favour, or believes its longer-term interests are better served by switching its fealty to the government rather than the Taliban (and vice versa), will do so. The result is a highly fluid environment in which the state has to deal with multiple and competing actors, each of whom has influence within a limited geographic space. This situation minimises the prospects of long-term allies. As such, the political terrain of central Helmand is far more comparable with the areas of limited statehood in the southern districts of Nangarhar than it is with the lower areas in the Kabul River valley where state–societal relations are more robust.

The rift between the rural elite and the population has also not been filled. In much of the canal command area, farmers talk of the local elite—*maliks* or *wakils*—as unrepresentative and absent from the village, typically living in Lashkar Gah. There are repeated references to the role that they play in corruption, colluding with district officials to share development assistance amongst themselves, or to distribute it through their patronage networks. They are accused of writing fictitious village lists for the distribution of aid, hiring men with false identity cards to collect it, and then selling the agricultural inputs on the open market. The rural elite are largely viewed as biased, greedy and unwilling to share the benefits of development assistance outside their own clique (Mansfield, Alcis, OSDR, 2011; Mansfield, 2012: 63–7).

In sum, it is clear that the political and physical landscape of central Helmand has changed dramatically since the construction of the canal system in the late 1950s. The amount of land under cultivation in central Helmand has grown to 129,581 hectares in 2010 from only 57,452 hectares in 1975. The canal system should have strengthened state control over the area, given the social structure it imposed on both settler communities and indigenous tribes and the land and public services it was designed to deliver to farming communities. However, ultimately, the picture is one in which government control has been weakened by atomised communities, and the incursions of indigenous tribes and *jihadi* commanders into the canal command area since the 1980s. The return of many of these commanders since the fall of the Taliban, their absorption of state power, the predatory nature of their *de jure* rule and the patronage systems they developed have further fractured the social fabric within the canal command area, fuelling resentment of the Karzai administration and providing multiple entry points for armed anti-government elements.

In addition, the number of armed local actors has increased with the 'surge' of foreign military forces into central Helmand and subsequent attempts to decentralise security to the local population. The establishment of the ALP, known locally as *arbaki* or *chawarki*, was one such initiative. It provided weapons, training and salaries to members of local communities to secure their area. Locally it is claimed that most of the forces that have been established in Marjeh and Nad e Ali are comprised of *naqel*. Scott has referred to their 'impotence' in the 1950s and 1960s, and there is a local perception that the settler communities were marginalised by the *mujahidin* in the 1980s and 1990s, and then by both the Taliban and the Karzai government. In contrast to this history of weakness, the *naqel* now find themselves armed and are being given a significant security role in a post-transition Afghanistan. It remains to be seen how the introduction of further groups of armed actors will impact on local bargaining in central Helmand after transition. Contemporary history suggests that, given the way that the indigenous tribes and their *jihadi* leaders have imposed themselves in the canal command area, resentment and outbreaks of violence may be as much about concerns over the empowerment of settler communities than opposing the ALP as a security instrument of the Afghan state.

A further development that has reshaped the political topography of central Helmand has been the counternarcotics effort. As we have seen in Nangarhar, opium production and counternarcotics policy form an important part of local patronage in rural Afghanistan. As a relatively high-value commodity, opium is a resource that can perform important functions in the pursuit of local power, particularly financing the acquisition of land, the purchase of weapons, and the means with which to bribe local officials.

In such a divided and competitive environment as central Helmand, opium production represents an important means of protection against contending rural elites and a way of gaining popular support among the rural population; denying cultivation is seen to undermine efforts to achieve these aims and weaken group survival. It is for these reasons that many people in rural areas of central Helmand assert that their support for the state is contingent on whether or not the governor allows them to cultivate poppy.

Livelihood Trajectories in Central Helmand

> ... It is easy to generalise, in ignorance, about the advantages of the 'Helmand farmers' as if they are some homogenous mass. There are many indigenous farmers of central Helmand who are well off thanks to the development activities of recent times. There are also indigenous farmers who are poorer now than a decade ago thanks to the changes in the water tables, e.g. drying up in the foothill regions and water logging in some areas near the main canals. The same kind of contrasts can be made of settlers, new and old. The variables are many .... The total farm-economic picture should be studied carefully. For example, the high rates of tractor use, high yielding varieties of wheat and fertiliser use found in Nad e Ali appear advantageous until it is realised that given the hard and poor clay soils of the area, those agricultural innovations are necessary to produce a crop that will result in net household income no better than in water-short Nawzad or Musa Qala, where fields are ploughed with oxen and the use of fertilizers and high yielding varieties are not common. Helmand province is full of such contradictions and requires more serious study. To generalise is to be wrong and regional development programs, like

academic stereotypes of 'Helmand farmers' are normally based on such generalisations. (Scott, 1980: 34)

The broader economic and social policies and processes that have contributed to profound changes in Helmand during the last decade have often yielded unanticipated and unintended consequences. This is particularly true of the dislocation of large sections of the rural population and their settlement in the desert lands on Afghanistan's frontiers. Scott makes a powerful case that external interventions like the Food Zone and the push to reduce opium poppy cultivation, as well as wider processes of social and economic change, will result in different responses depending on location, socio-economic group and economic opportunities. Table 1 presents a typology of the different agro-economic zones within central Helmand and the kinds of responses that have occurred. A more detailed analysis of livelihoods within each zone is provided in the rest of this section.

Zone 1: Well-irrigated Localities in the Canal Command Area in Proximity to Urban Centres

Amidst the stories in the media of protracted violence, insurgency and the failure of the international effort, there is evidence that the lives of some of the rural population in parts of the canal command area of central Helmand improved after 2012. In part this was a consequence of how much the security situation had deteriorated before September 2006, when UK military forces first established the PRT in Helmand and began to push into the rural areas and contest the Taliban's influence. This conflict was so intense throughout 2010, and even as late as the fall of 2011, that farmers in most of the twenty-nine sites that this research covered consistently complained of exposure to protracted firefights between ISAF and Taliban fighters, as well as the threat of improvised explosive devices (IEDs) and other acts of violence.

However, this appeared to have changed in the central part of the province between 2012 and 2013, particularly in the more restive districts of Marjeh and Nad e Ali, following the significant increase in ISAF and Afghan military forces, as well as the proliferation of development monies known as 'the surge'. By the end of 2013, farmers were not reporting the kinds of incidents that they had become so used to: requests for assistance and intimidation by Taliban fighters, firefights between the opposing military forces in the conflict and raids on household compounds by ANSF and ISAF troops. Rather, farmers talked of government security forces that were in control of much of the canal-irrigated area of central Helmand.

Table 1: Characteristics of Different Agro-Ecological Zones In Central Helmand Province

	Well irrigated canal command area in proximity to urban centres	Well irrigated canal command area but not in proximity to urban centres	Former desert areas in the area defined by the canal area but not receiving irrigation from the canal	Former desert areas north of the Boghra Canal
Landholdings	5–10 jeribs (1–2 ha)	5–20 jeribs (1–4 ha)	5–10 jeribs (1–2 ha)	5–30 jeribs (1–6 ha)
Irrigation	Canal	Canal	Deep or shallow well or pump from drainage	Deep well
Cropping Pattern	High degree of crop diversification, including movement into off-season 'green' vegetables and perennials; alfalfa cultivation for livestock and sales to urban centres	Few signs of crop diversification; continued reliance on low-risk low-return crops (e.g. wheat, cotton, maize and mung bean); alfalfa cultivation for livestock	Few signs of crop diversification; continued reliance on low-risk low-return crops (e.g. wheat, cotton, maize, mung bean); alfalfa cultivation for livestock	Intensive opium poppy cultivation with some wheat cultivation; alfalfa cultivation for livestock
Livestock	Dairy, cattle and small ruminants	Dairy, cattle and small ruminants	Limited numbers of largely small ruminants for consumption	Limited numbers of largely small ruminants for consumption
Non-farm Income	Increase in non-farm income opportunities, particularly in trade and transport, but also salaried employment in	Limited non-farm income opportunities Trade and transport opportunities largely restricted to relatively wealthy	Limited non-farm income opportunities Trade and transport opportunities largely restricted to relatively wealthy	Very few non-farm income opportunities; some trade in weekly markets or bazaars on Boghra Canal

	Lashkar Gah and Gereshk			
		ALP important source of local employment in rural areas. Still some reliance on wage income from opium harvest in former desert lands and other parts of Helmand	ALP important source of local employment in rural areas. Still some reliance on wage income from opium harvest in former desert lands and other parts of Helmand	ALP important source of local employment in rural areas. Still some reliance on wage income from opium harvest in former desert lands and other parts of Helmand
Opportunities for the Land-poor and Landless	Much fewer opportunities to sharecrop or lease land in the absence of opium poppy. Sharecropping arrangements 1/5 of final crop as opposed to 1/3 when opium poppy was grown	Far fewer opportunities to sharecrop or lease land in the absence of opium poppy. Sharecropping arrangements 1/5 of final crop as opposed to 1/3 when opium poppy was grown	No opportunities to sharecrop or lease land in the absence of opium poppy and little demand to do so	Many opportunities to sharecrop or lease land due to prevalence of opium poppy, but smaller share of the final crop than when sharecropped in canal command area
Security	Improved since 2012; ANSF dominate with more limited role of Afghan Local Police (ALP). Since 2013 fewer complaints about predation of ALP	Improved since 2012 and further improvements with departure of International Military Forces. Since 2013 fewer complaints about predation of ALP	Improved since 2012. Since 2013 fewer complaints about predation of ALP	Worsened in 2012 and 2013 with ASNF and NATO engagement in area. Regular complaints about predation of ALP but now largely limited

				to actions within the canal command area
Development Assistance	Focus of heaviest investment; agricultural inputs as well as significant investments in physical and social infrastructure, including education and health	Some investment; agricultural inputs as well as physical and social infrastructure, including education and health	Limited investment, primarily agricultural inputs captured by rural elite	No development assistance
Poppy Cultivation	None cultivated and little interest in returning to opium poppy cultivation	Small amounts cultivated (in particular behind walled compounds); economic pressure to return to opium poppy cultivation	Economic pressure to return to opium poppy cultivation	Intensive poppy cultivation but small amounts of wheat being cultivated after two consecutive years of low opium yield
Example of Area	Bolan, Qala Bost, Aqajan Kalay, Chanjir, Loy Bagh	Shin Kalay, Koshal Kalay, Marjeh	Dashte Aynak, Dashte Shersherak,	Shurawak, Dashte Shin Kalay, Dashte Loy Manda, Dashte Koshal Kalay, Dashte Ab Pashak

Perhaps ironically, a major contributing factor to improvements in the security situation in 2013 was the departure of the foreign military forces that had helped the ANSF secure the terrain in the first place. The rural population seemed especially pleased that ISAF had gone; in many areas of Afghanistan, farmers blamed the 'foreigners' for blocking the roads, searching household compounds and acting as a magnet for Taliban fire. With the departure of the bulk of the foreign military forces and the closure (or handing over) of many ISAF-led Forward Operating Bases in the summer of 2013, there was 'less to fight about'. In fact, at the end of 2013, those in the canal command area— even in places like Aqajan Kalay which straddles the Boghra Canal—reported that the ANSF were providing security and that their freedom of movement had improved. They expressed gratitude to the government because, in the words of one farmer, 'In the past there was always fighting and bombing in the area. Now there is peace and the government has brought security here.'

It was also claimed that many in the ALP—the vanguard of the security effort in the rural areas—were less prone to prey on their own communities than they had been when the ALP was initially established. Perhaps of even greater importance in terms of building local support was the income that the ALP had injected directly into the rural communities, providing salaries equivalent to between US$120 and US$155 each month[4] for those recruited. This kind of income could be transformative. A landowner in Chanjir had two sons in the ALP earning a total of US$310 per month—money that was paying for their brother to attend a private school in Lashkar Gah. He stated: 'I am always thinking of the government and pray for them. I think back to ten years ago and think about how much my life has improved, and not just mine but all the people. All of this is due to the government we have.'

It was not just the security situation that improved. In many parts of the canal command area of central Helmand farmers acknowledged a more fundamental change in their interactions with both economic and state institutions, and thereby in how they perceived the world. They no longer simply looked to their land for an income. As one farmer in Nad e Ali put it: 'Before people were not familiar with the bazaar. In the past I had a donkey; I had this donkey for ten years. I used to say if the donkey wants to go to the bazaar I will follow. Now everyone goes to the bazaar every day.' The farmers also looked to the services that were on offer—in particular schools and healthcare—and where public-sector options were deemed sub-standard, those with money turned to the private schools and doctors that have flourished in the last few years.

Some of this change in people's mindsets was attributed to the affordability of mechanised transport. For example, a new Chinese-made motorbike—

branded for sale in Afghanistan under names such as 'Helmand' and 'Pamir'—cost only US$460 to 560 in Helmand in late 2013, compared to around US$2,000 when only Japanese-manufactured bikes had been available in the late 1990s.[5] A 'Zarang'[6]—an Afghan-constructed three-wheeled vehicle and trailer that has become a common feature in Afghanistan since 2009—would set a family back US$1,340, while a secondhand version could be purchased for as little as US$522. More expensive forms of transport such as a Corolla, or perhaps a station wagon known as a *'saracha'*—all of which could be used to transport passengers as well as goods—could be purchased secondhand in Helmand for between US$5,000 and 8,000.[7] By contrast a tractor, which had been one of the only reliable ways of transporting goods and people to market in the past before the roads had improved, was more expensive in 2013 than it had been ten years earlier.[8]

The number of households that owned motorbikes, a Zarang or a car had increased significantly in 2013. Sales were aided by competition among sellers in Helmand, falling prices and improved roads paid for by international assistance. The result was a population more mobile than it had been a decade ago, with better access to food items in the bazaar, including meat and fruit, and to public services such as education and health. Vehicle ownership also contributed to family income, providing the equivalent of US$4.50 per day to a son or brother who might load up a Zarang and transport agricultural produce from the village to the district centre, or perhaps as much as US$11 per day to a household that owned a *saracha* and had a family member ply the roads taking passengers between the village and Lashkar Gah, Gereshk or other destinations.[9] Those leasing out their tractors often earned between US$730 and 910 a season transporting agricultural goods to the provincial centre, as well as taking fertiliser, diesel, water pumps, generators and building materials from the bazaar to the village.

However, it was not just better access to affordable transport and the availability of public and private goods in the district centres and village shops that changed the way of thinking of farmers in this part of central Helmand. Of particular interest is the way that some farmers—particularly those residing in the environs of Lashkar Gah—saw their lives had changed by giving up opium poppy since 2008.

Academics such as Jonathan Goodhand (2009) rightly point to the role that wide-scale opium production played in transforming rural areas like those of Helmand in the 1980s and 1990s, by supporting the development of a cash-based economy, the commercialisation of agricultural production and the closer integration of rural, and often peripheral, parts of the country into the national and international economy. In 2013, many farmers pointed to a further stage of agrarian change: one where the rural population was increasingly looking to the market for agricultural goods, wage labour and services as the way to earn a living, rather than relying on opium production. As one farmer described the change: 'when opium poppy was banned, we looked to the market'.

Ironically, in many cases this transition to a less opium-dependent livelihood was supported by the money earned from illicit opium production itself. Those who were in the fortunate position of having generated inventories of opium during the 'good years'—aided by land ownership, sizable plots and only a few household members who were unable to work—sold their opium at the inflated prices that followed the harvest of 2010, when prices rose to almost US$300 per kilogram. This provided the start-up costs to buy a shop, a car or a Zarang and to begin trading legal goods and services, replacing some of the income they had previously earned from opium.

Reducing opium poppy cultivation—a particularly labour-intensive crop requiring as much as 360 person days per hectare—also freed up family labour to staff the family shop, drive the vehicle or go to the bazaar or city and find employment. There was certainly greater evidence of non-farm income among rural households in the canal command area than there had been when opium poppy was grown more extensively. For example, while only one-quarter of the households interviewed for this research in late 2010 had one or more family members who earned a salary or daily wage, almost half of those interviewed in late 2013 had such a family member (Mansfield et al., 2011: 62).[10] It was this off-farm and non-farm income that played a critical role in improving the overall welfare of households in the absence of opium. Owning a shop, having a family member in the ALP, providing a son with a car, a Zarang, or even working in the construction industry in Lashkar Gah all provided valuable injections of cash into the household economy.

The benefits of non-farm income were not simply monetary; those with a family member working in the bazaar referred to their increased consumption of food items such as meat and fruit that had once been luxuries, eaten only when a family member was able to travel to the market, incurring transport costs, possibly having to pay bribes and risking physical harm, particularly at the peak of the conflict. In 2013, life was considered much easier with a son or brother in the bazaar who 'at the end of each day brings meat and sometimes fruit from the market'.

Greater market exposure also led to changes in agricultural production and a shift in the crops that farmers had grown following the reductions in opium poppy cultivation. It fostered improvements in security and the significant investments in rural infrastructure that central Helmand has seen since 2008. The initial response to the ban on opium poppy in the fall of 2008 was often to replace poppy with wheat, largely due to the significant rise in wheat prices and concerns over food security. Some farmers replaced their poppy with a low-return, low-risk cropping system that consisted of wheat in the fall, cotton, melon and watermelon in the spring, and maize and mung bean in the summer. Responses evolved, and by the 2009/10 growing season, many farmers in the environs of Lashkar Gah and Gereshk were cultivating a wide range of horticultural crops, both annual and perennial.

As time passed, this kind of mixed cropping system became more prevalent. It was not seen only in places like Bolan, Qala Bost, and Mohejerin, which were quick to diversify and meet the demands for agricultural produce from an expanding provincial capital; it also became visible across a wider geographical spread within the canal command area. A number of farmers were particularly enthusiastic about the shift to crops like grapes and apricots, and reflected nostalgically on how it had been more than twenty years since they had enjoyed 'gardens on their land'.

As the footprint of international military forces and the ANSF extended into the rural areas along the Boghra Canal in 2010 and 2011, and with it the ban on opium poppy cultivation, farmers adapted to the change in circumstances. Many invested in improved production techniques supported by donor-assisted programmes and their own ingenuity. For example, there was a rapid expansion in the number of polytunnels which could be seen across the canal command area in 2013. In 2011, these very same tunnels had not been erected in areas where the Taliban dominated, because farmers feared retaliation for advertising the fact that they had received development assistance (Mansfield et al., 2011: 64–5). Farmers also adapted the initial designs and took to building their own polytunnels from items that they purchased locally in the bazaar, including abandoning the more costly metal struts originally used in favour of wooden ones which were considered less likely to be stolen. Farmers across central Helmand also adopted other new technologies—waterpumps, generators, solar panels and mobile phones—as they became affordable, exploiting them to improve not only their agricultural productivity but also their quality of life.

Greater care was also given to crops that farmers had grown for many years and hence were already familiar with, improving the yields and economic returns on old staples like melon, watermelon and even wheat. A farmer in Chanjir commented on his change in perspective, saying: 'In the past we gave no attention to wheat', and the yield data for wheat supported his claim. For example, in 2009, wheat yields were typically between 140 to 170 *man* per *jerib* in the canal-irrigated areas of central Helmand (the equivalent of 3.1 to 3.6 metric tons per hectare). In late 2013, farmers rarely reported yields of less than 160 *man* per *jerib* in the irrigated areas, and 200 *man* per *jerib* (the equivalent of 4.5 metric tons per hectare) or more was not uncommon among those interviewed. Due to the expansion in wheat production and the improvements in security on the main highways, people trading wheat in the bazaars of Lashkar Gah and Gereshk reported that as much as two-thirds of the wheat grain that they purchased in Helmand was sold to traders in provinces like Kandahar, Kabul, Ghazni. Those trading fruit and vegetables in the cities made similar claims, and reported that traders from Kabul and Ghazni were regular buyers in Helmand, whereas a few years previously security concerns had significantly hampered trade both within Helmand and with other provinces.

The farmers who saw improvements in their welfare after 2008—combining remunerative cropping systems with non-farm income from one, two or even three family members—saw their capital grow. They took advantage of the increasing number of private schools and universities in Lashkar Gah and supplemented their children's public-school education with the growing number of private courses that became available. These farmers could still afford to marry their sons off despite the high bride prices that persisted[11] even in the absence of opium poppy across much of the canal command area. They could also meet the high costs of private healthcare when the public system was seen to be deficient, paying to send family members to private medical practitioners in Lashkar Gah, Kandahar and Quetta in Pakistan. Those communities experienced direct benefits from the investments in central Helmand and saw little reason to return to opium poppy cultivation.

Zone 2: Well-irrigated Localities in the Canal Command Area but not in Proximity to Urban Centres

There were households that had well-irrigated land in the canal command area of central Helmand but did not see the same welfare gains as those in the first agro-economic zone. This second zone was located in western Nad e Ali and across much of Marjeh, a greater distance from the agricultural and labour markets of Lashkar Gah and Gereshk and the associated multiplier effect of development investments. This is an area that has been subject to repeated rounds of eradication and where the population argues that it has abandoned opium poppy cultivation due to the coercive power of the state and foreign military forces.

In this second zone there was not the same evidence of a move into annual and perennial horticulture that could be seen closer to the urban centres; nor were there the same opportunities for non-farm incomes. In this zone there was growing anger towards the government, and farmers expressed a nostalgia for the Taliban. Crops such as wheat, maize, cotton and mung bean persisted despite falling prices, highlighting the absence of markets for higher-value production in these areas.

The complaints from those who persisted with staples like cotton, maize and mung bean were particularly pronounced in 2013 due to the low yields that they obtained following a particularly warm summer where temperatures reached 50 degrees centigrade. The mung bean harvest was especially poor, with yields of only 10 to 25 *man* per *jerib* (the equivalent of 45 to 112.5 kilograms), one-third of what they would usually be. Cotton yields were also low, typically ranging from 150 to 170 *man* per *jerib* (the equivalent of 675 to 765 kilograms), as opposed to 200 *man* per *jerib* (the equivalent of 900 kilograms) in 2012, a decrease of 15 to 20 percent. The troubles that had befallen the public gin in Lashkar Gah some years earlier, which many farmers believed had depressed the market for cotton in Helmand, remained a puzzle to those who juxtaposed the effort to ban opium with the failure to invigorate the other cash crop that they knew so well. As a struggling farmer in Louy Bagh asked: 'What do I do with this 6 *jeribs* of land? The government banned poppy and closed the cotton factory. Now no one buys our cotton.'

This group of farmers felt that the ban on opium poppy had subjected them to a large loss in income; many households had less than US$1 per person per day to meet family expenses, including food (see Table 3). A dwindling inventory of opium was all that allowed those in this group to meet their basic needs. For those without a store of opium from the 'good years', their consumption of meat and fruit declined; they complained of eating meat once every two to three weeks, and of having sold off their sheep before winter rather than slaughter them for dried meat known as '*landi*'. They relied on the public health clinic to treat their illnesses and had only a small amount of money to buy medicine when the public doctor ran out—a frequent experience. Such was the economic plight of this group that they had taken to selling long-term productive assets such as their dairy cows, and even their transport, including motorbikes and cars.

Table 3: Illustrative Gross Income on 15 *Jeribs* in Zone 2 (Pakistan Rupees)

	Jeribs	Yield (man)	Price (PR)	Landowner	Tenant[12]	Sharecropper[13]
Wheat	8	190	150	228,000	156,000	45,600
Alfalfa	1	NA	NA	0	0	0
Cotton	6	170	220	224,400	224,400	44,880
Maize	4	180	105	75,600	75,600	15,120
Mung bean	4	160	260	166,400	166,400	33,280
Total gross income[14]	–	–		694,400	622,400	138,880
Total gross income/person/ day[15]	–	–		190.25	170.52	38.05

Moreover, opium poppy maintained a foothold in the livelihoods of those who appeared to have abandoned the crop in recent years. Farmers continued to test the water each year, cultivating small amounts of opium poppy and seeing how the government responded. Small amounts of opium poppy persisted inside the compound walls of some farmers, in their gardens where fruits and vegetables were produced for household consumption.[16] And family members worked on the opium crop of others during the harvest in Bakwa in Farah, in Khanishin in Helmand, or in the former desert area north of the Boghra Canal.

This is also the zone where many of those who migrated to the former desert areas north of the Boghra Canal either had small amounts of land or were land-poor, leasing or sharecropping land until opium poppy was banned. The land-poor found it particularly difficult to survive in this zone once poppy was banned. Their scenario shifted from before 2008—when landowners would happily contract out their land to tenants and sharecroppers due to the amount of labour days required to grow poppy—to a situation where it was difficult to find land at all. Even worse, they experienced a reduction in the amount of crops that they received in return for their work. For instance, when the land-poor cultivated opium poppy as sharecroppers in the canal command area, they received one-third of the final crop—maybe even one-half if they paid for some of the agricultural inputs themselves. However, once opium poppy was banned, they not only found it hard to locate land in the canal command area; they received only one-fifth of the legal crops that were grown. This was not an attractive proposition, particularly in the case of low-value wheat, cotton, maize and mung bean.

This group had the added disadvantage of not being beneficiaries of either government or donor assistance. Those without land were not entitled to assistance; they did not belong to a specific community; they did not own land or water. Nor were they are well connected to the village elite—the elders and *khans*—who reaped most of the benefits distributed by government and international development programmes. Finally, given that much of the assistance was made up of agricultural inputs, it was of little benefit to those without land. At best, if they found land, they received a smaller share of a better yield of one of the improved crops being distributed, but this did not in any way make up for the losses in welfare they experienced due to the ban on opium.

The land-poor were thus marginalised by both the counternarcotics and statebuilding efforts in central Helmand, and saw themselves as having been impoverished by the international effort. They viewed the government and donor community as not having catered to their needs; they considered the government guilty of corruption and of distributing much needed development assistance to those with land, wealth and position. For the land-poor, the imposition of a ban on opium poppy restricted their access to other assets, including land, shelter, credit, income, food and health. With incomes of only a fifth of those who owned land in Marjeh, Koshal Kalay or Shin Kalay it is easy to see why they fell on such difficult times and why they believed that government that was out of touch with their needs and priorities: 'We request the Governor Sahib to help the people, to improve their lives, but they only know one thing and that is yelling to ban poppy.' In some cases, farmers blamed the deaths of family members on their loss of income due to the ban and their inability to afford basic healthcare.[17]

This was a group who suffered the most with the expansion of the opium ban, who had seen few benefits from the development of the rural economy that occurred, and who verbalised their resentment of the Afghan authorities and those whom they considered the authorities' international backers—the governments of America and Britain. This group was particularly profane in how they described Governor Baloch; his predecessor, Gulab Mangal; and the presidents of Afghanistan and the US (Mansfield, 2014). They often threatened violence towards the government and expressed a desire to see the return of the Taliban, who they believed would allow poppy cultivation to resume.

Zone 3: Former Desert Areas in the Area Defined by the Canal Area but not Receiving Canal Irrigation

The third agro-economic zone was largely populated by households that had some limited landholdings in non-irrigated parts of central Helmand—former uncultivated desert areas which are geographically very close to the irrigated land in the canal command area but do not have access to surface irrigation. This is a population that experienced the most significant losses in welfare due to the imposition of the opium ban under the Helmand Food Zone initiative.

In the late 1990s and in the early years of the Karzai administration, this desert land was taken over without legal authorisation by political–military actors, including those linked with former Governor Sher Mohammed Akhunzada (2002–8). The commanders who initially appropriated the desert area took significant amounts of land for themselves before distributing some of it to their extended families and subordinates. Over time this land was commoditised and sold, some of it many times after it was initially taken.

Many farmers welcomed the increased availability of land that this process of settlement brought about, particularly given the low price of land in these areas compared to prices for well-irrigated land in the canal command area. But the benefits were unevenly distributed and relatively short-lived. One of the main challenges was that, not being formally under the canal system, this land required irrigation by water pumps, shallow wells or tubewells. The fixed costs required to bring under cultivation, to build a household compound and the costs of diesel each year meant that these areas were heavily dependent on high-value cash crop cultivation, most notably opium poppy.

When farmers in these former desert lands were compelled to abandon opium poppy cultivation under the Helmand Food Zone initiative, they dramatically reduced the amount of land devoted to agricultural production of any kind during the winter growing season, and only a few crops were cultivated at all during the summer season. The Helmand Food Zone initiative did not in any way offset the adverse effects of sharp reductions in opium poppy cultivation on this socio-economic group, as these areas were not eligible for agricultural inputs.

Zone 4: Former Desert Areas North of the Boghra Canal

The fourth agro-economic zone in central Helmand is the area north of the Boghra Canal. The growth in the amount of land under agriculture in this area has been striking. In 2002, the land between the canal and south of Highway 1 was just desert, containing a few scattered communities whose residents had arrived in the late 1990s trying to escape the drought in Washir. By 2013, there were around 35,500 hectares of agricultural land: not just isolated fields primarily located on the north side of the canal, but contiguous fields stretching up to the outskirts of Camp Bastion/Leatherneck and home to as many as 160,000 people.[18]

The rapid expansion of land under cultivation in these former desert lands—much of it under poppy—is a direct result of the imposition of a ban on opium production in the canal command area of central Helmand and the continued high price of opium. For the land-poor, the ban on opium poppy cultivation and the shift to less labour-intensive crops in the canal command area meant that their services were no longer required by those who owned the land. Landowners could now farm their own land with family labour, and those who had relied on widespread opium poppy cultivation to obtain land and a place to live found themselves dispossessed. Without jobs or development assistance (and with landless households the least likely to receive what assistance was available), these farmers had little choice but to settle new land to the north in former desert areas, build homes there, and bring the area under agricultural production. Buoyed by the relatively high price of opium—a result of its illegality and recent counternarcotics efforts—these farmers have been able to purchase the land and the technology required to bring the land under cultivation, or have used their skills as opium producers to gain access to land through sharecropping arrangements.

While households in the former desert experienced dramatic reductions in income in 2012 and 2013 due to poor opium yields, the last decade has actually been one where many saw their capital grow. Coming from the canal command area with very few possessions, most of these settlers had a home by 2013, along with some productive land, a motorbike, a generator, a solar panel for power and, until very recently, a relatively regular supply of dried meat, with fresh meat and fruit 'once or twice a week'.

For those who came first it was hard work; they had no accommodation and had to clear and prepare the stark desert land for agricultural production. As time passed, life became a bit easier. The bazaars that sat astride the Boghra Canal grew in response to the increasing amounts of disposable income found in the former desert land, and a rising number of weekly markets began to emerge in the desert itself. Transport also became more available as all but a few households earned enough money to purchase a motorbike, or perhaps a car, so that they could travel to Lashkar Gah, Kandahar or even Quetta to get treatment for the sick or to buy agricultural inputs and consumer durables.

In addition, farmers took up new technologies as they became affordable, which made farming in such a harsh terrain more manageable. Once drilling equipment, as well as cheap Chinese and Pakistani generators and water pumps, became more available in the cities of Lashkar Gah and Gereshk, farmers abandoned less reliable shallow wells for deep tubewells, and now have a more consistent source of irrigation water. They began to use herbicides on their opium crops in order to manage weeds and limit the demand on family labour, and many have adopted solar technology, mobile phones and motorised transport.

An order was established in the rather atomised communities that initially sprang up in this former desert space. Tribes considered indigenous to Helmand dominate the former desert terrain—the Ishaqzai, Noorzai, Barakzai, Alkozai, Alizai, Baloch and formerly nomadic Kakar—all of whom claim a traditional right to the land and resist settlement by the *naqlin* (Mansfield, 2012).[19] Familial and tribal links, patronage networks and the Taliban offered a structure that appealed to many who had fled what they viewed as the intrusive and inequitable governance that they had found in the canal command area under the Karzai regime. In the absence of a government that the farmers considered legitimate and capable of delivering improvements to their lives, they looked only for a system that offered them physical security, a way of resolving disputes that was somehow considered 'fair', and to be left alone to earn a livelihood in whatever way they saw fit, including by cultivating opium poppy.

Despite the opportunities that life north of the canal offers, and the improvements that have occurred since the desert was first settled, it remains a tough life. Many of the settlers still complain about the summer heat, the lack of shade and, perhaps surprising to some, the fact that there is no schooling for their children. Since 2012, their life has become even harder due to the disease that affected their opium crop for two consecutive years.

While very likely a consequence of poor agricultural practice—the extensive monocropping of opium poppy that had taken place since 2010, the failure to rotate crops or rest the land and increasing salination—most farmers' view was that disease and lower yields were the result of a concerted campaign of crop destruction launched by the Americans. The anger directed towards the government for the loss in income that farmers experienced due to the poor harvests in 2012 and 2013 was extreme. There was little evidence of anything but contempt for the government, ranging from people who simply offered abuse and questioned the character of those in government, to others who expressed frustration and anger for what they felt was the government's relentless pursuit and the threat that the authorities posed to their way of life.

Governor Mangal remained the target of much of the opprobrium of this population even after he had left office. He was largely seen as having served the interests of the US and UK military and as acting independently of the government in Kabul. A common slur was to refer to him as 'the son of the British'; there were allegations that Mangal himself attributed his appointment to his links with the British and that he claimed to answer to the British Prime Minister and not President Karzai.[20] The perception that Governor Mangal was quick to react to foreign interests and neglected the concerns of rural Afghans was captured in the repeated use of the terms 'Murdagow' and 'Dowus' by respondents to describe Gulab Mangal.[21] More profane terms were common, as were the threats of violence, some of a sexual nature, made against the governor and anyone working in the government.[22]

In response to the economic downturn in 2012 and 2013, most farmers talked of cutting back on meat and fruit and of having trouble meeting the immediate costs of healthcare. Those with land recognised the severity of their situation as they did not have formal ownership of the land. Some resolved their financial difficulties by selling their opium stocks, others by marrying off their daughters. The situation for households sharecropping land was even more challenging. While many of those who rented or sharecropped land had contemplated moving in the immediate aftermath of the harvest, few appeared to have found land elsewhere. Many questioned where they could go without a return to widespread opium poppy in the canal command area, other than further into the desert. In fact, despite the obvious problems this area faced, the population north of the Boghra Canal keeps growing; even as late as the fall of 2013 farmers were still arriving. Most reassured themselves that 'a low yield of opium poppy is still better than wheat'—the option they saw for themselves in the canal command area—and just hoped that the opium yields would be better in 2013/14.

Without anywhere else to go, most farmers simply reduced the amount of opium poppy they cultivated and returned to a cropping system that included some wheat, a practice that they had pursued before the dramatic rise in opium prices in the spring of 2010. Some farmers even left land fallow, hoping that it would recover if rested and that better yields could be obtained in subsequent growing seasons. Others leased their land out or gave it to farmers to cultivate on a sharecropping basis and let them carry the risk of poor opium yields.

These were all rational responses designed to address uncertainty over poor opium yields and low farmgate prices, while ensuring a level of food security.

While some may celebrate what is likely to be a lower level of opium cultivation in these areas, the fundamental problem remains: what to do with a burgeoning population in the desert spaces of southern Afghanistan, who on the whole see their lives as having improved, not because of the interventions of the Afghan government and the Western donor community, but despite them. Moreover, for those currently residing north of the canal, the government is perceived as a threat to both their economic and physical security.[23] This is a population that had experienced life in 'state space' and has no wish to return to the canal command area for as long as the government is in Lashkar Gah and the ban on opium continues.

This section has shown just how varied the livelihood trajectories are for the different population groups within central Helmand and has examined the coping strategies households have adopted in response to both the ban on opium production in the Food Zone and the wider statebuilding effort that framed the ban. It has shown that, just as in the Kabul River valley of Nangarhar province, the people in the areas closest to the provincial centres of central Helmand were privileged by better resource endowments, market opportunities and preferential access to development assistance. They experienced improvements in their standard of living despite abandoning opium production after 2008.

This section has also documented how other communities less well endowed with land, water and patronage have seen significant losses in welfare once the prohibition of opium production became a priority of the provincial administration and the international community in Helmand. This loss in welfare subsequently led to a shift in the political fabric within the canal command area where the Food Zone was implemented, as well as in those areas beyond its boundaries. For those who experienced a deterioration in their standard of living within the Food Zone, the opium ban was perceived as a further act of predation; contrary to those who argue that prohibition serves to extend the writ of the state, the ban was seen as further evidence of state failure.[24] In fact, in those communities where the ban led to what Scott refers to as 'patterns of collective insecurity', prohibition was contextualised within a wider narrative of the state's inability to deliver improvements in the lives of the rural population, as well as its lack of legitimacy in light of prevailing corruption within the administration and the loss of state sovereignty attributed to the presence of foreign military forces. The belief that prohibition is the priority of Western powers and was implemented so that Governor Mangal could solicit the support of the US and

UK governments in his political rivalry with Sher Mohammed Akhunzada and President Karzai further weakened the administration in the minds of those made vulnerable by the ban.[25]

Perhaps the most significant change in the political topography caused by the ban on opium production in the canal command area has been the growth in the population and poppy cultivation in the area north of the Boghra Canal. This is a population that is hostile to the state; most have resided in the canal command area in the past and believe they were compelled to leave, forced out by prohibition and by what they perceive is the government's failure to generate sufficient economic opportunities. Moreover this is not a marginal population: they number around 160,000 in the area to the north of Boghra Canal and south of Highway One. More settlers can be found in the deserts to the north of Highway One in Nahre Seraj and in Nawzad; there is a further concentration of migrants in Bakwa, many of whom originate from Helmand, including those who have migrated from the canal command area following the imposition of the ban after 2008. This population is highly dependent on opium poppy due to the high costs of production in these desert spaces, and it is hard to see how they would sustain themselves if they could not grow poppy.

Conclusion

By the end of 2013, levels of opium poppy cultivation in Helmand had rebounded to the levels they were at before the Food Zone was implemented. Some attributed the resurgence in cultivation to the fact that the alternative livelihoods component—the wheat seed and fertiliser programme—had ceased at the end of the 2010/11 growing season. However, according to USG figures, cultivation within the Food Zone itself continued to fall even in 2013, and the increase was occurring in areas outside the Food Zone in the former desert areas and in the districts in the north of the province.

Advocates of the Food Zone initiative argued that little could be done to prevent the increases in those areas outside the Food Zone and that the growth in opium poppy in the former desert lands was a consequence of the failure to pursue a more comprehensive eradication effort in central Helmand. In fact, the increases in cultivation in areas beyond the perimeter of the Food Zone were taken as further evidence of the programme's success, and justification that similar initiatives should be launched in other provinces as a way of countering increasing levels of cultivation.

However, what was missing from this call for replication was a more detailed understanding of both the reasons why levels of opium poppy fell within the geographic boundaries of the Food Zone, as well as an analysis of why opium poppy cultivation increased outside. This chapter and the previous one have sought to answer these questions by examining the wider socio-economic and political processes that were occurring at the time of the Food Zone initiative, as well as developing a deeper understanding of how the ban on opium impacted on the different population groups within the canal command area of central Helmand through an analysis of both political economy and livelihood trajectories. This analysis has been particularly important given the dynamic environment; the sheer number of programmes and institutions operating in central Helmand at the time of the Food Zone, and how closely reductions in cultivation came to be tied to the success of the overall state-building effort in the province.

A further area of interest, particularly in light of the dramatic increases in cultivation in the southern districts of Nangarhar in 2013, is the question of the sustainability of the reductions in opium poppy that have been achieved in the Food Zone. My overall hypothesis is that an opium ban is likely to be more enduring in areas of consolidated statehood than in areas of limited statehood. As this chapter has shown, central Helmand offers a contrasting picture to that of Nangarhar. The degree of social fragmentation that has occurred in central Helmand over the last three decades, fuelled by conflict and the intrusion of armed *jihadist* commanders and their clients during the 1980s and 1990s, has imposed significant constraints on state power in the canal command area. Similar to those in government posts in Jalalabad engaged in bargains and deal-making with the tribal groups of southern Nangarhar, officials in Lashkar Gah are faced with multiple and competing tribal elites who only have a fragile hold over a limited geographic space.

These are not areas dominated by landed elites, as in the districts of Surkhrud or Kama in central Nangarhar, who preside over large tracts of land and have a symbiotic interest with the Afghan state. Instead, the state in central Helmand is confronted with divided tribal groups, engaged in intense competition as they contest control over natural resources, such as land and water, and for patronage from those wielding state power, as well as those aligned with anti-government elements. In this fragile and dynamic environment, favouring one group only serves to alienate another as each looks at how they might best protect their interests and the geographic territory that they currently control.

This is a highly fluid political context, in which it is difficult to sustain a ban on opium poppy cultivation in those areas where the population has endured significant losses in welfare, as to do so would risk alienating the rural population. Much will depend on the future coercive power of state actors, in particular the status and funding of the ALP. In the 2012/13 growing season many ALP units in central Helmand continued to impose a ban on opium, believing that their position and salaries depended on it. Growing resistance from within rural communities, increased attacks by insurgent groups, or the perception that donor money might dry up for the ALP and ANSF could soon change this calculation; forcing ALP units to take a more pragmatic position on an opium ban, not only to gain the consent of the rural population but also to gain a source of rent extraction, were funding from the state to cease.

At the start of the 2013/14 growing season it appeared that the population in much of the canal command area believed that the state had succeeded in concentrating the means of violence in the canal command area and had not sought to engage directly in rural rebellion. Instead, those who had been most adversely affected by the prohibition continued to relocate to the former desert area north of the Boghra Canal. Migration to this area cannot simply be dismissed as economic opportunism, but should be seen as an act of defiance. Many of those who have relocated were disadvantaged by the opium ban and could no longer obtain land or meet their basic needs in the canal command area without recourse to opium poppy cultivation. They departed the canal command area hostile to the government in Lashkar Gah and a rural elite that they believe had colluded with provincial and district officials to divert development assistance to the most powerful and the least needy. There is widespread support for the Taliban amongst those who settled in the desert land north of the Boghra to cultivate opium poppy, as well as those who remain in the canal command area and experienced a deterioration in their quality of life in the absence of opium poppy.

It seems unlikely that many of the farmers who have settled in the area north of the Boghra Canal will leave and that this area will return to desert. There is still plenty of potential for increasing rates of migration, especially were the government to persist with its opium ban in the canal command area of central Helmand and not take remedial action to meet the needs of the land-poor who have been most disadvantaged by current counternarcotics policies. With the prospect of a return to opium poppy cultivation in the Food Zone, and given how unlikely it is that settlers will abandon their new homes in the former desert lands, Helmand has the potential to reach new unprecedented levels of opium poppy cultivation after 2014.

It is notable that as the NATO combat mission comes to a close, levels of opium poppy cultivation in both Helmand and Nangarhar were in danger of reaching levels that would surpass previous records. This is despite the significant investments that have been made in pursuing counternarcotics objectives in both provinces and the successes that have been celebrated by the international community. In fact, in both provinces counternarcotics and the wider statebuilding project became indistinguishable. Low levels of cultivation became a proxy measure for strong and effective leadership by the governor, the PRT and international military forces. Once the success of the statebuilding effort became so intimately tied to this measure, and thereby institutional and individual performance, further reductions in cultivation had to be achieved almost regardless of the consequences. It is for this reason that Governor Gulab Mangal and his successor Naeem Baloch pressed for more aggressive eradication targets each year, just as Gul Aga Shirzai had done in Sherzad in 2010; and it is for this same reason that international forces *in situ* became so reluctant to be seen not to support the expansion proposed.

A further similarity between the bans imposed in Helmand and Nangarhar is how the boundaries between what some consider a distinct set of counternarcotics interventions and the wider statebuilding project became so blurred. This was in part because of the political pressure in each province for an array of national and international institutions to support the imposition of a ban at a time when rising cultivation was being seen as evidence of state failure. However, it was also because the boundaries between counternarcotics and statebuilding efforts are entirely artificial: defined by institutional mandates and budgets of Western organisations, and not consciously shaped. Too often there is too little understanding of the complex and dynamic processes that assist farmers with quite different resource endowments, histories of cultivation and local political structures to transition out of poppy cultivation and the kind of interventions that might support them.

The creation of the Food Zone, and in particular its simplified contractual approach, helped maintain the illusion of a recognisable set of boundaried counternarcotics interventions that could deliver a reduction in cultivation, and could be replicated elsewhere. This was despite the obvious exogenous factors that were at play at the time of the Food Zone, including the shift in the terms of trade between wheat and poppy and most importantly the dramatic increase in the presence of foreign military forces in many of the major poppy-growing areas of central Helmand. In Nangarhar there was no such pretence; there was no specific programme of wheat seed and fertiliser distribution and no attempt to solicit signed agreements from farmers to refrain from opium poppy cultivation. Moreover, Governor Gul Aga Shirzai made little effort to distinguish between interventions; he proved adept at conflating counterinsurgency and counternarcotics campaigns and using the threat of US military incursions to persuade farmers to desist from planting opium poppy in the 2007/8 growing season.

11

CONCLUSION

Introduction

This concluding chapter provides an overview of the main themes that emerge from a comparison of bans prohibiting opium poppy cultivation, and then outlines the contribution of the research to the broader literature on drugs, conflict and statebuilding. This research has examined the complex and dynamic political processes involved in prohibiting cultivation in a single source country. It has examined four distinct efforts to ban opium poppy cultivation, which offer scalability for drug control efforts in other parts of Afghanistan and beyond. The first, the Taliban ban, was a nationwide effort and resulted in the complete cessation across the country. The bans imposed by Hajji Din Muhammad and Gul Aga Shirzai were limited to the province of Nangarhar but succeeded in reducing cultivation to negligible levels, the latter over three consecutive seasons. The fourth ban was imposed in a more limited geographic area, centred on the canal command area of central Helmand by Gulab Mangal.

These bans were reviewed in detail in order to answer the first research question: what are the local, regional, national and international processes that contribute to the imposition of a ban on opium poppy cultivation? Detailed case study analysis illuminates why bans were imposed at specific moments in time, how institutions with very different interests, mandates and constituents aligned themselves behind efforts to enforce a ban across a given area, and how the act of prohibition itself played a role in reshaping the economic and political terrain which could lead to the collapse of a ban. Therefore, this research has situated efforts to ban opium in Afghanistan within a broader socio-economic and political context, including the international, national, provincial and local environments in which opium bans are imposed.

Each of the opium bans reviewed involved a multiplicity of actors and institutions, formal and informal, at the international, national and local levels. The timing of each of these bans, even the imposition of the Taliban prohibition of 2000/1, were contingent on the coincidence of the interests of these disparate institutions, as well as having the socio-economic and political conditions in place conducive to enforcing a ban across a wide geographic area. Table 4 outlines the main characteristics of each of the opium bans and the particular conditions that were in place when they were implemented. It outlines the wider external and internal political and economic factors that led to the enforcement of a ban at a particular time. It also offers a comparison of the different approaches used in the implementation of these bans and how this varied across the geographic space in which they were enforced. It is highlighted in the first part of this chapter how powerholders in Afghanistan have used prohibition to project the appearance of state power directed at external audiences, particularly Western donors and foreign powers. It goes on to highlight how the process of banning opium across the diverse political and economic landscape has involved quite different strategies. The process of enforcing a ban in areas of limited statehood—offering development assistance, payments to local elites and drawing on the coercive power of foreign military forces—has ultimately exposed the state as weak and undermined rural support for the political coalition that allowed a ban to be imposed.

The second research question addresses the impacts of the bans on a diverse rural population, exploring how farmers in different socio-economic groups and locations have responded to efforts to prohibit opium poppy over time, and in particular what are the conditions that lead to violent unrest. These differed according to sources of income and social protection, changes in patterns of food consumption, healthcare and assets, and finally collective responses to bans, including everyday acts of resistance and in extreme cases, armed resistance. The second part of the chapter highlights the role that the rural population plays in shaping the political terrain and reactions to a ban on opium. Farmers were largely compliant in areas of consolidated statehood due to the concentration of economic and political power in the hands of an amenable local elite, in contrast to the political vigour of rural communities in areas of limited statehood where there was growing rural dissent and support for the insurgency, compelling local elites in some cases to withdraw their support for the political coalition that had been instrumental in imposing the bans.

The third research question draws out the policy implications of the detailed case study research for counternarcotics interventions and statebuilding in Afghanistan and more widely.

In the final section the chapter examines how international civilians and military actors at the local and sub-national levels have been ill-equipped to deal with the complex and dynamic political terrain of rural Afghanistan, and how supporting a ban on opium has in the words of de Waal (2009) 'distorted the political marketplace', inflating the market value of those elites who favour prohibition in the eyes of the international community, while at the same time diminishing their status with the rural population. It also looks at how the prioritisation of counternarcotics has risen and fallen depending on levels of cultivation. It shows how counternarcotics institutions such as UNODC have tried to shape the policy debate and build coalitions across the international community in support of efforts to drive down levels of cultivation. It shows how temporary these coalitions are, inhibited by both a policy process that shifts rapidly from one problematic metric to another, and international institutions that have quite different mandates and understanding of the causes and consequences of opium production. The chapter concludes with a discussion of what these findings mean for both broader theory and policy.

Projecting the Appearance of Power: the Problematic Relationship Between Prohibition and Statebuilding

One of the most notable features of each of the bans is how at the national, provincial, district and local levels Afghan actors have instrumentalised bans in order to present an image of authority to the outside world. In fact, prohibition has often created the false impression of a Weberian state to the international community, and helped establish the political elites as credible interlocutors with whom the international community could engage. As already noted, the literature on opium bans in Afghanistan tends to take the 'narratives of the powerful' at face value, leading to inaccurate depictions of the role played by politico-military actors in restraining cultivation. These include the actions of Nasim Akhundzada in Helmand, early accounts of the Taliban during the 1994/5 growing season, and more recent efforts to prohibit cultivation in Nangarhar and Helmand.

The Taliban prohibition of 2000/1 exemplifies the way in which reductions in cultivation have come to symbolise state power in Afghanistan. The Taliban's success in securing a complete cessation of opium poppy cultivation was seen at the time as indicative of the regime's ability to subjugate the population. A closer examination of the motives behind the ban, as well as the highly localised and fragile political processes involved in negotiating compliance with rural communities, suggests a different picture: that the ban was a political gamble designed to reposition the Taliban on the international stage and attract development assistance at a time when the regime was facing increasing isolation, growing fissures within the leadership and signs of rural unrest (Crews and Tarzi, 2008: 263; Rashid, 2002: 103–4). Allegations that the ban was motivated by attempts to raise the price of opium and thereby increase revenues to the Taliban appear uninformed when greater consideration is given to the unregulated structure of the drugs trade, as well as the negotiated and fluid nature of the Taliban's authority over the regions at the time.

While members of the Taliban and their associates may well have been guilty of 'insider trading', simply dismissing the ban as a cynical attempt to manipulate prices ignores the complex political environment at the time and the growing international and domestic pressures on the Taliban movement. The ban gave the Taliban regime the appearance of moral authority with the international community, after being so frequently censured for its poor record on human rights and gender and for the sanctuary it gave to Osama Bin Laden. The ban embarrassed the United Front and challenged their international legitimacy as the recognised authority and occupiers of the official seat at the UN. The prohibition of opium production also forced Western nations to engage with the Taliban as a credible interlocutor, highlighted by the seniority of many of the members on the donors' mission sent to Afghanistan to investigate the impact and sustainability of the ban.

Finally, the prohibition compelled Western donors to provide short-term development assistance in response to the humanitarian impact of the ban, and to consider how they might engage with the regime through medium- to long-term development support (Donor Mission, 2001: 5). In fact, were it not for the tragic events of 11 September 2001 and the subsequent international intervention in Afghanistan, the Taliban's success in prohibiting opium production might well have succeeded in changing the way that the international community engaged with the regime.

Furthermore, if the Taliban are understood as proto-statebuilders (Goodhand, 2008), then drugs were one of several resources which contributed to a brutal but relatively effective process of state consolidation in Afghanistan. In fact, drugs were one of the sources of rent that glued together a dominant coalition in what was largely an endogenous process of political consolidation. The opium ban undercut these processes, fractured the political settlement on which order had been established, and exposed the rural population to the limits of the Taliban's coercive capacity.

Framing the Taliban prohibition within the broader international and national political environment in which it occurred also helps to clarify more recent efforts to ban opium in Afghanistan. These share many of the characteristics of the Taliban prohibition, particularly with regard to how the international community interpreted reductions in cultivation as an indicator of territorial control and strong leadership. For instance, Governors Gul Aga Shirzai, Gulab Mangal and Atta Mohammed Noor were all lauded for their counternarcotics efforts, establishing themselves as credible interlocutors with the national government and international institutions.

My research shows that political pressure to eliminate opium production is not only an exogenous factor. It took President Karzai several years in power before he realised that opium could not be eliminated in the short term. During the initial years of his tenure, he pressed for a policy of rapid reduction in cultivation, ignoring the arguments that a longer-term approach was required if reductions were to be enduring and not undermine statebuilding efforts (Ives, 2004).

The various governors who enforced bans did so with little consideration for the medium- and longer-term consequences of preventing opium production in areas where there were no economic alternatives for the local population. Governor Gul Aga Shirzai's eradication campaign in the district of Sherzad in 2010 and Gulab Mangal's desire to press north of the Boghra Canal were both indicative of the uncompromising position that several Afghan politicians adopted on counternarcotics, sometimes at odds with the policy positions of Western nations and institutions.

The often aggressive position adopted by state actors highlights the important role that counternarcotics can play in the 'political marketplace' in drug crop-producing countries (de Waal, 2009). Domestic actors were not merely 'innocent bystanders' (Keefer et al., 2010); they frequently sought political and economic benefits from imposing bans on cultivation, including consolidating their political careers and gaining recognition for their efforts from international agencies and central government. Governors such as Gul Aga Shirzai, Gulab Mangal, Hajji Din Muhammad and Atta Mohammed Noor used counternarcotics to consolidate and further their political careers and sought recognition for their efforts from international agencies and the central government. They leveraged patronage within the administration and international support and funding for their achievements in counternarcotics (UNODC/MCN, 2007; UNODC/MCN, 2008). The Karzai administration also sought to gain politically on the international stage from Governor Sherzai's and others' actions to ban opium production.

In all of these cases, prohibition was used by the authorities to press for further development assistance on the basis that prohibition imposed a significant economic burden on the rural population. For example, during the 2004/5 growing season there were concerted efforts by a range of Afghan ministers to use reductions in cultivation to leverage funds from the international community. These efforts took place against a backdrop of escalating violence in Iraq and concerns that the international efforts in Afghanistan would lose in a competition for reconstruction funding.

This strategy had the effect of raising expectations among rural communities that they would be rewarded for reducing opium poppy cultivation. Afghan elites also applied moral pressure by arguing that opium bans were imposed for the benefit of consumers in Western nations, in an attempt to leverage donor largesse.

Therefore one can understand these bans as part of a complicated bargaining game involving international, national and local actors. State sovereignty in the contemporary era is viewed less as a right than a responsibility (Chandler, 2010), and abiding by international drug control treaties is one of these responsibilities.Therefore, domestic elites aim to extract material and symbolic resources from international institutions by making a visible commitment to drug bans. These bans are theatrical and performative; they demonstrate a capacity and a will—paraphrasing Scott (1998)—to 'act like a state'. From the point of view of domestic elites (and perhaps also for counternarcotics policymakers) the long-term effects of bans are of less concern than the immediate benefits they generate. And in such an insecure and volatile environment, where actors in the marketplace are simply trying to survive or accumulate in the short term, the sustainability of bans may be a secondary issue.

External assistance is viewed by the producing country as compensation for the economic and political disruption that a ban on drug crops will cause, as illustrated by the concept of 'alternative development' that originated in Bolivia (Thoumi, 2003: 337). To a domestic audience, the ruling elite portrays itself as a benefactor extracting development funds from Western consumer countries for the benefit of those that have abandoned drug crop cultivation (ibid.). To Western donors these elites are potential statebuilders who, with the right support, can build the political coalition required to sustain a ban over an extended period. Yet there is a paradox in attempts to ban drug crop cultivation in the kind of political and physical terrain in which coca and opium poppy are currently concentrated. A sustainable shift out of drug cultivation requires a reasonably high-capacity, legitimate and developmental state; yet, as this research has shown, prohibition can undermine the possibility of the emergence of such a state.

Understanding the Diffuse Nature of Political Power in Rural Space

Those Afghan leaders who would best succeed during the [20th century] employed a 'Wizard of Oz' strategy. They declared their governments all-powerful but rarely risked testing their claim by implementing controversial policies. The leaders most prone to failure and state collapse were those who assumed that they possessed the power to do as they pleased, and then provoked opposition that their regimes proved incapable of suppressing. (Barfield, 2010: 164)

As Barfield indicates, 'state talk' creates an appearance of power, but Afghan leaders who act as though this power actually exists, particularly in areas of limited statehood, have rarely survived for long. Beneath the veneer of state power projected by Afghan leaders when imposing a ban on opium, and the associated threat of coercion linked to prohibition, is a far more opaque and complex picture of how prohibition was imposed in rural areas. The gap between the appearance of sovereign power and the practical limits to this power are most evident in the areas of limited statehood.

The case studies show that bans were more easily imposed in areas of consolidated statehood where there is a history of state encapsulation, agricultural surplus and better resource endowments. In these areas, a strong state presence reaches out into the spaces surrounding the provincial centres and alongside the arterial highways. In Nangarhar, this involved a movement out from districts like Behsud, Surkhrud and Kama to incorporate much of the Kabul River valley, including the canal-irrigated parts of Shinwar district, where even in the 2006/7 growing season opium poppy was grown extensively.

In these lower areas, the central and provincial authorities drew upon their common interests and bonds with a local elite that had largely succeeded in concentrating economic and political power through the opportunities derived from market and state penetration, colonial rule and foreign interventions. In districts such as Surkhrud and Kama, the prevalence of tenancy and sharecropping arrangements, as well as a rural elite that worked closely with Kabul and the provincial governor, helped impose a ban and maintain it even when other parts of Nangarhar returned to cultivation temporarily in the 2006/7 growing season and more extensively since 2010.

Since 2001, political offices in both Kabul and Jalalabad and positions in the administration provided a vehicle for the local leaders in these areas to strengthen patronage and gain a commanding position over goods and services. The elite drew on the support of the governor and their connections with Kabul to gain privileged access to development assistance and broaden their resource base through land grabs and a growing control over trade. The rural elites in these lowland areas did not represent local communities in their interactions with the state but were instead what Scott (1972:18) refers to as 'creatures of the centre who deal with the local community'.

While the state may be able to co-opt and incorporate the local elite in areas where resources and populations have been concentrated, this is not the case in rural areas where societal structures are more egalitarian and the population is more dispersed (Scott, 2009). In these areas of limited statehood, neither the rural elite nor the population simply acquiesce to the state. As the literature on political geography and political settlements indicates (Boone, 2003; Barkey, 1994; Parks and Cole, 2010), state power in these areas is negotiated and based on a constantly evolving process of deal-making between state power holders and the elites that work to maintain order in rural areas. Opium bans in areas of limited statehood can be characterised as 'spot bargains', involving brokerage between national governments, sub-national leadership and local elites, and, in the case of more recent bans, the intrusive presence of foreign militaries.

In fact, notwithstanding all that has been written about the coercive power of the Taliban regime, even the ban imposed in 2000/1 required negotiations and payments both in cash and in kind to communities in some of the more remote 'self-governing' parts of the country (Scott, 2009). Contemporary bans are also difficult to sustain in areas where the state had typically ceded authority to the local population. Hajji Din Muhammad, for example, failed to deliver a ban in the upper valleys of Achin and Khogiani during the 2004/5 growing season, and these areas increased levels of cultivation the following year when the ban continued to be effectively enforced in the lower parts of the province of Nangarhar. It was only with the increased presence of US military assets in the southern districts of Nangarhar in 2007, and with Governor Gul Aga Shirzai's success in bringing together counterinsurgency and counternarcotics efforts in the minds of the population, that a ban could effectively be imposed in these areas in the 2007/8 growing season. Even then, promises of development assistance were made to communities alongside the use of targeted violence to gain compliance.

In areas of limited statehood, where the rural elite are brokers rather than patrons, leaders such as Malik Niaz and Malik Usman in Achin have to negotiate with their rural constituencies. They have to be conscious of histories of armed resistance, of egalitarian tribal structures, and of political adversaries in the rural elite who are keen to capitalise on their failure to deliver improvements in welfare to the wider population. Consequently, in contrast to areas of consolidated statehood in Nangarhar, the local elite in the Spinghar piedmont is forced to be more responsive to their rural constituencies and to be perceived as serving the population's interests if they are not to find themselves outmanoeuvred by an opponent and rejected by the people they claim to represent.

In such contexts the state is working against the grain of prevailing social and political structures. It severely risks eroding its limited legitimacy and political capital by pushing policies which systematically undermine the population's economic welfare and exposes them to asset-depleting risks. The situation becomes even more precarious with the presence of armed opposition groups supported by neighbouring powers. Under these conditions, the secondary and tertiary political settlements on which prohibition is built are unlikely to be sustained.

Similar socio-economic and political processes can be seen at work in central Helmand. Apart from the Barakzai-dominated river plains around Gereshk, Lashkar Gah and Nawa Barakzai, the canal command area does not contain the more hierarchical and unitary tribal structures and senior aristocratic elites that can be found in the areas of consolidated statehood in the lower districts of Nangarhar. Instead, much of the canal command area of Helmand contains multiple tribal groups with their respective rural elites, all in intense competition for both resources and influence. While in theory the mix of tribal groups, both settler and indigenous, in the canal command area should have made it easier for the state to coerce the rural population, the effect of the protracted armed conflict in southern Afghanistan has undermined the state's capacity to concentrate the means of violence.

Furthermore, the political topography of the canal command area has gone through profound change over the last thirty years due to the penetration of former *mujahidin* fighters from areas of limited statehood in the northern parts of the province. These are the politico-military leaders who led the resistance against the Soviets, grabbed land in the canal area in the 1980s and 1990s and were then appointed to government office in the initial years of the Karzai administration. As in the southern districts of Nangarhar, the government in Helmand finds itself confronted with a myriad of competing interlocutors, each with limited control over geographic space even in an area close to the provincial centre that has only been settled due to government largesse. If needed, these interlocutors can look to patronage and the means of violence from the central and provincial administration, foreign military and civilian actors and insurgent groups, in order to gain the upper hand over rivals within the village or with the village next door. The most adept rural leadership in these areas maintains a relationship with all three groups, thereby ensuring access to powerful patrons while containing the coercive capacity of the Afghan state.

The state's capacity to enforce a ban in areas of limited statehood is not simply an issue of being able to accumulate sufficient coercive power; it is also a question of what economic impact a prohibition of opium has on the different groups involved. As the earlier chapters of this research show, when a ban is imposed on areas where the population has the capabilities and assets to adapt without a significant loss in welfare, conflict is less likely and the prevailing political settlement can be maintained. However, in areas where a ban on opium production prompts households to adopt coping strategies that generate high levels of economic stress, the population may look to the rural elite to renege on agreements reached with the state and support a return to opium poppy cultivation in subsequent seasons. In this situation, the state is forced to strengthen its coercive capacity and offer more financial incentives in order to impose a ban for longer than a single season, or, as was the case in Nangarhar under the governorship of Gul Aga Shirzai, borrow coercive power from the foreign military.

However, as the evidence from both Nangarhar and Helmand shows, in areas of limited statehood a strategy of using foreign military forces to project the appearance of state power can prove self-defeating. With regard to both the opium ban and the land conflict in Achin, drawing on the coercive power of foreign military forces undermined support for the provincial governor, and subsequently for the central authorities. The governor's reluctance to travel without foreign military support and the growing perception that he had put the concerns of his foreign patrons ahead of the needs of the rural population further weakened his position in the eyes of the rural population. These vulnerabilities were exploited by Shirzai's political rivals, whose election to national and provincial assemblies gave them greater access to formal positions of power and patronage, thereby creating a more volatile political environment (Giustozzi and Orsini, 2009). In Helmand, Governor Mangal was subjected to considerable and often profane criticism from the rural population for his close relationship with the UK and US military forces and the belief that he was answerable to foreign powers rather than to the Afghan population or President Karzai. This perception was of value to his political opponents in the province, such as former Governor Sher Mohammed Akhundzada and the insurgency.

Finally, it is important to note that the boundary between areas of consolidated and limited statehood is both blurred and dynamic. The drug economy has itself played a role in blurring this boundary; as a high-value commodity frequently grown in areas of limited statehood, opium poppy has acted as a gravitational pull on the state. Borderland regions that historically could not be profitably controlled and administered by the state have become an attractive resource, encouraging greater penetration of these regions (Goodhand, 2009).

The Rural Population as Political Actors

The drug economy has itself had transformational effects. It has led to new processes of capital accumulation, new forms of investment and new owners and distributors of capital; it has influenced local leadership and shifted bargaining relations between rulers and ruled. Any attempt to 'turn off' drug crop cultivation will inevitably influence and disrupt these relationships and will have a profound impact, given that the drugs economy is so deeply embedded in the social, political and economic life of a source country like Afghanistan, particularly at its periphery.

It is among the rural population that we find the inherent flaws in imposing a ban on drug crop cultivation in areas of limited statehood. These flaws are not adequately explained by the master narratives found in the drugs literature, with its focus on global supply and demand, rising opium prices and the subjugation of farmers by either state or non-state actors (Reuter, 2010; Caulkins, 2010). The case studies show that where opium bans have been imposed in areas of limited statehood, there was a disconnect between the 'outside world' of Western donors and national institutions that see prohibition as an expression of state power. This stands in stark contrast to the everyday reality of farmers and the rural elite who see a state interlocutor that negotiates, offers favours, makes promises and uses state violence sparingly for fear of provoking widespread dissent, and that draws on the threat of foreign military forces to compel the population to abandon poppy cultivation. On the ground, the Leviathan is less powerful than it appears from a distance.

In areas of limited statehood we see farmers adopting coping strategies that give indications of economic distress and undermine their future earning capacity: reducing the quality and quantity of food consumed; delaying expenditure on healthcare, even for life-threatening conditions; and pursuing livelihood options that expose their family members to injury and hazards (Kramer and Woods, 2012). Rather than moving into high-value crops, the predominant response to a ban is the adoption of low-risk return cropping systems with an emphasis on staples such as wheat and maize. In Helmand we have seen population groups depart from the main canal command area and settle in the former desert areas north of the Boghra Canal, expanding the territory over which the Afghan state has limited control. The vast majority of these migrants have been from what are considered the indigenous tribes of Helmand, many of them linked through patronage networks to armed actors within the government and/or insurgent groups.

At the same time, the rural population is aware of powerholders signalling that bans are contingent on improvements in welfare and the delivery of assistance. Indeed, opium bans in Afghanistan have been consistently presented to the rural population as the responsibility of the international community, thereby providing strategic distance for provincial and local elites who attempt to portray themselves as innocent bystanders in the process, even when they have been actively involved in enforcing a ban. The perception that those in political power in Afghanistan are serving foreign interests provokes considerable resentment among farmers most disadvantaged by prohibition.

It is these dual themes of state weakness and the primacy of foreign interests, as well as the collective impact of an opium ban combined with other shocks, that ultimately drive rural communities in areas of limited statehood to press local leaders to renege on their support for the continuation of an opium ban. It is almost inevitable that local elites—conscious of how fragile their position is with the rural population and, in Afghanistan, aware of the impact of the withdrawal of foreign military forces on political patronage—will look to their political survival rather than adhere to a position that they had insisted was conditional on increased development assistance. This position can be portrayed as entirely consistent with their initial support for an opium ban and, as seen in Nangarhar, can even be used to strengthen the local elites' negotiating position with the central and provincial authorities.

When the state maintained a ban that caused 'patterns of collective insecurity' (Scott, 1976: 196), as seen in the southern districts of Nangarhar in 2010 and 2011, rural communities shifted from acts of resistance aimed at deterring eradication to acts of rural rebellion designed to eject the state from the area. Simply attributing these acts of violence to insurgent groups like the Taliban, as if they are an external force, ignores local dynamics and the ability of armed opposition groups to embed themselves successfully in rural areas by appealing to local grievances and populist messages, including those condemning foreign occupation (Farrell and Giustozzi, 2013).

The collapse of the opium ban in the south-western districts of Sherzad, Hesarak and Khogiani in Nangarhar in 2010, followed by a return to cultivation in the upper parts of Achin in 2011 and significant rises in cultivation in the 2012/13 growing season, highlights the challenges of maintaining prohibition in areas where the state does not have a concentration of the means of violence and where the population questions the legitimacy of its actions. These are the same areas where the Taliban found itself having to negotiate to implement the ban in the 2000/1 growing season. To attribute the return of cultivation to simple recalcitrance on behalf of the population and a lack of political commitment by the governor is to fail to understand the nature of state power in these areas and the way in which opium bans have been implemented over the years. It also fails to reflect how much the impact of a ban on opium will vary depending on the assets and capabilities of individual households.

The reaction in areas of consolidated statehood in the lower valleys was quite different. There the livelihoods of households and communities were resilient in the face of a ban on opium poppy. More favourable resource endowments and improved access to private and public services have combined to support livelihood diversification and improvements in welfare, despite opium production being abandoned. In the areas where this kind of transformation occurred, there was little evidence of rural dissent or a resurgence in opium poppy cultivation. This experience in the lower valleys belies the claim that crop destruction automatically leads to growing support for insurgent groups.

Therefore, there have been quite different community responses to prohibition depending on the location, state–societal relations, resource endowments and local political structures. By drawing on the livelihoods framework, this research has shown that those located in areas of consolidated statehood have a greater capacity to carry the costs of prohibition with few negative consequences. These costs can be compensated by alternative revenue streams, existing assets, better integration into the wider economy, and the privileged access the rural elite has to patronage networks (Risse et al., 2011; Boone, 2003: 31).

Distorting the Political Marketplace

International actors have been key players in the Afghan political marketplace. On the whole, they have been ill-equipped to deal with this complex political terrain, its multiple centres of power and the array of competing and overlapping interests in rural Afghanistan (Gates, 2014: 589; Rohde, 2013). There has been a tendency among both civilian and military actors to accept the narratives of those in positions of power, as well as simplistic explanations of how bans on opium have been imposed in the past, particularly the ban enforced by the Taliban in the 2000/1 growing season. Too much emphasis has been placed on the role of coercion in imposing bans, with little regard to the economic circumstances of the population, state–societal structures or local configurations of power, and consequently the longer-term impact of prohibition on state formation.

In areas of limited statehood there has been a tendency to mistake local elites for patrons rather than brokers (Scott, 1972: 95) and to engage directly in bolstering those who have sought political favour and funding by supporting efforts to ban opium poppy cultivation. There has been little sense of the 'local rules of the game' (Schetter, 2013: 11) and of the reality that many local elites do not have the unequivocal support of the rural population and are required to be responsive to community needs if they are not to be deposed or subject to acts of violence. There has been even less appreciation that the direct threat of foreign power has undermined the support base of local elites in areas of indirect rule where there is a strong tradition of armed resistance to state and foreign intrusion.

Support by international actors directly to local elites has inflated their power and autonomy in relation to the centre. In an environment where low levels of cultivation have been viewed by international actors as evidence of good performance and strong leadership, provincial governors such as Gul Aga Shirzai imposed opium bans as a vehicle for furthering their longer-term political ambitions in Kabul. Local leaders such as Malik Niaz and Malik Usman also used the foreign patronage gained from their support of counternarcotics and counterinsurgency efforts to accrue land and development assistance, further undermining their position with the rural population. The perception of favouritism by international actors for those local leaders who were instrumental in banning opium in Nangarhar also led to growing resentment amongst excluded rural elites, further undermining the fragile political settlements on which the ban was based.

There has also been a lack of awareness of the changing political geography in rural Afghanistan and how Western policies and strategies, including in the field of counternarcotics, have contributed to these changes. The land dispute in Achin, driven by the 'Shinwari Pact' of 2010, was catalytic; taken in conjunction with the continued imposition of the opium ban in the southern districts, it exposed the limits of state power, undermined the position of the governor, fractured the political settlement in Nangarhar and, ultimately, offered a further entry point for insurgent groups. International civilian and military actors were important protagonists in these developments, but did not seem to be aware of the likely consequences of their actions or of events as they unfolded. The dramatic increase in the settlement of former desert land to the north of the Boghra Canal and the contributing role of the Food Zone are further examples of the international community's failure to consider the unintended consequences of its actions. It illustrates how some parties have simply considered second-order effects of much less importance—something for their successor to deal with—in light of their limited time in the country and the political pressure to deliver on key metrics.

It is also possible to see from the different bans imposed how individual and institutional incentives shaped the nature of the international engagement on counternarcotics. The perception in the minds of many Western officials that the amount of opium poppy cultivation in an area is a proxy indicator of state power led to a growing reluctance to preside over high or rising levels of cultivation. This view, combined with the rapid turnover of civilian and military staff in Afghanistan, led to strategies that gave precedence to reductions in cultivation rather than livelihood outcomes and interdiction, both of which have greater support amongst the rural population.

Periods of increased cultivation had the effect of inflating the influence of international counternarcotics institutions in shaping the policy agenda in Afghanistan. In this regard, both 2004 and 2007 were watersheds for counternarcotics for the county as a whole, and the period between 2004 and 2008 was of particular significance for the province of Helmand. In these years counternarcotics gained ascendancy among competing policy priorities and institutional mandates. The upward trends in levels of cultivation meant that those in the US administration pressing for aerial spraying had the rest of the international community and the Afghan government on the defensive.

The 2004/5 growing season was particularly significant, as opium poppy cultivation had increased dramatically, and for the first time was reported in every province of Afghanistan. With the rise in opium production contrasting with what was generally seen as 'the good news story' emanating from Afghanistan in 2004, and the low levels of cultivation achieved by the Taliban regime, there was a clear political imperative within the international community, and particularly the US, for a correction. Similar responses in the policy debate between international and national actors were seen following the rise in cultivation in the 2006/7 growing season at a national level, and in the provinces of Helmand and Nangarhar.

During these years there was a genuine fear that if cultivation continued to rise, it would be difficult to resist the pressure to introduce the kind of aerial eradication campaign that had been implemented in Colombia. The threat of crop spraying led to a coalition of disparate national, international, civilian and military institutions pressing for reductions in cultivation in Afghanistan, with some unlikely individuals and agencies even supporting increasing levels of manual eradication. The imposition of both the bans in Nangarhar during the 2004/5 and the 2007/8 growing seasons should be seen as a direct consequence of the need to counter the upward trend in levels of opium poppy cultivation and to avert the introduction of an aerial eradication campaign. The fact that Nangarhar province was under the jurisdiction of US military and civilian forces in the PRT, with the resources that this entailed, made it the most likely candidate for an invigorated counternarcotics effort during these years. In Helmand the British PRT feared further damage to its reputation and a renewed campaign to press for aerial eradication from advocates within the USG if it did not actively engage in efforts to reduce opium poppy cultivation in 2008, despite the high cost and conceptual weaknesses of the plan.

It is also apparent that UNODC played a decisive role in shaping counternarcotics policy in Afghanistan, including the imposition of opium bans. For example, it strongly encouraged the Taliban to eliminate opium poppy cultivation prior to the 2000/1 growing season. In discussions with the leadership of the regime, the prospects of future development assistance were often raised as a quid pro quo for the elimination of cultivation. As an institution, UNODC sought to benefit from its role as the primary interlocutor on the drugs issue with the Taliban regime and as an implementer of the drug control programme.

Since the collapse of the Taliban, UNODC has continued to shape the policy narrative on counternarcotics through the publication of the Annual

Afghan Opium Survey. The former Executive Director of UNODC, Antonio Maria Costa, often used his preface to the Survey to press for a more aggressive counternarcotics policy in Afghanistan during the years when cultivation increased; he actually came out in support of crop spraying in late 2007 (Semple and Golden, 2007; UNODC/MCN, 2007). Despite concerns over the integrity of the data, UNODC statistics also featured heavily in the arguments of those pressing for aerial spraying.

Bans as Temporary Coalitions of Interest

The major challenge for international drug control institutions has been how to maintain support for an effective opium ban once cultivation has begin to fall. In fact, what is perhaps most striking in each of these efforts to ban opium in Afghanistan is how diffuse political power is amongst both international and national actors, and how the successful imposition of each ban has been a function of the alignment of an array of disparate international, national, regional and local institutions. Often these institutions have little direct interest in eliminating opium but are responding to the market signals that led to counternarcotics gaining ascendancy among the range of competing policy objectives and institutional interests that exist in Afghanistan.

We have also seen that the alignment of these institutional interests is often temporary, especially in areas of limited statehood. On the international stage the political pressure to 'do something' means that once a metric can be corrected (or other metrics become worse), policy priorities shift and institutional interests realign to resolve another more pressing problem (Arjomand, 2013). The reordering of priorities leads to a reallocation of resources and a shift in the lexicon and narratives used to describe certain problems. Ongoing projects and programmes may re-label themselves to align with the new priorities, or seek justification as to how they might contribute to the new preferred policy priority. The rush to categorise an array of disparate interventions, including the National Solidarity Program, as 'counternarcotics' in the 2004/5 growing season and then to re-categorise some of these same projects and programmes as 'counterinsurgency' after 2008 is illustrative of this process. This 'theatre of counternarcotics'—labelling a wide range of interventions with quite different objectives as drug control when the circumstances dictate and realigning different programmes to contribute to counternarcotics objectives—points out the challenges of being guilty of drugs fetishism and attributing any changes in cultivation to what are perceived to be drug control programmes.

The market signal that typically led to counternarcotics rising up the priority list was an increase in the level of cultivation. The rise in this metric, often accompanied by a narrative of the failure of the statebuilding project in Afghanistan, created the political pressure to respond, and to respond quickly with efforts that might lead to a dramatic reduction in opium production almost regardless of whether these reductions would endure.

Following this 'call to action', a wide range of international and national institutions were mobilised, over and above organisations with a drug control mandate that were dealing with the drugs issue on a day-to-day basis. However, when cultivation subsequently fell, for example after a ban was successfully imposed, the attention of these institutions at the periphery of the drug control debate, including national actors, was diverted to other poor performing metrics, thereby making it difficult to maintain the institutional alignment that supported a reduction in opium production in the first place.

The challenge, however, is not just one of the constantly shifting priorities of the different institutions involved in policy in Afghanistan and how to maintain some kind of quorum. There is also the challenge that the many institutions involved in the drugs issue during periods of rising cultivation were shaped by different motives, mandates and understandings of the problem and did not agree as to how it related to the wider statebuilding project in Afghanistan. This made it particularly challenging to maintain an appropriate and consistent strategy on counternarcotics and led to a process where institutions engaged and disengaged according to the booms and slumps in levels of cultivation.

As we have seen, a rise in cultivation often led to the closer involvement of a multitude of development institutions, including Afghan line ministries, bilateral donors, international financial institutions such as the World Bank, and NGOs. When engaged, these development institutions realigned elements of their programming to offset some of the humanitarian and presentational problems created by the imposition of an opium ban. In the case of aerial spraying, some development institutions became far more proactive in counternarcotics simply to deter what they believed was a bad policy that would ultimately affect their capacity to implement development programmes on the ground. Typically the engagement of development organisations was short-term and waned when cultivation fell. Moreover, their interest did not lead to a deeper understanding of the multifunctional role of opium poppy in the lives and livelihoods of farmers; nor did it foster a shift to a medium- to longer-term development response designed to address the causes of cultivation. Throughout this process there was often the public spectacle of being seen to do something about the drugs issue—'the theatre of drug control'—while the policy and operational programmes of these institutions remained largely unchanged.

Ownership of the drugs issue among Afghan actors at the national, sub-national and local levels also ebbed and flowed. It ranged from playing a pro-active role in reducing cultivation in order to show strong leadership and gain favour, to indifference, or in some cases active encouragement of cultivation as a mark of defiance or as a basis for soliciting development funds on behalf of an increasingly hostile rural population. Other priorities or shifts in the political fabric could also diminish the importance of the drugs issue in the minds of the political elite. The breakdown in the political settlement between Gul Aga Shirzai and the old *jihadi* elite and their scions, as they competed for office, influence and rent, meant that there was little interest in maintaining low levels of cultivation, knowing that it was the governor who would gain the political kudos from such an achievement. The unpopularity of a policy that imposed economic hardship on the rural population, and that had not been accompanied by a sufficient rise in development assistance, also led local elites to consider the political capital that they had expended and to recalibrate their position on the ban, particularly in light of the withdrawal of interna-tional military forces.

A policy environment made up of a multitude of agencies with different mandates who sometimes become involved because they are compelled to, or because they see short-term advantages, but who look to exit as soon as they can, is clearly not an optimal one. It is important to recognise that some par-ties may have little interest in reducing drug crop cultivation permanently but, like David Keen's (2012) observations of 'war and war making as business', may see political and financial advantage in engaging in the 'war on drugs' and help to impose a ban, only to encourage cultivation in subsequent years to prolong the benefits they receive by acting as an interlocutor between the state and local communities. Managing the numerous temporary bargains between national, sub-national and local elites and the rural population is almost impossible without a permanent shift in the state's capacity to enforce a ban within its territory and a clear development strategy that mitigates the impact of an opium ban on the rural population.

On this basis, the potential for opium to return to areas of limited statehood following the withdrawal of NATO forces is high. What remains less clear is what will happen to those areas where the population has graduated out of opium poppy cultivation without losses in welfare, and where the state has built an effective social compact by providing goods and services to the rural population and political positions to the local elite. A poorly managed transition by international forces and the Afghan government may result in a reduction in areas of consolidated statehood and lead to opium poppy once again being cultivated adjacent to the main highways and provincial centres. Alternatively, a diminished foreign footprint could open up political space for endogenous settlements at the local level and perhaps even at the national level.

Contribution to Policy

By combining political economy and livelihoods analysis it is possible to develop a far more nuanced understanding of the profoundly political processes involved in imposing a ban on drug crop cultivation and how this impacts on political settlement, the economy and rural resistance across diverse political geography.

What can be derived from the Afghan case study is the fact that drug production and drug control are only one element in the political accommodation and bargaining processes in which sub-national and local elites are engaged. There are many other resources and opportunities for rent-seeking over which local and sub-national leaders collude and compete. They may place a higher priority on gaining control over political office with its opportunities for earning the patronage of international and national institutions and influencing the allocation of development funds and the security apparatus of the state.

Drug control can serve as a means for elites to present themselves as credible interlocutors and behave in a 'state-like' way to gain patronage and support, almost regardless of their past or current misdemeanours. To the outside world a ban is an expression of power, control and territorialisation. The interactions of the domestic political leadership with the international community and the public support they receive reinforces the image of leadership. In territory where the state has a history of encapsulation, the assistance offered might help shore up patronage networks, contribute to the consolidation of control over the means of violence and thereby help build a more stable political settlement.

Prohibition is much easier to impose in areas where the state has a history of direct rule, in part because drug crop cultivation is not at the forefront of the livelihood portfolios of the rural population. There are other economic opportunities that farmers can draw upon in areas of consolidated statehood; and in the context of a significant international effort, their privileged position—a function of location, history, resource endowments and the close bond between local and sub-national elites—can result in increased public- and private-sector investment and welfare gains. A ban on cultivation in these areas does have a short-term impact, but it is neither experienced by a significant proportion of the population nor severe enough to provoke widespread unrest and rural rebellion. There are too many other advantages associated with the current political order, coupled with a belief that further benefits will accrue if stability is maintained, given the population's physical proximity to the state's security institutions and the local elite's domination of physical resources and patronage networks. And there is, of course, recognition of the serious potential risks associated with revolt.

A ban on opium poppy cultivation in this kind of terrain can in fact reinforce political order and aid statebuilding by removing a 'lootable commodity' that is often a source of financing for political rivals. Moreover, a ban can eliminate the rent on opium production extracted by competitors to the current political order without antagonising large sections of the rural population. This in turn can strengthen relationships of patronage and resource flows between the state, the periphery and the rural population that support the development of more hierarchical societal structures and consolidate the power of local leaders who have already been co-opted by the state.

There is contrasting experience in the more remote border areas of limited statehood. In these areas drug crop cultivation is more embedded in the livelihoods of the rural population. It is the cornerstone of the economy and provides a variety of functions that cannot be easily replaced. Prohibition in these areas inflicts immediate and dramatic losses on the welfare of the vast majority of the rural population. Households are compelled to pursue activities that undermine their future earning capacity or expose family members to greater hazards. The prospects of even significant development investments offering respite from the impact of a ban are limited by location, terrain and sparse resources.

The highly contested nature of political leadership in these areas means that the local elite risk their political position if they are seen to support a ban on drug crop cultivation for more than a single season, perhaps more so when the elite is seen to be benefitting from the patronage of sub-national, national or even international actors. In these circumstances the rural elite faces immediate opprobrium from the local population; this disaffection can become violent and more widespread when the state can no longer maintain the appearance of order. The fact that drug control is presented as an international priority—something imposed from outside—offers elites the political space with which to distance themselves from a ban and renege on their commitments when their political survival demands it.

The wider and changing political environment and economy make maintaining a ban all the more challenging in areas of limited statehood, given how susceptible the population is to exogenous shocks, particularly after prohibition has been imposed. Further economic shocks will have a powerful effect on the population, as will natural disasters such as drought or crop failure. Elections can undermine the political coalitions that supported the imposition of a ban, prompting the formation of new alliances as political rivals within the local and sub-national elite seek to gain support from a disaffected population. This all points to the fact that prohibition in areas of limited statehood is doomed to fail not simply because of the impact a ban might have on farmgate prices, or because of corruption and insurgency, but because the bargains on which these bans are built are inherently unstable, constrained by state–societal relations, local configurations of power, the resource endowments of the population and the sheer number of disparate and competing institutions involved.

In areas of limited statehood, a ban on opium poppy cultivation is counterproductive. It fuels instability precisely because it exposes the rural population to significant economic shocks; it destabilises the political order due to the fluid and fragile nature of local leadership and the perceived failure of the local elite to deliver improvements in welfare and state patronage; and finally it damages the bond between state and periphery, fuelling violence and rural rebellion, precisely because prohibition presents an image of a state and a local leadership that does not care about the welfare of the population but prioritises its own interests and those of foreign benefactors. In this kind of terrain—where the state does not have a history of encapsulation, where there is a history of resistance and where there is a high dependency on opium poppy cultivation—a ban on opium production should not be considered.

The implications of this analysis are that international statebuilders need to have a more variegated and spatially informed approach to stabilisation; they cannot act geographically if they are blind to the nuances. As such, it is less about either a 'heavy' or 'light' footprint than about calibrating that footprint so that it works with, rather than against, the grain of society.

CONCLUSION

Contribution to Theory

From a theoretical perspective, this research has provided a number of valuable contributions to the literature on political economy, rural livelihoods and illicit drugs. Primarily it has shown how central politics and power are critical to the way that rural households earn a living in areas of conflict. It has highlighted the importance of understanding the messiness of local politics; of challenging the narratives of those who appear to be powerful patrons; and of investing in a deeper understanding of the underlying societal structures and the concentration of economic power that determine patterns of local leadership.

Secondly, this research has illustrated that drug crop cultivation is concentrated in an acutely political environment, where rural communities are often vibrant political actors. It has shown that it is a mistake to ignore the role that these communities can play in shifting the political terrain; how they have established room for negotiation with the state through acts of resistance; and how they can engage in violent dissent to repel the state and its representatives. Arguing that rural communities are the passive recipients of acts of violence by state and non-state actors, who ultimately determine whether drug crop cultivation occurs, lacks a clear understanding of the complex and multifaceted bargains and political arrangements that are so common in areas where drug crop cultivation is concentrated. The narrative of the passive farmer also ignores the fact that rural households and communities in drug-producing areas are not simply economic actors seeking to maximise income but social, cultural, political and economic beings engaged in a wide range of activities, many of which are non-monetary.

A third contribution of this research is an analysis of the complex institutional environment in which bans are imposed, and the multiplicity of international, national, sub-national and local actors involved. It has exposed how much easier it is to maintain the alignment of the disparate and competing interests of formal and informal institutions in areas of consolidated statehood where hierarchical structures are more prevalent and where international actors tend to operate through, and support, state institutions. This is in contrast to areas of limited statehood where, in the words of Risse et al. (2011: 245), multilevel governance dominates and where sovereignty is shared by local, national and global actors. However, as opposed to the more structured model of interactions between these institutions depicted by Risse et al., and de Waal's model of the political marketplace, this research has offered a more unruly and fluid reality, where some local actors operate in strategic locations, including on the interstices of national borders, to negotiate directly with national, sub-national and international actors. It is in this context that opium production and efforts to curb it are simply another commodity that local elites look to trade upon, but which are not fully in their capacity to deliver.

Finally this research has illustrated the methodological challenges associated with integrating power and politics into livelihoods analysis. It shows that this kind of inquiry, immersed not just in the secondary political settlements between national and sub-national actors but in the myriad local deals and bargains—the tertiary settlements—that are often the building blocks of political order in conflict-prone societies, takes time, patience and caution. This is not something that can be achieved through short-term one-off studies, reviews of secondary literature and interviews with policy-makers in capital cities or military bases. There is a need to engage in primary data collection with rural communities themselves and to conduct, as de Haan and Zoomers (2005: 44) suggest, comparative research that examines 'livelihood decisions in different geographical, socio-economic, cultural and temporal contexts'. Methodological pluralism is critical, and in a setting where high-resolution geospatial imagery is becoming increasingly affordable, there is a real need to invest in a variety of data collection methods that can help overcome some of the challenges of conducting primary research in insecure and contested space, particularly when examining sensitive issues such as the drugs economy. The integration of in-depth fieldwork and imagery has been a particularly innovative part of this research. It has shown the synergies that can be developed through feedback loops between high-resolution geospatial analysis and long-term fieldwork in insecure terrain.

CONCLUSION

Table 4: Comparison of Selected Opium Bans in Afghanistan

	National	Nangarhar		Helmand
	Taliban Ban	*Hajji Din Muhammad*	*Gul Aga Shirzai*	*Gulab Mangal*
Wider drugs context	Cultivation reached 91,000 hectares in 1999, bringing widespread condemnation. Fell to 82,000 hectares in 2000 after initial statement of ban, but reductions largely attributed to drought. Increasing calls for Taliban to act against opium poppy cultivation. Allegations of taxation of production and trade of narcotics against regime. UNODC actively engaged in persuading Taliban to impose ban since 1997.	Cultivation in Afghanistan reached an unprecedented level of 131,000 hectares in 2004. Cultivation in Nangarhar reached highest level of 28,213 hectares in 2004. Growing references to Afghanistan as a 'narco state' in policy circles and media. Pressure to introduce crop spraying by parts of USG, but rejected by Karzai.	Cultivation in Afghanistan reached a new peak of 193,000 hectares in 2007. Resurgence in Nangarhar in 2007 to 18,739 hectares. Pressure to introduce crop spraying by USG, but rejected by Afghan cabinet.	Decline in national figures, but Helmand reached a new peak of 103,590 hectares in 2009. Pressure to introduce crop spraying dissipated, but continued concerns that a failure to reduce cultivation in Helmand in coming year may lead to a renewed effort by advocates within USG. Counternarcotics operations, and reduction in levels of cultivation, increasingly seen as part of COIN efforts as illicit drugs regarded as major source of funding for Taliban in south.
Wider political environment	International criticism of Taliban as pariah regime. Aid flow limited, despite drought and ongoing conflict. UN sanctions imposed.	Afghan government concerned over maintaining aid flows following invasion of Iraq. Hajji Din Muhammad fearful he would be replaced if failed to deliver	Karzai keen to keep Shirzai contained due to presidential ambitions and rivalry with Ahmed Wali Karzai in the south. Gul Aga Shirzai concerned over	Karzai favoured reinstating Sher Mohamed Akhundzada as governor of Helmand; blamed resurgence of Taliban on his removal as governor in

	National	Nangarhar		Helmand
	Taliban Ban	*Hajji Din Muhammad*	*Gul Aga Shirzai*	*Gulab Mangal*
	Number of attempts by Taliban to recast themselves on international stage, including in the hijack of Indian airliner and arrest of Christian NGOs. Divisions in Taliban leadership and growing dissent in some rural areas due to opposition to conscription, ongoing drought and lack of development assistance.	on counter-narcotics. Presidential elections have high turnout and won by Karzai. US and UK concerned about perceived success of Afghan statebuilding project, particularly in light of situation and media coverage in Iraq; conscious that rising levels of cultivation do not marry well with narrative of success in Afghanistan.	position following removal from Kandahar and rise in cultivation; political ambitions meant he was keen to show leadership to potential international backers. USG concerned about impact of rising levels of cultivation in Nangarhar on their reputation, given leading role in PRT. Increase in US military presence in province, including in remote southern districts, as part of COIN effort.	2006, done at insistence of the British. Relationship between Gulab Mangal and Karzai strained; Mangal looked to US and UK for patronage and political support in face of president who wanted to see him removed, particularly in run-up to presidential election in 2009. UK government concerned about reputation with USG, particularly in light of campaign in Basra, Iraq and role as lead/ partner nation on CN. Increase in UK and US military presence in central and southern Helmand in 2008; followed by dramatic uplift in both ANSF and international military forces with the 'surge' and Operation Moshtarak.

	National	Nangarhar		Helmand
	Taliban Ban	Hajji Din Muhammad	Gul Aga Shirzai	Gulab Mangal
Wider economic environment	Concerns over food security due to drought. Increasing wheat prices. Fall in opium prices.	Concerns over food security due to increasing wheat prices and restrictions imposed on wheat exports by government of Pakistan. Fall in opium prices.	Concerns over food security due to increase in global wheat prices and trade restrictions imposed by government of Pakistan. Fall in opium prices. Significant recipient of aid with further increases associated with military surge in late 2007 and as part of COIN efforts in the province.	Continued concerns over food security due to high global wheat prices, trade restrictions imposed by government of Pakistan, and over-production of opium in Helmand in 2008. Continued fall in opium prices until winter of 2010. Food Zone and agricultural inputs seen as part of stabilisation efforts by military, governor and district officials. Rise in levels of development assistance in 2008, followed by significant increase in aid to the province associated with the surge in 2009 and 2010.
Strategy to reduce cultivation	Drew on religious credentials of Mullah Omar, leader of Taliban, to declare opium poppy un-Islamic.	Karzai elected president; used inauguration to launch *jihad* against opium poppy.	Governor visited rural areas, including areas of limited statehood in southern districts.	Conditional assistance; agricultural inputs were provided in return for commitment to

	National	Nangarhar		Helmand
	Taliban Ban	Hajji Din Muhammad	Gul Aga Shirzai	Gulab Mangal
	Focus on preventing planting: mount early eradication campaign in strategic districts in planting season, and compel farmers to eradicate their own crops.	Focus on preventing planting.	Offers of development assistance combined with (implicit) threat of US military power.	refrain from opium poppy cultivation.
	Resistance limited to civil disobedience in southern districts of Nangarhar.	Mounted early eradication campaign in strategic districts in planting season and compelled farmers to eradicate their own crops.	Successful linking of counternarcotics and COIN objectives in minds of rural population.	Major programme for delivery of agricultural inputs launched with US and UK funds, as well as technical and logistical support.
	Rural elite from key tribes given preferential access to international donors.	Rural elite from key tribes given preferential access to international donors.	Focus on preventing planting.	Outreach by governor as part of pre-planting campaign, but limited mobility; largely confined to Lashkar Gah and Gereshk and district centres and relied on attendees to cascade message to farmers *in situ*.
			Rural elite from key tribes given preferential access to international donors.	
			Mounted early eradication campaign in planting season in strategic districts.	Eradication campaign restricted to spring season after crop had already been planted; conducted in areas where the population was considered marginal and outside the Food Zone until 2009, when security situation in districts like Nad e Ali had improved.

CONCLUSION

	National	Nangarhar		Helmand
	Taliban Ban	Hajji Din Muhammad	Gul Aga Shirzai	Gulab Mangal
Local bargains	Rural elite co-opted into implementation. Negotiation with key tribes, including allegations of payments made to key tribal elders, particularly Shinwaris.	District governors and security commanders, many of whom were long-term allies of governor, co-opted into implementation. Allegations of payments made to key tribal elders.	Rural elite co-opted into implementation. Investment in building patronage through salary stipends and gifts to maliks. Allegations of payments made to key tribal elders.	Engagement with rural elite limited, as many in local elite confined to Lashkar Gah in initial years of Food Zone and seen as unrepresentative of what are often heterogeneous communities in canal command area.
	Rural elite from key tribes given preferential access to international donors during mission.	Rural elite from key tribes given preferential access to international donors.	Rural elite from key tribes given preferential access to international donors.	Rural elite and district officials considered primary beneficiaries of agricultural inputs distributed.
Coercion	Implicit but rarely used.	Early eradication campaign mounted with little resistance. Resistance limited to civil disobedience in southern districts of Nangarhar.	Perceived threat of foreign military power supported by greater US and UK military presence in southern districts and increase in security infrastructure, including bases in southern districts of Achin and Khogiani.	Perceived threat of foreign military power supported by greater US and UK military presence and increase in security infrastructure.
Durability	Significant economic impact of opium ban and absence of alternatives.	Governor removed in August 2005. Increased cultivation in	Growing disputes over official positions, contracts and rent extraction between	Reductions in canal command area compensated by concentration of opium

	National	Nangarhar		Helmand
	Taliban Ban	Hajji Din Muhammad	Gul Aga Shirzai	Gulab Mangal
	Fissures in leadership. Growing dissent in some rural areas. Continued opposition to conscription. 11 September 2001.	southern districts in 2006, followed by widespread cultivation in 2007.	governor and Nangarhar political elite leave Shirzai isolated. Poorly handled eradication campaign in Sherzad in 2010 led to deaths and increased levels of cultivation in the district in 2011. Local resistance to government and removal of key Maliks in upper parts of Achin in 2011. Significant upswing in violent resistance to eradication in 2012 growing season, including fifty-two killed. PRT closes April 2013. Eradication largely cosmetic, limited to lower valleys and involving security forces bargaining with local communities. Low levels of cultivation maintained in areas of consolidated	cultivation and those disadvantaged by the Food Zone Programme to former desert areas north of Boghra Canal. Coping strategies adopted in response to ban on opium poppy cultivation under stress. For example, reduction in non-farm income opportunities and falling real wage labour rates in Lashkar Gah and Gereshk in 2013 and 2014; as well as reduction in off-farm income opportunities north of the Boghra Canal due to failing opium harvest. Significant reductions in international troop numbers in central Helmand and transition to ANSF; despite this, some units of Afghan Local Police keen to engage in

National	Nangarhar		Helmand
Taliban Ban	Hajji Din Muhammad	Gul Aga Shirzai	Gulab Mangal
		statehood, but overall cultivation increases from 3,151 hectares in 2012 to 15,719 hectares in 2013.	counternarcotics efforts, including deterring cultivation.
			Closure of PRT in August 2014.
			Uncertainty as to future levels of development assistance to province and status of ALP.

NOTES

1. ESTABLISHING THE CONTEXT

1. For example, William Byrd (2006, 2008), Jonathan Caulkins (2010, 2011), Daniel Mejia (2010) and Peter Reuter (2010) write on drugs issues largely from an economics perspective. Letizia Paoli (2010) comes from a criminology background, while Pierre-Arnaud Chouvy (2011) is a geographer. Julia Buxton (2006, 2011) and Vanda Felbab Brown (2006, 2010), are political scientists. Alfred McCoy (1980, 1992, 2004), Daniel Weimer (1971) and William Walker (1996) are historians. However, many of these scholars adopt an interdisciplinary approach to their study of drugs and drugs policy.
2. There are, of course, exceptions to this which provide a well-grounded political economy analysis of drug crop-producing countries. These include Alfred McCoy (1980), Pierre-Arnaud Chouvy (2011), Jonathan Goodhand (2004a, 2004b, 2009, 2012) and Tom Kramer (2012).

2. POWER, CORRUPTION AND DRUG CROP CULTIVATION

1. While the International Opium Commission, held in Shanghai in 1909, is seen as one of the first steps toward international drug control and pre-dates the Opium Convention of 1912, the delegates had no plenipotentiary powers and the meeting led to 'weak recommendations that were largely ignored' (Collins, 2015: 3).
2. Political declaration: Guiding Principles of Drug Demand Reduction and Measures to Enhance International Cooperation to Counter the World Drug Problem, Action Plan on International Cooperation the Eradication of Illicit Drug Crops and Alternative Development, page 33.
3. These laws include Section 489 of the Foreign Assistance Act; Section 804 of the Narcotics Control Trade Act of 1974; Section 591 of the Kenneth M. Ludden Foreign Operations, Export Financing and Related Appropriations Act; and Section 706 of the Foreign Relations Authorization Act of 2003.

4. 'Our common efforts remain the same: .... to ensure that Afghanistan 'never again' is used as a breeding and staging ground for terrorism or for traffic in drugs': Lakdar Brahimi, Briefing to the Security Council, 13 Nov. 2001, www.un.org/News/dh/latest/afghan/brahimi-sc-briefing.htm
5. The exceptions are the recent scholarly work of Mukhopadhyay (2014), and my own primary research for AREU.
6. 'That model was monarchical, patriarchal and authoritarian. It presumed a king at the centre of every polity, a chief on every piece of administrative ground, and a patriarch in every homestead or kraal. Whether in the homestead, the village or the kingdom, authority was considered an attribute of a personal despotism.' (Mamdani, 1996: 39).

3. RURAL LIVELIHOODS PERSPECTIVES ON DRUG CROP PRODUCTION

1. Chouvy (2011: 158) cites a counternarcotics official in the British Embassy saying in reference to Helmand Province: 'My feeling is that a lot of the poppy is grown here by people who are greedy, not needy; not by people who have to grow poppy. They are growing it for profit. They are not being forced to grow it, they choose to grow it, and they do it because they can get away with it.'
2. McCoy highlights some of the excesses of hyperbole in Steinberg et al. (2004: 68) when he writes, 'Through this twenty-fold increase during two decades of warfare, Afghanistan was transformed from a diverse agricultural system—with herding, orchards, and 62 field crops—into the world's first opium monocrop. With much of the arable land, labour, water and capital devoted to opium, the drugs trade became the dominant economic force shaping the nation's destiny.'

4. RESEARCH METHODOLOGY

1. Strategic Study #1: An analysis of the process of expansion of opium poppy to new districts in Afghanistan (UNDCP, 1998b); Strategic Study #2: The dynamics of the farmgate trade and the coping strategies of opium traders (UNDCP, 1998c); Strategic Study #3: The role of opium as a source of informal credit (UNDCP, 1999a); Strategic Study #4: Access to labour: The role of opium in the livelihood strategies of itinerant harvesters working in Helmand province, Afghanistan (UNDCP, 1999b); Strategic Study #5: An analysis of the process of expansion of opium poppy to new districts in Afghanistan (UNDCP, 1999c); Strategic Study #6: The role of women in opium poppy cultivation in Afghanistan (UNDCP, 2000); Strategic Study #9: Opium poppy cultivation in a changing environment: Farmers intentions for the 2002/3 growing season (UNODC, 2004).
2. See UNDCP Strategic Studies Series.
3. Anonymous UK official in his request for fieldwork on opium poppy cultivation, August 2009.

5. AN HISTORICAL OVERVIEW: STATEBUILDING AND DRUG PRODUCTION IN AFGHANISTAN

1. For instance, my own experience of managing the UNDCP annual opium poppy survey between 1997 and 1999 tells me that we often only assessed the amount of opium production in those areas where we already knew it could be found and we did not survey areas that were hard to reach for either logistical or security reasons. This included areas such as Ghor, where opium was reported in the districts of Taiwara and Pasaband in the late 1990s but was not reported by the UN until 2002.

2. INCB (1989: 16) reported that 'information on the extent of opium production in Afghanistan, as well as the amount of opium abuse is unclear'.

3. The Helmand Food Zone was a counternarcotics initiative launched in late 2008 under then Governor Gulab Mangal with financial and logistical backing from the UK and US governments. It consisted of three strands of activities over the course of the growing season: (i) a counternarcotics information campaign aimed at deterring planting; (ii) the provision of agricultural inputs, mainly wheat seed and fertiliser; and (iii) an eradication campaign (Mansfield et al., 2011).

6. REPOSITIONING A PARIAH REGIME—THE TALIBAN BAN OF 2000/1

1. UNDCP is the predecessor to the United Nations Office for Drug Control.

2. Claims of the repressive way in which the ban was imposed need to be seen in contrast to the findings of the Donor Mission (2011: 6–7), as well as the loss of life associated with subsequent efforts to eradicate opium.

3. 'In October 2001, just a few days before the start of the war against the Taliban, Tony Blair told the Labour Party Conference that "the biggest drugs hoard in the world is in Afghanistan, controlled by the Taliban.... The arms the Taliban are buying today are paid for with the lives of young British people, buying their drugs on British streets."' (cited in Johnson and Leslie, 2004: 128)

4. 'Due to a lack of funds, UNDCP could not complete projects agreed in the Drugs Control Action Plan (DCAP). UNDCP did not fulfil its commitment' (Mullah Kabir, personal communication, 2 May 2001).

5. 'Over the past five years we have been talking with UNDCP on how to have a slow reduction in poppy but I do not believe this is possible. We have also eradicated poppy in accordance with UNDCP agreements but they still could not deliver assistance' (Mullah Hassan Rahmani, personal communication, 26 April 2001).

6. 'Where agreements have been reached and signed, UNDCP's critics have suggested that there has been considerable pressure exerted by external factors. For instance it is argued that the DCAPs have only been signed once strong pressure was applied raising concerns over whether Taliban have ownership over these plans. Indeed, it is reported that the DCAP for Shinwar was only signed after the coordinator of the DCCU exerted considerable pressure on the district *shura* during the donors'

mission in October/November 1997. Prior to this pressure there was little confidence that the District *Shura* would sign the DCAP. Similarly, reports suggest that the DCAP [in Kandahar] was only signed after the UN suspension of activities in the south-western region. It has been suggested that prior to the suspension there were protracted negotiations with every indication that the DCAP would not be signed by the authorities. The final decision to sign prompted some critics to suggest that the DCAP was only signed to elicit positive publicity at a time when the Taliban's actions in the south were receiving considerable criticism.' Mansfield (1999), unpublished note to file 1999 x:talib

7. 'On 10 September 1997, the State High Commission for Drug Control stated that: "The Islamic State of Afghanistan informs all compatriots that as the use of heroin and hashish is not permitted in Islam, they are reminded once again that they should strictly refrain from growing, using and trading in hashish and heroin. Anyone who violates this order shall be meted out a punishment in line with the lofty Mohammed and Sharia Law and this shall not be entitled to launch a complaint." This declaration was subsequently amended by a clarification issued on October 1997 which specifically banned the cultivation and trafficking of opium.' (UNDCP, 1998a: 6)

8. The ban caused considerable consternation amongst the donor community in Afghanistan. For example, Erick de Mul referred to 'the absence of watertight guarantees from the Taliban with regards to the ban' but was of the view that because the ban was expressed in religious terms, 'it was more likely to be complied with' (De Mul, personal communication, 23 April 2001). At the same time, he also stated: 'Nobody could predict the ban would happen; nobody could predict it would be implemented.' (personal communication, 23 April 2001)

9. During the donors' mission, Erick de Mul stated that 'UNDCP asked the Taliban to ban poppy' (personal communication, 23 April 2001).

10. Farrell and Thorne (2005) cite: 'According to a senior UN official at the time, the only major international agency that maintained contact with the Taliban was the United Nations Office on Drugs and Crime.'

11. 'UNDCP should be aware of recognising presumptive authorities through this programme of building institutions for presumptive authorities or of strengthening rival factions in the establishment of DCCU's' (UNDCP, 1997: 17).

12. 'UNDCP needs to consider whether investments in infrastructure might free up resources for the prosecution of war' (ibid.).

13. 'The proposed programme attributes a major role to the presumptive authorities in Afghanistan and proposes to support these through institution and governance building. This comes close to recognition of the presumptive authorities and contravenes present UN policies.' (Ibid.: 15)

14. 'UNDCP to recommend robust enforcement as a last resort only, and not in early years of poppy reduction projects.' (UNDCP Summary of Lessons Learned from UNDCP Afghanistan Programme, unpublished paper, 26 Nov. 1999)

15. 'The description of events given to the authors by a UN official suggest that UNODC diplomats were able to exploit three key levers to encourage the Taliban to seek to reduce poppy cultivation. First, the Taliban were facing increasing international pressure and UN sanctions. In this context, UNODC established initial trust and influence with the Taliban who gained some positive recognition in return. This "foot in the door" tactic included the offer of some UNODC financial resources. Second, it is possible that UNODC officials were able to play upon the hard line anti-drugs position inherent to the fundamentalist teachings of the Taliban.... Third, after the initial progress had been made, UNODC officials were subsequently able to play upon Taliban pride which was wounded when the one third reduction in poppy target announced by Mullah Omar in 1999 was not achieved. If this diplomatic combination of carrots and sticks was responsible for including the forced eradication and total elimination of poppy that followed, then UNODC could arguable claim it as one of the most significant negotiated drug control efforts to date.' (Farrell and Thorne, 2005: 85)

16. This states that 'The Office for Drug Control and Crime Prevention has reported that in 1998 total opium production in Afghanistan was about 2,500 tons. This nearly doubled, to 4,600 tons in 1999. These figures, plus the 3,100 tons produced in 2000, appear to confirm the view that the Taliban has accumulated a sizable stock of opium and heroin and wanted to stop production to prevent prices from further spiralling downward. This situation also puts into question the sincerity of Mullah Omar's fatwah. If Taliban officials were sincere in stopping the production of opium and heroin, then one would expect them to order the destruction of all stocks existing in areas under their control.'

17. 'Traditionally [*ushr*] was paid to the village mullahs for their service to the community; however, in the eastern region this tax was paid directly to the local authorities under the mujahidin. Under the Taliban it is thought that this system of direct payment to the district administrator, or woliswal, continues in the eastern region. However, in the southern region it is reported that payments are still paid directly to the mullahs.' (UNDCP, 1999c: 26, ftn 26).

18. Mansfield, 1998 field notes.

19. 'Hajji Bashir comes from a well-known Kandahari family. He has no title, although he is a member of the 'outer shura' of the movement. He is very close to Omar, hailing from Omar's Kandahar district, Maiwand. Although ostensibly a legitimate businessman, there are plenty of reports that Hajji Bashir is a key player in the drugs trade and that he controls various gangs that run drugs to Quetta and through Iran. He seems to play the role of moneybags for the Taliban. He is said to pass them a lot of cash.' (United States Department of State, American Embassy Islamabad, Dec. 1998, http://www.gwu.edu/~nsarchiv/NSAEBB/NSAEBB295/doc13.pdf p. 6)

20. 'Hajji Bashir Noorzai also stands accused of being closely associated with senior

members of the administration in Kabul and, Kandahar and having maintained contacts with NATO forces.' (Naval Postgraduate School, 2010; Risen, 2007; Goodhand and Mansfield, 2010: 21)

21. This comment referred to the limited tenure of Mullah Omar, also known as Amir ul momineen, if the Taliban were to persist with the ban into a second consecutive year.

22. 'At the time of the fieldwork for the Taliban ban, a Taliban commander was killed in the Pekhar valley in Achin and the Taliban advised team members not to go to the area' (Mansfield, 2001: 28).

7. NANGARHAR–A MODEL PROVINCE

1. A *karez* uses a series of access shafts that make it possible to dig and clean out the underground channels (tunnels) which eventually reach the surface far from the source of the water.

2. I have heard these claims from farmers in Nangarhar, as well as diplomats in Kabul.

3. Prior to this, the CN effort was led by the Counter Narcotics Directorate in the National Security Council.

4. William Wood served as ambassador in Colombia (2003–7) before being appointed in Afghanistan. Anne Patterson was his predecessor in Colombia (2000–3).

5. Tom Schweich also worked as chief of staff for Anne Patterson when she was US ambassador to the United Nations in New York. Schweich was promoted to ambassadorial rank 'after Patterson's intervention' (Schweich, 2008).

6. Typically, these raids were poorly understood by farmers who did not see themselves as opium traders and believed the intrusion into their homes dishonoured the female members of their household and scared their children. The discovery of weapons during such raids and the subsequent arrest of the homeowner were also misunderstood, given the fact that the vast majority of households have one or more guns in their possession 'for protection'.

7. UNODC estimated that there were 218 hectares of opium poppy cultivation in the 2000/1 growing season.

8. THE BAN UNRAVELS

1. Abdul Haq was captured and then killed by the Taliban in October 2001.

2. For instance in Jani Khel, another long-term respondent who cultivated wheat and opium poppy in the winter of 2007 produced cucumber (50,000 PR), sugar cane (300,000 PR), okra (10,000 PR), squash (consumed), bean (10,000 PR), onion (60,000 PR), clover (intercropped with apricot) and wheat (140 PR per *seer*) in 2011. He diversified even further in the 2011/12 growing season.

3. The equivalent of between 2.8 and 3.5 metric tons per hectare.

4. 'My hand is open in the summer, I always have yoghurt and milk, I have good food,

and I can buy meat and fruit for guests.' (Farmer, Lower Mizakhel, Kama District, personal communication, April 2012)

5. In Deha Ghazi, a tenant recalled: 'In Khogiani there is nothing but killing and explosions. But here I can go to the farm each day and my children can sleep safe at night. I hope that the situation improves more and I will find some land to build a house.'

6. In 2008 Achin was subsequently subdivided into the districts of Achin and Spinghar, with both the administrative centres remaining in Kahi.

7. A further twelve Sepai were alleged to have been killed in the initial outbreak of violence between the Alisherkhel and the Sepai in March 2010.

8. 'For 1000 years there has been a desert and Malik Niaz did not come and capture this land. Now that he has the guns of Gul Aga Shirzai and the US, he brings his people and takes this land.' Member of Alisherkhel tribe, April 2010.

9. International development worker, Jalalabad, April 2010.

10. This was the first time since this study began in April 2005 that researchers were unable to visit this part of Achin.

11. 'Malik Usman and Niaz have two hands: one belongs to the government, the other to the Taliban.' Farmer in Achin, April 2012.

12. This is confirmed by aerial photography taken by Alcis Ltd at the time.

13. For example, the district governor is alleged to have sent a message to the valleys of Pekhar and Abdul Khel saying that the authorities would not come to the area to destroy the crop but requesting that the population 'destroy small parts of the crop and take pictures'. Respondents in Batan and Asadkhel, April 2013.

9. THE HELMAND FOOD ZONE—A TECHNOCRATIC RESPONSE TO A COMPLEX PHENOMENON

1. These figures include the costs of the air assets used in support of the AEF. For example, GAO (2007: 16) reported that, 'State provided $104 million to support the AEF's operating costs and purchase of additional equipment, and $124 million to purchase and lease aircraft to move the force around the country'.

2. While much is made of the reluctance of the UK military to engage in counternarcotics effort, exemplified by the campaign in the fall of 2006 where farmers were leafleted by the PRT and told that their crop would not be destroyed (Schweich, 2008: 4), individual officers have often expressed support for an aggressive eradication campaign. The author also witnessed one former head of the UK military effort in Helmand call for aerial eradication during a meeting with senior US military officials visiting from Washington DC.

3. See UNODC/MCN Annual Opium Poppy Survey 2008, page 10, where photographs from Helmand are accompanied by captions that make reference to the purported wealth of farmers both within the canal and in the former desert land. A senior USG official also used such images in presenting his arguments for aerial

spraying to the staff of various congressional committees (Anonymous staff, personal communication, 2008). The challenge is that these pictures of what appear to be large fields of opium poppy do not convey the boundaries of individual farmers' fields and may be farmed by a number of different households including those leasing or sharecropping the land for others, a common phenomenon in central Helmand.

4. 'UNODC calculates that eradicating 25% of the opium crop will introduce sufficient fear of future eradication into farmers' minds to prevent planting next year. The Afghan government wants to reach the 25% eradication threshold. This may prove impossible, however, without the use of herbicides.' (Schweich, 2007: 52)

5. Also cited in the US Counternarcotics Strategy for Afghanistan, August 2007 (Schweich, 2007: 30).

6. Mohammed Daud was killed by a bomb in the provincial centre of Takhar, the province where he was born, on 28 May 2011. In 2010 he was appointed Police Chief of Northern Afghanistan and Commander of the 303 Pamir Corps. Prior to this appointment he was Deputy Minister of Interior, responsible for the Counter Narcotics Police and the eradication effort across Afghanistan.

7. In May 2011 Razik was appointed Provincial Police Chief for Kandahar and promoted to Brigadier General. In conjunction with this new post, he retained his position as head of the border police in Spin Boldak.

8. Accusations of involvement in the drugs trade are also made against Mir Wali's son, Hekmattullah Khan, who has served as Chief of Police in Garmsir, and more recently Gereshk (Davies, 2013).

9. In the 2007 Annual Opium Poppy Survey, UNODC reported that 'the Taliban are again using opium to suit their interest. Between 1996 and 2000 in Taliban controlled areas 15,000 tons of opium were produced and exported—the regime's sole source of foreign exchange at the time. In July 2000, the Taliban leader, Mullah Omar, argued that opium was against Islam and banned its cultivation (but not its export). In recent months the Taliban have reversed their position once again and started to extract from the drugs economy for arms, logistics and militia pay.' (UNODC/MCN, 2007: iv) The statement that opium was the sole source of foreign exchange at the time stands in contrast to UNODC (then UNDCP)'s own analysis at the time and work of other Afghan analysts (Rubin, 2000: 1796).

10. In this part of Nad-e-Ali, one *forma* is the equivalent of 30 *jeribs*. Over the years, this land has typically been fragmented and split between brothers, or perhaps part of it may have been sold. In this case, farmers will pay a proportion of land tax according to the amount of land they own.

11. For a more detailed discussion of the different systems of rural taxation that can be found in Afghanistan, see Mansfield (2013b, 2014).

12. The US GAO report that 'State originally intended a central eradication force comprised of Afghan counternarcotics police to be augmented by aerial herbicide spraying' (GAO, 2010: 15).

13. Both USAID and DFID had funded a US$25 million countrywide wheat seed and fertiliser distribution programme in the 2005/6 growing season, known as the Agricultural Inputs Supply Programme. The reasons for supporting the programme were driven largely by a need to respond to the reductions in levels of opium poppy cultivation in the 2004/5 growing season and prevent resurgence the following year. At the time there were some concerns about the efficacy of the programme, given its focus on wheat, and in particular the potential for the fertiliser to be diverted to opium poppy cultivation (DFID, 2005: 13).

14. It is perhaps ironic that both Gulab Mangal and Gul Aga Shirzai were keen to be promoted out of their respective governorships and drew on their achievements in counternarcotics as evidence of their performance as strong leaders when soliciting support for promotion from Western donors. At the same time it was precisely because they presided over such dramatic reductions in cultivation and because of concerns that production might rise in their absence that made both the US and UK eager to see Shirzai and Mangal stay in post.

15. This commitment was made through local elders prior to the much publicised attack on Marjeh. It was part of the campaign to win over the support of the local population and was reminscent of the UK military campaign when it first arrived in Helmand in May 2006, where it leafleted the local population informing them that the British had not come to Helmand to destroy their opium poppy. Following increasing criticism from Mangal and other international agencies, the USMC adopted a programme called the Marjeh Accelerated Agricultural Transition Program (MAAT-P) which provided US$300 per hectare to farmers to destroy their crops and plant licit spring crops. The timing of this programme, coming so late in the poppy season, meant that many farmers could harvest some of their crop and then receive a payment to clear their fields and subsequently plant the spring crop they would have grown anyway (Mansfield, 2010c: 9).

16. For example in the 2009/10 growing season a package of vegetable seeds for the spring and summer cropping season, along with fertiliser, was offered by USAID. In the fall of 2010 farmers were offered a choice of a base package of 50 kilogram certified wheat seed, 100 kilogram urea and 100 kilogram DAP, combined with either a 'Forage Package' or a 'Winter Vegetable Package'. The Forage Package contained 10 kilograms of alfalfa seeds and the Winter Vegetable Package contained seeds for spinach (500 grams), cauliflower (100 grams), cabbage (100 grams), cucumber (500 grams) and white radish (400 grams). The Food Zone Programme was also supported by the distribution of grape vine and saplings as well as vegetable seeds, fertiliser and polytunnels under the Afghanistan Vouchers for Increased Production in Agriculture (AVIPA) Plus programme implemented by International Relief and Development.

17. In the 2009/10 growing season, it took ISAF ten days to escort a convoy of agricultural inputs to Musa Qala, a journey that had originally been planned to take three days.

18. These payments rose from around 7 per cent in the initial year of the programme to 35 per cent in the fall of 2010. This increase was at the behest of MAIL to ensure consistency across the country and compliance with the National Wheat Seed Distribution Programme.

19. Daniel Green (2012: 140–41) describes the wheat seed programme in Uruzgan as an 'unmitigated disaster that deepened resentment against the local government and embarassed the PRT even though we had nothing to do with it'. He refers to some of the problems with wheat seed distribution in the province, suggesting that those implementing the programme 'defined distribution as getting the wheat seed to the distritc chief without detemining whether deserving families had received it or not'.

20. These examples of fraud are not unique to Helmand. For example, the Office of the Inspector General of USAID conducted an audit of the 2008/9 wheat seed and fertiliser distribution programme under AVIPA, covering 4,563 farmers from 183 villages in seven provinces. Of these entries the OIG identified 2,582 (56.5 per cent) cases of what appeared to be matching fingerprints in the list of beficiaries (USAID, 2010: 6–7).

21. Over the course of the programme there were numerous allegations against the contractor in Herat who was responsible for the seed procurement, and considerable confusion as to the quality of the seed and whether it was certified as improved or not. It was not until the 2010/11 growing season that many of the issues with the seed quality were addressed and certified seed was distributed (MacKenzie, 2010).

22. For an account of the AEF in action it is worth reading Jon Lee Anderson's 2007 article in *The New Yorker*, 'The Taliban's Opium War: The difficulties and dangers of the eradication program'.

23. This project began in 2004/5 and was known as the 'Support to the Verification Process of Opium Poppy Eradication'; it was implemented together with the MCN and the MoI and focused on verifying GLE. Prior to this UNODC there was no independent monitoring of the eradication effort and serious concerns that a number of provinces, including Helmand, were over-reporting the scale of eradication. For example in the 2002/3 growing season the Afghan authorities reported that 21,430 hectares of opium were eradicated. UNODC cited these figures in their annual survey but commented that 'the Afghanistan Opium Survey 2003 neither monitored, nor assessed the effectiveness of the eradication campaign' (UNODC/CND, 2003: 53). In 2004 UNODC/CND did not report any eradication figures (UNODC/MCN, 2004: 77).

24. Concerns over the veracity of the figures were most pronounced in 2006 and 2007 when the total amount of crop destroyed was reported at 15,300 hectares and 19,510 hectares respectively (UNODC, 2010: 42). These figures were markedly higher than levels of eradication before or since. An account of the challenges asso-

ciated with the eradication verification process during these initial years and an outline of the methodology can be found in the Afghanistan Opium Poppy Survey (2006: 64–5).

25. Cranfield used AEF reporting and satellite imagery taken both before and after the 2006/7 eradication campaign to illustrate the extent of over-reporting and crop recovery (Cranfield, 2007).

26. This was initially a payment of US$120 per hectare of opium poppy destroyed, before being increased to US$135 per hectare in 2009 and then US$250 in 2010. Between 2011 and 2012 the USG made payments only for the areas destroyed within the eradication target area. In 2013 the US reverted to paying governors' compensation regardless of the location, including those areas outside the Helmand Food Zone.

27. The area for which the USG estimated cultivation approximated to the boundaries of the Food Zone in 2009. UNODC did not produce separate estimates for the Food Zone until 2012 and 2013. In contrast to the USG figures, UNODC reported rising levels of opium poppy cultivation in the Food Zone between 2012 and 2013, with cultivation rising from 24,241 hectares in 2012 to 36,244 in 2013 (UNODC/MCN, Afghanistan Opium Risk Assessment 2013: 26).

28. The imagery analysis presented by the US does not appear to control for the significant increase in security infrastructure.

29. USG reported the same recovery, with cultivation having reached 94,500 hectares in 2008, subsequently declining to a low of 61,500 hectares in 2011, and then returning to 95,500 hectares in 2013.

10. SHIFTING SANDS: MOVEMENTS IN GEOGRAPHY AND POPPY CULTIVATION

1. There is considerable speculation about Mullah Nasim's role in opium production, including the claim that he compelled farmers in the canal command area to cultivate opium, imposing quotas on them and threatening those who did not comply with torture or even death. These are the same claims that were made about the Taliban in the 1990s and the twenty-first century. It is hard to see why a farmer would need to be compelled, under threat of torture and death, to cultivate a crop that fits well into the cropping patterns and ecological conditions in central Helmand, provides preferential access to credit, offers increased wage labour opportunities and obtains a relatively good price from traders who will travel to the farm-gate to purchase.

2. The claim that Nasim Akhundzada was killed by Hezbe Islami is based on the assessment that the ban that he imposed in Helmand adversely affected the party's heroin-refining interests. It is unclear whether there is evidence to support this claim or whether it is 'tea house chatter'. The same claims were made following the death of Haji Qadir, former Governor of Nangarhar and at the time Minister of Interior,

after his involvement in the compensated eradication campaign in Nangarhar in the spring of 2002. Given the particular career paths both men had followed, it is clear that they would have had numerous enemies.

3. This kind of land grab can be seen in places like Dashte Shin Kalay and Dashte Koshal Kalay in western Nad e Ali.

4. Those in the ALP reported salaries of between 7,000 and 9,000 Afghanis per month. In December 2013 there were 58 Afghani to US$1.

5. In 1999 a new motorbike cost around 100,000 PR in Helmand. At that time there were 50 PR to US$1. In December 2013 a new motorbike sold for between 50,000 and 60,000 PR, at a time when US$1 was the equivalent of 110 PR.

6. The Zarang is named after Zarang Ltd, an Afghan company established in 2005 in Herat to assemble motorcycles. While Zarang Ltd sells a range of different two-wheel motorbikes, it is particularly well-known for the three-wheel vehicles and trailers that it produces; see http://www.Zarangltd.com/products_list/&pmcId=df8bfcd1-cac6–4f00–8659-bafc5635aa9a.html

7. This is for an earlier model; a post-2000 model of a Corolla or *saracha* might cost between US$10,000 and 16,000.

8. In 2013 an Iranian Massey Ferguson cost between US$5,200 and 8,400 second-hand, depending on its condition; and around US$12,000 new. In 2003 this same tractor cost US$9,224 (Anthony Fitzherbert, unpublished report, Sep. 2003: 10).

9. The importance of a motorcycle to the everyday life of a rural Helmandi family could be seen by the reaction that one respondent from Aqajan Kalay in Nad e Ali had to the theft of his motorbike in the district centre: 'When I had a motorbike I always went to the bazaar and bought meat and fruit and other goods. Now I do not have a motorbike I cannot go to the bazaar as it costs too much to rent a vehicle.' (Aqajan Kalay #1).

10. Of the 319 households interviewed in the twenty-one research sites south of the Boghra Canal, 154 reported a family member earning an off-farm or non-farm income, the vast majority from owning a shop, leasing out a tractor or renting out their car as a taxi. Of these 154 households, fifteen had family members in the ANSF, something that did not feature in the results of any of the previous rounds of fieldwork up until December 2012.

11. Bride prices reported during this round of fieldwork ranged from 600,000 PR to 1,000,000 PR.

12. Tenant farmers in Marjeh were typically paid 60–70 *man* of wheat per *jerib* in the 2012/13 growing season.

13. Sharecroppers receive one fifth of the final crop.

14. This is simplified data for illustrative purposes; in reality farmers would look to retain sufficient wheat, maize and mung bean for family consumption, to make contributions to the local mullah (around 3% of the total crop) and to keep some crop for seed for the subsequent season. It is also important to note that very few farmers in the canal command area would cultivate as much as 15 *jeribs* of land.

15. This assumes a household of ten members, of which typically two or three are fully working members.

16. Cultivating opium poppy within a walled compound is considered much less risky in areas where there is an effective opium ban, since for a variety of reasons (including in particular that the women of the household are there and are in seclusion from strangers) it is considered that security forces are unlikely to go into household compounds for the purpose of poppy eradication.

17. One respondent blamed the death of his daughter on a lack of income due to the ban on poppy (Doh Bandi #2); another the death of his son (Dasht e Shersherak #7).

18. This estimate is based on a population density of 0.9 persons per *jerib* of cultivated land. Ibid.: 54.

19. It is alleged that some Naqlin have purchased land north of the Boghra but lie about their tribal affiliation as they know that this would lead to conflict with those from tribes who consider themselves indigenous to Helmand.

20. It is claimed that the tendency of successive British Prime Ministers to fly into Lashkar Gah and visit the governor before travelling to Kabul to meet with President Karzai had reinforced this impression.

21. 'Don't ask about the Government because people who work in Government are pimps and they sold the country to foreigners' (Nawabad Shawal, 10 *jerib*, sharecropper (1/5), Ishaqzai, arrived 2009). 'Now we have life and we know the meaning of life because we have money. The Government is the slave of the foreigners, we cannot accept that. Next year if the Mujahidin is still here we will again grow poppy' (Shna Jama, 13 *jerib*, owner cultivator, Ishaqzai, arrived 2004).

22. 'I will F*** the mother of those people who work for the Government' (Dashte Loy Manda, 10 *jerib*, sharecropper, Ishaqzai, arrived 2010). 'In this government, all the way up to Karzai, I will F*** their wives by donkey' (Shen Ghazi, 9 *jerib*, sharecropper (1/3), Ishaqzai, arrived in 2010). 'Here is the Islami Emirate and these people F*** the wife of this Government' (Shna Jama, 12 *jerib*, owner cultivator, Noorzai, arrived 2003).

23. 'I don't like the government as if they come here the fighting will start and the poppy will be banned' (Dashte Shin Kalay 13).

24. 'For the last three years we have had the government in Marjeh but we did not see anything from them to improve our lives. There is just one thing to improve our lives here and that is poppy' (Marjeh F4D5, 17 *jeribs*, rented, Noorzai).

25. 'The government destroyed my crop, they destroyed my house. If they were a man they would go to the Dashte and destroy the crop there. But they don't have power to go there to destroy the crop. They receive money from the Americans. If they don't destroy the crop how do they answer to their fathers [the Americans]?' (Khoshal Kalay, 10 *jeribs*, owner cultivator, Kharoti).

BIBLIOGRAPHY

Ahmed, A. S. (1977). *Social and Economic Change in the Tribal Areas*. Karachi, Pakistan: Oxford University Press.

Aikins, M. (2009). 'The Master of Spin Boldak: Undercover with Afghanistan's Drug Trafficking Border Police'. *Harper's Magazine*, retrieved from http://www.harpers.org/archive/2009/12/0082754

Anderson, J. L. (2007). 'The Taliban's opium war: the difficulties and dangers of the eradication program'. *New Yorker*, 9 Jul. 2007.

Arjomand, N. (2013). *Eagle's Summit Revisited: Decision Making in the Kajaki Dam Refurbishment Project*. Kabul, Afghanistan: Analysts Network.

Asad, A. Z. & Harris, R. (2003). *The Politics and Economics of Drug Production on the Pakistan–Afghanistan Border*. Aldershot, UK: Ashgate Publishing.

Auty, R. M. (2001). *Resource Abundance and Economic Development*. Oxford: Oxford University Press.

Babor, T., Caulkins, J. et al. (2010). *Drug Policy and the Public Good*. Oxford: Oxford University Press.

Baldauf, S. (2003). 'Afghan Military Tied to Drug Trade'. *Christian Science Monitor*, 4 Sep. 2003, retrieved from http://www.csmonitor.com/layout/set/r14/2003/0904/p06s01-wosc.html

Barakat, S., Chard, M., Jacoby, T. & Lume, W. (2002). 'The Composite Approach: Design in the Context of War and Armed Conflict'. *Third World Quarterly*, 23(5).

Barfield, T. (2000). *The Political Implications of Pashtun Tribal Organisation for War and Peace*. Paper presented at Monterrey, CA, 22 September 2000.

——— (2004). 'Problems in Establishing Legitimacy in Afghanistan'. *Iranian Studies*, 37(2): 263–93.

——— (2010). *Afghanistan: A Cultural and Political History*. Princeton, NJ: Princeton University Press.

Barkey, K. (1994). *Bandits and Bureaucrats: The Ottoman Route to State Centralisation*. New York: Cornell University Press.

Barlett, P. F. (1980). Adaptive Strategies in Peasant Agricultural Production. *Annual Review of Anthropology*, 9: 545–73.

Barnett, M., Fang, S. & Zuercher, C. (2008). *The Peacebuilder's Contract: How External State-building Reinforces Weak Statehood*. Paper presented at the annual meeting of the ISA's 49th Annual Convention, Bridging Multiple Divides, Hilton, San Francisco, CA, 26 Mar. 2008, retrieved from http://citation.allacademic.com/meta/p250944_index.html

Batterbury, S. (2008). *Sustainable Livelihoods: Still Being Sought, Ten Years on*. Paper given as part of the African Environments Programme, Oxford University Centre for the Environment (OUCE), 24 Jan. 2008.

Baumann, P. (2000). *Sustainable Livelihoods and Political Capital: Arguments and Evidence From Decentralization and Natural Resources Management in India*. Working Paper, 136. London: Overseas Development Institute.

BBC News (2012). 'A Glimpse of Life after NATO in Afghanistan's Wild East'. 18 May 2012, retrieved from http://www.bbc.co.uk/news/world-asia-18118781

Bearak, B. (2001). 'At Heroin's Source Taliban do what 'Just say no' could not'. *New York Times*, 24 May 2001, retrieved from http://www.nytimes.com/2001/05/24/world/at-heroin-s-source-taliban-do-what-just-say-no-could-not.html?pagewanted=all&src=pm

Berg, B. L. (2007). *Qualitative Research Methods for the Social Sciences*. Boston, MA: Pearson Education.

Bergen, P. L. (2011). *The Longest War: The Enduring Conflict Between America and Al Qaeda*. New York: Free Press.

Bever, J. A. (2010). 'Threats to Global Stability and US Policy Responses'. Statement for the Record of James A. Bever, Director of USAID's Afghanistan Pakistan Task Force. US House Committee on Oversight and Government Reform, Subcommittee on National Security and Foreign Affairs, Hearing on Transnational Drug Enterprises (Part II).

Binswanger, H. P. (1981). 'Attitudes Toward Risk: Theoretical Implications of an Experiment in Rural India'. *Economic Journal*, 91(364): 867–90.

Blair, D. & Morgan Edwards, L. (2002). 'Assassins of Afghan Leader Linked to Drug Trade'. *Daily Telegraph*, 8 Jul. 2002, retrieved from http://www.telegraph.co.uk/news/worldnews/asia/afghanistan/1400723/Assassins-of-Afghan-leader-linked-to-drug-trade.html

Blanchard, C. M. (2009). 'Afghanistan: Narcotics and US Policy'. *Congressional Research Service*, 12 Aug. 2009.

Boege, V., Brown, A., Clements, K. & Nolan, A. (2008). *On hybrid political orders and emerging states: State formation in the context of 'fragility'*. Berghof Research Center for Constructive Conflict Management.

Boege, V., Brown, B., Clements, K. & Nolan, N. (2009). 'Building Peace and Community in Hybrid Political Orders'. *Journal of International Peacekeeping*, 16(9): 599–615.

Bonner, A. (1987). *Among the Afghans*. Durham, OH: Duke University Press.

Boone, C. (2003). *Political Topographies of the African State: Territorial Authority and Institutional Choice*. New York: Cambridge University Press.

Boone, J. (2008). 'Afghan Drug Body Hit by UK Funding Reversal'. *Financial Times*, 25 February 2008.

Bourgois, P. (1990). Confronting Anthropological Ethics: Ethnographic Lessons From Central America. *Journal of Peace Research*, 27(1): 43–54.

Bradford, J. (2013). *Opium in a Time of Uncertainty: State Formation, Diplomacy, and Drug Control in Afghanistan During the Musahiban Dynasty, 1929–1978*. PhD thesis, Department of History, Northeastern University, Boston, MA.

—— (2015). 'Drug control in Afghanistan: Culture, politics, and power during the 1958 prohibition in Badakhshan'. *Iranian Studies*, 48(2): 223–48.

Brailsford, G. (1989a). *Opium Crop Substitution Programme: Achin District, Nangarhar. Evaluation Report*. Peshawar, Pakistan: Afghan Aid.

—— (1989b). *A Survey of Opium Cultivation in Badakhshan Province, Afghanistan. Evaluation Report*. Peshawar, Pakistan: Afghan Aid.

Brass, T. (2008). 'Moral Economists, Subalterns, New Social Movements, and the (re)Emergence of a (Post-)Modernized (Middle) Peasant'. *Journal of Peasant Studies*, 18(2): 173–205.

Bray, D. (2011). 'The Opium Trade in Nahre Seraj. Network Report'. Unpublished report by Etihad.

Brick, J. (2010). *The Political Economy of Customary Village Organizations in Rural Afghanistan*, retrieved from http://www.bu.edu/aias/brick.pdf

Brown, C. (1999). 'Burma: The Political Economy of Violence'. *Disasters*, 23(3): 234–56.

Buddenberg, D. & Byrd, W. (eds.) (2006). *Afghanistan's Drugs Industry: Structure, Functioning, Dynamics and Implications for Counter Narcotics Policy*. Kabul, Afghanistan: UNODC/World Bank.

Burawoy, M. (1998). 'The Extended Case Method'. *Sociological Theory*, 16(1).

Buxton, J. (2006). *The Political Economy of Narcotics, Production, Consumption and Global markets*. London: Zed Books.

—— (ed.) (2011). *The Politics of Narcotic Drugs—A Survey*. London: Routledge.

Byrd, T. & Marshall, A. (2011). *Afghanistan: How the West Lost Its Way*. New Haven, CT: Yale University Press.

Byrd, W. A. (2008). *Responding to Afghanistan's Opium Economy Challenge: Lessons and Policy Implications From a Development Perspective*. Policy Research Working Paper 4545. Washington, DC: World Bank.

Canfield, R. L. (1972). 'The Ecology of Rural Ethnic Groups and the Spatial Dimensions of Power'. *American Anthropologist*, 75(5): 1511–28. DOI: 10.1525/aa.1973.75.5.02a00200.

Carney, D. (ed.) (1998). *Sustainable Rural Livelihoods: What Contribution Can We Make?* London: DFID.

—— (1999). *Approaches to Sustainable Livelihoods for the Rural Poor*. ODI Poverty Briefing, 2 Jan. 1999. London: Overseas Development Institute.

Caulkins, J. P., Kulick, J. D. & Kleiman, M. A. R. (2010). *Drug Production and Trafficking Counterdrug Policies and Security and Governance in Afghanistan*. New York: Center on International Cooperation, New York University.

—— (2011). *Think Again: The Afghan Drug Trade*. retrieved from http://www.foreignpolicy.com/articles/2011/04/01/think_again_the_afghan_drug_trade

Chandrasekaran, R. (2010). 'The Afghan Robin Hood'. *Washington Post*, 4 Oct. 2010.

—— (2012). *Little America: the War Within the War for Afghanistan*. New York: Alfred A. Knopf.

Chayanov, A. V. (1966). *The Theory of Peasant Economy*, ed. D. Thorner, B. Kerblay, R. Smith. Homewood, ILL: American Economic Association.

Chayes, S. (2006). *The Punishment of Virtue: Inside Afghanistan after the Taliban*. New York: Penguin Press.

Chin, K. (2007). 'Into the Thick of it: Methodological Issues in Studying the Drug Trade in the Golden Triangle'. *Asian Criminology*, 2: 85–109.

—— (2009). *The Golden Triangle Inside Southeast Asia's Drug Trade*. Ithaca, NY: Cornell University Press.

Chisholm, M. (2010). 'Marines Offer Cash in Fight Against Afghan Opium'. Reuters, 21 Mar. 2010.

Chouvy, P. (2009). *Opium: Uncovering the Politics of Poppy*. London: I. B. Tauris.

Clapp-Wincek, C. & Baldwin, E. (1983). *The Helmand Valley Project in Afghanistan*. Washington, DC: US AID Evaluation Special Study 18.

Clawson, P. L. & Lee III, Rensselaer W. (1996). *The Andean Cocaine Industry*. New York: St Martin's Press.

Coburn, N. (2013). 'The Political Economy of Withdrawal and Transition in an Afghan Market Town'. *Central Asia Policy Brief No. 12*, Oct. 2013. Washington, DC: Elliott School of International Affairs, George Washington University.

Coffey International Development (2012). *Helmand Monitoring and Evaluation Programme Focus Study: Helmand Provincial Conflict Assessment*. DFID, UK.

Coghlan, T. (2009). 'The Taliban in Helmand: an Oral History'. In A. Giustozzi (ed.), *Decoding the New Taliban: Insights From the Afghan Field*. London: Hurst & Co.

Coll, S. (2004). *Ghost Wars: the Secret History of the CIA, Afghanistan and Bin Laden, From the Soviet Invasion to September 10, 2001*. London: Penguin Books

Collins, J. (2015). *Regulations and Prohibitions: Anglo-American Relations and International Drug Control, 1939–1964*. PhD thesis, Department of International History, London School of Economics.

Collinson, S. (2003). 'Power, Livelihoods and Conflict: Case Studies in Political Economy Analysis for Humanitarian Action'. *HPG Report 13*, Feb. 2003. London: Overseas Development Institute.

Costa, A. M. (2007). 'An Opium Market Mystery'. *Washington Post*, 25 Apr. 2007.

Counter Narcotics Directorate (2004). *Counter Narcotics Mainstreaming and Conditionality*. Working Group Session of Alternative Livelihoods Technical Working Group, 22–23 Jun. 2004.

Cowper-Coles, S. (2011). *Cables from Kabul: The Inside Story of the West's Afghanistan Campaign*. London: Harper Press.

Cramer, C. & Goodhand, J. (2011). 'Hard Science or Waffly Crap? Evidence-based Policy Versus Policy-based Evidence in the Field of Violent Conflict'. In Baylss, K., Fine, B. & Waeyenberge, E. (2011). *The Political Economy of Development: The World Bank, Neo-Liberalism and Development Research*. London: Pluto Press, 215–38.

Cranfield University (2007). *Verification of AEF Eradication in Helmand Province 2007*. Unpublished report.

——— (2009). *Poppy and Cereal Cultivation in Helmand 2007 to 2009*. Unpublished report.

Crews, R. D. & Tarzi, A. (ed.) (2008). *The Taliban and the Crisis of Afghanistan*. Cambridge MA: Harvard University Press.

Cullather, N. (2002). 'Damming Afghanistan: Modernization in a Buffer State'. *Journal of American History*, ed. Joanne Meyerowitz, 512–37.

Dalrymple, W. (2013). *Return of a King: The Battle for Afghanistan 1839–42*. New York: Alfred A. Knopf.

de Haan, L. & Zoomers, A. (2005). 'Exploring the Frontier of Livelihoods Research'. *Development & Change*, 36(1): 27–47.

Department for International Development Afghanistan (2005). *Agricultural Input Supply Programme, Programme Document, 2005*.

——— (2009). *Helmand Growth Programme, Programme Document, December 2009*.

Dessaint, A. Y. (1971). 'Lisu Migration in the Thai Highlands'. *Ethnology*, 10: 329–48.

——— (1972). 'The Poppies are Beautiful This Year'. *Natural History*, 81: 31–6.

de Waal, A. (2009). 'Mission Without End? Peacekeeping in the African Political Marketplace'. *International Affairs*, 85(1): 99–113.

——— (2010). 'Dollarised'. *London Review of Books*, 32(12): 38–41.

Di John, J. & Putzel, J. (2009). *Political Settlements. Issues Paper*. Governance and Social Development Resource Centre, International Development Department, University of Birmingham.

Dion, M. L. & Russler, C. (2008). 'Eradication Efforts, the State, Displacement and Poverty: Explaining Coca Cultivation in Colombia During Plan Colombia'. *Journal of Latin American Studies*, 40: 399–421.

Donini, A., Niland, N. & Wermester, K. (eds.) (2004). *Nation-building Unraveled? Aid, Peace and Justice in Afghanistan*. West Hartford, CT: Kumarian Press.

Donor Mission (2001). 'The Impact of the Taliban Prohibition on Opium Poppy Cultivation in Afghanistan'. 25 May 2001.

Dorronsoro, G. (2005). *Revolution Unending: Afghanistan, 1979 to the Present*. New York: Colombia University Press.

Dressler, J. A. (2009). 'Securing Helmand Understanding and Responding to the Enemy'. *Afghanistan Report 2*, Sep. 2009. Washington, DC: Institute for the Study of War, www.understandingwar.org

—— (2010). 'Marjah's Lessons for Kandahar'. *Backgrounder*, 9 Jul. 2010. Washington, DC: Institute for the Study of War, www.understandingwar.org

Dupree, Louis (1997). *Afghanistan*. Karachi, Pakistan: Oxford University Press.

Dupree, N. H. (1977). *An Historical Guide to Afghanistan*. Kabul: Afghan Tourist Organization Publication No. 5.

Durrenberger, P. (1976). 'The Economy of a Lisu Village'. *American Ethnologist*, 3: 633–43.

Durrenberger, P. E. (1980). 'Chayanov's Economic Analysis in Anthropology'. *Journal of Anthropological Research*, 36(2): 133–48.

Edwards, D. B. (1996). *Heroes of the Age: Moral Fault Lines on the Afghan Frontier*. Berkeley, CA: University of California Press

—— (2010). 'Counterinsurgency as a Cultural System'. *Small Wars Journal*, 27 Dec. 2010.

—— (2012). *Before Taliban Genealogies of the Afghan Jihad*. Berkeley, CA: University of California Press.

Egnell, R. (2011). 'Lessons From Helmand, Afghanistan: What Now for British Counterinsurgency?' *International Affairs*, 87(2): 297–315.

Eide, K. (2012). *Power Struggle Over Afghanistan: an Inside Look at What Went Wrong—and What we Can do to Repair the Damage*. New York: Skyhorse Publishing.

Elias, B. (2009). *The Taliban Biography Documents on the Structure and Leadership of the Taliban 1996–2002*. Retrieved from http://www.nsarchive.org/NSAEBB/NSAEBB295

Ellis, F. (2000). *Rural Livelihoods and Diversity in Developing Countries*. Oxford: Oxford University Press.

Fafchamps, M. (1992). 'Cash Crop Production, Food Price Volatility and Rural Market Integration in the Third World'. *American Journal of Agricultural Economics*, 74(1): 90–99.

Farrell, G. & Thorne, J. (2005). 'Where Have All the Flowers Gone? Evaluation of the Taliban Crackdown Against Opium Poppy Cultivation in Afghanistan'. *International Journal of Drug Policy*, 16: 81–91.

Farrell, T. & Gordon, S. (2009). 'COIN Machine: The British Military in Afghanistan'. *Orbis*, Fall 2009.

Farrell, T. & Giustozzi, A. (2013). 'The Taliban at War: Inside the Helmand Insurgency, 2004–2012'. *International Affairs*, 89(4): 845–71.

Feinstein, D. (2012). *Support Afghan Farmers, Cut off Taliban's Drug Funding*. Letter to Secretary Clinton, 7 Feb. 2012.

Felbab-Brown, V. (2006). 'Kicking the Opium Habit? Afghanistan's Drug Economy and Politics Since the 1980s'. *Conflict, Security and Development*, 6(2): 127–49.

—— (2010). *Shooting Up: Counterinsurgency and the War on Drugs*. Washington, DC: Brookings Institute Press.

Ferguson, J. (2010). *Taliban: the Unknown Enemy*. Cambridge: Da Capo Press.

Filipov, D. (2002). 'Drug Trade Flourishes Again in Afghanistan'. *Boston Globe*, 31 Oct. 2002.

Fitzherbert, A. (2004). *Planning Alternative Livelihoods in Nangarhar*. Unpublished notes, 11 Nov. 2004.

Forsberg, C. (2009). 'The Taliban's Campaign for Kandahar'. *Afghanistan Report 3*, Dec. 2009. Washington, DC: Institute for the Study of War.

Foschini, F. (2011a). *Sherzai Staying or Leaving? A Nangarhar Tug of War*. Kabul: Afghanistan Analysts Network, 8 Mar. 2011.

—— (2011b). *How Outside Interference Politicized the Achin Land Conflict*. Kabul: Afghanistan Analysts Network, 20 Oct. 2011.

Foust, J. (2008). 'Warlord for Afghanistan's 'Person of the Year''. *Central Asia News*, 20 March 2008.

Gall, C. (2008). 'Governor of Afghan Opium Capital Pushes for Crop Replacement'. *New York Times*, 3 October 2008.

Gallant, T. (1999). 'Brigandage, Piracy and Capitalism, and State-Formation Transnational Crime: a Historical World Systems Perspective'. In Heyman, J. (ed.), *State and Illegal Practices*. Oxford: Berg.

Gannon, K. (2005). *I is for Infidel: From Holy War to Holy Terror: 18 Years Inside Afghanistan*. New York: Public Affairs.

Gates, R. M. (2014). *Duty: Memoirs of a Secretary at War*. New York: Alfred A. Knopf.

Gebert, R. (2000). *UNDCP/UNOPS Poppy Crop Reduction (Alternative Development Pilot Project) AD/AFG/97/C28. An Assessment of Social Impact and Community Development*. Unpublished report.

Geddes, W. R. (1970). 'Opium and the Miao: A Study in Ecology and Adjustment'. *Oceania*, Sept.

George, R. & Dante, P. (2011). 'The Case for Wartime Chief Executive Officer, Fixing the Interagency Quagmire in Afghanistan'. *Foreign Affairs*, 21 Jun. 2011.

Ghani, A. & Lockhard, C. (2008). *Fixing Failed States: A Framework for Rebuilding a Fractured World*. Oxford: Oxford University Press.

Ghanizada (2012). 'Anti-corruption Protests Erupt in Helmand and Takhar'. *Khaama Press*, 13 May 2012.

Giustozzi, A. (2003). 'Respectable Warlords? The Politics of State-Building in Post-Taleban Afghanistan'. *Crisis States Programme Working Paper 1*. London: London School of Economics.

—— (2004). 'Good State Versus Bad Warlord. A Critique of Statebuilding Strategies in Afghanistan. Crisis States Programme'. *Working Papers Series no. 1*. London: LSE.

—— (2007). 'War and Peace Economies of Afghanistan's Strongmen'. *International Peacekeeping*, 14(1): 75–89.

—— (ed.) (2009a). *Decoding the New Taliban: Insights from the Afghan Field*. London: Hurst & Co.

—— (2009b). *Empires of Mud. Wars and Warlords in Afghanistan*. London: Hurst & Co.

—— (2009c). 'The Eye of the Storm: Cities in the Vortex of Afghanistan's Civil Wars'. *Working Paper 62*. Crisis States Research Centre, London School of Economics, retrieved from http://eprints.lse.ac.uk/28123/1/WP62GiustozziR.pdf

—— (2010). 'The Taliban Beyond the Pashtuns'. *Afghanistan Papers 5*, Jul. 2010, Ontario: Centre for International Governance Innovation.

—— (2011). *The Art of Coercion: The Primitive Accumulation and Management of Coercive Power*. London: Hurst & Co.

—— & Orsini, D. (2009). 'Centre–periphery Relations in Afghanistan: Badakhshan Between Patrimonialism and Institution Building'. *Central Asian Survey*, 28(1): 1–16.

—— & Ullah, N. (2006). 'Tribes and Warlords in Southern Afghanistan, 1980–2005'. *Working Paper 7*. Crisis Research Centre.

Goodhand, J. (2000). 'Research in conflict zones: ethics and accountability'. *Forced Migration Review*, 8: 12–15.

—— (2004a). 'Afghanistan in Central Asia'. In Pugh, M. & Cooper, N. with Goodhand, J. (eds.), *War Economies in a Regional Context: Challenges for Transformation International Peace Academy*. London: Lynne Rienner Publishers, 45–91.

—— (2004b). 'From War Economy to Peace Economy? Reconstructing and State Building in Afghanistan'. *Journal of International Affairs*, 58(1), Fall 2004.

—— (2008). 'Corrupting or Consolidating Peace? The Drugs Economy and Post Conflict Peacebuilding in Afghanistan'. *International Peacekeeping*, 15(3): 405–23.

—— (2009). 'Bandits, Borderlands and Opium Wars. Afghan State Building Viewed From the Margins'. *DIIS Working Paper*, Nov. 2009.

—— (2012). *Contested Transitions: International Drawdown and the Future State in Afghanistan*. Norwegian Peacebuilding Resources Centre, Nov. 2012.

—— & Cramer, C. (2002). 'Try Again, Fail Again, Fail Better. War the State and the Post Conflict Challenge in Afghanistan'. *Development and Change*, 33(5): 885–909.

—— & Mansfield, D. (2010). 'Drugs and (Dis)order: A Study of the Opium Economy, Political Settlements and State Building in Afghanistan'. *LSE Conflict and Crisis States working paper series 83*.

Goodson, L. P. (2001). *Afghanistan's Endless War: State failure, regional politics, and the rise of the Taliban*. Seattle: University of Washington Press.

Gootenburg, P. 'Talking Like a State'. In van Schendel, W. & Abraham, I. (eds.), *Ilicit*

Flows and Criminal Things: States, Borders and the other Side of Globalisation. Indiana: Indiana University Press.

Gordon, S. (2010). *Aid and Stabilisation: Helmand Case Study*. Unpublished paper.

—— (2011). *Winning Hearts and Minds? Examining the relationship between aid and security in Afghanistan's Helmand Province*. Medford, MA: Feinstein International Center, Tufts University.

Goudsouzian, T. (2004). 'Interview: Nangarhar Province Governor on Elections, Drugs and Security'. *Radio Free Europe*, 31 Aug. 2004.

Gough, I. & Wood, G. (2004). *Insecurity and Welfare Regimes in Asia, Africa and Latin America: Social Policy in Development Contexts*. Cambridge: Cambridge University Press.

Gough, I. & McGregor, J. A. (2007). *Wellbeing in Developing Countries: from Theory to Research*. Cambridge: Cambridge University Press.

Government of the Islamic Republic of Afghanistan (2005). *An Overview of Committed expenditure and Funding Gaps for Counter-Narcotics related Projects in the 1384 National Development Budget*. Kabul: Author.

——, Ministry of Counter Narcotics (2006). *National Drug Control Strategy: An updated Five Year Strategy for tackling the Illicit Drug Problem*. Kabul: Author.

—— (2009). *Afghanistan Statistical Yearbook 2008/09*. Central Statistics Organisation, retrieved from http://www.cso.gov.af/

Green, D. (2012). *The Valley's Edge: A Year with the Pashtuns in the Heartland of the Taliban*. Washington, DC: Potomac Books.

Gregorian, V. (1969). *The Emergence of Modern Afghanistan: Politics of reform and Modernization 1880–1946*. Stanford: Stanford University Press.

GTZ (2003). *Drugs and Poverty: The Contribution of Development-Oriented Drug Control to Poverty Reduction*. A cooperative study of the Drugs and Development Programme (ADE) and the Poverty Reduction Project of GTZ, June 2003.

Guardian (2010a). *US Embassy Cables: Allies Praise for Helmand Governor*, 2 Dec. 2010.

—— (2010b). *US Embassy Cables: Gordon Brown Urges Karzai not to Replace Helmand Governor*, 2 Dec. 2010.

—— (2010c). *US Embassy Cables: Hamid Karzai Threatens a Tribal Solution in Helmand 2010*, 2 Dec. 2010.

—— (2010d). *US Embassy Cables: Karzai's Attempt to Appoint 'Known Warlord and Criminal'*, 2 Dec. 2010.

—— (2010e). *US Embassy Cables: Taliban Using Opium Stocks Like Savings Nest*, 20 Dec. 2010.

Hafvenstein, J. (2007). *Opium Season: a Year on the Afghan Frontier*. Guildford, CT: Lyons Press.

Hammond, R. (2011). 'The Battle Over Zomia'. *Chronicle Review*, 4 September 2011.

Harding, L. (2001). 'Taliban Rulers get no Thanks for Ending Afghanistan's Opium

Production'. *Guardian*, 5 Apr. 2001, http://www.mapinc.org/drugnews/v01/n622/a04.html

Harris, P. (2001). 'With Taliban Gone, Afghans Look Forward to Bumper Opium Crops'. *Observer*, 30 Nov. 2001, http://rense.com/general17/withtalibangone.htm

Hashimi, A. M. (2010a). '10 Dead as Poppy Growers and Security Personnel Clash'. *Pajhwok Afghan News*, 27 Apr. 2010.

—— (2010b). 'Public Reps, Elders Declare War on Graft'. *Pajhwok Afghan News*, 10 May 2010.

—— (2012a). 'Zakhilwal is a Liar, says Sherzai'. *Pajhwok Afghan News*, 24 June 2012.

—— (2012b). 'Arrest Warrants for Provincial Council Member Issued'. *Pajhwok Afghan News*, 4 Feb. 2012.

Helbardt, S., Hellmann R. & Korf, R. (2010). 'War's Dark Glamour: Ethics of Research in War and Conflict Zones'. *Cambridge Review of International Affairs*, 23(2): 349–69.

Hewad, G. (2011). *The New National Front: A Dark Horse Returns—with Three Riders*. Kabul: Afghanistan Analysts Network, 1 Dec. 2011.

Heyman, J. & Smart, A. (1999). 'States and Illegal Practices: An Overview'. In Heyman, J. (ed.), *States and Illegal Practices*. Oxford: Berg.

Hodge, N. (2012). 'US Finds Graft by Favoured Afghan Leader'. *Wall Street Journal*, 2 Nov. 2012.

Hodge, N. & Zia al Haq Sultani (2012). 'US Ally is Fired in Afghan Shake-up'. *Wall Street Journal*, 20 Sep. 2012.

Holbrooke, R. (2006). 'Afghanistan: The Long Road Ahead'. *Washington Post*, 2 April 2006.

—— (2008). 'Still Wrong in Afghanistan'. *Washington Post*, 23 Jan. 2008.

Holzmann, R., Sherburne-Benz, L. & Tesliuc, E. (2003). *Social Risk Management: The World Bank's Approach to Social Protection in a Globalizing World*. Washington, DC: World Bank.

Hopkins, B. D. (2008). *The Making of Modern Afghanistan*. London: Palgrave Macmillan.

Hopkins, B. D. & Marsden, M. (2011). *Fragments of the Afghan Frontier*. London: Hurst & Co.

Hyman, A. (1982). *Afghanistan Under Soviet Domination 1964–81*. New York: St Martin's Press.

Inkster, N. & Comolli, V. (2012). *Drugs Insecurity and Failed States: the Problems of Prohibition*. London: International Institute for Strategic Studies.

International Commission on Intervention and State Sovereignty (2001). *The Responsibility to Protect*. Report of the International Commission on Intervention and State Sovereignty, co-chaired by Gareth Evans and Mohamed Sahnoun, Dec. 2001.

International Narcotics Control Board (1989). *Vienna Report 1989*, retrieved from https://www.incb.org/documents/Publications/AnnualReports/AR1989/1989_ANNUAL_REPORT_eng.pdf

IRIN (2004). *In-depth: Bitter-Sweet Harvest: Afghanistan's New War*. Afghanistan: Interview with Antonio Maria Costa, executive director of the UN Office of Drugs and Crime.

Ives, N. (2004). 'Karzai Plans to Destroy Poppy Fields in 2 Years'. *New York Times*, 13 Dec. 2004.

Jackson, R. (1990). *Quasi-States: Sovereignty, International Relations and the Third World*. New York: Cambridge University Press.

Jacobsen, K. & Landau L. (2003). 'Researching Refugees: Some Methodological and Ethical Considerations in Social Science and Forced Migration'. *New Issues in Refugee Research*. Working Paper 19, UNHCR, Evaluation and Policy Analysis Unit.

Jaggia, A. K. & Shukla, S. (2000). *IC 814 Hijacked!* New Delhi: Lotus Collection.

Jawad, K. (2011). 'Is the Bulldozer Running out of Fuel?' *Afghanistan Today*, 26 March 2011.

Jelsma, M. (2005). 'Learning Lessons From the Taliban Opium Ban'. *International Journal of Drug Policy*, 16: 98–103.

Jenkins, J. C. (1982). 'Why do Peasants Rebel? Structural and Historical Theories of Modern Peasant Rebellions'. *American Journal of Sociology*, 88(3): 487–514.

Johnson, C. & Leslie, J. (2004). *Afghanistan: the Mirage of Peace*. London: Zed Books.

Johnson, R. (2011). The *Afghan Way of War—Culture and Pragmatism: A Critical History*, London: Hurst & Co.

——— (2012). 'Managing Helmand Province: From Bost to Bastion'. *International Area Studies Review*, 15: 279. DOI: 10.1177/2233865912453903.

Jones, J. (1991a). 'Farmer Perspectives on the Economics and Sociology of Coca Production in the Chapare'. *Institute for Development Anthropology, Working Paper 77*. Binghamton, New York.

——— (1991b). 'Economics, Political Power and Ethnic Conflict on a Changing Frontier: Notes from the Beni Department, Eastern Bolivia'. *Institute for Development Anthropology, Working Paper 58*. Binghamton, New York.

Kakar, H. (1971). *Afghanistan: A Study in Internal Political Developments, 1880–1896*. Lahore: Punjab Educational Press.

——— (1979). *Government and Society in Afghanistan: The Reign of Amir Andal-Rahman Khan*. Austin: University of Texas Press.

——— (1997). *Afghanistan: The Soviet Invasion and the Afghan Response, 1979–1982*. Berkeley, CA: University of California Press.

Kalyvas, S. N. (2006). *The Logic of Violence in Civil War*. Cambridge: Cambridge University Press.

Kandiyoti, D. (1999). 'Poverty in Transition: An Ethnographic Critique of Household Surveys in Post Soviet Central Asia'. *Development and Change*, 30: 499–524.

Kanji, N., MacGregor, J. & Tacoli, C. (2005). 'Understanding Market-based Livelihoods in a Globalizing World: Combining Approaches and Methods'. *Paper for the International Institute for Environment and Development.*

Kantor, P. & Pain, A. (2011a). Running out of Options: Tracing Rural Afghan Livelihoods. Kabul: Afghanistan Research and Evaluation Unit, Briefing Paper 1.

—— (2011b). The Role of Social Resources in Securing Life and Livelihood in Rural Afghanistan. *Bath Papers in International Development 12,* Jan. 2011. Bath, UK: Centre for Development Studies, University of Bath.

Keefer, P. & Loayza, N. (eds.) (2010). *Innocent Bystanders: Developing Countries and the War on Drugs.* Washington, DC: Palgrave Macmillan and World Bank.

Kemp, R. (2010). 'Counterinsurgency in Nangarhar Province, Eastern Afghanistan 2004–2008'. *Military Review,* Nov-Dec 2010.

Kerkvliet, B. & Tria, J. (2009). 'Everyday Politics in Peasant Societies (and Ours)'. *Journal of Peasant Studies,* 36(1): 227–43.

Kiani, K. (2006). 'Torkham–Jalalabad Road Opened'. *Dawn Newspaper,* 14 Sep. 2006, Lahore, Pakistan, http://www.dawn.com/2006/09/14/top5.htm

Kilcullen, D. (2009). *The Accidental Guerrilla: Fighting Small Wars in the Midst of a Big One.* London: Hurst & Co.

King, A. (2012). 'Operation Herrick: The British Campaign in Helmand'. In Hynek, N. & Martin, P. (eds.), *State Building in Afghanistan: Multinational Contributions to Reconstruction.* London: Routledge.

Kirk, R. (1995). *More Terrible Than Death: Violence, Drugs and America's War in Colombia.* New York: Public Affairs.

Koehler, J. (2005). *Project for Alternative Livelihoods in Eastern Afghanistan. Conflict processing and Opium Poppy Economy in Afghanistan.* Jalalabad.

Kovats-Bernat, C. (2002). 'Negotiating Fields: Pragmatic Strategies for Fieldwork Amid Violence and Terror'. *American Anthropologist,* New Series, 104(1): 208–22.

Kramer, T. & Woods, K. (2012). *Financing Dispossession—China's Opium Substitution Programme in Northern Burma.* Amsterdam: Trans National Institute.

Krasner, S. (1999). *Sovereignty: Organised Hypocrisy.* Princeton, NJ: Princeton University Press.

Kulick, J. D., Caulkins, J. P. & Kleiman, M. A. R. (2011). 'Material support: Counternarcotics vs. Counterinsurgency in Afghanistan'. *School of Public Policy Working Papers19.* Malibu, CA: Pepperdine University, http://digitalcommons. pepperdine.edu/sppworkingpapers/19

Lancaster, J. (2004). 'Karzai Urges War on Opium Trade: Leaders Says Cultivation Imperils Attempts to Rebuild Afghanistan'. *Washington Post Foreign Service,* 10 December 2004.

Landay, J. S. (2007). 'US Ignores Angry Reaction to Secret Poppy Spraying Test'. *McClatchy Newspapers,* 26 October 2007.

Lautze, S. & Raven-Roberts, A. (2006). 'Violence and Complex Humanitarian Emergencies: Implications for Livelihoods Models'. *Disasters*, 30(4): 383–401.

Le Billon, P. (2001). 'The Political Ecology of War: Natural Resources and Armed Conflicts'. *Political Geography*, 20: 560–84.

—— (2007). 'Geographies of War. Perspective on 'Resource Wars''. *Geography Compass* 1(2): 162–83.

Ledwidge, F. (2011). *Losing Small Wars: British Military Failure in Iraq and Afghanistan.* New Haven, CT: Yale University Press.

Leithead, A. (2008). 'New Hope for Helmand Province', BBC News, 23 Mar. 2008.

Lintner, B. (1999) *Burma in Revolt: Opium and Insurgency Since 1948.* Bangkok, Thailand: Silkworm Books.

Luckham, R. & Kirk, T. (2013). 'Understanding Security in the Vernacular in Hybrid Political Contexts: a Critical Survey'. *Conflict, Security & Development*, 13(3): 339–59. DOI: 10.1080/14678802.2013.811053.

Lund, C. (2006). 'Twilight Institutions: An Introduction'. *Development and Change*, 37: 673–84.

Macdonald, D. (2007). *Drugs in Afghanistan: Opium, Outlaws and Scorpion Tales.* London: Pluto Press.

MacKenzie, J. (2009). 'The Great Poppy Seed Caper'. *Global Post*, 22 June 2009.

—— (2010a). 'The Battle for Afghanistan—Militancy and Conflict in Helmand'. *Counter terrorism Strategic Initiative Policy Paper.* Washington, DC: New America Foundation, www.Newamerican.net

—— (2010b). 'Good Money After Bad in Afghanistan?' *Global Post*, 18 January 2010.

Mackrell, D. (1999). *Review of Strategy in Shinwar District.* UNDCP Afghanistan Programme, unpublished report.

Maley, W. (ed.) (1998). *Fundamentalism reborn? Afghanistan and the Taliban.* New York: New York University Press.

—— (2009). *The Afghanistan Wars* (2nd edn). London: Palgrave Macmillan.

Malik, N. J. (1994). *Proposal for High Value Cropping Systems for Dir District Development Project.* Islamabad, Pakistan: United Nations Drug Control Programme.

Malkesian, C. (2013). *War Comes to Garmser: Thirty Years of Conflict on the Afghan Frontier.* New York: Oxford University Press.

Mamdani, M. (1996). *Contemporary Africa and the Legacy of Late Colonialism.* Princeton, NJ: Princeton University Press.

Mankin, J. (2009). 'Gaming the System: How Afghan Opium Underpins Local Power'. *Journal of International Affairs*, 63(1): 195–209.

Mansfield, D. (1998). *UNDCP's Relationship with the Taliban.* Note to file, personal correspondence.

—— (2001). *The Impact of the Taliban Prohibition on Opium Poppy Cultivation in*

Afghanistan. Unpublished paper prepared for the Donor Mission to Afghanistan, 23 April–4 May 2001.

—— (2002a). *The Economic Superiority of Illicit Drug Production: Myth and Reality—Opium Poppy Cultivation in Afghanistan*. Paper prepared for the International Conference on Alternative Development in Drug Control and Cooperation, Feldafing, 7–12 Jan. 2002.

—— (2002b). *The Failure of Quid Pro Quo: Alternative Development in Afghanistan*. Paper prepared for the International Conference on Alternative Development in Drug Control and Cooperation, Feldafing, 7–12 Jan. 2002.

—— (2004c). *What is Driving Opium Poppy Cultivation? Decision Making Amongst Opium Poppy Cultivators in Afghanistan in the 2003/4 Growing Season*. Paper for the UNODC/ONDCP Second Technical Conference on Drug Control Research, 19–21 Jul. 2004.

—— (2005). *Pariah or Poverty? The Opium Ban in the Province of Nangarhar in the 2004–05 Growing Season and Its Impact on Rural Livelihood Strategies*. GTZ Project for Alternative Livelihoods in Eastern Afghanistan: Internal Document No. 11.

—— (2006a) *Opium Poppy Cultivation in the Provinces of Nangarhar and Ghor. A report for AREU's Applied Thematic Research into Water Management, Livestock and the Opium Economy*. Kabul: AREU.

—— (2006b). 'Responding to the Challenge of Diversity in Opium Poppy Cultivation in Afghanistan'. In Buddenberg, D. & Byrd, W. (eds.), *Afghanistan's Drugs Industry: Structure, functioning, dynamics and implications for counter narcotics policy*. Kabul: UNODC/World Bank.

—— (2007a). 'Economical with the Truth: The Limits of Price and Profitability in both Explaining Opium Poppy Cultivation in Afghanistan and in Designing Effective Responses'. In Pain, A. & Sutton, J. (eds.), *Reconstructing Agriculture in Afghanistan*. Rugby: Practical Action Publishing.

—— (2007c). *Beyond the Metrics: Understanding the Nature of Change in the Rural Livelihoods of Opium Poppy Growing Households in the 2006/07 Growing Season*. Report for the Afghan Drugs Inter Departmental Unit of the UK Government.

—— (2008a). *Resurgence and Reductions: Explanations for Changing Levels of Opium Poppy Cultivation in Nangarhar and Ghor in 2005–2007*. A report for AREU's Applied Thematic Research into Water Management, Livestock and the Opium Economy. Kabul: AREU.

—— (2008b). *Responding to Risk and Uncertainty: Understanding the Nature of Change in the Rural Livelihoods of Opium Poppy Growing Households in the 2007/08 Growing Season*. A Report for the Afghan Drugs Inter Departmental Unit of the UK Government.

—— (2009a). *Poppy Free Provinces: Measure or a Target?* Report for AREU's Applied Thematic Research into Water Management, Livestock and the Opium Economy. Kabul: AREU.

—— (2009b). *Sustaining the Decline? Understanding the Nature of Change in the Rural Livelihoods of Opium Poppy Growing Households in the 2008/09 Growing Season*. A Report for the Afghan Drugs Inter Departmental Unit of the UK Government.

—— (2010a). *Where Have all the Flowers Gone? Assessing the Sustainability of Current Reductions in Opium Production in Afghanistan*. Afghanistan Research and Evaluation Briefing Paper. Kabul: AREU.

—— (2010b). *Helmand Eradication Impact Study 2009*. A Report for the Afghan Drugs Inter Departmental Unit of the UK Government, 25 Jan. 2010.

—— (2010c). *Helmand Counter Narcotics Impact Study, May 2010*. A Report for the Afghan Drugs Inter Departmental Unit of the UK Government, 10 May 2010.

—— (2011a). 'The Ban on Opium Production Across Nangahar: A risk too far?' *International Journal of Environmental Studies*, 68: 381–95.

—— (2011b). *Between a rock and a hard place: Counternarcotics efforts and their effects in the 2011/12 growing season*. Kabul: AREU.

—— (2012). *Briefing Paper 3: Central Helmand in the 2011/12 Growing Season*. A Report for the British Embassy, Kabul.

—— (2013a). *All Bets are Off; Prospects for (B)reaching Agreements and Drug Control in Helmand and Nangarhar in the run up to Transition*. AREU Case Study Series. Kabul: AREU.

—— (2013b). *Briefing paper 7: Taxation in Central Helmand and Kandahar*. An Unpublished Paper for the British Embassy, Kabul.

—— (2014). *'From Bad they Made it Worse': The Concentration of Opium Poppy in areas of Conflict in the Provinces of Helmand and Nangarhar*. AREU Case Study Series. Kabul: AREU.

Mansfield, D., Alcis Ltd and OSDR (2011). *Managing Concurrent and Repeated Risks: Explaining the Reductions in Opium Production in Central Helmand 2008–2011*. Kabul: AREU.

Mansfield, D. & Fishstein, P. (2013). *Eyes Wide Shut: Counter Narcotics in Transition*. Afghanistan Research and Evaluation Unit Briefing Paper. Kabul: AREU.

Mansfield, D. & Pain, A. (2005). *Alternative Livelihoods: Substance or Slogan?* Afghanistan Research and Evaluation Unit Briefing Paper. Kabul: AREU.

—— (2006). *Opium Poppy Eradication: How do you Raise Risk where there is Nothing to Lose?* Afghanistan Research and Evaluation Unit Briefing Paper. Kabul: AREU.

—— (2008). *Counter Narcotics in Afghanistan: The Failure of Success?* Afghanistan Research and Evaluation Unit Briefing Paper. Kabul: AREU.

Mansfield, D. & Sage, S. (1997). 'Drug Crop Producing Countries: A Development Perspective'. In R. Coomber (ed.), *The Control of Drugs and Drug Users: Reasons or Reactions*. London: Harwood Academic Press.

Marsden, M. & Hopkins, B. D. (2011). *Fragments of the Afghan Frontier*. New York: Columbia University Press.

Marsden, P. (2009). *Afghanistan Aid, Armies and Empires*. London: I. B. Tauris.

Martin, M. (2011). *A Socio-Politico History of Helmand*. PhD thesis.

Matinuddin, K. (1999). *The Taliban Phenomenon: Afghanistan 1994–1997*. Karachi: Oxford University Press.

Maxwell, D. & Vaitla, B. (2012). *Livelihoods Change over Time Study: Analytical Methodology Paper*. Paper delivered as part of the university study of the same name. Medford, MA: Tufts University.

McChrystal, S. Gen. (2013). *My Share of the Task: A Memoir*. New York: Portfolio.

McCoy, A. W. (2003). *The Politics of Heroin: CIA Complicity in the Global Drug Trade* (revised edn). Chicago: Lawrence Hill Books.

McCoy, A. (2004). 'The Stimulus of Prohibition: A Critical History of the Global Narcotics Trade'. In Steinberg, M., Hobbs, J. J. & Mathewson, K. (eds.), *Dangerous Harvest: Drug Plants and the Transformation of Indigenous Landscapes*. New York: Oxford University Press.

McPherson, S. & Hannah, C. (2010). *Review of the Helmand Provincial Counter-Narcotics Strategy: Third Report*. Unpublished review for the Counter Narcotics Team, Provincial Reconstruction Team, Helmand.

Meehan, P. (2011). 'Drugs, Insurgency and State-building in Burma: Why the Drugs Trade is Central to Burma's Changing Political Order'. *Journal of Southeast Asian Studies*, 23: 376–404.

Mejia, D. (2010). 'Evaluating Plan Colombia'. In Keefer, P. & Loayza, N. (eds.), *Innocent Bystanders: Developing Countries and the War on Drugs*. Washington, DC: Palgrave Macmillan and World Bank.

Mejia, D. & Posada, C. E. (2010). 'Cocaine Production and Trafficking: What do we Know?' In Keefer, P. & Loayza, N. (eds.), *Innocent Bystanders: Developing Countries and the War on Drugs*. Washington, DC: Palgrave Macmillan and World Bank.

Menkhaus, K. (2007). 'Governance without Government in Somalia: Spoilers, State Building, and the Politics of Coping'. *International Security*, 31(3): 74–106.

Mercille, J. (2013). *Cruel Harvest: US Intervention in the Afghan Drug Trade*. New York: Pluto Press.

Merk, W. R. H. (1984). *The Mohmands*. Lahore: Vanguard Books.

Migdal, J. (1994). 'State Building and the Non Nation State'. *Journal of International Affairs*, 58(1).

Miles, D. (1979). 'The Finger Knife and Ockham's Razor: A Problem in Asian Culture, History and Economic Anthropology'. *American Ethnologist*, 6: 223–43.

Ministry of Counter Narcotics (2012). *National Drug Control Strategy, 2012–2016*. Kabul: MCN.

Moore, B. (1966). *Social Origins of Dictatorship and Democracy: Lord and Peasant in the Making of the Modern World*. Boston, MA: Beacon Press.

Morgan Edwards, L. (2011). *The Afghan solution: The inside story of Abdul Haq, the CIA and how Western hubris lost Afghanistan*. London: Bactria Press.

Moscardi, E. & de Janvry, A. (1977). 'Attitudes Towards Risk Amongst Peasants: an Econometric Approach'. *American Journal of Agricultural Economics*, 50(2): 252–7.

Moser, C. O. N. (2006). *Asset-based Approaches to Poverty Reduction in a Globalized Context*. Global Economy and Development Working Paper, Nov. 2006. Washington, DC: Brookings Institute.

Mosse, D. (2004). 'Is Good Policy Unimplementable? Reflections on the Ethnography of Aid Policy and Practice'. *Development and Change*, 35(4): 639–71.

Mukhopadhyay, D. (2009a). *Warlords as Bureaucrats: The Afghan Experience*. Carnegie Endowment for International Peace, Middle East Program, 101.

—— (2009b) 'Disguised Warlordism and Combatanthood in Balkh: the Persistence of Informal Power in the Formal Afghan State'. *Conflict Security and Development*, 9(4): 535–64.

—— (2014) *Warlords, Strongman Governors, and the State in Afghanistan*. Cambridge: Cambridge University Press.

Naim, M. (2005). *Illicit: how Smugglers, Traffickers and Copycats are Hijacking the Global Economy*. London: Arrow Books.

Neumann, R. E. (2009). *The Other War: Winning and Losing in Afghanistan*. Washington, DC: Potomac Books.

Nissenbaum, D. (2010). 'Afghan Poppy Harvest is Next Challenge for US Marines'. *MacClatchy Newspapers*, 16 March 2010.

Noelle, C. (1997). *State and Tribe in Nineteenth-century Afghanistan: the Reign of Amir dost Muhammad Khan (1826–1863)*. Richmond: Curzon Press.

Nojumi, N. (2002). *The Rise of the Taliban in Afghanistan: Mass Mobilization, Civil War, and the Future of the Region*. New York: Palgrave.

Nordland, R. (2010a). 'Afghan Warlord with Many Enemies, and Possibly One Notorious Ally, Killed by Suicide Bomber'. *New York Times*, 23 Feb. 2010.

—— (2010b). 'US Turns a Blind Eye to Opium in Afghan Town'. *New York Times*, 20 March 2010.

North, D. C., Wallis, J. J., Webb, S. B. & Weingast, B. R. (2007). 'Limited Access Orders in the Developing World: A New Approach to the Problems of Development'. *Policy Research Working Paper 4359*. Washington, DC: World Bank, Independent Evaluation Group, Country Relations Division.

North, D. C., Wallace, J. J. & Weingast, B. R. (2009). *Violence and Social Orders: A Conceptual Framework for Interpreting Recorded Human History*. Cambridge: Cambridge University Press.

Nugent, P. (2002). *Smugglers, Secessionists and Loyal Citizens on the Ghana–Togo Frontier*. Oxford: James Currey.

Office of the Governor of Helmand (2008). *Short Term Provincial Counternarcotics Strategy, Proposal, 2nd Draft*, 6 July 2008.

—— (2009). *Helmand Provincial Counternarcotics Strategy, Proposal*, 28 May 2009.

Orkand Corporation (1989). *Afghanistan: The Southern Provinces*. Final Report, April 1989. Silver Spring, MD: Orkand Corporation.

Owens, G. P. (1971). *1970 Farm Economic Survey: Helmand and Arghandab Valleys of Afghanistan*. USAID/University of Wyoming Contract Team, unpublished report.

Owens, G. P. & Clifton, J. H. (1972). *Poppies in Afghanistan*. Kabul: US Agency for International Development.

Paige, J. (1975). *Agrarian Revolution: Social Movements and Export Agriculture in the Underdeveloped World*. New York: Free Press.

Pain, A. (2004). *The Impact of the Opium Poppy Economy on Household Livelihoods: Evidence from the Wakhan Corridor and Khustak Valley in Badakhshan*. Study for AKDN, Badakhshan Programme, funded by GTZ.

—— (2006a). *Cultivation in Kunduz and Balkh Provinces: a scoping study*. A report for AREU's Applied Thematic Research into Water Management, Livestock and the Opium Economy. Kabul: AREU.

—— (2006b). *Opium Trading Systems in Helmand and Ghor*. Afghanistan Research and Evaluation Unit Issues Paper Series. Kabul: AREU.

—— (2007a). *The Diffusion and Spread of Opium Poppy Cultivation in Balkh*. A report for AREU's Applied Thematic Research into Water Management, Livestock and the Opium Economy. Kabul: AREU.

Painter, J. (1994). *Bolivia and Coca—A study in Dependency*. Boulder, CO: Lynne Rienner Publishers.

Paoli, L., Greenfield, V. A. & Reuter, P. (2009). *The World Heroin Market: Can Supply be Cut?* Oxford: Oxford University Press.

Paris, R. & Sisk, T. (2007). *Managing Contradictions: The Inherent Dilemmas of Post War State Building*. International Peace Academy.

Parks, T. & Cole, W. (2010). *Political Settlements: Implications for International Development Policy and Practice*. Occasional Paper 2. Asia Foundation.

Partlow, J. & Jaffe, G. (2010). 'US Military Runs into Tribal Politics after Deal with Pashtuns'. *Washington Post Foreign Service*, 10 May 2010.

Patton, M. Q. (1990). *Qualitative Evaluation and Research Methods* (2nd edn). Newbury Park, CA: Sage Publications.

Pearson, G. & Hobbs, D. (2001). *Middle Market Drug Distribution*. Home Office Research Study.

Perl, R. (2001). Taliban and the Drug Trade. *CRS Report for Congress, RS21041*, 5 Oct. 2001, retrieved from http://fpc.state.gov/documents/organization/6210.pdf

Peters, G. (2009a). *How Opium Profits the Taliban*. Washington, DC: United States Institute for Peace.

—— (2009b). *Seeds of Terror: How Heroin is Bankrolling the Taliban and Al Qaeda*. New York: Thomas Dunn Books.

Pinney, A. (2010). *DFID Afghanistan Data Quality Assessment of the Asia Foundation Surveys of the Afghan People 2006–2009*, Sep. 2010. Unpublished report.

Popkin, S. (1979). *The Rational Peasant: the Political economy of Rural Society in Vietnam*. Berkeley, CA: University of California Press.

Radio Free Europe (2008). 'Afghanistan: Radio Free Afghanistan Names Person of the Year', 20 March 2008.

Radin, C. & Roggio, B. ((2008). 'Afghanistan Mapping the Violence'. *The Long War Journal*, 5 Aug. 2008, retrieved from http://www.longwarjournal.org/archives/2008/08/afghanistan_mapping.php

Rashid, A. (2001). *Taliban: Islam, Oil and the New Great Game in Central Asia*. London: I. B. Tauris.

—— (2012). *Pakistan on the Brink: the Future of America, Pakistan and Afghanistan*. New York: Viking.

Rawlinson, P. (2007). 'Look who's Talking: Interviewing Russian Criminals'. *Trends in Organised Crime*, 11: 12–20.

Renard, R. D. (1996). *The Burmese Connection: Illegal drugs and the Making of the Golden Triangle*. Boulder, CO: Lynne Rienner Publishers.

—— (2001). *Opium Reduction in Thailand 1970—2000 A Thirty-Year Journey*. Chiang Mai: Silkworm Books.

Reuter, P. (2010). 'Can Production and Trafficking of Illicit Drugs be Reduced or Only Shifted?' In Keefer, P. & Loayza, N. (eds.), *Innocent Bystanders, Developing Countries and the War on Drugs*. Washington, DC: Palgrave Macmillan and World Bank.

Reuters (2007). 'Pressure for Tougher Afghan Anti Drugs Drive—UN'. 5 Sep. 2007.

Risen, J. (2006). *State of War: the Secret History of the CIA and the Bush Administration*. New York: Free Press.

—— (2008). 'Afghanistan: Reports Link Karzai's Brother to Heroin Trade'. *New York Times*, 5 Oct. 2008.

Risse, T. (ed.) (2011). *Governance without a State: Policies and Politics in Areas of Limited Statehood*. New York: Colombia University Press.

Rodgers, D. (2001). 'Making Danger a Calling: Anthropolgy, Violence and the Dilemmas of Participant Observation'. *Working Paper 6*, LSE Crisis States Programme.

Rohde, D. (2013). *Beyond War: Reimagining American Influence in a New Middle East*. New York: Viking.

Rosenberg, M. (2009). 'US Courts Former Warlords in its Bid for Afghan Stability'. *Wall Street Journal*, 20 March 2009.

Roy, O. (1990). *Islam and Resistance in Afghanistan* (2nd edn). Cambridge: Cambridge University Press.

Rubin, A. J. & Rosenberg, M. (2012). 'US Efforts Fail to Curtail Trade in Afghan Opium'. *New York Times*, 26 May 2012.

Rubin, B. (2000). 'The Political Economy of War and Peace in Afghanistan'. *World Development*, 28(2): 1789–803.

Rubin, B. & Sherman, J. (2008). *Counter-narcotics to Stabilize Afghanistan: the False Promise of Crop Eradication*. New York: Center on International Cooperation.

Ruttig, T. (2009a). 'Dimensions of the Afghan Insurgency: Causes, Actors and Approaches to 'Talks''. *Afghanistan Analysts Network*, July 2009.

—— (2009b). 'UNODC Sees Afghan Drug Cartels Emerging—With One Eye Closed'. *Afghanistan Analysts Network*, Sep. 2009.

Ryder, M. & Read, C. (2009). *Review of the Helmand CN Plan*. Unpublished document for the Afghan Drugs Interdepartmental Unit.

Saikal, A. (2004). *Modern Afghanistan: A History of Struggle and Survival*. London: I. B. Tauris.

Salmon, G. (2009). *Poppy: Life, Death and Addiction Inside Afghanistan's Opium Trade*. North Sydney: Ebury Press.

Scheper-Hughes, N. (1995). 'The Primacy of the Ethical: Propositions for a Militant Anthropology'. *Current Anthropology*, 36(3): 409–40.

Schetter, C. (ed.) (2012). *Local Politics in Afghanistan: A Century of Intervention in Social Order*. London: Hurst & Co.

Schmink, M. (1984). 'Household Economic Strategies: Review and Research Agenda'. *Latin American Research Review*, 19(3): 87–101.

Schulenberg, M. Von der (2000). *Letter of Resignation to Mr Pino Arlacchi, Executive Director of UNODCCP-UNOV*, 4 Dec. 2000, retrieved from http://www.tni.org/sites/www.tni.org/archives/drugsungass-docs/resignation.pdf

Schweich, T. (2007). *US Counternarcotics Strategy for Afghanistan*. Washington, DC: US Government Printing Office.

—— (2008). 'Is Afghanistan a Narco State?' *New York Times*, 27 July 2008.

Scoones, I. (1998). 'Sustainable Rural Livelihoods: A Framework for Analysis'. *IDS Working Paper 72*. Brighton: Institute of Development Studies.

—— (2009). 'Livelihoods, Perspectives and Rural Development'. *Journal of Peasant Studies*, 36(1): 171–96.

Scott, J. C. (1972a). 'The Erosion of Patron–Client Bonds and Social Change in Rural Southeast Asia'. *Journal of Asian Studies*, 32(1): 5–37.

—— (1972b). 'Patron–Client Politics and Political Change in Southeast Asia'. *American Political Science Review*, 66(1): 91–113.

—— (1976). *The Moral Economy of the Peasant Rebellion and Subsistence in Southeast Asia*. New Haven, CT: Yale University Press.

—— (1985). *Weapons of the Weak: Everyday Forms of Peasant Resistance*. New Haven, CT, Yale University Press.

—— (1987). 'Resistance without Protest and without Organization: Peasant Opposition to the Islamic Zakat and the Christian Tithe'. *Comparative Studies in Society and History*, 29(3): 417–52.

——— (1990). *Domination and the Arts of Resistance: Hidden Transcripts*. London: Yale University Press.

——— (1998). *Seeing like a State: How Certain Schemes to Improve the Human Condition have Failed*. New Haven, CT: Yale University Press.

——— (2009). *The Art of NOT Being Governed: an Anarchist history of Upland South East Asia*. New Haven, CT: Yale University Press.

Scott, P. D. (2003). *Drugs, Oil and War: the United States in Afghanistan, Colombia and Indochina*. New York: Rowman & Littlefield.

Scott, R. (1980). 'Tribal and Ethnic Groups in the Helmand Valley'. *Asia Society, Occasional Paper No. 21*.

Semple, K. & Golden, T. (2007). 'Afghans pressed by US to Spray Poppies'. *New York Times*, 8 October 2007.

Sen, A. (1984). *Resources, Values and Development*. Oxford: Basil Blackwell.

——— (1999). *Development as Freedom*. Oxford: Oxford University Press.

Shairzai, F., Farouq, G. & Scott, R. (1975). *Farm Economic Survey of the Helmand Valley*. Unpublished report for USAID/DP Kabul, Afghanistan.

Shanty, F. (2011). *The Nexus: International Terrorism and Drug Trafficking from Afghanistan*. Santa Barbara, CA: Praeger.

Shuljgin, G. (1969). 'Cultivation of the Opium Poppy and the Oil Poppy in the Soviet Union'. *UN Bulletin of Narcotics*, 1(1): 1–8.

Siegel, D. (2008). 'Conversations with Russian Mafiosi'. *Trends in Organised Crime*, 11: 21–9.

Sinno, A. H. (2008). *Organizations at War in Afghanistan and Beyond*. Ithacha, NY: Cornell University Press.

Skocpol, T. (1982). 'What Makes Peasants Revolutionary? Peasants, Politics and Revolution: Pressures toward Political and Social Change in the Third World'. *Comparative Politics*, 14(3): 351–75.

Smith, Jr, D. (2010). *US Peacefare: Organizing American Peace Building Operations*. Washington, DC: Center for Strategic International Studies.

Smith, G. (2009). 'Afghan Officials in Drug Trade cut Deal Across Enemy Lines'. *Globe and Mail*, 21 March 2009.

——— (2013). *The Dogs are Eating Them Now: Our War in Afghanistan*. Toronto: Alfred A. Knopf.

Smith, T. J., Sgt (2010). 'Afghan Border Police Enlist Tribal Leaders to Protect Eastern Borders'. *Digital Video & Imagery Distribution System*, 15 Feb. 2010.

Snyder, R. (2006). 'Does Lootable Wealth Breed Disorder? A Political Economy of Extraction Framework'. *Comparative Political Studies*, 39: 943–68. DOI: 10.1177/0010414006288724.

Solesbury, W. (2003). 'Sustainable Livelihoods: A Case Study of the Evolution of DfID Policy'. *Working Paper 217*. London: Overseas Development Institute.

Special Inspector General for Afghanistan Reconstruction (2010). 'Weakness in

Reporting and Coordination of Development Assistance and Lack of Provincial Capacity Pose Risks to US Strategy in Nangarhar Province'. SIGAR Audit 11–1.

Spencer, D. K., Major (2009). 'Afghanistan's Nangarhar Inc., A Model for Interagency Success'. *Military Review*, July–August 2009.

Staniland, P. l. (2012). 'States, Insurgents, and Wartime political Orders'. *Articles*, 10(2). DOI: 10.1017/S1537592712000655.

Steinberg, M., Hobbs, J. J. & Mathewson, K. (2004). *Dangerous Harvest: Drug Plants and the Transformation of Indigenous Landscapes*. New York: Oxford University Press.

Stevens, I. M. & Tarzi, K. (1965). *Economics of agricultural production in Helmand Valley, Afghanistan*. Report for US Department of the Interior, Bureau of Reclamation.

Stewart, R. & Knaus, G. (2011). *Can Intervention Work?* New York: W. W. Norton.

Stinchcombe, A. (1961). 'Agricultural Enterprise and Rural Class Relations'. *American Journal of Sociology*, 67: 165–76.

Stockman, F. (2009). 'Karzai's Pardon Nullifies Drug Court Gains'. *Boston Globe*, 4 July 2009.

Streatfeild, D. (2001). *Cocaine: An Unauthorised Biography*. London: Virgin Publishing.

Strick van Linschoten, A. & Kuehn, F. (2012). *An Enemy We Created*. New York: Oxford University Press.

Strong, S. (1992). *Shining Path: the World's Deadliest Revolutionary Force*. London: Fontana.

Suhrke, A. (2006). *The Limits of State-building: The Role of International Assistance in Afghanistan*. Paper presented at the International Studies Association annual meeting, San Diego, 21–24 March 2006.

——— (2009). 'Reconstruction as Modernisation. The 'post conflict' project in Afghanistan'. *Third World Quarterly*, 28(7): 1291–308.

——— (2011). *When More is Less: the International Project in Afghanistan*. New York: Colombia University Press.

Swedish Committee for Afghanistan (1992). 'Farming systems of Nad e Ali District, Helmand Province'. *Afghanistan Agricultural Survey*, 15th Report, part VI.

Synovitz, R. (2006). 'Afghanistan: UN Antidrug Chief Wants NATO to Destroy Opium'. RFE/RL, 12 Sep. 2006, www.rferl.org/content/article/1071273.html

Taylor, J. (2007). *Verification of AEF Eradication in Helmand Province 2007*. Personal correspondence and presentation. Cranfield, UK: Cranfield University.

Thorne, J. & Farrell, G. (2003). *Where Have All the Flowers Gone? Evaluation of a Law Enforcement Crackdown Against Opium Poppy Cultivation in Afghanistan*. Paper presented to the annual meeting of the American Society of Criminology 2003 in Denver, CO, 18–23 Nov. 2003.

Thoumi, F. E. (2002). 'Can the United Nations Support 'Objective' and Unhampered

Illicit Drug Policy Research? A Testimony of a UN Funded Researcher'. *Crime, Law and Social Change*, 38: 161–83.

—— (2003). *Illegal Drugs, Economy, and Society in the Andes*. Washington, DC: Woodrow Center Press.

—— (2005). 'The Numbers Game: Let's All Guess the Size of the Illegal Drug Industry.' *Journal of Drug Issues*, 0022–0426/05/01: 185–200.

Tilly, C. (1985). 'War Making and State Making as Organised Crime'. In Evans, P., Rusechemeyer, D. & Skocpol, T. (eds.), *Bringing the State Back In*. Cambridge: Cambridge University Press.

Trans National Institute (2001). 'Afghanistan, Drugs and Terrorism: Merging Wars'. *Drugs & Conflict Debate Papers. TNI Briefing Series No. 3*, Dec. 2001. Amsterdam: Trans National Institute.

—— (2003). 'Cross Purposes: Alternative development and conflict in Colombia'. *TNI Briefing Series No. 7*, Jun. 2003. Amsterdam: Trans National Institute.

Transitional Islamic State of Afghanistan (2003). *National Drug Control Strategy*, 18 May 2003. Personal copy; can be retrieved from www.afghandata.org

Tullis, L. (1995). *Unintended Consequences: Illegal Drugs and Drug Policies in Nine Countries*. Boulder, CO: Lynne Rienner Publishers.

Turse, N. (2012). 'Tomgram. The Pentagon's Bases of Confusion'. Retrieved from www.tomdispatch.com/dilogs/print/?id=175588

The 'United Nations (1998)' reference needs to be swapped with the (1972) reference below it so that the dates are in the correct order

United Nations (1998). *Political declaration: Guiding Principles of Drug Demand Reduction and Measures to Enhance International Cooperation to Counter the World Drug Problem*. Action Plan on International Cooperation: the eradication of illicit drug crops and alternative development.

—— (1972). *Single Convention on Narcotics Drugs, 1961, as amended by the 1972 Protocol Amending the Single Convention on Narcotics Drugs, 1961*. New York: United Nations Publication.

—— (1998). *Convention against Illicit Traffic in Narcotics Drugs and Psychotropic Substances, 1988*. New York: United Nations Publication.

United Nations Commission on Narcotic Drugs (1995). 'Illicit Drug Traffic and Supply: Strategies for Illicit Supply Reduction'. *Commission on Narcotic Drugs, March 1995, E/CN.7/1995/1*. Vienna: UNDCP.

United Nations Drug Control Programme (1994). *Afghanistan Opium Poppy Survey: Main Report*. Islamabad: UNDCP.

—— (1995a). *Afghanistan: Assessment Strategy and Programming Mission to Afghanistan*, May–July 1995.

—— (1995b). *Afghanistan Opium Poppy Survey*. Islamabad: UNDCP.

—— (1996). *Afghanistan Opium Poppy Survey*. Islamabad: UNDCP.

—— (1997). *Afghanistan: Aide-Memoire prepared by the Appraisal Team*. Islamabad, 10 Nov. 1997.

—— (1998a). *Afghanistan Annual Opium Poppy Survey, 1998.* Islamabad: UNDCP.

—— (1998b). *Strategic Study #1: An analysis of the process of expansion of opium poppy to new districts in Afghanistan.* Preliminary report by D. Mansfield. Islamabad: UNDCP.

—— (1998c). *Strategic Study #2: The dynamics of the farmgate trade and the coping strategies of opium traders.* Final report by D. Mansfield. Islamabad: UNDCP.

—— (1999a). *Strategic Study #3: The role of opium as a source of informal credit.* Preliminary report by D. Mansfield. Islamabad: UNDCP.

—— (1999b). *Strategic Study #4: Access to labour: The role of opium in the livelihood strategies of itinerant harvesters working in Helmand province, Afghanistan.* Final report by D. Mansfield. Islamabad: UNDCP.

—— (1999c). *Strategic Study #5: An analysis of the process of expansion of opium poppy to new districts in Afghanistan.* Second report by D. Mansfield. Islamabad: UNDCP.

—— (2000). *Strategic Study #6: The role of women in opium poppy cultivation in Afghanistan.* Final report by D. Mansfield. Islamabad: UNDCP.

United Nations Office on Drugs and Crime (2003). *The Opium Economy in Afghanistan: An International Problem.* New York: United Nations.

—— (2004). *Strategic Study #9: Opium Poppy Cultivation in a Changing Environment: Farmers' Intentions for the 2002/03 Growing Season by D. Mansfield.* Kabul: UNODC.

—— (2005). *Thematic Evaluation of UNODC's Alternative Development Initiatives. Independent Evaluation Unit, November 2005.* Vienna: UNODC.

—— (2008a). *Thematic Evaluation of the Technical Assistance Provided to Afghanistan by the United Nations Office on Drugs and Crime: Volume 6: Illicit Crop Monitoring Program,* A report for the Independent Evaluation Unit, May 2008. Vienna: UNODC.

—— (2008b). *Discussion Paper: Is poverty Driving the Afghan Opium Boom?* March 2008.

United Nations Office on Drugs and Crime/Ministry of Counter Narcotics (2003–2013). *United Nations Afghanistan Opium Surveys.* Kabul: UNODC/MCN.

—— (2011). *Afghanistan: Poppy Eradication and Verification, Final Report.* Kabul: UNODC/MCN, Sep. 2011.

United Nations Office of Internal Oversight Services (2001). *Report on the Inspection of Programme Management and Administrative Practices in the Office for Drug Control and Crime Prevention,* 1 June 2001. http://www.un.org/Depts/oios/reports/a56_83.htm

United Nations Security Council (2001). *Report of the Committee of Experts Pursuant to Security Council Resolution 1333 (2000) Paragraph 15a, Regarding the Monitoring of the Arms Embargo Against the Taliban and the Enclosure of Terrorist training Camps in the Taliban-held Areas of Afghanistan, S/2001/501.* Retrieved from

http://www.sipri.org/databases/embargoes/un_arms_embargoes/afghanistan/
un-committee-of-experts-report-s-2001–511

United States Agency for International Development, Afghanistan (2010). *Final
Evaluation of Alternative Development Program South (ADP/S) for USAID in the
Islamic Republic of Afghanistan*, 11 Jan.—19 Apr. 2010.

——— (2011). *Fact Sheet, Helmand Province*, Jun. 2011.

United States Agency for International Development, Office of Inspector General
(2010). 'Audit of USAID/Afghanistan's Vouchers for Increased Productive
Agriculture (AVIPA) Program', *Audit Report No. 5–306-10–008*, 20 Apr. 2010.

——— (2011). 'Audit of USAID/Afghanistan's Afghanistan Stabilisation Initiative
for the Southern Region', *Audit Report No. F-306-12–001-P*, 13 Nov. 2011.

United States Congressional Research Service (2001). 'Report RS1041, Taliban and
the Drug Trade. Ralph F. Perl, Foreign Affairs, Defense, and Trade Division'.
WikiLeaks Document Release, 2 Feb. 2009.

United States Department of State (2007). *US Counter Narcotics Strategy for
Afghanistan*. US report compiled by the Coordinator for Counternarcotics and
Justice Reform in Afghanistan.

United States Department of State, Bureau for International Narcotics and Law
Enforcement Affairs (2010a). *International Narcotics Control Strategy Report
(INCSR), Vol 1: Drug and Chemical Control, March 2010*. Washington, DC: US
Government Printing Office.

——— (2010b). *The INL Beat*, Jan. 2010.

——— (2012). *International Narcotics Control Strategy Report*, 7 Mar. 2012.

United States Government (2011). *Measuring the Deterrent Effect of Poppy Eradication
in the Helmand Food Zone*. Unpublished image and analysis presented at conference, 26 Jan. 2011.

United States Government Accountability Office (2005). *Afghanistan Security: Efforts
to Establish Army and Police Have Made Progress, but Future Plans Need to be Better
Defined*.

——— (2006). *Afghanistan Drug Control: Despite Improved Efforts, Deteriorating
Security Threatens Success of US Goals*. Report to Congressional Committees,
GAO-07-078.

——— (2010). *Afghanistan Drug Control: Strategy Evolving and Progress Reported, but
Interim Performance Targets and Evaluation of Justice Reform Efforts Needed*. GAO-
10–291, March 2010.

United States House of Representatives, 94th Congress (1975). *Subcommittee on
Future Foreign Policy Research and Development of the Committee on International
Relations*. Hearing on the Proposal to Control Opium from the Golden Triangle
and Terminate the Shan Opium Trade.

——— (2003). *Legislation on Foreign Relations through 2002*. Committee on
International Relations Committee on Foreign Relations, Jul. 2003.

—— 108th Congress (2004). 'Afghanistan: Are the British Counter Narcotics efforts going wobbly?' *Subcommittee on Criminal Justice, Drug Policy and Human Resources of the Committee on Government Reform*, 1 Apr. 2004, serial no. 108–224.

United States Senate (2009). *Afghanistan's Narco War: Breaking the Link between Drug Traffickers and Insurgents*. Report to the Committee on Foreign Relations, United States Senate, 111st Congress, First Session, 10 Aug. 2009, http://www.gpoaccess.gov/congress/index.html

—— (2010). *US Counternarcotics Strategy in Afghanistan*. A report to the Senate, Caucus on International Narcotics Control, 111st Congress, Second Session, July 2010, http://drugcaucus.senate.gov

Vistisen, N. K. (2011). 'When Governance is Individuals: One Heart Attack away From a Really Big Problem'. *Small Wars Journal*, 7 November 2011.

Vlassenroot, K. (2006). 'War and Social Research: The Limits of Empirical Methodologies in Wartorn Environments'. *Civilisations*, 54:191–8.

Von Lampe, K. (2008). 'Introduction to the Special Issue on Interviewing Organised Criminals'. *Trends in Organised Crime*, 11: 1–24.

Wafa, A. W. & Gall, C. (2009). 'Afghan Governor Leaves Presidential Race'. *New York Times*, 2 May 2009.

Walker, A. R. (1992). 'Opium: Its Production and Use in a Lahu Nyi (Red Lahu) Village Community'. In A. R. Walker (ed.), *The Highland Heritage: Collected Essays on Upland Northern Thailand*. Singapore: Suvarnabhumi Books.

Ward, C. & Byrd, W. (2004). 'Afghanistan's Opium Drug Economy'. *World Bank South Asia Region PREM Working Paper Series, Report No. SASPR-5*. Washington, DC: World Bank.

Ward, C., Mansfield, D., Oldham, P. & Byrd, W. (2008). *Afghanistan: Economic Incentives and Development Initiatives to Reduce Opium Production*. Report for the World Bank and the Department for International Development.

Watson, P. (2005). 'The Lure of Opium Wealth is a Potent Force in Afghanistan'. *Los Angeles Times*, 29 May 2005.

Wayne, A. E. (2009). Transcript of Ambassador E. Anthony Wayne remarks at GPI signing ceremony. 23 Nov. 2009.

Westermeyer, J. (1982). *Poppies, Pipes and People: Opium and its Use in Laos*. Berkeley, CA: University of California Press.

Windle, J. (2011). 'Ominous Parallels and Optimistic Differences: Opium in China and Afghanistan'. *Law, Crime and History*, 2.

Windle, J. & Farrell, G. (2012). 'Popping the Balloon Effect: Assessing Drug Law Enforcement in terms of Displacement, Diffusion, and the Containment Hypothesis'. *Informa*. USA: Healthcare USA, Inc.

Wolf, E. (1966). *Peasants*. Englewood Cliffs, NJ: Prentice Hall.

—— (1969). *Peasant Wars of the Twentieth Century*. New York: Harper and Row.

—— (2006). The Ethical Challenges of Field Research in Conflict Zones. *Qualitative Sociology*, 29: 373–86.

Wood, G. (2003). Staying Secure, Staying Poor: The 'Faustian Bargain'. *World Development*, 31(3): 455–71.

—— (2007). *Social Policy in Unsettled Societies: the Case for a Wellbeing Regime Framework*. Prepared for a lecture at a workshop on 'Comprehensive Social Policies as a Concept for Development in the Global South', comprising Austrian Development Agency, Ministry of European and Foreign Affairs, NGOs and Vienna University, held in Vienna, 20 Nov. 2007. Bath: University of Bath Online Publication.

—— & Gough, I. (2006). 'A Comparative Welfare Regime Approach to Global Social Policy'. *World Development*, 34(10): 1696–712.

World Bank (2011). *World Development Report 2011: Conflict, Security an Development*. Washington, DC: Word Bank.

Yin, R. K. (1994). Case Study Research: Design and Methods (2nd edn). *Applied Social Research Methods*, 5.

Young, H., Osman, A. & Dale, R. (2007). *Strategies for Economic Recovery and Peace in Darfur: Why a Wider Livelihoods Approach is Imperative and Inclusion of the Abbala (Camel Herding) Arabs is a Priority*. Feinstein International Center Briefing Paper. Medford, MA: Tufts University.

Young, H., Osman, A. M., Abusn, A. M., Asher, M. & Egemi, O. (2009). *Livelihoods, Power and Choice: The Vulnerability of the Northern Rizaygat, Darfur, Sudan*. Feinstein International Center Paper. Medford, MA: Tufts University.

Zaeef, A. S. (2010). *My Life with the Taliban*. London: Hurst & Co.

Zaher, A. (2012). 'Sherzai Accused of Grabbing State Land'. *Pajhwok Afghan News*, 2 April 2012.

Zaitch, D. (2001). *Traquetos: Colombians involved in the Cocaine Business in the Netherlands*. PhD thesis, Amsterdam School for Social Science Research, University of Amsterdam.

Zebedee, G. (2010). *Review of the Helmand Provincial Counternarcotics Plan: Second Report*. Review commissioned by the Counternarcotics Team, Provincial Reconstruction Team, Helmand.

INDEX